FACTASTIC
BOOK OF
1001
LISTS

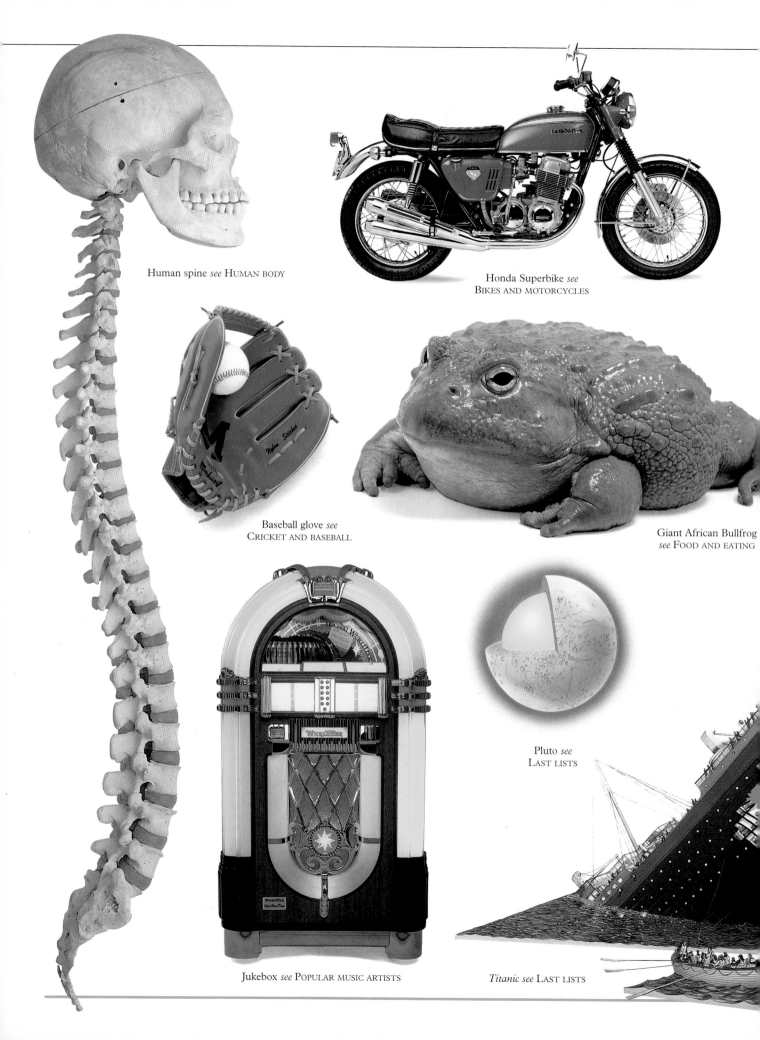

Human spine *see* HUMAN BODY

Honda Superbike *see*
BIKES AND MOTORCYCLES

Baseball glove *see*
CRICKET AND BASEBALL

Giant African Bullfrog
see FOOD AND EATING

Pluto *see*
LAST LISTS

Jukebox *see* POPULAR MUSIC ARTISTS

Titanic see LAST LISTS

FACTASTIC
BOOK OF
1001
LISTS

RUSSELL ASH

Football helmet *see*
FOOTBALL AND RUGBY

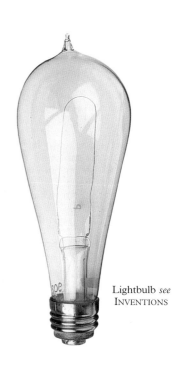

Lightbulb *see*
INVENTIONS

DK PUBLISHING, INC.
www.dk.com

LIST OF EDITORS

A DK PUBLISHING BOOK
www.dk.com

Produced for Dorling Kindersley by
PAGEOne, Cairn House, Elgiva Lane, Chesham,
Buckinghamshire HP5 2JD

EDITORIAL DIRECTOR Helen Parker
ART DIRECTOR Bob Gordon
PROJECT EDITOR Sarah Watson
EDITOR Sophie Williams
EDITORIAL CONSULTANT Jane Yorke
PROJECT ART EDITOR Chris Clark
DESIGNERS Melanie McDowell, Suzanne Tuhrim

FOR DORLING KINDERSLEY
MANAGING EDITOR Jayne Parsons
MANAGING ART EDITOR Gill Shaw
PROJECT EDITOR Maggie Crowley
US EDITORS Julee Binder-Shapiro, Constance Robinson
DTP DESIGNER Nomazwe Madonko
PRODUCTION Kate Oliver
PICTURE RESEARCH Christine Rista
DK PICTURE LIBRARY Sally Hamilton
JACKET DESIGN Mark Richards

First American Edition, 1999
2 4 6 8 10 9 7 5 3 1
Published in the United States by DK Publishing, Inc.
95 Madison Avenue, New York, New York 10016

Published in Great Britain by Dorling Kindersley Limited.

Library of Congress Cataloging-in-Publication Data
Ash, Russell.
Factastic book of 1001 lists / written by Russell Ash. – 1st
American ed.
p. cm.
Includes index.
ISBN 0-7894-3412-1 (paperback)
ISBN 0-7894-3769-4 (hardcover)
1. Handbooks. vade-mecums, etc. I. Title.
AG106.A85 1999   98-7701
031.02–dc21   CIP
Color reproduction by GRB Editrice, Italy
Printed and bound by Artes Graficas Toledo, S. A.
D.L. TO: 1470-1998

CONTENTS

INTRODUCTION

Why lists? Every day of our lives the media bombards us with information through print, TV, CD-ROMs, and the Internet. Lists enable us to make sense of what might otherwise be a mass of data and figures that no one has time to absorb, and provide us with summaries of important events. They help to simplify or organize information in a form that we can easily digest and remember.

What sort of lists? In this book I have brought together 1,001 lists of all sorts, biggests and fastests, firsts and lasts, checklists, and lists of milestone events. Each list is easily identifiable by the colored band at the top. I call them factastic because they are facts, and many of them are also fantastic, a mixture of serious and fun. This is not a book of "bests" and "worsts," which contain someone's personal opinion. The only bests here are bestsellers, and the worsts are worst disasters, all of which can be measured.

Who says so? My main source of data is my own library of reference books. I also use specialized library collections and, increasingly, information that is available on

CD-ROM and the Internet. I make a lot of use of "official" sources, such as the United Nations and sports governing bodies, as well as commercial organizations and research groups, many of whose publications are not easily available to the public. The best source of all are private individuals who are happy to share their specialist knowledge – particularly on the Internet.

How accurate are these lists?

Like all reference book compilers, I strive to be 100 percent accurate, but it can be difficult: sources often disagree as to even basic figures, such as the areas and populations of countries, and even the height of Mount Everest can appear to change, as new survey methods are used. In addition, lists change all the time. By the time you read this, certain sports records may have been broken, and long-running shows will have run for even longer – or perhaps closed!

New ideas?

If you have any factastic ideas for lists please send them to me and I'll try to include them in the next book! Equally, if you have any corrections to my lists, you can contact me on our World Wide Web site at www.dk.com (where you will also find details about other DK books), e-mail me direct at ash@pavilion.co.uk, or write to me at the publisher's address. And remember – if you enjoy this book, look out for my annual, The Top 10 of Everything!

SPACE

THE UNIVERSE

EVOLUTION OF THE UNIVERSE

THE BIG BANG Many scientists believe that the Universe was created by a huge explosion called the Big Bang, which occurred 15 billion years ago.

THE FIRST ATOMS Within minutes of the Big Bang the first atoms, the basis of all matter, were formed.

THE FIRST MOLECULES After about 10,000 years, temperatures of more than 10 billion degrees forced atomic particles to come together to form the gases hydrogen and helium.

GASES FORM STRANDS About 700,000 years after the Big Bang, gases in space started to form into strands.

GASES FORM NEBULAE About 1 billion years after the Big Bang, the strands of gases swirled together to form clouds of dust and gas called nebulae.

THE FIRST STARS As the clumps of dust and gas in a nebula were drawn together by their own gravity, the increasing pressure made gases at the center very hot. Once the core reached 18 million °F (10 million °C), nuclear reactions occurred and the first stars were born.

BIRTH OF THE FIRST GALAXIES About 1.5 billion years after the Big Bang, the first galaxies were formed as spinning clouds of stars, dust, and gas.

CONTINUALLY EXPANDING UNIVERSE Scientists have proved that the galaxies of the Universe are moving farther and farther apart. This means that the Universe is getting bigger and bigger.

THE BIG CRUNCH Most scientists believe that the Universe will expand only so far. Once the energy from the Big Bang is used, it will fall inward to a Big Crunch.

SPACE WORDS

ASTEROIDS Chunks of rock of varied size that are found mainly between Mars and Jupiter.

BLACK HOLE Formed when a star more than three times as heavy as the Sun collapses at the end of its life, and becomes more compact and dense. This black hole drags in material and nothing, not even light, can escape its gravity.

COMET An object composed of snow and dust that orbits the Sun. If a comet approaches the Sun, it forms a tail of gas and dust particles.

CONSTELLATION A group of stars around which astronomers have drawn imaginary lines to form a memorable image, for example, a horse.

GALAXY An enormous collection of stars. The Universe has about 100,000 million galaxies. The Earth is just one star in the Milky Way galaxy.

GRAVITY The invisible force that attracts two masses to each other. It holds the Solar System and galaxies together.

METEOR A piece of dust that falls off speeding comets and forms showers, or "shooting stars."

MOON A ball of rock that spins on its own axis while orbiting a planet. All the planets have moons except Venus and Mercury.

NEBULA A cloud of dust and gas in space.

NEUTRON STAR A star that has collapsed into a superdense form of matter. Some neutron stars are seen as pulsars.

PULSAR A neutron star that emits pulses of radiation toward Earth as it spins (like a lighthouse). It gets its energy from rotation.

QUASAR Thought to be the most distant and luminous objects in the universe, quasars are probably the cores of the first galaxies to be formed.

STAR A spinning ball of hot, luminous gas, which releases energy through nuclear reactions.

SUPERNOVA The explosion of a large star, which may briefly produce more light than a galaxy.

GALAXY FACTS

TYPES OF GALAXY There are three types of galaxy: spiral, elliptical, and irregular.

SPIRAL GALAXIES These are disk-shaped and contain young and old stars.

ELLIPTICAL GALAXIES These are the most common type of galaxy and are made up of flat, round collections of old stars.

IRREGULAR GALAXIES These do not form a specific shape, and are rare.

OUR GALAXY The Sun is only one of 100–200 billion stars in the Milky Way galaxy, which is 100,000 light-years in diameter.

NEAREST GALAXY Andromeda is our nearest neighboring galaxy – 2.2 million light-years away from the Milky Way. It contains 300 billion stars and is 180,000 light-years wide.

LARGEST GALAXY The central galaxy of the Abell 2029 galaxy cluster is 5.6 million light-years wide – 80 times wider than ours.

BRIGHTEST GALAXY The galaxy known as IRAS F10214+4724 is 300,000,000,000,000 times brighter than the Sun!

MOST COMMON ELEMENTS

ELEMENT	PERCENTAGE
Hydrogen	73.90
Helium	24.00
Oxygen	1.07
Carbon	0.46
Neon	0.14
Iron	0.12
Nitrogen	0.10
Silicon	0.06
Magnesium	0.05
Sulfur	0.04

DID YOU KNOW? The elements hydrogen and helium together comprise almost 98 percent of all matter in the Universe.

DISTANCES IN THE UNIVERSE

BODY	TIME TAKEN FOR LIGHT FROM THESE BODIES TO REACH EARTH
Moon	1.26 sec
Sun	8 min 17 sec
Pluto (farthest planet)	5 hr 20 min
Nearest star	4.22 years
Most distant star in our galaxy	62,700 years
Nearest body outside our galaxy	174,000 years
Farthest visible star	2,309,000 years
Most distant known quasar	13,200,000,000 years
Edge of universe	14,000,000,000 years

BRIGHTEST STARS FROM EARTH

STAR	CONSTELLATION
Sun	Solar System
Sirius	Canis Major
Canopus	Carina
Alpha Centauri	Centaurus
Arcturus	Boötes

DID YOU KNOW? This is a list of the brightest stars as viewed from Earth. Sirius, which has a diameter of 900,988 miles (1,450,000 km) is, in fact, more than 24 times brighter than the Sun, but its distance from the Earth puts it in second place.

DID YOU KNOW? Proxima Centauri is the closest star to Earth, but it is too small to be seen without a telescope!

AMAZING FACT! The temperature on the surface of the Sun is about 9,932°F (5,500°C)!

ALL 88 CONSTELLATIONS

ANDROMEDA (princess) • ANTLIA (air-pump) • APUS (bird-of-paradise) • AQUARIUS (water-bearer) • AQUILA (eagle) • ARA (altar) • ARIES (ram) • AURIGA (charioteer) • BOÖTES (herdsman) • CAELUM (chisel) • CAMELOPARDALIS (giraffe) • CANCER (crab) • CANES VENATICI (hunting dogs) • CANIS MAJOR (big dog) • CANIS MINOR (little dog) • CAPRICORN (goat) • CARINA (keel) • CASSIOPEIA (seated lady) • CENTAURUS (centaur) • CEPHEUS (king) • CETUS (sea monster) • CHAMELEON • CIRCINUS (compass) • COLUMBIA (dove) • COMA BERENCIES (Bernice's hair) • CORONA AUSTRINA (southern crown) • CORONA BOREALIS (northern crown) • CORVUS (crow) • CRATER (cup) • CRUX (cross) • CYGNUS (swan) • DELPHINUS (dolphin) • DORADO (swordfish) • DRACO (dragon) • EQUULEUS (colt) • ERIDANUS (river) • FORNAX (furnace) • GEMINI (twins) • GRUS (crane) • HERCULES (hero) • HOROLOGIUM (clock) • HYDRA (sea serpent) • HYDRUS (water snake) • INDUS (North American) • LACERTA (lizard) • LEO (lion) • LEO MINOR (lion cub) • LEPUS (hare) • LIBRA (scales) • LUPUS (wolf) • LYNX (lynx) • LYRA (lyre) • MENSA (table) • MICROSCOPIUM (microscope) • MONOCEROS (unicorn) • MUSCA (fly) • NORMA (carpenter's square) • OCTANS (octant) • OPHIUCHUS (serpent holder) • ORION (hunter) • PAVO (peacock) • PEGASUS (winged horse) • PERSEUS (hero) • PHOENIX • PICTOR (easel) • PISCES (fishes) • PISCIS AUSTRINUS (southern fish) • PUPPIS (stern) • PYXIS (sailor's compass) • RETICULUM (net) • SAGITTA (arrow) • SAGITTARIUS (archer) • SCORPIO (scorpion) • SCULPTOR • SCUTUM (shield) • SERPENS (snake) • SEXTANS (sextant) • TAURUS (bull) • TELESCOPIUM (telescope) • TRIANGULUM (triangle) • TRIANGULUM AUSTRALE (southern triangle) • TUCANA (toucan) • URSA MAJOR (large bear) • URSA MINOR (small bear) • VELA (sail) • VIRGO (virgin) • VOLANS (flying fish) • VULPECULA (little fox)

STAR FACTS

HOW A STAR IS BORN All stars begin as vast clouds of dust and gas. As this cloud collapses under gravity, parts contract into clumps called protostars, which spin and flatten into disks. Nuclear reactions begin, dust is blown away, and the star is born. It radiates energy and starts to shine, as it gradually burns up.

CLOSEST STAR The closest star to the Earth is the Sun, which is 92.9 million miles (149.6 million km) away.

HEAVIEST STAR The variable Eta Carinae, 9,100 light-years away in the Carinae Nebula, is 200 times heavier than our own Sun.

LARGEST STAR The diameter of the supergiant Betelgeux (the top left star of the Orion constellation) is about 400 million miles (700 million km) – about 500 times that of the Sun.

SMALLEST STAR The white dwarf L362-81 has an estimated diameter of just 3,500 miles (5,632 km) – almost 50 times smaller than the Sun.

BRIGHTEST SUPERNOVA First seen in 1993, the supernova 1993 J in the galaxy M81 is the brightest to have appeared in the northern sky for 20 years.

SUPERNOVA ENERGY The energy released by a supernova in one minute is equivalent to the total energy radiated by the Sun in 900 million years.

HOW A STAR DIES The life of a star ends in either a supernova explosion or a planetary nebula.

COMET FACTS

WHAT IS A COMET? Billions of icy lumps called comets fly around the Solar System. Some are knocked onto a path toward the Sun, which melts the lump so it becomes a large head and a long, streaky tail. As comets travel, they shed dust, seen from Earth as meteors.

FIRST COMETS In ancient times, people did not know what comets were. Their sudden appearance made superstitious people regard them as omens.

SHOEMAKER-LEVY In 1993, Comet Shoemaker-Levy passed close to Jupiter and was broken into fragments by Jupiter's immense gravity. During July 1994, these fragments crashed into Jupiter, causing a series of huge explosions in Jupiter's atmosphere.

ENCKE'S COMET Encke is the comet that appears the most frequently. It returns every 3.3 years. It is named after German astronomer Johann Encke (1791–1865), who studied its orbit.

HALLEY'S COMET Named after the English scientist Edmond Halley, (1656–1742), this comet was first seen in ancient times. Halley became the first to show that some comets return regularly because they follow predictable orbits that bring them close to the Sun. Halley predicted that the comet he saw in 1682 would return in 1759.

HALE-BOPP One of the brightest comets seen in recent years, Hale-Bopp came nearest to Earth on March 22, 1997, when it was viewed by millions.

THE SOLAR SYSTEM

SUN FACTFILE

DIAMETER At its equator, the Sun is 865,121 miles (1,391,980 km).

DISTANCE FROM EARTH The Sun is estimated to be 93,026,724 miles (149,680,000 km) away.

SUN'S SURFACE Magnified, the Sun's surface looks grainy. These grains are columns of gas, each 620 miles (1,000 km) wide – the size of France! The columns flare at 5-minute intervals!

TEMPERATURE The core of the Sun reaches a temperature of 27,720,000°F (15,400,000°C)!

SURFACE AREA The Sun's surface area covers 2,350,982,700,000 sq miles (6,088,575,000,000 sq km)!

ENERGY OUTPUT The Sun's hydrogen core works like a nuclear reactor – converting hydrogen to helium at a rate of 590 million tons (600 million tonnes) every second. In doing this, the Sun loses four million tons of its mass per second. In the same time, it gives out 35 million times as much electricity as the US uses in a year!

SOLAR PROMINENCE Sometimes gigantic jets of flaming gas shoot off the surface of the Sun, stretching thousands of miles (kilometers) into space. The energy released from these prominences, or flares, can be a million million times that of the first nuclear bomb!

LIGHT Just 10.8 sq ft (1 sq m) of the Sun's surface shines as brightly as 600,000 100-watt light bulbs!

⚠ **DON'T TRY IT YOURSELF! Never** look directly at the Sun, even through a camera or with sunglasses, because it could damage your eyes.

⚠ **TRY IT YOURSELF!** You can cover the Moon in the sky with a coin held at arm's length. In fact, it is a quarter the diameter of the Earth – nearly as big as Australia!

MOON DATA

SIZE Earth's Moon has a diameter of 2,161 miles (3,477 km).

AGE Like Earth, the Moon is an incredible 4.6 billion years old!

DISTANCE FROM EARTH The Moon is 238,866 miles (384,400 km) away.

SURFACE TEMPERATURE Ranges from -247°F to 221°F (-155°C to 105°C).

SURFACE The Moon is littered with craters formed by meteorites and dark seas of solidified lava from billions of years ago.

MOON MISSIONS Neil Armstrong and Edwin E. "Buzz" Aldrin, from the US, landed in 1969 in *Apollo XI*. There have been six landings in total with 12 astronauts. Since there is no air or water on the Moon, the tracks of the astronauts will remain there forever.

BLUE MOON In 1950, the Moon appeared to turn blue after a forest fire in Canada threw up smoke particles.

ASTEROID FACTS

WHAT IS AN ASTEROID? Sometimes called "minor planets," asteroids are lumps of rock that orbit the Sun.

TOTAL MASS The total mass of all asteroids is less than that of the Moon!

FIRST FOUND AND LARGEST Ceres was discovered in 1801 and is the largest asteroid. It is 582 miles (936 km) wide.

DO THEY COME NEAR EARTH? On average, a 0.25-mile (0.4-km) diameter asteroid hits Earth every 50,000 years. In 1991, one came within 106,000 miles (170,600 km) of Earth!

ASTEROID DISASTER An asteroid that collided with Earth 65 million years ago may have caused dinosaur extinction.

ASTEROID NAMES

Every asteroid is numbered in the order of its discovery. The discoverer usually names it after whatever he or she chooses.

1652 Hergé, the creator of the popular Belgian comic strip *Tintin*.

2309 Mr. Spock, after a ginger cat!

2865 (Stan) Laurel, comedy star.

3534 Sax, in honor of Adolphe Sax, inventor of the saxophone.

4147 Lennon, musician, The Beatles.

5050 Doctor Watson, after the friend of fictional detective Sherlock Holmes.

5405 Neverland, after the fantasy island in children's story *Peter Pan*.

COMPARATIVE WEIGHTS

Gravity is a force that pulls objects together. The heavier and farther apart objects – such as planets – are, the stronger the gravitational pull will be. If you weigh 110 lb (50 kg) on Earth, this is what you will weigh elsewhere in space thanks to gravity:

PLANET/STAR	WEIGHT	
	LB	KG
Pluto	7.3	3.3
Moon	18.7	8.5
Mercury	29.8	13.5
Mars	40.8	18.5
Venus	94.8	43.0
Uranus	101.4	46.0
Earth	110.0	50.0
Saturn	128.9	58.5
Neptune	158.7	72.0
Jupiter	291.0	132.0
Sun	3064.4	1,390.0

DID YOU KNOW? The Moon's gravity is less than Earth's because it is smaller than Earth. On Earth, an astronaut weighs 298 lb (135 kg); on the Moon he weighs 48 lb (22 kg)!

THE NINE PLANETS

PLANET	DISTANCE FROM SUN		LENGTH OF ORBIT	DIAMETER		MOONS
	MILLION MILES	MILLION KM		MILES	KM	
Mercury	36.0	57.9	87.97 days	3,031	4,878	0
Venus	67.2	108.2	224.70 days	7,520	12,104	0
Earth	93.0	149.7	365.30 days	7,296	12,756	1
Mars	141.6	227.9	687.00 days	4,217	6,794	2
Jupiter	483.6	778.3	11.86 years	88,846	142,984	16
Saturn	886.0	1,427.0	29.46 years	74,898	120,536	18
Uranus	1,784.0	2,871.0	84.01 years	31,763	51,118	15
Neptune	2,794.0	4,497.0	164.80 years	30,775	49,528	8
Pluto	3,675.0	5,914.0	247.70 years	1,419	2,284	1

NAMING THE PLANETS

PLANET	NAME MEANING
Mercury	Roman messenger of gods
Venus	Roman goddess of love
Earth	Land
Mars	Roman god of war
Jupiter	Chief god of the Romans
Saturn	Roman god of farming
Uranus	First Greek sky god
Neptune	Roman god of water
Pluto	Roman god of underworld

TEN LARGEST PLANETARY MOONS

MOON	ORBITS PLANET	DIAMETER	
		MILES	KM
Ganymede	Jupiter	3,274	5,269
Titan	Saturn	3,200	5,150
Callisto	Jupiter	2,995	4,820
Io	Jupiter	2,257	3,632
Moon	Earth	2,159	3,475
Europa	Jupiter	1,942	3,126
Triton	Neptune	1,708	2,750
Titania	Uranus	982	1,580
Rhea	Saturn	951	1,530
Oberon	Uranus	942	1,516

DID YOU KNOW? One of Jupiter's moons, Europa, has a surface of ice that measures at least 60 miles (97 km) thick! Another, Io, was investigated by the 1979 *Voyager* probe, sent to observe the moon. It showed that Io experiences volcanic eruptions that hurl sulfur 186 miles (300 km) high!

HOTTEST PLANETS

PLANET	HIGHEST TEMPERATURE	
	°F	°C
Venus	+868	+464
Mercury	+806	+430
Earth	+140	+60

DID YOU KNOW? These three planets are the only ones above freezing!

COLDEST PLANETS

PLANET	LOWEST TEMPERATURE	
	°F	°C
Pluto	-382.0	-230
Uranus	-369.4	-223
Mercury	-328.0	-200
Neptune	-364.0	-220
Saturn	-256.0	-160

PLANET FACTS

MERCURY This planet, the nearest to the Sun, has the greatest temperature extremes, ranging from -328°F (-200°C) to 806°F (430°C). On Mercury, which has much weaker gravity than Earth, an athlete could leap over an elephant!

VENUS The closest planet to Earth, Venus could not be more different. Its inhospitable atmosphere is very hot, dense, and acidic.

EARTH This is the only planet that can support life because it has the right balance of water, light, and air.

MARS This red planet is completely free of water, but dry riverbeds suggest that water once flowed on the planet.

JUPITER This fast-spinning planet is bigger than all the others put together! On Earth, a flea can jump 13 in (33 cm), but on Jupiter, where gravity is 2.6 times that on Earth, the flea could jump only 5 in (13 cm).

SATURN A giant planet, Saturn is surrounded by rings of icy rock and dust. These rings are 656 ft (200 m) thick, and more than 167,800 miles (270,000 km) in diameter.

URANUS Named after Uranus, the first Greek sky god, this planet is one of the coldest, with an average temperature of -369°F (-223°C). It is made mainly of hydrogen, and has a barren landscape apart from frozen methane clouds. It is surrounded by dark rings.

NEPTUNE Pictures of Neptune taken by the *Voyager* probe show that it is a blue planet, with icy clouds of methane very similar to those on Uranus. It has a Great Dark Spot, a giant storm where winds blows at 1,240 mph (2,000 km/h).

PLUTO The smallest, darkest, and coldest planet, Pluto was discovered in 1930 by American farmer Clyde Tombaugh (1906–1997).

SPACE EXPLORATION

EARLY ASTRONOMERS

EUDOXUS OF CNIDUS (408–355 BC) According to Greek thinker Eudoxus, the Earth was at the center of the Universe.

PTOLEMY (c.AD 120–180) Greek astronomer Ptolemy compiled a book called the *Almagest*, which provided the basis of scientific astronomy for more than 1,000 years.

AL-SUFI (903–986) A Persian nobleman and one of the leading astronomers of his time, Al-Sufi listed the position and brightness of more than 1,000 stars, in his *Book of Fixed Stars*.

NICOLAUS COPERNICUS (1473–1543) Copernicus was a Polish monk who wrote a book in which he stated that the Sun was at the center of the Universe.

GALILEO GALILEI (1564–1642) Italian scientist Galileo discovered Jupiter's four largest moons, supporting the theory that the Sun is the center of the Universe.

JOHANNES KEPLER (1571–1630) German astronomer Kepler established three laws ruling planetary movement.

ISAAC NEWTON (1642–1727) This English scientist's theory of gravity explained why planets orbit the Sun.

WILLIAM HERSCHEL (1738–1822) German-born Herschel found Uranus and four of its moons.

ASTRONOMY MILESTONES

1543 Nicolaus Copernicus (1473–1543) shows that Sun is center of the Solar System.

1608 First telescope invented by Dutch scientist Hans Lippershey (1570–1619).

1609 German Johannes Kepler (1571–1630) describes laws of planetary motion.

1668 Isaac Newton (1642–1727) builds first reflecting telescope.

1705 British Edmond Halley (1658–1742) predicts return of Halley's comet in 1758.

1781 German musician William Herschel (1738–1822) discovers Uranus.

1801 First asteroid, Ceres, discovered by Italian Giuseppe Piazzi (1746–1826).

1846 German Johann Galle (1812–1910) discovers Neptune.

1905 German physicist Albert Einstein (1879–1955) proposes the theory of relativity.

1924 British Edwin Hubble (1889–1953) discovers galaxies beyond the Milky Way.

1924–1930 "Big Bang" theory formulated independently by Belgian Abbé Lemaitre (1894–1966) and Russian A. Friedmann (1888–1925).

1930 Clyde Tombaugh (US, 1906–1997) discovers Pluto.

1932 US engineer Karl Jansky (1905–1950) picks up first radio waves from outside Earth.

1949 3K cosmic background radiation, believed to be remains of Big Bang, is discovered by Americans Arno Penzias (b.1933) and Robert Wilson (b.1936).

1967 Discovery of pulsars by British astronomer Jocelyn Bell (b.1943).

1986 *Giotto* space probe sends back first pictures of a comet's nucleus.

1990 Hubble space telescope is launched above Earth's atmosphere.

1994 People on Earth see comet Shoemaker-Levy crashing into Jupiter.

1995 *Galileo* probe reaches Jupiter.

PROBLEMS OF SPACE TRAVEL

WEIGHTLESSNESS Away from the Earth's gravity, objects float unless they are fixed, and injuries may result.

EATING Astronauts eat about 70 percent less in space than on Earth. They can choose from an extensive menu of preserved foods.

ILLNESS Viruses, such as colds, spread quickly in the confines of the cabin. Astronauts exercise to overcome motion sickness and muscle-wasting.

TOILETS Early astronauts wore diapers, but toilets with hand and toe holds are installed on modern space stations. The waste is shredded by machine, and dumped into space.

SHAVING Astronauts must shave with foam, or an electric razor with a vacuum attachment to suck away whiskers, which can jam equipment.

BURPING AND FARTING Burping in space often brings up vomit, which floats around the cabin in globules. In the confined area, farts are antisocial!

SPACE JUNK

Junk left in space does not decay and can pose a threat to spacecraft. It includes the following:

• "Dead" satellites

• Tools and equipment lost during spacewalks

• Chunks of discarded booster rockets

• The descent stages of six *Apollo* modules

• Three Lunar Rover vehicles left on the Moon

COUNTRIES WITH MOST SPACEFLIGHT EXPERIENCE

COUNTRY	ASTRONAUTS	DURATION OF MISSIONS			
		DAYS	HR	MIN	SEC
USSR/Russia	85	13,094	2	7	17
US	234	5,768	3	44	1
Germany	9	298	11	30	13
France	7	137	20	8	27
Kazakhstan	2	133	21	6	15

DID YOU KNOW? Up until January 1, 1998, Soviet and Russian cosmonauts accounted for 66 percent of the total time spent by humans in space, largely through the long-duration stays on board the *Mir* space station, which has been occupied since 1986.

ASTRONAUT RECORDS

Record	Astronaut	Country	Date	Spacecraft/ Space station
First to orbit Earth	Yuri Gagarin	USSR	1961	*Vostok 1*
First woman in space	Valentina Tereshkova	USSR	1963	*Vostok 6*
First spacewalker	Alexei Leonov	USSR	1965	*Voskhod 2*
First man on Moon	Neil Armstrong	US	1969	*Apollo 11*
Most experienced spaceman	Valeri Polyakov	USSR	1988	*Mir* space station
Longest spacewalk	Thomas Akers Richard Hieb Pierre Thut	US	1992	*STS-49*
Most experienced spacewoman	Shannon Lucid	US	1996	*STS-76 Atlantis,* *Mir* space station *STS-79 Atlantis*

AMAZING FACT! Leonov's first spacewalk almost ended in disaster, when his spacesuit "ballooned." He was unable to return through the air lock into the capsule until he reduced pressure in his suit to a dangerously low level.

SPACE EXPLORATION MILESTONES

1926 US engineer Robert Goddard designs and launches first liquid-fueled rocket.

1942 First German V2 rockets tested against Britain in World War II.

1957 First satellite *Sputnik 1* (USSR) in orbit.

1958 NASA (National Aeronautics and Space Administration) founded; first US satellite, *Explorer 1*.

1961 First humans in space: Yuri Gagarin, of the USSR, and Alan Shepard, of the US. Gagarin is also the first man to orbit Earth.

1963 Valentina Tereshkova of the USSR is the first woman launched into space. First spacewalk achieved by Alexei Leonov of the USSR.

1969 First manned Moon landing (*Apollo 11*, US). Neil Armstrong is first to walk on Moon.

1970 *Venera 7* is first probe to land on another planet, Venus.

1986 *Mir* space station becomes operational; *Voyager 2* observes Uranus.

1996 *Galileo* mini probe is first to enter the atmosphere of a giant planet.

1997 US *Pathfinder* lands on Mars.

FIRST IN-FLIGHT SPACE FATALITIES

1967 Launched on April 24, Soviet spaceship *Soyuz 1* had technical problems during its 18th orbit. The capsule parachute tangled and it crash-landed near Orsk in the Ural Mountains, killing astronaut Viktor Komarov.

1971 After a then record 23 days in space, on June 29, the Soviet *Soyuz 9*'s capsule depressurized. Although it landed intact, all three cosmonauts – Georgi Gobrovolsky, Vladislav Volkov, Viktor Patsayev, who were not wearing spacesuits, were found dead.

1986 On January 28, *Challenger STS-51-L*, the US's 25th space shuttle mission, exploded on takeoff from Cape Canaveral, Florida, killing astronauts Gregory Jarvis, Christa McAuliffe, Ronald McNair, Ellison Onizuka, Judith Resnik, Francis Scobee, and Michael Smith. The disaster was watched by thousands on the ground and millions on worldwide television. It prompted a full review of the engineering problems and revision of the safety methods undertaken. It was not until September 29, 1988, that the next space shuttle, *Discovery STS-26*, was successfully launched.

ANIMALS IN SPACE

Dogs Early Soviet space experiments involved launching several dogs into space, including Laika, a female Samoyed husky, launched in 1957.

Mice In 1958, two mice called Laska and Benjy became the first living creatures the US sent into space.

Chimpanzees The US launched Ham, a male chimpanzee, on a premanned flight test in 1961.

Cat In 1963, a cat called Félicette was launched in a suborbital flight in a French *Veronique* rocket.

Spiders Two spiders, Anita and Arabella, took part in experiments in the US's *Skylab 3*, 1973, to see whether they could spin their webs in zero gravity.

Jellyfish Apart from bacteria, the largest group of creatures in space was the 2,478 jellyfish on space shuttle *STS–40* in 1991.

THE EARTH

ROCKS and MINERALS

GEOLOGICAL TIMECHART

Geologists divide the Earth's history into three different time spans called eras, periods, and epochs. Eras are the longest, and epochs the shortest. Each interval marks a particular stage in our planet's history.

mya = millions of years ago

ERA	PERIOD	EPOCH	MYA	EVENTS
CENOZOIC	Quaternary	Holocene	0.01	Humans farm and develop technology.
		Pleistocene	1.6	Ice ages. *Homo sapiens* evolves. Saber-toothed cats and mammoths die out.
	Tertiary	Pliocene	5.3	Many modern mammals appear.
		Miocene	23	Deerlike hoofed mammals flourish. First hominids (humanlike primates).
		Oligocene	34	First humanlike creatures appear. Hunting birds thrive.
		Eocene	53	Mammals grow larger. Primates evolve.
		Palaeocene	65	Mammals, insects, and flowering plants flourish.
MESOZOIC	Cretaceous		135	First flowering plants. Mass extinction of dinosaurs at end of period.
	Jurassic		205	Dinosaurs flourish. First birds evolve.
	Triassic		250	Dinosaurs and mammals appear.
PALAEOZOIC	Permian		300	Reptiles diversify. Conifers replace tree ferns.
	Carboniferous		345	Swampy forests. First reptiles.
	Devonian		410	Age of sharks and fish. Insects and amphibians appear. Giant tree ferns.
	Silurian		438	First jawed fish and giant scorpions. Small land plants colonize shore.
	Ordovician		510	First crustaceans and early jawless fish. Coral reefs form.
	Cambrian		570	First molluscs and trilobites.
	Precambrian		4,650+	First single-celled life forms.

MEMORY TIP! Remember the order of the periods and epochs, from Cambrian up to Pleistocene, with the following phrase: **C**hina **o**wls **s**eldom **d**eceive **c**lay **p**igeons. **T**hey **j**ust **c**hase **p**ast **e**ach **o**ther **m**aking **p**reposterous **p**uns.

ROCK TYPES

All rocks fit into one of the following three categories:

IGNEOUS Igneous rocks form as molten magma or lava solidifies. The oldest igneous rocks date back at least 3.6 billion years, while the youngest are still forming.

SEDIMENTARY About 75 percent of the Earth's surface is covered with thin layers of debris. These sediments settle on the beds of oceans, lakes, and rivers, and are compacted over millions of years to form sedimentary rock.

METAMORPHIC When rocks are baked by the heat of molten magma or squeezed by the movements of vast tectonic plates, they are transformed into new, metamorphic rocks.

AMAZING METEORITE FACTS

WHAT IS A METEORITE? Lumps of rock called meteoroids that move around in space sometimes fall to Earth as meteorites.

LARGEST IN THE WORLD The Hoba meteorite was found on a farm in Grootfontein, South Africa, in 1920. It is a 9 x 8-ft (2.73 x 2.43-m) slab of 82 percent iron and 16 percent nickel.

LARGEST ON EXHIBITION Named *Ahnighito*, or "the tent," by local Inuit, this meteorite was found in 1897 at Cape York in Greenland by US explorer Robert Peary. Weighing 30.4 tons (30 tonnes) – as much as six bull elephants – it is in the American Museum of Natural History.

HOW OFTEN DO THEY FALL? It has been calculated that about 500 meteorites fall to Earth every year, although many fall in the sea and in unpopulated areas.

WHAT IS THE RISK OF BEING STRUCK? There is no recorded case of a person being killed by a meteorite, although animals are occasional victims. In the US, it is estimated that one meteorite death could occur every 9,300 years.

LAYERS OF THE EARTH

OCEANIC CRUST This layer of rock has an average thickness of 2.2 miles (3.2 km). It lies under the ocean floor.

CONTINENTAL CRUST Lying beneath the continents, this layer is older than the oceanic crust, and is 44 miles (60 km) thick.

MANTLE This layer of hot, often molten, rock is 1,780 miles (2,865 km) thick.

OUTER CORE At 1,404 miles (2,260 km) thick, the outer core of molten nickel and iron gives the Earth its magnetic field.

INNER CORE At the center of the Earth, the solid, inner core is 759 miles (1,222 km) thick.

BASIC ELEMENTS OF ROCK

About 99 percent of all rocks contain the eight main elements in the Earth's crust.

ELEMENT	PERCENTAGE OF EARTH'S CRUST
Oxygen	46.5
Silicon	28.9
Aluminium	8.3
Iron	4.8
Calcium	4.1
Potassium	2.4
Sodium	2.3
Magnesium	1.9

BIRTHSTONES

Some birthstones are linked with the months of the year.

January	Garnet
February	Amethyst
March	Aquamarine
April	Diamond
May	Emerald
June	Pearl
July	Ruby
August	Peridot
September	Sapphire
October	Opal
November	Topaz
December	Turquoise

ROCKS AND MINERALS

ROCKS Three types of rock are found on Earth: igneous, sedimentary, and metamorphic. Within each type, rocks can be further identified by their color, structure, and texture.

Examples Granite and marble

MINERALS These natural, nonliving substances grow from elements in the Earth and are shaped by temperature and pressure. They can be identified by their hardness, specific gravity, color, and the symmetry of their crystals.

Examples Sulfur and copper

CRYSTALS Derived from the Greek word *kryos* meaning "cold," crystals are formed from molten or dissolved minerals. Crystal symmetry or shape is grouped into six main shapes or "systems": monoclinic, triclinic, trigonal/hexagonal, cubic, orthorhombic, and tetragonal.

Examples Quartz and pyrite

GEMSTONES These are minerals whose color, rarity, or hardness makes them valuable. There are 100 types of gems.

Examples Diamond and ruby

MOHS' SCALE

DID YOU KNOW? German mineralogist Friedrich Mohs (1773–1839) devised a rating system for minerals, known as Mohs' scale. It defines the hardness or the ability of a mineral to resist scratching. A mineral with a high Mohs' score can scratch any material with a lower rating.

HARDNESS		SCRATCH TOOL	MINERAL
10	Very hard	Steel file	Diamond
9	Very hard	Steel file	Corundum
8	Very hard	Steel file	Topaz
7	Very hard	Steel file	Quartz
6	Hard	Heavy penknife	Orthoclase
5	Hard	Heavy penknife	Apatite
4	Semi-hard	Window glass	Fluorite
3	Soft	Copper wire or coin	Calcite
2	Soft	Fingernail	Gypsum
1	Very soft	Fingernail	Talc

FAMOUS ROCKS

ULURU Looming up from the Australian desert, this giant block of red sandstone, once known as Ayers Rock, is the world's largest free-standing rock. It is more than 1.5 miles (2.4 km) long, 1,142 ft (348 m) high, and has a perimeter of 5.8 miles (9.4 km). Uluru, meaning "great pebble," is the name given to the rock by Aboriginal Australians, for whom it is sacred.

BLACK STONE OF MECCA The Black Rock is located in the Eastern corner of the Ka'ba, the Great Mosque in Mecca, Islam's holiest shrine. According to legend, it was once white, but by absorbing the sins of the countless pilgrims who touch it, it has turned black.

DEVIL'S TOWER The tallest rock formation in the US, this giant monolith in Wyoming is visible from 100 miles (160 km) away. Its fluted columns rise 865 ft (265 m) high into the sky.

BALANCING ROCKS OF EPWORTH Just outside Harare, Zimbabwe, granite boulders teetering on top of each other have been formed by erosion from an ancient mass of granite. The rocks will sway from side to side, but always return to their original position.

GIANT'S CAUSEWAY Said to have been built by Irish giant Finn MacCool in pursuit of his Scottish counterpart Finn Gall, this rock formation in Northern Ireland, UK, comprises 40,000 rock columns which range from sea level to 18 ft (6 m) high. From overhead, they look like paving stones, many of which are perfect hexagons.

ROCK OF GIBRALTAR This long, steep mountain lies in the British colony of Gibraltar at the southernmost tip of Spain. At 1,396 ft (426 m) high and 2.25 miles (4 km) long, it is known as one of the Pillars of Hercules. The other Pillar of Hercules is the Jebel Musa in Africa, which lies opposite at the narrowest point of the Strait of Gibraltar.

15

PHYSICAL FEATURES

HIGHEST MOUNTAINS

All 35 of the highest mountains in the world are found in the Himalaya-Karakoram range in Asia.

MOUNTAIN	COUNTRY	HEIGHT	
		FT	M
Everest	Nepal/Tibet	29,022	8,846
K2	Kashmir/China	28,250	8,611
Kangchenjunga	Nepal/Sikkim	28,208	8,598
Lhotse	Nepal/Tibet	27,890	8,501
Makalu I	Nepal/Tibet	27,790	8,470
Dhaulagiri I	Nepal	26,810	8,172
Manaslu I	Nepal	26,760	8,156
Cho Oyu	Nepal	26,750	8,153
Nanga Parbat	Kashmir	26,660	8,126
Annapurna I	Nepal	26,504	8,078

DID YOU KNOW? On May 29, 1953, Edmund Hillary from New Zealand and Sherpa Tenzing Norgay from Nepal became the first people to reach the summit of Mount Everest.

LONGEST CAVE SYSTEMS

CAVE SYSTEM	COUNTRY	FT	M
Mammoth Cave system	US	1,837,270	560,000
Optimisticeskaja	Ukraine	583,989	178,000
Hölloch	Switzerland	449,475	137,000
Jewel Cave	US	416,667	127,000
Siebenhengsteholensystem	Switzerland	360,892	110,000

AMAZING FACT! The Mammoth Cave system is longer than the world's longest glacier, and even longer than the length of all the tunnels of the London underground tube system. The opening was discovered in 1799 by a hunter chasing a bear. Once a source of saltpeter, an ingredient of gunpowder, the caves became a major tourist attraction. The Mammoth Cave National Park, in Kentucky, was established in 1941.

LONGEST MOUNTAIN RANGES

RANGE	LOCATION	LENGTH	
		MILES	KM
Andes	South America	4,500	7,242
Rocky Mountains	North America	3,750	6,035
Himalayas/Karakoram/ Hundu Kush	Asia	2,400	3,862
Great Dividing Range	Australia	2,250	3,621
Trans-Antarctic Mountains	Antarctica	2,200	3,541
Brazilian East Coast Range	Brazil	1,900	3,058
Sumatran/ Javan Range	Sumatra, Java	1,800	2,897
Tien Shan	China	1,400	2,253
Eastern Ghats	India	1,300	2,092
Altai	Asia	1,250	2,012
Central New Guinean Range	Papua New Guinea	1,250	2,012
Urals	Russia	1,250	2,012

DID YOU KNOW? The longest undersea mountain range, the Mid-Atlantic Ridge, is 7,000 miles (11,265 km) long.

EARTH'S LOWEST POINTS

DEAD SEA Lying between Israel and Jordan, the Dead Sea's shore is the lowest exposed ground below sea level, at 1,312 ft (400 m). The seabed actually reaches 2,388 ft (728 m) below sea level. If there was a flight of stairs to take you back up to sea level, you would have to climb about 2,000 steps.

TURFAN DEPRESSION China's Turfan Depression is the second lowest point in the world, at 505 ft (154 m) below sea level.

QATTARA DEPRESSION The world's third lowest point is Egypt's Qattara Depression, at 436 ft (133 m) below sea level. It is on the Mediterranean coast, near the Libyan border.

ISLAND RECORDS

RECORD	ISLAND	MEASUREMENTS
Largest island	Greenland (Kalaatdlit Nunaat)	840,070 sq miles (2,175,600 sq km)
Smallest island country	Nauru (Pacific Ocean)	Nauru has an area of 8.2 sq miles (21.2 sq km)
Remotest island	Bouvet Island	1,056 miles (1,700 km) from Queen Maud Land, east Antarctica
Longest island arc	Indonesia	Covers 3 million sq miles (8 million sq km)
Highest island	Irian Jaya	Mount Jaya in Irian Jaya rises 16,500 ft (5,030 m)

AMAZING FACT! Although Australia looks to be the largest island on the map, it is actually regarded worldwide as a continental landmass, and not an island. It has an area of 2,941,517 sq miles (7,618,493 sq km), which is three times the size of Greenland.

HIGHEST ACTIVE VOLCANOES

VOLCANO	LOCATION	LATEST ACTIVITY	HEIGHT FT	M
Guallatiri	Chile	1987	19,882	6,060
Lááscar	Chile	1991	19,652	5,990
Cotopaxi	Ecuador	1975	19,347	5,897
Tupungatito	Chile	1986	18,504	5,640
Popocatépetl	Mexico	1995	17,887	5,452
Ruiz	Colombia	1992	17,716	5,400
Sangay	Ecuador	1988	17,159	5,230
Guagua Pichincha	Ecuador	1988	15,696	4,784
Purace	Colombia	1977	15,601	4,755
Kliuchevskoi	Russia	1995	15,584	4,750

DID YOU KNOW? In 1985 and 1987, Guallatiri, the southernmost volcano in the Andes, ejected whitish-yellow fumes up to 1,648 ft (500 m) high every half-hour.

LARGEST METEORITE CRATERS

CRATER	WIDTH MILES	KM
Sudbury, Ontario, Canada	87	140
Vredefort, South Africa	87	140
Manicouagan, Quebec, Canada	62	100

DID YOU KNOW? Recently, by using photographs taken from space, many new possible astroblemes (impact sites) have been discovered, including a massive site in Prague, Czech Republic, which measures 199 miles (320 km).

DEEPEST CAVES

CAVE SYSTEM	LOCATION	FT	M
Réseau Jean Bernard	France	5,256	1,602
Lampreschtsofen	Austria	5,036	1,535
Gouffre Mirolda	France	4,987	1,520
Shakta Pantjukhina	Georgia	4,947	1,508
Sistema Huautla	Mexico	4,839	1,475

LARGEST DESERTS

SAHARA North Africa's Sahara Desert is the world's largest, covering 3,500,000 sq miles (9,000,000 sq km). This hot, sandy desert is rapidly encroaching on grazing land.

AUSTRALIAN The Australian Desert covers 1,470,000 sq miles (3,800,000 sq km), but is made up of smaller desert regions – the Gibson, Simpson, and Great Sandy Desert.

ARABIAN The Arabian Desert covers 502,000 sq miles (1,300,000 sq km) of southwest Asia. Part of this desert is the Empty Quarter, a vast expanse of sand, which covers 250,000 sq miles (647,500 sq km).

GOBI Central Asia's barren Gobi Desert covers 400,000 sq miles (1,036,000 sq km). It has scorching summers and bitterly cold winters. Its name comes from *kobi*, the Mongolian word for desert. The Chinese call it *shamo*, or "sandy sea."

KALAHARI Covering 201,000 sq miles (520,000 sq km), an area larger than France, the Kalahari, in southern Africa, is the fifth largest desert. Its name comes from a local word that means torture, or suffering, but the Boer (Dutch) settlers called it *Bosjeveld*, or "thorn field."

RIVERS and LAKES

WORLD'S LONGEST RIVERS

RIVER	COUNTRIES	LENGTH	
		MILES	KM
Nile	Tanzania, Uganda, Sudan, Egypt	4,145	6,670
Amazon	Peru, Brazil	4,007	6,448
Yangtze–Kiang	China	3,915	6,300
Mississippi–Missouri–Red Rock	US	3,710	5,971
Yenisey–Angara–Selenga	Mongolia, Russia	3,442	5,540
Huang He (Yellow River)	China	3,395	5,464
Ob'–Irtysh	Mongolia, Kazakhstan, Russia	3,362	5,410
Zaïre (Congo)	Angola, Congo, Democratic Republic of the Congo	2,920	4,700
Lena–Kirenga	Russia	2,734	4,400

DID YOU KNOW? The River Nile could stretch all the way from New York to Berlin, Germany! The source of the river, Lake Victoria, Central Africa, was identified in 1858 by British explorer John Hanning Speke (1827–1864).

LARGEST LAKES

LAKE	LOCATION	APPROX. AREA	
		SQ MILES	SQ KM
Caspian Sea	Azerbaijan/Iran/Kazakhstan/Russia/Turkmenistan	143,205	371,000
Superior	Canada/US	31,820	82,414

DID YOU KNOW? Lake Superior, one of the Great Lakes in eastern North America, is the world's largest freshwater lake. It is 350 miles (564 km) in length – almost as long as Florida!

Victoria	Kenya, Tanzania, Uganda	26,570	68,800
Huron	Canada, US	23,010	59,596
Michigan	US	22,400	58,016
Aral Sea	Kazakhstan, Uzbekistan	15,444	40,000
Tanganyika	Burundi, Tanzania, Congo, Zambia	13,860	32,900
Great Bear	Canada	12,270	31,790
Baikal	Russia	11,775	30,500

DID YOU KNOW? Lake Baikal (or Baykal), Siberia, has a depth of up to 1.02 miles (1.63 km) in parts and contains one-fifth of the world's fresh water.

Great Slave	Canada	10,980	28,440

AMAZING RIVERS

GREATEST OUTFLOW The River Amazon, Brazil, discharges 2.5 cubic miles (10.5 cubic km) of water a minute into the Atlantic Ocean. That is enough for everyone in the world to have a bath every 44 minutes, allowing 17.5 gallons (80 liters) per bath.

LARGEST RIVER DELTA A delta is a wide, flat floodplain where a river becomes blocked with sediment and splits into many separate streams. The largest is the Ganges and Brahmaputra delta, which covers about 30,000 sq miles (75,000 sq km) – Sri Lanka could fit into this with room to spare!

LONGEST EUROPEAN RIVER The River Volga, Russia, flows for a distance of 2,194 miles (3,531 km).

LONGEST AUSTRALASIAN RIVER Australia's Murray River travels 1,609 miles (2,589 km)!

DID YOU KNOW? All rivers receive their water from rain or melting snow.

RIVER TYPES

PERENNIAL Usually found in temperate and tropical areas, perennial rivers flow year round. Although in mountain areas, such as the Rockies, river levels vary greatly between winter and summer, the river never dries up.

EPHEMERAL Many desert rivers are ephemeral. These rivers are usually dry and hardly ever have water flowing in them. The Todd River in central Australia is an ephemeral river.

SEASONAL Found in many areas of the Mediterranean, seasonal rivers are only full for part of the year. Often, they are rocky streams that flow in the winter and are bone dry during the summer.

AMAZING LAKES

LARGEST MAN-MADE RESERVOIR Owen Falls, in Uganda, has a volume of 49 cubic miles (205 cubic km). Completed in 1954, it generates hydroelectricity by waterfalls driving turbines.

LARGEST AUSTRALASIAN LAKE Australia's Lake Eyre has an area of 3,600 sq miles (9,323 sq km). It loses a lot of water by evaporation due to the heat of the sun. This process leaves the lake very salty.

OLDEST LAKE While most lakes are short-lived geological features, lasting only a few hundred thousand years, Lake Baikal, in Siberia, is 25 million years old.

LARGEST SOUTH AMERICAN LAKE Lake Titicaca, which sits in both Peru and Bolivia, has an area of 3,200 sq miles (8,288 sq km).

DID YOU KNOW? Lake Geneva will be filled in by sediment from the Rhone River and disappear in approximately 40,000 years!

HIGHEST WATERFALLS

WATERFALL	LOCATION	TOTAL DROP	
		FT	M
Angel Falls	Venezuela	3,212	979
Tugela	South Africa	3,107	947
Utigård	Norway	2,625	800
Mongefossen	Norway	2,540	774
Yosemite	US	2,425	739
Østre Mardøla Foss	Norway	2,152	656
Tyssestrengane	Norway	2,120	646
Cuquenán	Venezuela	2,000	610
Sutherland	New Zealand	1,904	580
Kjellfossen	Norway	1,841	561

AMAZING FACT! The longest single drop in the Angel Falls is 2,648 ft (807 m) – twice the height of the Eiffel Tower, France!

FRESHWATER ISLANDS

We think of islands as being in seas, and surrounded by seawater, but some are found in rivers and lakes, with fresh water around them. Here are six of the largest:

MARAJÓ Found at the mouth of the River Amazon, Brazil, Marajó has an area of 18,500 sq miles (48,000 sq km).

BANANAL Bananal Island, River Araguaia, Brazil, measures 7,720 sq miles (20,000 sq km).

MANITOULIN The island of Manitoulin, in Lake Huron, Canada, has an area of 1,068 sq miles (2,766 sq km).

ROYALE Surrounded by Lake Superior, US and Canada, Royale is 210 sq miles (544 sq km).

SAINT JOSEPH Saint Joseph, Lake Huron, has an area of 141 sq miles (365 sq km).

DRUMMOND Also surrounded by Huron, Drummond covers 136 sq miles (352 sq km).

INLAND WATER FACTS

LONGEST CANAL The Suez Canal links the Mediterranean with the Red Sea and stretches 108 miles (174 km).

MOST CANALS The Netherlands has 4,971 miles (8,000 km) of canals.

OLDEST CANALS These were built in Sumer (now Iraq) around 4000 BC.

WHAT IS A FJORD? In regions where deep valleys have been scoured by glaciers, the sea level often rises and floods the valleys, forming fjords.

LONGEST FJORD Nordvest Fjord, Greenland, extends for 194 miles (313 km) inland.

GLACIER FACTS

HOW ARE GLACIERS MADE? Layers of snow build up over years, turning into an icy mass called a firn. Eventually the firn becomes an ice cap and gravity forces it to flow down to lower ground.

LONGEST GLACIER Antarctica's Lambert-Fisher glacier is the longest in the world, at 320 miles (515 km) in length. It is 2.2 miles (3.5 km) deep and 40 miles (64 km) wide. It was discovered as recently as 1956.

MOST GLACIATED REGIONS More than one-tenth of the Earth's surface is permanently covered with ice. About 90 percent of this occurs in Antarctica. The South Polar region has 4,610,610 sq miles (12,588,000 sq km) of permanent snow and ice.

AVERAGE GLACIER FLOW Many of the world's glaciers begin high up in the mountains, and flow at a rate of 7 ft (2 m) per day.

THE GREAT LAKES

The Great Lakes are a group of freshwater lakes in North America.

SUPERIOR The farthest north, Superior covers 31,820 sq miles (82,414 sq km).

ONTARIO At 7,520 sq miles (19,477 sq km), Ontario means "beautiful lake."

HURON Named by French settlers, Lake Huron covers 23,010 sq miles (59,596 sq km).

MICHIGAN The only great lake contained in the US, Michigan measures 22,400 sq miles (58,016 sq km).

ERIE Lake Erie covers 9,930 sq miles (25,719 sq km). Its name comes from the Iroquois *erie*, meaning "cat."

MEMORY TIP! Think of **HOMES** to remember the Great Lakes: **H**uron, **O**ntario, **M**ichigan, **E**rie, **S**uperior.

OCEANS and SEAS

OCEANS AND SEAS

NAME	APPROXIMATE AREA	
	SQ MILES	SQ KM
Pacific Ocean	64,185,629	166,240,000

! DID YOU KNOW? The Pacific Ocean contains more water than all the world's other seas and oceans put together!

NAME	SQ MILES	SQ KM
Atlantic Ocean	33,421,006	86,560,000
Indian Ocean	28,351,484	73,430,000
Arctic Ocean	5,108,132	13,230,000
Arabian Sea	1,492,000	3,864,000
South China Sea	1,148,499	2,974,600
Caribbean Sea	1,062,939	2,753,000
Mediterranean Sea	969,116	2,510,000
Bering Sea	872,977	2,261,000
Bay of Bengal	839,000	2,173,000
Gulf of Mexico	595,749	1,542,985
Sea of Okhotsk	589,798	1,527,570
East China Sea	482,299	1,249,150
Sea of Japan	391,100	1,012,945
Andaman Sea	307,993	797,700
Hudson Bay	282,001	730,380
North Sea	222,124	575,300
Red Sea	168,996	437,700

! DID YOU KNOW? Most oceans are about 3.5 percent salt, but the Red Sea is 4.2 percent salt.

NAME	SQ MILES	SQ KM
Black Sea	168,495	436,400
Baltic Sea	160,000	414,400
Caspian Sea	143,552	371,800
Yellow Sea	113,514	294,000
Persian Gulf	92,197	238,790
Gulf of California	62,548	162,000
Irish Sea	40,000	103,600
English Channel	34,710	89,900

! AMAZING FACTS! The world's oceans and seas together make up 94 percent of all the water on Earth! • The Atlantic Ocean grows by 1 in (2.5 cm) every year, and it sinks about 4 in (10 cm) every 100 years! • The oldest parts of the ocean floor are about 200 million years old! • The Persian Gulf, in the Indian Ocean, is the warmest sea. • The highest tides occur in Canada's Bay of Fundy, rising more than 49 ft (15 m)!

WAVE HEIGHT SCALE

This wave height scale describes the sort of waves that sailors might encounter at sea. Wave height varies according to wind speed, and the higher ranges may prove dangerous, especially to small boats.

CODE	DESCRIPTION	HEIGHT RANGE	
		FT	M
0	Glassy	0	0
1	Calm	0–1	0–0.3
2	Rippled	1–2	0.3–0.6
3	Choppy	2–4	0.6–1.2
4	Very choppy	4–8	1.2–2.4
5	Rough	8–13	2.4–4
6	Very rough	13–20	4–6
7	High	20–30	6–9
8	Very high	30–45	9–14
9	Ultra high	45+	14+

! DID YOU KNOW? When the waves in an ocean or sea form white frothy tips, they are called "white horses."

ELEMENTS IN SEAWATER

The world's oceans and seas contain various minerals. Rain dissolves minerals from rocks, and washes them into the oceans. The most abundant are sodium and chlorine, which together form salt (sodium chloride).

ELEMENT	AVERAGE PERCENTAGE
Chlorine	55.29
Sodium	30.79
Magnesium	3.66
Sulfur	7.94
Calcium	1.19
Potassium	1.13

! AMAZING FACT! The total amount of salt in the world's oceans and seas would cover Europe to a depth of 3 miles (5 km).

UNDERWATER FEATURES

HIGHEST UNDERWATER SEAMOUNT The Great Meteor Tablemount in the north Atlantic Ocean is a huge submerged mountain – the tallest underwater mountain in the world. It was formed from a volcano erupting on the sea bed. The mountain measures 13,123 ft (4,000 m) high and is more than 62 miles (100 km) wide at its base.

LONGEST OCEAN MOUNTAIN RANGE The Atlantic Ocean's Mid-Atlantic Ridge is a line of rocks that marks the point where two of the Earth's tectonic plates meet. It stretches 7,000 miles (11,265 km) from a point north of Iceland to Bouvet Island in the South Atlantic Ocean. Some of its mountains are 13,123 ft (4,000 m) high.

TALLEST MOUNTAIN RISING FROM THE OCEAN Mauna Kea rises up 33,480 ft (10,205 m) from the floor of the Pacific Ocean to form the island of Hawaii. It is the world's tallest mountain from base to peak.

DEEPEST SUBMARINE CANYON A canyon 5,906 ft (1,800 m) deep is found 25 miles (40 km) south of Esperance, Australia. It is even deeper than the Grand Canyon!

BLACK SMOKERS Smokers are tall towers of mineral deposits that form on the ocean floor. Occurring in areas of volcanic activity, they erupt jets of hot water every few minutes. They were first discovered in 1977 by marine biologists in the American submersible, *Alvin*.

! AMAZING FACT! Legend has it that a fantastic city called Atlantis once existed in the center of the Atlantic Ocean. It was apparently destroyed by an earthquake, and lost beneath the surface forever.

SEA ICE FACTS

WHEN DOES THE SEA FREEZE? Oceans and seas freeze over only when the temperature falls below 28°F (-1.9°C).

LARGEST ICEBERG The biggest iceberg recorded was over 208 miles (335 km) long and 60 miles (97 km) wide – an area three times as big as Cyprus!

HOW OLD ARE ICEBERGS? Scientists estimate that the average age of the ice that forms icebergs is 5,000 years!

TALLEST ICEBERG A 550-ft (167-m) iceberg was seen off Greenland in 1958.

LONGEST GLACIER The Lambert-Fisher Ice Passage, in Antarctica, extends for a distance of 320 miles (515 km).

FASTEST-MOVING GLACIER Greenland's Quarayaq glacier flows as fast as 65–80 ft (20–24 m) every day!

DID YOU KNOW? Only about 12 percent of an iceberg is visible above the surface of the water – the rest is hidden below the surface.

DEEPEST DEEP-SEA TRENCHES

TRENCH	OCEAN	DEEPEST POINT	
		FT	M
Marianas	Pacific	35,837	10,924
Tonga	Pacific	35,430	10,800
Philippine	Pacific	34,436	10,497
Kermadec	Pacific	32,960	10,047
Bonin	Pacific	32,786	9,994
New Britain	Pacific	32,609	9,940
Kuril	Pacific	31,985	9,750
Izu	Pacific	31,805	9,695
Puerto Rico	Atlantic	28,229	8,605
Yap	Pacific	27,973	8,527
Japan	Pacific	27,599	8,412
South Sandwich	Atlantic	27,313	8,325

AMAZING FACT! Eight of the deepest ocean trenches would be deep enough to submerge Mount Everest!

DEEPEST OCEANS AND SEAS

OCEAN/SEA	GREATEST DEPTH	
	FT	M
Pacific Ocean	35,837	10,924
Atlantic Ocean	30,246	9,219
Indian Ocean	24,460	7,455
Caribbean Sea	22,788	6,946
Arctic Ocean	18,456	5,625
South China Sea	16,456	5,016
Bering Sea	15,659	4,773
Mediterranean Sea	15,197	4,632
Gulf of Mexico	12,425	3,787
Japan Sea	12,276	3,742

DID YOU KNOW? The deepest point in the deepest ocean is close to 6.8 miles (11 km) down, almost 29 times the height of the Empire State Building!

DID YOU KNOW? The Arctic Ocean has an average depth of only 3,953 ft (1,205 m), making it the shallowest ocean in the world. It is frozen solid for most of the year.

MOST RECENT UNDERWATER DESCENT RECORDS

PERSON	COUNTRY	SUBMARINE	LOCATION	DATE	DEPTH	
					FT	M
William Beebe Otis Barton	US	Bathysphere	Bermuda	August 15, 1934	3,028	923
Otis Barton	US	Benthoscope	Santa Cruz, USA	August 16, 1949	4,500	1,372
Georges Houot and Pierre Willm	France	F.R.N.S. 3 bathyscaphe	Toulon, France	August 12, 1953	5,085	1,550
Georges Houot and Pierre Willm	France	F.R.N.S. 3 bathyscaphe	Cap Ferrat, France	August 14, 1953	6,890	2,100
Auguste and Jacques Piccard	France	Trieste bathyscaphe	Ponza, Italy	September 30, 1953	10,335	3,150
Georges Houot and Pierre Willm	France	F.R.N.S. 3 bathyscaphe	Dakar, Senegal	February 14, 1954	13,287	4,050
Jacques Piccard and Donald Walsh	Switzerland US	Trieste 2 bathyscaphe	Marianas Trench, Pacific Ocean	November 14, 1959	18,600	5,669
Jacques Piccard and Donald Walsh	Switzerland US	Trieste 2 bathyscaphe	Marianas Trench, Pacific Ocean	January 7, 1960	24,000	7,315
Jacques Piccard and Donald Walsh	Switzerland US	Trieste 2 bathyscaphe	Marianas Trench, Pacific Ocean	January 23, 1960	35,814	10,916

DID YOU KNOW? Because the Marianas Trench is the deepest known place in the world's oceans, the 1960 descent of the *Trieste 2* to its lowest point set a record that can never be broken. Scientists on board traveled in an observation capsule with thick walls to withstand the pressure.

AMAZING FACT! Joint record-holder Jacques Ernest Jean Piccard (b.1922) is the son of Auguste. As well as their ocean descent records, three members of the Piccard family – Auguste (1884–1962), his twin brother, Jean Félix (1884–1963), and Jean's wife, Jeanette (1895–1981) – set balloon altitude records!

WEATHER

WEATHER RECORDS

WINDIEST PLACE In Port Martin, Antarctica, the wind speed averaged 65 mph (105 km/h) for a whole month.

BIGGEST HAILSTONES On September 3, 1970, hailstones weighing 1 lb 11oz (760 g) and the size of tenpin bowling balls fell on Kansas.

BIGGEST SNOWFALL Single snowstorms have resulted in almost 16 ft (5 m) of snow – the equivalent of three adults standing on each others' shoulders! However, the greatest snowfall ever occurred in Paradise, Mount Rainier, Washington, between February 1971 and February 1972, when 102 ft (31 m) of snow fell!

DRIEST PLACE Chile's Atacama Desert is so dry that it receives an average rainfall of only 0.02 in (0.51 mm) per year.

MOST RAINY DAYS Hawaii's Mount Wai-'ale-'ale experiences up to 350 days of rain per year.

RAINING FROGS Although as yet there are no reports of any cats and dogs falling from the sky, the people of Trowbridge, UK, were amazed and bewildered when there was a downpour of live frogs! Strong winds had sucked them up from local ponds and rivers.

MOST THUNDERY DAYS Thunder occurs on 200–250 days of the year in Java, Indonesia and also around Lake Victoria, Africa.

SUNNIEST PLACE In the Eastern Sahara Desert, Africa, the Sun shines for 97 percent of the time.

LEAST SUNSHINE At the North Pole, the freezing cold winters last 182 days during which the Sun never shines.

DID YOU KNOW? In any one day, there may be 44,000 storms over the Earth!

TRY IT YOURSELF! To find out how far away a storm is, count slowly between the flash and the rumble. Every five is a mile; each three is a kilometer.

HIGHEST RECORDED RAINFALL

TOWN	COUNTRY	RECORD RAINFALL	
		IN	MM
Cherrapuni	India	425	10,795
Andagoya	Colombia	281	7,137
Pago Pago	Samoa	194	4,928
Moulmein	Burma	190	4,826
Tabing	Indonesia	175	4,445
Monrovia	Liberia	175	4,420

TRY IT YOURSELF! If you are caught in a thunderstorm, to avoid being struck by lightning, crouch down low and keep your feet together. Keep away from trees.

RECORD HIGH TEMPERATURES

TOWN	COUNTRY	HIGHEST TEMPERATURE	
		°F	°C
Arouane	Mali	130	54.4
Abadan	Iran	127	52.8
Cloncurry	Australia	127	52.8
Wadi Halfa	Sudan	127	52.8
Aswan	Egypt	124	51.1
Fort Flatters	Algeria	124	51.1
Mosul	Iraq	124	51.1
Cufra	Libya	122	50.0
Gabes	Tunisia	122	50.0

CONTINENTAL HIGHS

CONTINENT	TEMPERATURE	
	°F	°C
Africa	136	57.8
North America	134	56.7
Asia	129	53.9
Australasia and Oceania	128	53.3
Europe	122	50.0
South America	120	48.9
Antarctica	58	14.4

DID YOU KNOW? The sizzling temperature that tops this list was recorded in Azizia, Libya, Africa in 1922.

RECORD COLD TEMPERATURES

Although it is not a country, but a dependency of Denmark, Greenland, is included in this list – the town of Eismitte is the world's oldest inhabitable place.

TOWN	COUNTRY/ DEPENDENCY	COLDEST TEMPERATURE	
		°F	°C
Eismitte	Greenland	-85	-64.8
Yakutsk	Russia	-84	-64.3
Fairbanks	US	-66	-54.4
Aklavik	Canada	-62	-52.2
Ulan Bator	Mongolia	-48	-44.4

CONTINENTAL LOWS

CONTINENT	TEMPERATURE	
	°F	°C
Antarctica	-128.6	-89.2
Australasia and Oceania	-8	-22.2
South America	-27	-32.7
Europe	-67	-54.9
Asia	-90	-67.7
North America	-81	-62.7
Africa	-11	23.9

DID YOU KNOW? No one lives in Antarctica because of its harsh climate, but visiting scientists work in research stations.

BEAUFORT SCALE FOR MEASURING WIND SPEED

The Beaufort scale, which was introduced in 1806 by British Admiral Sir Francis Beaufort (1774–1857), describes the effects of wind on land and sea. The scale is divided into a series of values, known as forces, from 0 for total calm to 12 and above for hurricanes. Each value represents a specific range and classification of wind speeds with accompanying descriptions of the effects on surface features.

FORCE	DESCRIPTION	SPEED		CHARACTERISTICS
		MPH	KM/H	
0	Calm	1	1.6	Smoke rises vertically; sea surface is mirror smooth
1	Light air	1–3	1.7–5	Rising smoke indicates the direction of the wind
2	Slight breeze	4–7	6–12	Wind can be felt on the face and leaves rustle in trees
3	Gentle breeze	8–12	13–20	Wind extends a light flag
4	Moderate wind	13–18	21–30	Loose paper blows around; frequent whitecaps at sea
5	Fresh wind	19–24	31–39	Small trees sway
6	Strong wind	25–31	40–50	Wind whistles in telephone wires; some spray on the surface of the ocean
7	High wind/ near gale	32–38	51–61	Large trees sway
8	Gale	39–46	62–74	Twigs break from trees; long streaks of foam appear on the surface of the sea
9	Strong gale	47–54	75–87	Branches break from trees
10	Whole gale/ storm	55–63	88–102	Trees uproot; sea takes on a white appearance
11	Severe storm	64–72	103–116	Widespread damage
12+	Hurricane	73–82	117–132	Structural damage on land; storm waves at sea

CLOUD LAYERS

STRATUS The lowest of all clouds, stratus form below 1,456 ft (450 m) and often hide hills and tall skyscrapers with fog.

CUMULUS Puffy cumulus clouds are gray at the bottom and brilliant white on top and form between 1,476–6,562 ft (450–2,000 m).

STRATOCUMULUS These clouds are recognizable by a low sheet of gray or white lumpy clouds, forming at 1,476–6,562 ft (450–2,000 m) high.

CUMULONIMBUS When there is a heavy shower, thunderstorm, or tornado, blame these massive, dark cumulonimbus clouds. They stretch as high as 1,476–6,562 ft (450–2,000 m).

NIMBOSTRATUS Thick, multi-layered clouds, nimbostratus bring only rain and snow. They form at 2,953–9,843 ft (900–3,000 m) above the ground.

ALTOSTRATUS Forming a thin, watery layer 6,562–22,966 ft (2,000–7,000 m) above the ground, altostratus clouds make a colored ring around the Sun and Moon.

CIRRUS The highest in the sky, wispy cirrus clouds are 16,404 ft (5,000 m) higher than Mount Everest. They drift above us at between 16,404–44,291 ft (5,000–13,500 m).

CIRROCUMULUS Also at 16,404–44,291 ft (5,000–13,500 m), cirrocumulus clouds are made of icy particles and resemble fishscales in appearance – hence the phrase "a mackerel sky."

DID YOU KNOW? The highest thunderclouds in the sky are black, flat-topped cumulonimbus, which loom above us at 10 miles (16 km) high. They often bring hail showers or tornadoes.

HOW FAR CAN YOU SEE?

EXTREMELY CLEAR In good, clear conditions, you can see for more than 31 miles (50 km).

LIGHT HAZE In a light haze or mist, visibility is reduced to about 6 miles (10 km) – a vast difference from a clear day.

LIGHT FOG Ground level cloud or light fog drastically reduces the distance you can see to only about 0.6 mile (1 km).

VERY DENSE FOG Extremely dense fog is a hazard to vehicle traffic, but it is possible to see up to 50 ft (15 m). Fortunately, fog that, as in the expression, is so thick that you "can't see your hand in front of your face" is exceptionally rare.

DID YOU KNOW? Some people use the expression "a pea souper" to describe a very dense fog – comparing it to thick pea soup!

NATURAL DISASTERS

WORST AVALANCHES AND LANDSLIDES OF THE 20TH CENTURY

LOCATION	INCIDENT	DATE	ESTIMATED NUMBER KILLED
Yungay, Peru	Landslide	May 1970	17,500
Italian Alps	Avalanche	December 1916	10,000
Huarás, Peru	Avalanche	December 1941	5,000
Nevada Huascaran, Peru	Avalanche	January 1962	3,500
Medellín, Colombia	Landslide	September 1987	683
Chungar, Peru	Avalanche	March 1971	600

DID YOU KNOW? This list includes only incidents where deaths occurred as a direct result of the avalanche or landslide itself, rather than by flooding or earthquakes. The worst incident of all was the destruction of Yungay in Peru, which was part of a much larger cataclysm that left up to 70,000 dead. Following an earthquake and flooding, the town was wiped out by an avalanche that left 2,500 survivors out of a population of 20,000.

MOST DESTRUCTIVE FLOODS AND STORMS OF THE 20TH CENTURY

LOCATION	DATE	ESTIMATED NUMBER KILLED
Huang He River, China	August 1931	3,700,000
Bangladesh	November 1970	300–500,000
Henan, China	September 1939	200,000
Chang Jiang River, China	September 1911	100,000
Bengal, India	November 1942	40,000

DID YOU KNOW? The Earth's surface is made up of "plates" that move constantly but very slowly. When two plates collide, pressure builds up and the result is an earthquake.

HURRICANE NAMES

1998	1999	2000	2001	2002	2003
Alex	Arlene	Alberto	Allison	Arthur	Ana
Bonnie	Bret	Beryl	Barry	Bertha	Bill
Charley	Cindy	Chris	Chantal	Cristobal	Claudette
Danielle	Dennis	Debby	Dean	Dolly	Danny
Earl	Emily	Ernesto	Erin	Edouard	Erika
Frances	Floyd	Florence	Felix	Fay	Fabian
Georges	Gert	Gordon	Gabrielle	Gustav	Grace
Hermine	Harvey	Helene	Humberto	Hanna	Henri
Ivan	Irene	Isaac	Iris	Isidore	Isabel
Jeanne	José	Joyce	Jerry	Josephine	Juan
Karl	Katrina	Keith	Karen	Kyle	Kate
Lisa	Lenny	Leslie	Lorenzo	Lili	Larry
Mitch	Maria	Michael	Michelle	Marco	Mindy
Nicole	Nate	Nadine	Noel	Nana	Nicholas
Otto	Ophelia	Oscar	Olga	Omar	Odette
Paula	Philippe	Patty	Pablo	Paloma	Peter
Richard	Rita	Rafael	Rebekah	Rene	Rose
Shary	Stan	Sandy	Sebastien	Sally	Sam
Tomas	Tammy	Tony	Tanya	Teddy	Teresa
Virginie	Vince	Valerie	Van	Vicky	Victor
Walter	Wilma	William	Wendy	Wilfred	Wanda

This is a list of the agreed names given to hurricanes, or tropical cyclones, in the order in which they occur in the Atlantic, the US, and the Caribbean. The lists are reused every six years, so the 1998 list will be reused in 2004.

GREAT VOLCANIC ERUPTIONS

VESUVIUS, ITALY In AD 79, Mount Vesuvius erupted, engulfing and preserving the Roman cities of Herculaneum and Pompeii. As many as 20,000 people lost their lives.

LAKI, ICELAND Iceland is highly volcanic but as it is thinly populated, eruptions seldom result in major loss of life. However, when the Laki volcanic ridge erupted in 1783, it engulfed villages in a river of lava 50 miles (80 km) long and 100 ft (30 m) deep, releasing poisonous gases that killed about 9,350 people.

TAMBORA, INDONESIA The eruption of Tambora in 1815 killed about 10,000 islanders outright, with 82,000 more dying later from disease and the famine caused by the destruction of crops. No other volcano has caused such a loss of human life.

KRAKATOA, SUMATRA After a series of eruptions in August 1883, the island of Krakatoa exploded with a tremendous bang that was recorded 3,000 miles (4,800 km) away. Officially 36,417 people were killed, but some sources put the fatalities at 200,000.

MONT PELÉE, MARTINIQUE After lying dormant for centuries, in 1902 Mont Pelée burst apart, showering the island with molten lava, ash, and gas, and destroying all life.

EARTHQUAKE RECORDS

WORST EVER If historical records are to be believed, an earthquake affecting the Middle East and North Africa in 1202 killed as many as one million people.

WORST 20TH-CENTURY In 1920, an earthquake and resulting landslides in Kansu Province, China, left 180,000 dead.

LONGEST-LASTING Most earthquakes last less than a minute and there are no accurate records of durations of many. However, an earthquake in 1964 in Alaska lasted five minutes, and killed 131 people.

MOST POWERFUL In 1906, an earthquake 200 miles (322 km) off the Colombian coast measured 8.9 on the Richter scale.

MODIFIED MERCALLI SCALE FOR MEASURING EARTHQUAKES

Using a range of I–XII, the Mercalli scale, devised by Italian geologist Giuseppe Mercalli (1850–1914), indicates an earthquake's intensity by observing its effects.

I Movement detected by instruments

II Felt by people resting

III Hanging lights sway

IV Windows rattle; parked cars rock

V Small objects move; doors swing

VI Felt by all; trees sway; objects fall off shelves; window glass shatters

VII Difficult to stand; bricks and tiles fall; chimneys crack

VIII Hard to steer a car; tree branches snap; chimneys fall

IX General panic; ground cracks; damage to underground pipes

X Pipes burst; rivers flood; buildings collapse

XI Few structures survive; bridges destroyed, large gaps in ground

XII Total destruction; waves ripple ground

WORST DISASTERS

FAMINE A famine in China in 1959–1961 is believed to have killed at least 30 million people. Just ten years later, in 1969–1971, another famine caused 20 million more deaths.

FIRE The Peshtigo forest fire, which broke out in Wisconsin in 1871, resulted in 2,682 deaths. Bush fires in Australia, in 1983, devastated vast areas of Victoria and destroyed seven towns and 2,000 homes.

HAILSTONES In 1888, in Moradabad and Beheri, India, 246 people and more than 1,600 sheep and goats were killed by hailstones as big as baseballs.

TORNADO In 1989, a tornado at Shaturia, Bangladesh, left around 1,300 people dead and 50,000 homeless.

TSUNAMI In 1960, the combined effect of a tornado and tsunami, or tidal wave, killed 12,000 Moroccans. A tsunami that hit Papua New Guinea in 1998 is believed to have killed more than 6,000.

RICHTER SCALE

Invented in 1935 by US seismologist (earthquake expert) Charles F. Richter (1900–1985), the Richter scale is used to indicate the magnitude or strength of an earthquake, based on the size of seismic waves (vibration of the ground). Each level on the scale is ten times higher than the one before it.

0 Detected by sensitive seismographs

1 Detected by instruments

2 Lowest felt by humans

3 Slight vibration; more than 100,000 a year around the world

4 Up to 15,000 a year; 4.5 is detected by seismographs worldwide, but causes little damage

5 3,000 a year; the 1960 Agadir, Morocco, earthquake was 5.6

6 100 a year worldwide

7 20 a year; the 1995 Kobe, Japan, earthquake was 7.2

8 Major destructive earthquakes; average two a year. The 1907 San Francisco earthquake was estimated at 8.25

9 No quake higher than 8.9 has been recorded, but 9.0 or even higher is theoretically possible

25

LIFE ON EARTH

CLASSIFICATION

HOW TO CLASSIFY A SPECIES

Living things are classified according to the features they have in common. This is how a tiger would be classified.

KINGDOM Animals (Animalia) A kingdom is the largest grouping in the classification.

PHYLUM Chordates (Chordata) A phylum is a major group within a kingdom. It is sometimes called a division in the classification of plants.

CLASS Mammals (Mammalia) A class is a major part of a phylum or subphylum. A subclass is a large group within a class.

FAMILY Cats (Felidae) A family is a large collection of species that have several features in common.

GENUS Big cats (*Panthera*) A genus is a small collection of similar species.

SPECIES Tiger (*Panthera tigris*)

THE FIVE KINGDOMS

All living things are divided into five groups, called kingdoms, based on the different ways in which they work.

MONERANS This kingdom includes the single-celled organisms, such as bacteria. Monerans were the first life forms, and there are now more than 5,000 species. The kingdom of Monerans also includes blue-green algae.

PROTISTS This kingdom contains simple organisms, most of which have only a single cell. There are at least 65,000 species of protist.

FUNGI Fungi, such as mushrooms and toadstools, absorb food that has been made by plants and animals. The kingdom has thousands of species.

PLANTS Plants cannot move. They reproduce by making spores or seeds. The kingdom contains more than 400,000 species.

ANIMALS The animal kingdom contains organisms that cannot make their own food and must therefore feed themselves. Most animals are able to move around in search of food, but some spend their adult lives in one place.

KINGDOM OF MONERANS

PHYLUM	LATIN NAME	SPECIES
Typical bacteria	Eubacteria	5,000
Primitive bacteria	Archaebacteria	500

KINGDOM OF PROTISTS

COMMON NAME	PHYLUM	SPECIES
Algae	Several	20,000
Amoebas	Sarcodina	20,000
Flagellates	Zoomastigina	15,000
Ciliates	Ciliophora	8,000
Sporozoans	Sporozoa	5,000

KINGDOM OF FUNGI

PHYLUM	LATIN NAME	SPECIES
Sac fungi	Ascomycota	30,000
Fungi imperfecti	Deuteromycota	25,000
Club fungi	Basidiomycota	25,000
Molds	Zygomycota	750
Water molds	Oomycota	600

KINGDOM OF PLANTS

Most plants are organisms that produce food from sunlight. Most phyla contain nonflowering plants, including the spore- and the cone-bearing phyla. There is only one phylum of flowering plants, which produce flowers, fruits, and seeds.

PHYLUM	LATIN NAME	SPECIES
Flowering plants	Angiospermophyta	250,000
Mosses, liverworts	Bryophyta	15,000
Ferns	Pteridophyta	12,000
Club mosses	Lycopodophyta	1,000
Gymnosperms	Gymnospermophyta	1,000
Horsetails	Sphenophyta	15

DID YOU KNOW? Gymnosperms are nonflowering plants, and include conifers (pine trees) and cycads (palm trees).

FLOWERING PLANTS

There are more than 250,000 species of flowering plants, of which there are two groups: monocotyledons and dicotyledons.

MONOCOTYLEDONS Plants whose seeds have one cotyledon (seed-leaf) and that have leaves with parallel veins are called monocotyledons. The flower parts are usually in threes, or multiples of three. Examples of monocotyledons are irises, grasses, and orchids.

DICOTYLEDONS Plants that have seeds with two cotyledons (seed-leaves) and leaves with a branching network of veins are called dicotyledons. Flower parts are usually in fours or fives, or multiples of these numbers. Many species have woody stems. Examples of dicotyledons are beans, roses, cacti, carrots, and oak trees.

KINGDOM OF ANIMALS

PHYLUM	LATIN NAME	SPECIES
Arthropods	Arthropoda	1,000,000+
Molluscs	Mollusca	110,000
Chordates	Chordata	45,000
Roundworms	Nematoda	20,000
Segmented worms	Annelida	18,600
Flatworms, flukes	Platyhelminthes	15,000
Corals, jellyfish	Cnidaria	9,500
Sponges	Porifera	9,000
Echinoderms	Echinodermata	6,000
Moss animals	Bryozoa	4,000
Rotifers	Rotifera	2,000
Spiny-headed worms	Acanthocephala	1,500
Water bears	Tardigrada	600
Lampshells	Brachiopoda	300
Horsehair worms	Nematomorpha	250
Velvet worms	Onychophora	100
Comb jellies	Ctenophora	90

CLASSES OF MOLLUSKS

CLASS	LATIN NAME	SPECIES
Snails	Gastropoda	35,000
Mussels, clams	Bivalvia	15,000
Octopuses, squids	Cephalopoda	600
Deep-sea limpets	Monoplacophora	500
Chitons	Polyplacophora	500
Tusk shells	Scaphopoda	350
Solenogasters	Aplacophora	250

CLASSES OF ARTHROPODS

CLASS	LATIN NAME	SPECIES
Insects	Insecta	1,000,000+
Millipedes	Diplopoda	10,000
Centipedes	Chilopoda	2,500
Sea spiders	Pycnogonida	1,000
Horseshoe crabs	Merostomata	4

ARACHNID ORDERS

Camel spiders • Harvestmen • Micro-whip scorpions • Mites • Pseudoscorpions • Ricinuleids Scorpions • Spiders • Whip scorpions and spiders

CLASSES OF VERTEBRATES

Animals in the phylum Chordata have a stiff cord running down their bodies. Most are vertebrates (animals with backbones). Sea squirts – a subphyla of about 2,500 species – have a cord, but it is not a true backbone.

CLASS	LATIN NAME	SPECIES
Bony fish	Osteichthyes	20,000
Birds	Aves	9,000
Reptiles	Reptilia	6,000
Mammals	Mammalia	4,600
Amphibians	Amphibia	4,200
Sharks and rays	Chondrichthyes	800
Jawless fish	Agnatha	75

MAMMAL ORDERS

Aardvarks • Bats • Carnivores • Colugos Elephant shrews • Elephants • Even-toed hoofed mammals • Hares, rabbits, pikas Hyraxes • Insectivores • Manatees and dugongs Marsupials • Monotremes • Odd-toed hoofed mammals • Pangolins • Primates • Rodents Seals, sealions, walruses • Sloths, anteaters, armadillos • Tree shrews • Whales and dolphins

CLASSES OF CRUSTACEANS

Crustaceans are a subphylum of arthropods. There are about 40,000 species.

CLASS	LATIN NAME	SPECIES
Crabs, lobsters, shrimps	Malacostraca	20,000
Copepods	Copepoda	7,500
Mussel shrimps	Ostracoda	2,000
Barnacles	Cirripedia	1,220
Branchiopods	Branchiopoda	1,000
Spiny sand shrimps	Branchiura	125
Mystacocarideans	Mystacocarida	10
Sand shrimps	Cephalocarida	9

INSECT ORDERS

Ants, bees, wasps • Beetles • Bugs • Butterflies, moths • Caddisflies • Cockroaches • Diplurans Dragonflies • Earwigs • Fleas • Grasshoppers, crickets • Grylloblattids • Lacewings, ant lions Lice • Mayflies • Praying mantises • Proturans Scorpionflies • Silverfish • Springtails • Stick and leaf insects • Stoneflies • Stylopids • Termites Thrips • True flies • Webspinners • Zorapterans

AMPHIBIAN ORDERS

Caecilians • Frogs, toads Newts, salamanders

REPTILE ORDERS

Crocodiles, alligators Snakes and lizards • Tuatara Turtles and tortoises

BONY FISH ORDERS

Carp, characins • Catfish Eels • Flying fish, garfish Herrings, anchovies Perches, cichlids, gobies, wrasses • Salmon, trout

CARTILAGINOUS FISH ORDERS

Sharks, skates, and rays

BIRD ORDERS

Albatrosses, petrels, shearwaters • Cranes, rails, coots, bustards • Divers Ducks, geese, swans Eagles, hawks, vultures Emus, cassowaries Frogmouths, nightjars Grebes • Herons, storks, ibises, spoonbills, flamingos Kingfishers, bee-eaters, rollers, hornbills • Kiwis Mousebirds • Ostriches Owls • Parrots • Pelicans, gannets, frigate birds, cormorants, anhingas Penguins • Perching birds Pheasants, partridges, grouse, turkeys • Pigeons, doves • Rheas • Sandgrouse Swifts, hummingbirds Tinamous • Trogons, quetzals • Turacos, cuckoos, roadrunners • Waders, terns, gulls, auks • Woodpeckers, barbets, honeyguides, puffbirds, toucans

DID YOU KNOW?
Bird species outnumber mammals by two to one.

TREES and PLANTS

THE LANGUAGE OF FLOWERS

In the 19th century, flowers and plants were given symbolic meanings, and by choosing which flowers were used in a bouquet, the sender could convey a hidden message.

PLANT	MEANING
Bluebell	Permanence
Carnation	Pure love
Daffodil	Admiration
Forget Me Not	True, lasting love
Geranium (scarlet)	Comfort/stupidity
Hollyhock	Ambition
Lavender	Distrust
Poppy	Extravagance
Rose	Love

MOST FORESTED LANDS

These are the countries with the greatest area of forest and woodland as a percentage of their total land area. With increasing deforestation, the world average of forest area has fallen to about 31 percent.

COUNTRY/ DEPENDENCY	PERCENT COVERED BY FOREST
Surinam	92
Papua New Guinea	91
Solomon Islands	85
French Guiana (French dependency)	81
Guyana	77

DID YOU KNOW? The least forested large countries in the world are the desert lands of the Middle East and North Africa, such as Libya. Less than 0.5 percent of the land area of these countries is covered by forest or woodland.

TOP NONFOOD CROPS IN THE WORLD

CROP	USE	ANNUAL PRODUCTION TONS	TONNES
Cotton	Clothing	19,250,9520	19,560,00
Tobacco	Cigarettes	6,858,866	6,968,996
Rubber	Tires, shoes, balls, erasers	6,718,720	6,826,580
Jute	Sacks, rope	2,742,625	2,786,654
Castor beans	Oil	1,304,312	1,325,251
Coir	Mats	644,051	654,390
Flax	Linen	525,611	534,049
Sisal	String	319,986	325,123
Hops	Flavoring beer	120,257	122,188

STRANGE PLANTS AND TREES

SEE THE LIGHT The Japanese fungus *Mycaena lux-coeli* produces phosphorescent enzymes that make it glow like a miniature lantern. It can be seen in the dark from 50 ft (15 m) away.

CATCHING FLIES *Rafflesia*, a parasitic plant that grows in the forests of Southeast Asia, has the largest and possibly the smelliest flower in the world. It looks and smells like a lump of decaying flesh, and is visited by swarms of flies, which pollinate the flower while crawling over it.

DRINK YOUR MILK The South American milk tree, *Brosimum utile*, belongs to the fig family, and produces a sap that looks, tastes, and is used just like cows' milk!

PLANT PARTS

LEAF A leaf traps the energy in sunlight to make food – a process called photosynthesis.

STEM The part of a plant that supports the buds, leaves, and flowers, and carries water and nutrients throughout the plant.

SHOOT A plant shoot consists of a stem, bud, leaves and flowers. It normally grows toward the light.

BUD An undeveloped shoot that is protected by scales. When conditions are favorable, the scales fold back, the bud bursts, and the shoot starts to grow.

ROOT The part of a plant that collects water, minerals, and, in some, food.

POISONOUS PLANTS

Many common plants, such as buttercups, are poisonous if they are eaten, because they contain harmful chemicals known as phytotoxins.

ACONITE Also called Wolf's Bane or Monkshood, the plant is found in Europe and North America. It can cause death within minutes.

CURARE Extracted from the bark of certain trees, it is used by South American Indian tribes to tip their poison arrows.

DEADLY NIGHTSHADE Also known as Belladonna, it contains a tiny amount of the poison atropine, enough to kill a child.

HEMLOCK Water hemlock and spotted hemlock contain some of the most deadly poisons known, even though carrots, celery, and parsnips belong to the same family!

PLANT MYTHOLOGY

ROWAN Rowan used to be made into garlands, then placed around the necks of pigs to fatten them up.

OAK An old rhyme warned that oak trees should be avoided in thunderstorms since they were believed to be good conductors of electricity: "Beware the oak, it draws the stroke."

MISTLETOE If mistletoe was hung in a house before Christmas, it is believed that a death would occur.

LAUREL Laurel has long been associated with victory – soldiers who had won battles wore laurel wreaths.

TREE RECORDS

LARGEST FORESTS/MOST COMMON TREES Russia has 20 percent of the world's total forest area. The Siberian larch accounts for 38 percent of the total tree cover in Russia. The huge Tongass National Forest, Sitka, Alaska, which is the largest forest in the US, occupies some 26,125 sq miles (67,664 sq km), an area almost as large as the whole of Ireland!

FASTEST-GROWING TREES A eucalyptus tree in New Guinea grew 35 ft (10.6 m) in 15 months. One in Zimbabwe reached 100 ft (30.48 m) in seven years and one in New Zealand 150 ft (45.72 m) in 15 years.

SLOWEST-GROWING TREES *Puya raimondii*, a rare South American evergreen, is one of the slowest to grow and takes the longest to flower – its panicle (flower tuft) appears after 80 to 150 years, after which the plant dies. *Fitzroya*, a Chilean conifer, can take 300 years to reach 66 ft (20 m).

OLDEST TREE SPECIES Imprints of leaves of the maidenhair tree (*Ginkgo biloba*) have been found in sedimentary rocks of the Jurassic and Triassic Periods (135–210 million years ago). This means they must have been living at the same time as the dinosaurs.

LARGEST TREE The General Sherman giant sequoia in Sequoia National Park, California, is 998 in (2,535 cm) in circumference, and 275 ft (83.8 m) tall – the tallest living thing on the planet. It has been calculated that if it were converted into pencils, end to end, they would more than reach round the Equator, a distance of 24,901.46 miles (40,075.02 km)!

MOST DROUGHT RESISTANT Africa's baobab tree stores up to 30,000 gallons (136,000 liters) of water in its trunk.

PLANT RECORDS

FASTEST-GROWING PLANTS A *Hesperoyucca whipplei*, a shrub also known as "Our Lord's Candle," grew 12 ft (3.65 m) in 14 days in 1978 – an average of approximately 9.8 in (25 cm) a day. There are also examples of sunflowers growing to 20 ft (6 m) in one season, and some bamboos can spurt by 35.4 in (90 cm) a day, and reach 98.4 ft (30 m) high in three months.

SLOWEST-GROWING PLANTS *Dioon edule*, an evergreen shrub found in Mexico that resembles a tree fern, measured just 3.9 in (10 cm) high when it was 120 years old. It grew by 0.03 in (0.76 mm) a year. It is the slowest-growing flowering plant – one aged 1,000 years was only 6 ft 6 in (2 m) high.

OLDEST PLANT SPECIES A hollylike bush in Tasmania is thought to have been growing for more than 43,000 years! Various lichens on rocks grow only a few millimeters a century, and may be thousands of years old. The trunk of a vine planted in 1768 at Hampton Court, Middlesex, UK, now measures 7 ft (2.16 m) in diameter.

LARGEST FRONDS The Pacific giant kelp seaweed (*Macrocystis pyrifera*) has the largest fronds of any plant. Each one may grow up to 394 ft (120 m) – taller than the Statue of Liberty!

LARGEST SEED The huge seed of the coco de mer palm can weigh as much as 55 lb (25 kg) – the equivalent of about 30 coconuts!

PLANTS NAMED AFTER PEOPLE

CAMELLIA Georg Joseph Kamel, a Moravian missionary.

FREESIA Friedrich Heinrich Theodor Friese, a German doctor.

GREENGAGE Sir William Gage, a British collector.

MAGNOLIA Pierre Magnol, a French botanist.

ANIMAL RECORDS

MOST INTELLIGENT ANIMALS

Edward O. Wilson, Professor of Zoology at Harvard University, observed animal intelligence, and measured learning performance over a wide range of tasks, taking account of the animal's brain size. Here are his findings:

1	Human	9	Dolphin
2	Chimpanzee	10	Elephant
3	Gorilla	11	Pig
4	Orangutan		
5	Baboon		
6	Gibbon		
7	Monkey		
8	Smaller toothed whale		

! DID YOU KNOW? A chimpanzee's brain weighs 0.97 lb (0.44 kg).

ANIMAL RECORDS

TALLEST ANIMAL Adult giraffes, from the African savanna, reach an average height of 19.4 ft (5.9 m), including horns of about 6–9 in (15–22 cm).

LOUDEST INSECT You can hear the familiar noise of a cicada from 1,312 ft (400 m) away.

LOUDEST LAND ANIMAL Howler monkey calls echo through the rainforest for more than 2 miles (3 km).

HEAVIEST SEA MAMMAL The blue whale is probably the largest animal ever to have lived, weighing in at 128 tons (130 tonnes) and stretching 110 ft (33.5 m) long.

TALLEST BIRD The ostrich, of eastern and southern Africa, is the world's tallest bird, measuring 9 ft (2.75 m) in height, but it cannot fly.

LOUDEST SEA MAMMAL Registering up to 188 decibels, the call of the blue whale can be heard by other whales up to 1,000 miles (1,600 km) away.

LONGEST LAND ANIMAL The Royal Python grows up to 35 ft (10.7 m).

HEAVIEST LAND ANIMAL African elephants are about 24 ft (7.3 m) long and weigh 14,432 lb (7,000 kg).

SMALLEST PET DOG A tiny chihuahua weighs as little as 1 lb (0.45 kg).

SLEEPIEST CREATURES

ANIMAL	AVERAGE HOURS OF SLEEP PER DAY
Koala	22
Two-toed sloth	20
Little brown bat	19
Giant armadillo	18

! DID YOU KNOW? The shrew has no time for sleep. It must constantly hunt and consume food or it will perish.

WHAT'S THE BIGGEST?

CLASS	ANIMAL	LENGTH
Fish	Whale shark	59 ft (18 m)
Land mammal	African elephant	13.1 ft (4 m)
Sea mammal	Blue whale	110 ft (33.5 m)
Mollusk	Atlantic giant squid	20 ft (6.1 m)
Reptile	Asian saltwater crocodile	32 ft (10 m)
Amphibian	Chinese giant salamander	5.9 ft (1.8 m)
Bird	Ostrich	9 ft (2.75 m)
Crustacean	Japanese spider crab	9 ft (2.75 m)
Arachnid	Indian scorpion	11.5 in (29.2 cm)
Insect	Goliath beetle	4.3 in (11 cm)

! AMAZING FACT! Groups of giant squid live in the Atlantic Ocean. Their eyes alone have a diameter of 19.7 in (50 cm).

WHAT'S THE SMALLEST?

CLASS	ANIMAL	LENGTH
Fish	Dwarf pygmy goby	0.31 in (8 mm)
Mammal	Kitti's hog-nosed bat	6.25 in (160 mm)
Mollusk	*Ammonicera*	A granule of sugar
Reptile	Virgin Island gecko	0.75 in (18 mm)
Amphibian	*Psyllophryne didactyla* (frog)	0.41 in (10.4 mm)
Bird	Bee hummingbird	2.2 in (56 mm)
Crustacean	*Alonella* flea	A grain of salt
Arachnid	Midget spider	Microscopic
Insect	Mymarid wasp	0.0067 in (0.17 mm)

! AMAZING FACT! Bee hummingbirds are so tiny, weighing just 0.056 oz (1.6 g), that they need to eat half their body weight in food every day just to stay alive!

FASTEST ANIMALS IN THE SEA

ANIMAL	MPH	KM/H
Sailfish	68	110
Marlin	50	80
Bluefin tuna	46	74
Yellowfin tuna	44	70
Blue shark	43	69
Wahoo	41	66

FASTEST ANIMALS ON LAND

ANIMAL	MPH	KM/H
Cheetah (over short distance)	65	105
Pronghorn antelope	55	89
Mongolian gazelle	50	80
Springbok	50	80
Lion (over short distance)	50	80
Thomson's gazelle	47	76

FASTEST ANIMALS IN THE AIR

ANIMAL	MPH	KM/H
Peregrine falcon (diving)	185	298
Golden eagle	150	240
Spine-tailed swift	106	171
Frigate bird	95	153
Spur-winged goose	88	142
Red-breasted merganser	80	129

HOW FAST IS ITS HEART?

ANIMAL	HEARTBEATS PER MINUTE
Hummingbird	1,000+
Bat	750
Mouse	500–600
Chicken	250–300
Cat	120
Sheep	75
Human/Cow	60–80
Horse/Lion	40
Frog/Camel	30

DID YOU KNOW? In subzero conditions, a frog's heart rate dips as low as 6–8 beats per minute.

HOW LONG CAN THEY LIVE?

TYPE	ANIMAL	YEARS
Mollusk	Marine clam	200
Reptile	Giant tortoise	150
Land mammal	Human	121
Sea mammal	Killer whale	90
Fish	European eel	88
Bird	Andean condor	72
Crustacean	North American lobster	50
Amphibian	Common toad	40
Arachnid	Theraphosid spider	28
Insect	Queen ant	18

DID YOU KNOW? Common male houseflies complete their entire life cycle in just 17 days, giving them the shortest animal lifespan.

ANIMAL REPRODUCTION RECORDS

QUICKEST COURTSHIP After a year or more as a larva, the adult mayfly has one day to find a mate and lay its eggs before it dies.

GREATEST EGG LAYERS Tapeworms, which live inside the gut of other animals, release up to a million eggs a day for several years but hardly any survive. The giant clam lays as many as a billion eggs once a year for up to 40 years.

LONGEST GESTATION The pregnancy of an Asian elephant lasts 660 days, about 22 months – more than twice that of a human mother.

SHORTEST GESTATION The young of the Virginian opossum develop fully in just 12 days.

LARGEST ANIMAL BABY Blue whales are 20–26 ft (6–8 m) long and weigh 1.9–2.9 tons (2–3 tonnes) at birth. Every day, the baby drinks 360 pints (200 liters) of its mother's milk.

MOST PROLIFIC FISH On average, ocean sunfish lay about 30 million eggs, although one female was found to be carrying 300 million eggs. They do this because so few of the young survive.

YOUNGEST MAMMAL BREEDER Female Norway lemmings can breed when they're just 14 days old!

LARGEST MAMMAL LITTER Tailless tenrecs from Madagascar may produce up to 31 young in a single birth.

HEAVIEST BIRDS' NEST Bald eagles build huge nests. The largest recorded weighed 2.9 tons (3 tonnes) – equal to three cars.

MOST MAMMAL YOUNG PER YEAR The prairie vole rears 17 litters in quick succession, bringing up to 150 young into the world.

MAMMALS

HOW BIG ARE THE BIG CATS?

The length of tails among members of the cat family varies considerably – it may be as much as 55 in (140 cm) in the case of the leopard, or as little as 3 in (8 cm) in the lynx. The measurements are from the nose to the tip of the tail.

SPECIES	WHERE FOUND	MAX. LENGTH	
		IN	CM
Tiger	Asia	130	330
Leopard	Asia, Africa	126	320
Lion	Africa, Asia	110	280
Jaguar	North, Central, and South America	107	271
Mountain lion	North, Central, and South America	96	245
Snow leopard	Asia	94	240
Cheetah	Africa, Asia	87	220
Clouded leopard	Asia	78	197
Ocelot	North, Central, and South America	67	170
Lynx	Europe, Asia, North America	54	138
Golden cat	Africa	54	138
Serval	Africa	49	125
Caracal	Africa	47	120
Bobcat	North and Central America	47	119
Wild cat	Europe, Asia	41	103
Pampas cat	South America	40	102
Domestic cat	Worldwide	38	97

MAMMAL HOMES

MAMMAL	HOME
Badger	Earth, sett
Beaver	Lodge
Bear	Den
Fox	Burrow, earth, kennel
Hare	Form
Otter	Holt
Rabbit	Burrow, warren
Squirrel	Drey

MAMMAL GROUPS

MAMMAL	GROUP
Bats	Colony
Bears	Sloth, sleuth
Camels	Caravan, flock
Cows	Kine
Lions	Pride
Mice	Nest
Monkeys	Troop
Pigs	Litter, herd
Porpoises	School
Tigers	Ambush
Wolves	Pack

WHAT DO YOU CALL A YOUNG...?

MAMMAL	YOUNG CALLED
Antelope	Calf, kid
Bear	Cub
Beaver	Kit, kitten
Bobcat	Kit, kitten
Buffalo	Calf
Camel	Calf
Cat	Catling, pussy, kit, kitten
Cow	Calf, heifer (female only), stirk
Deer	Fawn, yearling
Dog	Pup, puppy, whelp
Donkey	Foal, colt (male), filly (female)
Elephant	Calf
Elephant seal	Weaner
Elk	Calf
Fox	Cub, kit, kitten, whelp
Giraffe	Calf
Goat	Kid
Hamster	Kit, kitten
Hare	Leveret
Hippopotamus	Calf
Horse	Foal, yearling, colt (male), filly (female)
Kangaroo	Joey
Lion	Cub, lionet, whelp
Moose	Calf
Pig	Farrow, grice, piglet, shoat, suckling
Rabbit	Bunny, kit, kitten
Seal	Pup
Sheep	Cosset, hog, lamb, lambkin
Wolf	Cub, whelp

BEARS OF THE WORLD

BEAR	WHERE FOUND	WEIGHT		LENGTH	
		LB	KG	IN	CM
Brown (grizzly) bear	North America, Europe, Asia	300–860	136–390	114	up to 290
Polar bear	Arctic	440–1,760	200–800	101	up to 257
American black bear	North America	130–660	60–300	50–75	127–191
Sloth bear	Asia	175–310	80–140	60–75	152–191
Asiatic black bear	Southern Asia	220–440	100–200	50–74	127–188
Spectacled bear	South America	150–250	70–113	60–72	152–183
Sun bear	Asia	60–145	27–65	48–60	122–152

 DID YOU KNOW? The Giant panda bear is usually considered a member of the racoon family, and not a true bear, but it would come eighth in this list, at 48–60 in (122–152 cm) in length.

HOW LONG CAN THEY STAY UNDERWATER?

MAMMAL	UNDERWATER SURVIVAL (MINS)
Human	1
Polar bear	1.5
Human pearl diver	2.5
Sea otter	5
Platypus	10
Muskrat	12
Hippopotamus	15
Sea cow	16
Seal	22
Sperm whale	112

SMALLEST MAMMALS

MAMMAL	WEIGHT		LENGTH	
	OZ	G	IN	CM
Kitti's hog-nosed bat	0.07	2.0	1.1	2.9
Pygmy shrew	0.05	1.5	1.4	3.6
Pipistrelle bat	0.11	3.0	1.6	4.0
Little brown bat	0.28	8.0	1.6	4.0
Masked shrew	0.08	2.4	1.8	4.5
Southern blossom bat	0.42	12.0	2.0	5.0
Harvest mouse	0.18	5.0	2.3	5.8
Pygmy glider	0.42	12.0	2.4	6.0
House mouse	0.42	12.0	2.5	6.4
Common shrew	0.18	5.0	2.5	6.5
Water shrew	0.42	12.0	2.8	7.0
Bank vole	0.53	15.0	3.2	8.0
Pygmy possum	0.53	15.0	3.4	8.5

Ranked by length

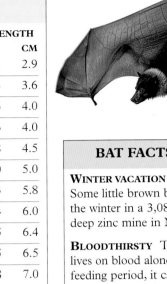

BAT FACTS

WINTER VACATION
Some little brown bats spend the winter in a 3,085-ft (1,160-m) deep zinc mine in New York.

BLOODTHIRSTY The vampire bat lives on blood alone. During its brief feeding period, it can consume more than its own body weight in blood.

ON THE WING Flying foxes of the Pteropus group are the largest bats in the world, with wingspans of up to 6.6 ft (2 m) across.

COMPLETELY BATS During World War II, the US Air Force captured millions of bats. They planned to make all the bats carry tiny bombs, fly into buildings, and explode. Fortunately, the war ended before the plan could be put into action!

AMAZING MAMMALS

MARSUPIALS The male red kangaroo can grow to more than 6.6 ft (2 m) tall and 8 ft (2.5 m) in overall length.

SWIMMERS A shark's skin is rough enough to be used as sandpaper, and its teeth are literally as hard as steel.

CAMOUFLAGE To complete their camouflage, polar bears cover their black noses with their paw as they stalk prey in the snow.

BURROWERS The badger has strong front legs and long claws so that it can dig underground burrows up to 66 ft (20 m) long.

LONGEST LIVING Humans are the longest-living mammals, but Asian elephants come a close second. The oldest recorded example of the species died at 78 years old.

LONGEST SLEEPING The barrow ground squirrel of Alaska hibernates for nine months at a time.

MAMMALS WITH THE LONGEST TAILS

DID YOU KNOW?
The flying squirrel uses its flattened tail as a rudder for steering as it leaps from tree to tree. The tail also acts as an air brake.

MAMMAL	TAIL LENGTH	
	IN	CM
Asian elephant	59	150
Leopard	55	140
African elephant	51	130
African buffalo	43	110
Giraffe	43	110
Red kangaroo	43	110
Langur	39	100

DID YOU KNOW?
Camels can drink 200 pints (113 liters) of water in half an hour.

UNDERWATER CREATURES

REPRODUCTION FACTFILE

MALE MOTHER The female seahorse lays her eggs in her partner's pouch. He carries the tiny, developing seahorses until they are ready to be born, between two and six weeks later.

LARGEST EGG The whale shark lays an egg about 14 in (30 cm) in length.

ONE YOUNG Some sharks give birth to just one pup because the first to develop inside the mother eats all the other eggs!

MERMAID'S PURSES Hard, horny "mermaid's purses" found on the sea shore are the dried-out egg cases of dogfish, skates, and rays. The embryos grow inside, wriggling out after six to nine months.

SHARK PUPS It takes sharks 9–22 months to grow inside their mother, and up to 100 pups can be born at one time.

DEEP-SEA DIVERS

BIRDS Some emperor penguins have been recorded 870 ft (265 m) deep.

TURTLES In 1987, a leatherback turtle was fitted with a depth-gauge that recorded 3,937-ft (1,200-m) dives. Turtles may go even deeper for food.

WHALES Sperm whales regularly dive to 3,937 ft (1,200 m), and sometimes descend to twice this depth!

DEEP-SEA FISH Fish in the brotulid group have been found in deep-sea trenches, such as the Puerto Rico Trench, at 27,230 ft (8,300 m) – almost as deep as Mount Everest is high!

DID YOU KNOW? In a record-breaking mission in the bathyscaphe *Trieste*, scientists Jacques Piccard and Donald Walsh observed creatures living as far down as 35,814 ft (10,916 m) in the Marianas Trench, Pacific Ocean.

LARGEST MARINE MAMMALS

MAMMAL	LENGTH		WEIGHT	
	FT	M	TONS	TONNES
Blue whale	110.0	33.5	127.95	130.0
Fin whale	82.0	25.0	44.29	45.0
Right whale	57.4	17.5	39.37	40.0
Sperm whale	59.0	18.0	35.43	36.0
Gray whale	46.0	14.0	32.18	32.7
Humpback whale	49.2	15.0	26.08	26.5
Baird's whale	18.0	5.5	10.83	11.0
Southern elephant seal	21.3	6.5	3.54	3.6
Northern elephant seal	19.0	5.8	3.35	3.4
Pilot whale	21.0	6.4	2.85	2.9

DID YOU KNOW? The herbivorous dugong, a type of sea cow, is the largest mammal to live in inland waters, weighing up to 2,000 lb (907 kg) and measuring 13.5 ft (4.1 m) in length.

DID YOU KNOW? The gray whale travels farther than any other whale. It swims about 12,500 miles (20,000 km) each year from its winter breeding grounds in Mexico to the Bering Sea.

SMALLEST MARINE MAMMALS

SMALLEST WHALE The pygmy right whale grows to 21 ft (6.45 m) and weighs 3.15 tons (3.2 tonnes) – less than a quarter of the length and under 3 percent of the weight of the largest, the blue whale.

SMALLEST DOLPHIN There are several contenders for smallest dolphin, one of which is Hector's dolphin, found off New Zealand. It is 5 ft (1.53 m) long and weighs under 126 lb (57.27 kg).

SMALLEST SEAL The rare Galápagos fur seal reaches a maximum weight of 142 lb (64 kg) and a length of 4 ft 11 in (1.5 m).

SMALLEST SEA MAMMAL Found off the western coast of South America, the marine otter weighs a maximum of 10 lb (4.5 kg). It measures only about 3 ft 9 in (1.15 m) long. Marine otters sometimes come ashore, unlike the slightly larger sea otters, which spend their lives in the water.

FACTASTIC MARINE CREATURES

SMALLEST MOLLUSK The gastropod *Ammonicera* is only 0.04 in (1 mm) long.

LARGEST INVERTEBRATES Giant squid can grow 50 ft (15 m) long and weigh 1.9 tons (2 tonnes). Imagine coming face to face with 15.7-in (40-cm) wide eyes!

ITS ELECTRIFYING! The electric eel, from the Amazon, kills fish with 500-volt shocks from muscles that act like tiny batteries.

LEAVING A LEG BEHIND Crabs and other crustaceans can escape danger by simply discarding an injured or trapped limb!

NO EYES Some cave-dwelling fish have no eyes because they spend their lives in darkness and don't need them!

LARGEST CRUSTACEAN The Japanese spider crab has a leg span of 13 ft (4 m).

LOBSTER MARCH Hundreds of spiny lobsters often walk one after another for 60 miles (100 km) in search of an area to settle. They make sounds, which are thought to coordinate the journey!

HEAVIEST CRUSTACEAN The North Atlantic lobster weighs up to 44 lb (20 kg).

DANGEROUS UNDERWATER CREATURES

BLUEFISH Considered the fiercest fish, the bluefish of the Americas attacks and eats other fish: a 5-lb (2-kg) bluefish can devour a ton of fish a year – 500 times its body weight!

LIONFISH The fins of this brightly colored fish contain a deadly poison!

CONE-SHELL Found in the South Pacific and Indian Oceans, the poisonous barbs of the cone-shell cause paralysis and death. The geographer cone is the most dangerous.

SEA WASP Also known as the box jellyfish, found off the Australian coast, it has 30-ft (9-m) tentacles. Its venom is as powerful as that of a cobra.

JAPANESE PUFFER Also known as the maki-maki, or "deadly death puffer fish," certain parts of a Japanese puffer's body contain a nerve poison that, if eaten, can kill a person. There is no known antidote. Despite the danger, they are eaten as a delicacy in Japan. Although chefs are trained to prepare them, 50 people a year die from negligence in the kitchen.

OCTOPUS The bites of several species, especially the blue-ringed octopus found off Australia, are dangerous, often causing paralysis.

SEA URCHIN If trodden on, several sea urchins cause severe paralysis or death.

SEA LAMPREY Not a good ingredient for a fish stew! These eel-like creatures may be poisonous – English king Henry I died after gorging himself on "a surfeit of lampreys."

PORTUGUESE MAN-OF-WAR Found in tropical seas, this vicious jellyfish-like creature has 70-ft (21-m) tentacles! It can cause very painful stings that affect the nerves.

SEA SNAKE All sea snakes are dangerous, but *Hydrophis belcheri* has a deadly venom that is stronger than that of many land snakes.

PIRANHA Living in South America, these fish will strip a human to the bone in minutes!

STINGRAY Lurking in most coastal waters, the stingray has a highly venomous spine above its tail. A sting can hinder breathing, but rarely kills.

DID YOU KNOW? The teeth of the great white shark are 5 in (12 cm) long. New ones grow forward to replace them as they wear out.

UNDERWATER LIFESPANS

ANIMAL	LONGEST IN YEARS
Quahog (marine clam)	200
Deep-sea clam	100
Killer whale	90
Sea anemone	80
Sperm whale	65
Whale shark	60
North American lobster	50
Gray seal	46
Blue whale	45
Australian school shark	32
California sea lion	30
Starfish	15

At the other end of the scale, some fish have lifespans of less than a year, among them the white goby, seahorse, and dwarf pygmy goby.

BIG FISH RECORDS

WHALE SHARK Not only the biggest shark, but also the biggest fish, the gigantic whale shark can grow to a length of 39 ft (12 m)!

OARFISH Also called ribbonfish, oarfish are the biggest bony fish, growing up to 30 ft (9 m) long. They live in deep tropical waters.

EUROPEAN CATFISH A catfish weighing 720 lb (363.3 kg) was allegedly caught in the 1800s in the Dnieper River, in Russia.

PLA BUK Found in the waters of the Mekong River, China, the giant pla buk can weigh as much as 553 lb (242 kg).

WHITE STURGEON Caught by a lucky angler in California in 1983, this huge fish weighed 468 lb (212.28 kg)!

TRY IT YOURSELF! You can measure a fish's top swimming speed per second by multiplying its length by ten. So, a trout 6 in (15 cm) long swims at 5 ft (1.5 m) per second!

HEAVIEST SHARKS

SPECIES	LB	KG
Whale shark	46,297	21,000
Basking shark	32,000	14,515
Great white shark	7,300	3,314
Greenland shark	2,250	1,020
Tiger shark	2,070	939
Great hammerhead shark	1,860	844
Six-gill shark	1,300	590
Gray nurse shark	1,225	556
Mako shark	1,200	544
Thresher shark	1,100	500

DID YOU KNOW? Although whale sharks are huge, you needn't worry, they're not dangerous! Whale sharks eat only plankton and couldn't swallow a person whole because their throats are only 4 in (10 cm) in diameter.

BIRDS

ONE AND ONLY BIRDS

HIBERNATING BIRD The only bird to hibernate is the North American poorwill (*Phalaenoptilus nuttallii*). During the cold winters, its metabolism slows down and its body temperature drops from 106°F (41°C) to 55°F (13°C).

POISONOUS BIRD The only poisonous bird known is the black and orange hooded pitohui (*Pitohui dichrous*) from New Guinea. The poisons it gives off are similar to those secreted by poison-dart frogs.

LANNER
FALCON

DID YOU KNOW?
A bird's strong, broad wing or flight feathers provide the surface needed to produce lift.

DID YOU KNOW?
Long, strong tail feathers help the bird steer, balance, and brake in the air.

DID YOU KNOW?
Sleek body feathers give the bird the streamlined shape it needs for flight.

DID YOU KNOW?
Beneath its body feathers, a bird has soft, fluffy down feathers to keep it warm

AMAZING MIGRATIONS

LONGEST Each year, the sun-loving Arctic tern flies from the Arctic to the Antarctic and back – a round trip of about 25,000 miles (40,000 km).

UNLIKELIEST Even though it weighs only 0.1 oz (3.5 g), the ruby-throated hummingbird flies nonstop for about 500 miles (800 km) from North to South America every autumn. It flies back in the spring

YOUNGEST Left behind by their parents, young shining bronze cuckoos migrate 4,000 miles (6,400 km) from New Zealand to Australia and then on to the Bismarck archipelago.

BON APPETIT!

Ostriches appear to be indiscriminate in their choice of food. A director of the London Zoological Society, E. G. Boulenger, listed the following objects as having been extracted from the stomach of one unfortunate ostrich at its postmortem in the 1930s:

1 key	2 collar studs
1 part of a gold necklace	1 glove fastener
1 5-in (12.5-cm) piece of wood	1 bicycle tire valve
1 part of a comb	2 handkerchiefs
1 pencil	1 35-in (90-cm) length of thick string
3 gloves	8 coins
1 film spool	

LARGEST WINGSPANS

	MAXIMUM WINGSPAN	
BIRD	**FT**	**M**
Marabou stork	13	4.0
Albatross	12	3.7

DID YOU KNOW?
The wingspan of an adult albatross is greater than the length of a small car!

Trumpeter swan	11	3.4
Mute swan	10	3.1
Whooper swan	10	3.1
Gray pelican	10	3.1
California condor	10	3.1
Black vulture	10	3.1
Great bustard	9	2.7
Kori bustard	9	2.7

FEATHER FACTS

WHAT ARE THEY MADE OF? Feathers are made of dead cells and composed of keratin, the same material as our hair and nails.

PARTS OF A FEATHER The shaft of a feather is the rachis; the body is the vane; and the strands are barbs. Barbs have tiny hooks on them called barbules, which cling to each other like Velcro.

UNLUCKY FEATHERS Peacock feathers are believed to represent the evil eye, and are considered unlucky in many cultures.

EDIBLE FEATHERS? Grebes eat their own feathers. This may help them to digest food by forming pellets that enable them to regurgitate the bones and scales of the fish they eat.

LONGEST FEATHERS The tail feathers of the Japanese phoenix fowl, or onagodori, may measure up to 34.7 ft (10.6 m) – the longest of any bird – although these birds cannot fly!

WHY ARE FLAMINGO FEATHERS PINK?
A flamingo's fishy diet keeps its feathers pink. Flamingos in captivity have to eat a special diet rich in carotene – the orange coloring in carrots – otherwise their feathers turn white!

LARGEST FLYING BIRDS

BIRD TYPE	WEIGHT		
	LB	OZ	KG
Great bustard	46	1	20.9
Trumpeter swan	37	1	16.8
Mute swan	35	15	16.3
Albatross	34	13	15.8
Whooper swan	34	13	15.8
Manchurian crane	32	14	14.9
Kori bustard	30	0	13.6
Gray pelican	28	11	13.0
Black vulture	27	8	12.5

BIRD GROUP NAMES

Most of the following names are still used, but some, such as a murmuration of starlings, a murder of crows, and an unkindness of ravens, are now out of fashion.

A bevy of quail

A bouquet of pheasants

A brood of hens

A cast of hawks

A charm of finches

A colony of penguins

A covey of partridges

An exaltation of larks

A flight of swallows

A gaggle of geese

A siege of herons

A skein of geese

A trip of dotterel

A wisp of snipe

TEN FASTEST BIRDS

Birds are among the fastest animals on Earth. When diving, peregrine falcons can reach speeds of almost 185 mph (298 km/h). However, most comparisons of air speed in birds rule out diving or wind-assisted flight. This list picks out star performers among medium to large-sized birds (mainly waterfowl) that can hit their top speed without help from wind or gravity.

BIRD	MAXIMUM RECORDED SPEED	
	MPH	KM/H
Spine-tailed swift	106	171
Frigate bird	95	153
Spur-winged goose	88	142
Red-breasted merganser	80	129
White-rumped swift	77	124
Canvasback duck	72	116
Eider duck	70	113
Teal	68	109
Mallard	65	105
Pintail	65	105

AMAZING FACT! The speediest of flightless birds is the ostrich, which can run at 45 mph (72 km/h) and can maintain this speed for nearly 20 minutes.

RARE AND ENDANGERED BIRDS

Rare birds are most under threat in places where they are unable to seek refuge, such as on islands like Mauritius, where the dodo became extinct in the 17th century.

BIRD	COUNTRY	BREEDING PAIRS
Spix's macaw	Brazil	1
Cebu flower pecker	Philippines	1
Hawaiian crow	Hawaii	5
Black stilt	New Zealand	12
Echo parakeet	Mauritius	13
Imperial Amazon parrot	Dominica	15
Magpie robin	Seychelles	20
Kakapo	New Zealand	24
Pink pigeon	Mauritius	70
Mauritius kestrel	Mauritius	100

RARE RECOVERY! The Mauritius kestrel was once the second rarest bird, now recovered to more than 100 pairs.

LARGEST FLIGHTLESS BIRDS

BIRD	WEIGHT			HEIGHT	
	LB	OZ	KG	IN	CM
Ostrich	345	0	156.5	108.0	274.3
Emu	88	3	40.0	60.0	152.4
Cassowary	73	14	33.5	60.0	152.4
Rhea	55	2	25.0	54.0	137.1
Emperor penguin	64	13	29.4	44.0	114.0
Flightless cormorant	9	15	4.5	37.4	95.0

BIRDS' EGGS

SMALLEST EGGS The minuscule eggs of the bee hummingbird are as small as peas and weigh just 0.008 oz (0.25 g).

LARGEST EGGS Ostrich eggs can measure up to 8 in (20 cm) long and weigh up to 3.5 lb (1.65 kg) – equal to about 24 hens' eggs.

LARGEST CLUTCH The gray partridge may lay as many as 19 eggs in a single clutch.

DID YOU KNOW? Webbed feet prevent water birds from sinking into the mud.

INSECTS and SPIDERS

INSECT RECORDS

LONGEST Stick insects are the longest insects! Some measure up to 20 in (51 cm), in length.

HEAVIEST A goliath beetle may be as long as 4 in (11 cm), and can weigh 2.5–3.5 oz (70–100 g), almost as heavy as a small apple!

SMALLEST Battledore wing fairy flies, a kind of parasitic wasp, measure just 0.0083 in (0.21 mm).

LONGEST-LIVED Jewel beetle larvae may live inside wood for 30 years or more before the insect emerges.

NOISIEST The mating calls from a male cicada colony can measure 80–100 decibels from 60 ft (18.28 m) – as noisy as heavy traffic!

TOUGHEST Snow fleas can live in temperatures of -59°F (-15°C)!

MOST NUMEROUS There are about 5,000 springtails per sq ft (50,000 per sq m) of grassland in the world.

FACTASTIC MOTHS AND BUTTERFLIES

SO MANY SPECIES There are at least 170,000 different species of butterflies and moths.

LARGEST MOTH The Atlas moth is the largest in the world.

SMALLEST MOTH The *Stigmella ridiculosa* moth measures only 0.08 in (2 mm) across.

SMALLEST BUTTERFLY The grass jewel butterfly has a wingspan of only 0.39–0.59 in (1–1.5 cm).

LONG-DISTANCE FLIERS Butterflies have been tracked traveling 3,000 miles (4,828 km)! Monarch butterflies regularly migrate a distance of 1,864 miles (3,000 km) from Canada and the US to Mexico.

AMAZING ANTENNAE The antennae of male longhorn moths are six times as long as their bodies.

HUNGRY CATERPILLAR In its lifetime, a black arches moth caterpillar can eat about 1,000 pine needles and damage another 1,000 at the same time.

REPRODUCTION RECORDS

LARGEST EGGS Malaysian stick insects lay eggs that measure 0.5 in (1.3 cm) in diameter.

MOST EGGS LAID The Queen *Macrotermes* termite can lay up to 40,000 eggs per day!

LONGEST IN EGG The cerambycid beetle *Saperda carcharia* takes nine and a half months to hatch.

DID YOU KNOW? Butterflies flap their wings about 640 times a minute when flying!

DID YOU KNOW? The female Queen Alexandra birdwing butterfly of Papua New Guinea, has the largest wingspan of any insect, at 11 in (28 cm)

DEADLY SPIDERS

Spiders are the number one phobia of many people. Most spiders are harmless, but some species are lethal killers, such as the following examples:

• Black widows
• Brown recluse spiders
• Hobo spider
• Tarantulas
• Banana spider
• Sydney funnel web
• Redback
• White-tailed spider
• Mouse spider

SPIDER AND SCORPION FACTFILE

LARGEST SPIDER The goliath bird-eating spider is 11 in (28 cm) in diameter – as big as a dinner plate!

SPEEDY SPIDER Watch out at home – ordinary house spiders can speed at 1 mph (1.9 km/h)!

LARGEST SPIDER WEB The orb weaver spider group can make 10-ft (3-m) webs – as large as bedsheets!

SMALLEST SPIDER WEB A midget spider weaves the world's tiniest web, at 0.39 in (10 mm) – that's smaller than your fingernail.

LARGEST SCORPION *Heterometrus swannerdami* measures 7 in (18 cm) from its pincers to its tail.

SMALLEST SCORPION *Microbothus pusillus* is just 0.5 in (13 mm) long.

MOST POISONOUS SCORPION The Israeli gold scorpion has the most poisonous sting known.

HOW LONG DO INSECTS LIVE?

ANIMAL	LIFESPAN
Wood-boring beetle	45 years
Jewel beetle	30 years
Periodic cicada	17 years
Indian meal moth	4 weeks
Housefly	17 days
Mayfly	1 hour

THESE ARE NOT INSECTS!

Here are some creatures that are often mistaken for insects: Spiders • Scorpions Crabs • Shrimp • Woodlice • Centipedes Millipedes • Worms • Slugs • Snails

HAVE YOU SEEN...?

You are not likely to come across a Queen Alexandra Birdwing butterfly – they are the rarest butterflies in the world.

DANGEROUS INSECTS

BEES AND HORNETS Stings may be painful, and multiple stings may cause an allergic reaction or death. More people are killed by bees than by snakes!

COCKROACHES As well as devouring food, cockroaches transmit diseases.

HARVEST MITES In some tropical countries, harvest mites transmit typhus to people.

KISSING BUGS The bite of these insects spreads Chagas' disease, which kills some 45,000 people a year.

LOCUSTS Locusts are responsible for destroying crops, leaving some human populations destitute. It has been estimated that a swarm of 50 billion desert locusts can eat in a day enough food for 500,000 people for a year.

MOSQUITOES These insects carry diseases such as malaria, which causes between 1,500,000 and 2,700,000 deaths a year, in tropical countries. Malaria has killed about half of all the human population since the Stone Age.

TERMITES Hordes of these demon insects can destroy entire buildings by eating away at the wooden structure.

FASTEST INSECTS

INSECT	TOP SPEED	
	MPH	KM/H
Dragonfly	20.0	32.0
Hornet	13.39	21.5
Horsefly	8.93	14.3
Bee	11.0	18.0

DID YOU KNOW? A bee could travel 4 million miles (6.5 million km) at 7 mph (11 km/h) on the energy it would obtain from 1 gallon (4.5 liters) of nectar.

USEFUL INSECTS

BEES Worldwide, bees produce over 0.9 million tons (1 million tonnes) of honey annually and help to pollinate crops. Beeswax is also used in furniture polish.

LAC INSECT This scaled insect secretes a resin that is used to make varnish for furniture and leather goods.

SILKWORMS Silkworm larvae are used commercially to make silk. About 40,000 silkmoth cocoons could provide enough silk to circle the earth in a single thread.

SCALE INSECTS The crushed bodies of Mexican scale insects produce cochineal, a red food coloring.

EDIBLE INSECTS

AUSTRALIA Aboriginal Australians eat witchety grubs (giant moth caterpillars). They also tap the hollow logs where beetles live to catch beetle larvae.

CAMBODIA People sit around campfires at night and attract cicadas by clapping. They then cook them by roasting them on the fires, like sausages on sticks.

CENTRAL AND SOUTH AMERICA The wings, heads, and legs of parasol ants are removed, and their bodies are eaten raw or toasted.

CHINA Grasshoppers (*Tsa ku meng*) are fried in sesame oil until crisp, then served and eaten like roasted nuts.

INDIA To make red ant chutney (*Chindi chutney*), ants are cooked on a fire, then ground into a paste, which is salted, mixed with chilies, and baked.

MEXICO A delicacy in parts of Mexico is a giant water bug – so huge that it eats frogs! Waterboatmen eggs are served like caviar.

BEST JUMPERS

HIGH JUMPER Fleas can leap 12 in (30 cm) into the air – about 200 times their own height!

LONG JUMPER The desert locust, a type of grasshopper, can leap distances of 19.5 in (50 cm) – ten times the length of its body!

NAMES OF INSECT ORDERS

INSECT	ORDER	MEANING
Beetles	Coleoptera	Hard wings
Butterflies	Lepidoptera	Scaly wings
Midges	Diptera	Two wings
Aphids	Hemiptera	Half wings
Grasshoppers	Orthoptera	Straight wings
Caddisflies	Trichoptera	Hairy wings
Springtails	Collembola	Sticky peg
Dragonflies	Odonata	Toothed flies
Thrips	Thysanoptera	Fringed wings
Lacewings	Neuroptera	Net-veined wings
Cockroaches	Blattodea	Insect avoiding light
Bark lice	Pscoptera	Milled wings
Stick insects	Phasmatodea	Like a ghost
Fleas	Siphonaptera	Tube without wings
Termites	Isoptera	Equal wings
Mayflies	Ephemeroptera	Living for a day

AMPHIBIANS and REPTILES

FROG RECORDS

OLDEST FROG The Stephens Island frog evolved on Earth 170-275 million years ago, and is thought to be the ancestor of all frogs. Discovered in 1917, it is found only in New Zealand.

SMELLIEST FROG The Venezuela skunk frog (*Aromobates nocturnus*), discovered in 1991, deters enemies by releasing a stinky chemical identical to the one that skunks spray as a defense!

POISON-ARROW
FROG

LARGEST FROGS The Rana goliath frog, found in the African countries of Cameroon, Democratic Republic of Congo, and Equatorial Guinea, is the largest frog ever known. In 1949, a bullfrog weighing about 8 lb (3.5 kg) and allegedly 3.3 ft (1 m) long was found in Martha Lake, Washington.

LARGEST TREE FROG *Hyla vasta*, found only on Hispaniola, in the Caribbean, is 7.1 in (18 cm) long. It has huge round fingers and toes that grip like superglue.

LARGEST TOAD The bodies of some South American marine toads (*Bufo marinus*) measure 9 in (23 cm) long. They can weigh almost 3 lb (1.5 kg). They come from South America, but have been introduced around the world to control sugar beetles that destroy crops. In Australia, marine toads have been moving south from Queensland, allegedly by stowing away on trucks.

SMALLEST TOAD The East African toad (*Bufo taitanus beiranus*), from Mozambique, rarely grows more than 1 in (2.5 cm) long.

RECORD EGG-LAYER The female marine toad (*Bufo marinus*) can lay as many as 35,000 eggs a year.

DEFENSIVE FROGS

DON'T PICK ME UP! The dagger frog (*Babini holsti*), found in Okinawa, Japan, has a sharp spiny "thumb" to stab anyone who picks it up!

DON'T BREATHE ON ME! In Germany, spadefoot toads are called the *Knoblauchskrote*, or "garlic toads," because of the smelly substance they give off!

DON'T TOUCH ME! Deadly "poison-arrow" frogs from Central and South America include the golden-dart frog, which has enough poison to kill 1,000 people!

FACTASTIC FROGS

WHEN IS A FROG A TOAD? It is not always easy to distinguish between frogs and toads. Frogs tend to live in water, while toads live on land and breed in water. Technically they all belong to the genus *Rana*, so are all frogs!

GIGANTIC EGGS The male red-eyed tree frog (*Agalychnis callidryas*) is half the size of the female, but her egg cluster is bigger than both of them!

MALE MIDWIFE The male European midwife frog carries 35–50 eggs wrapped around his hind legs. After three weeks, he takes them into the water to hatch.

LARGE LARVA The tadpoles of the paradoxical frog (*Pseudis paradoxus*), from Trinidad and the Amazon, can be 10 in (25 cm) long – three times bigger than the frogs they turn into, which are rarely more than 3 in (7.6 cm).

SEE-THROUGH FROGS Some frogs, such as the African lesser banana frog (*Megalixalus stuhlmanni*), have such transparent flesh that you can see their bones through it.

THROATY NOISES The white-lipped frog that lives in the Puerto Rican rainforests communicates by thumping the ground with its throat pouch. This is detected by other frogs up to 18 ft (5.5 m) away.

FUNNY FROG AND TOAD NAMES

Many frogs have strange common and Latin names

COMMON NAME	LATIN NAME
Catholic frog	*Notaden bennetti*
Cricket frog	*Acris gryllus gryllus*
Fire-bellied toad	*Bombina bombina*
Little green toad	*Bufo debilis*
Meadow frog	*Rana pipiens pipiens*
Mountain chicken	*Leptodactylus fallax*
Mountain chorus frog	*Pseudacris brachyphora*
Oregon red-legged frog	*Rana aurora aurora*
Peeper	*Hyla crucifer crucifer*
Texan cliff frog	*Eleutherodactylus latrans*
Warty frog	*Rana tuberculosa*

LEAP FROGS

BEST JUMPER Cricket frogs leap 36 times their own length: if a human did this, the record could be 216 ft (65.8 m).

WORST JUMPER The tiny greenhouse frog jumps less than 5 in (13 cm).

FROG AND TOAD SOUNDS

Not all frogs and toads "ribbit" – according to the American Audubon Society, which, in 1975, published a report to identify frog and toad sounds.

FROG/TOAD	SOUND
American toad	Trilling
Fowler's toad	Nasal bleat
Green frog	Like a plucked banjo string
Gray tree frog	Short, harsh trill
Leopard and pickerel frogs	Resembles snoring
Spring peeper	Like sleigh bells
Wood frog	Creaky clatter

HAVE YOU EVER HEARD...? The carpenter frog, which sounds like a carpenter hammering nails; the pig frog, which grunts like pigs; or the sheep frog, which resembles bleating sheep?

LIZARD FACTS

COLOR CHANGE Chameleons such as the Parson's chameleon change color to hide themselves from predators or to show their mood.

LONG TONGUE A chameleon has a sticky tongue as long as its body and tail together!

SMALLEST LIZARD The Virgin Island gecko is just 0.7 in (18 mm) in length.

BIGGEST LIZARD Komodo Dragons, from Indonesia, can grow up to 10 ft (3 m) long.

WALKING ON WATER To escape predators, basilisk lizards drop onto water and run across the surface!

HEAVIEST TURTLES AND TORTOISES

TURTLE/TORTOISE	MAXIMUM WEIGHT	
	LB	KG
Pacific leatherback turtle	1,908	865
Atlantic leatherback turtle	1,000	454
Green sea turtle	900	408
Aldabra giant tortoise	900	408
Loggerhead turtle	850	386
Galápagos giant tortoise	849	385

DID YOU KNOW? Aldabra giant tortoises may live 50 years and are probably the longest-lived of their kind!

TERRIFIC TURTLES

PREHISTORIC MONSTER All living turtles would be dwarfed in size by prehistoric monster turtles, such as *Stupendemys geographicus*, which were 10 ft (3 m) long and weighed more than 4,497 lb (2,040 kg).

EGG DELAY Some female turtles produce eggs four years after mating!

TURTLES IN DANGER In 1947, 40,000 Kemp's Ridley turtles laid eggs on their nesting beach in Mexico. By 1995, hunting had reduced numbers to less than 5,000.

DID YOU KNOW? This harmless Sinaloan milk snake looks like the poisonous coral snake – so predators stay away!

TWELVE DEADLY SNAKES

The world's most dangerous snakes, listed here, are all from the poisonous Elapidae family of reptiles, except the rattlesnake, which belongs to Viperidae.

SNAKE	FOUND IN	DEATH RATE %
Black mamba	Africa	95–100
Common krait	Asia	77–93
Russell's viper	Asia	30–65
Taipan	Australia	25–50
Indian cobra	Asia	33
Cape cobra	Africa	25
Egyptian cobra	Africa/Asia	unknown
Multibanded krait	Asia	unknown
King cobra	Asia	18
Green mamba	Africa	unknown
Tropical rattlesnake	C./S. America	15–25
Tiger snake	Australia	20

DID YOU KNOW? The Black mamba, from parts of Africa, is not only a vicious killer, but it is reputed to be the fastest-moving land snake. It is capable of chasing after prey at 10–12 mph (14–19 km/h).

AMAZING ALLIGATORS AND CROCODILES

LARGEST CROCODILE The saltwater crocodile measures up to 33 ft (10 m) long! As well as being the largest, it is the most dangerous of all crocodiles.

SMALLEST CROCODILE South America's dwarf caimans hardly ever grow more than 5 ft (1.5 m) long.

STONE SWALLOWERS Crocodiles swallow stones! These accumulate in the stomach and help the animal to remain submerged under the water.

SUPERSHARP TEETH Crocodiles and alligators have sharp, pointed teeth for tearing prey apart. As they wear, new teeth appear – as many as 50 new sets in a lifetime.

LONGEST SNAKES

SNAKE	MAXIMUM LENGTH	
	FT	M
Reticulated python	35	10.7
Anaconda	28	8.5
Indian python	25	7.6
Diamond python	21	6.4
King cobra	19	5.8
Boa constrictor	16	4.9
Bushmaster	12	3.7
Giant brown snake	11	3.4
Diamondback rattlesnake	9	2.7
Indigo or gopher snake	8	2.4

DID YOU KNOW? Reports of monster 120-ft (36.5-m) anacondas have been published, but there is no evidence to prove this. Even so, a 25-ft (8-m) anaconda can eat a 6-ft (2-m) caiman; digesting it takes a week!

EXTINCT and ENDANGERED

MOST ENDANGERED ANIMALS

YANGTZE RIVER DOLPHIN Pollution has reduced the number of river dolphins in China to fewer than 200.

SIBERIAN TIGER Hunted for their fur and body parts, tigers are becoming increasingly rare. There are only between 250 and 400 Siberian tigers remaining in their natural habitat.

MONK SEAL There are now fewer than 400 Mediterranean monk seals. Their habitats have been polluted by oil, sewage, and industrial chemicals, making survival difficult.

MOUNTAIN GORILLA Only 400 gorillas remain in central Africa. Destruction of their forest habitat and hunting to supply the trade in body parts have led to declining numbers.

GIANT PANDA There are only about 1,000 pandas left in China. As their forest habitat is destroyed, their supply of food and shelter is reduced.

JAVAN RHINOCEROS Only about 70 rhinoceros are left in Java, Indonesia. Their habitat is being destroyed and they are hunted for their tusks.

BLUE WHALE About 9,000 blue whales swim in the world's oceans, but they are hunted for trade and suffer from pollution in the oceans.

ASIAN ELEPHANT Although 34,000–50,000 elephants remain in Southeast Asia, India, and China, their numbers are rapidly decreasing due to hunting for their ivory tusks, and the destruction of their habitat for farmland and buildings.

JAGUAR Poachers hunt the jaguar and its relative, the ocelot, for their attractive, spotted coats. These are then made into coats, shoes, or bags. Most of this killing is illegal, but while demand for these goods is high, it will continue.

PAMPAS DEER Large herds once grazed on the pampas of South America, but the introduction of farm mammals has drastically reduced the number of pampas deer.

KAKAPO This flightless bird from New Zealand has become endangered because animals such as cats, rats, stoats, and ferrets eat their eggs and young.

DID YOU KNOW? This black rhinoceros is very agile, and despite its hefty weight, it can gallop at 30 mph (48 km/h)!

THREATS TO WILDLIFE

HABITAT DESTRUCTION More and more land is being claimed by humans for planting crops and building settlements and roads.

POACHING Many animals are killed for their skins horns or tusks, and bones. Animal body parts are used in some traditional medicines.

POLLUTION Industry and farming can poison wildlife. Chemical spills, drainage, and acid rain can kill river wildlife. Farming pesticides can upset the natural balance and the habitat's food chains.

NON-NATIVE SPECIES When humans introduce new animals to a habitat, competition can lead to the demise of some species.

HOW RARE?

Listed below are the first in a range of categories in which the International Union for the Conservation of Nature places the species of animals and plants that it considers under threat.

EXTINCT Used when there are no definite reports of species of animals or plants for 50 years.

ENDANGERED Describes species of animals or plants that are in danger of extinction.

VULNERABLE Species likely to become endangered unless threats can be removed.

RARE Used to describe species that are at risk through low numbers, but are not yet endangered.

THREATENED A term for species that are under threat in various different ways.

COMMERCIALLY THREATENED Describes species whose survival is threatened by exploitation for commercial purposes.

EXTINCT ANCIENT ANIMALS

SABER-TOOTHED TIGER Also called *Smilodon*, the saber-toothed tiger of North and South America was one of the most ferocious carnivores. It had 6-in (15-cm) front teeth to slice through flesh.

WOOLLY MAMMOTH The woolly mammoth lived during the Ice Age in the cold tundra of North America, Europe, and Asia. It stood 10 ft (3 m) tall at the shoulder and had huge ivory tusks.

FIRST BIRD *Archaeopteryx* lived 150 million years ago. It is recognized as the first bird, evolving from a small group of meat-eating dinosaurs.

DINOSAUR RECORDS

ASTEST CARNIVORE Coelurosaurs could travel at about 25 mph (40 km/h) hen chasing prey.

ARGEST EGG Just one of the giant eggs id by *Hypselosaurus* was about the same olume as 60 chickens' eggs!

ARGEST BRAIN Small, speedy meat aters, such as *Troodon*, had the largest rain in proportion to their size, but ere not necessarily the most telligent.

SMALLEST BRAIN *Stegosaurus* had a rain smaller than a walnut.

SMALLEST CARNIVORE The tiny, hicken-sized *Compsognathus* was ss than 28 in (70 cm) long.

ARGEST CLAWS *Therizinosaurus* had he largest claws known, measuring bout 35 in (90 cm) long!

SMALLEST EVER FOUND *Mussaurus* as only 8 in (20 cm) long. However, ecause only one skeleton was found, inosaur experts think that it could have een a hatchling.

ARGEST FOOTPRINT Footprints made y a duck-billed dinosaur were 4.25 ft 1.3 m) long and 31 in (80 cm) wide.

ONGEST SKELETON The longest omplete skeleton found is that of *Diplodocus*, a long-necked sauropod hat grew to 85.25 ft (26 m) long. As many as 50 people could stand side y side next to *Diplodocus*!

BEST DEFENSE *Ankylosaurus* had a hard one at the end of its tail that could be wung at an enemy to keep it away.

ONGEST TAIL *Barosaurus* had the ongest tail, measuring 43 ft (13 m)!

DID YOU KNOW?
Tyrannosaurus rex had a gigantic mouth, full of huge, serrated teeth, each measuring up to 7 in (18 cm) in length!

DINOSAUR NAMES

1824 *Megalosaurus*, meaning "great lizard," was named by William Buckland (1784–1856).

1825 Gideon Mantell (1790–1852), a doctor with an interest in the study of geology, named *Iguanodon*, meaning "iguana tooth", after finding the first *Iguanodon* teeth in 1822. It was among a pile of stones used for road repairs!

1841 Richard Owen (1804–1892) named *Cladeiodon*, or "branch tooth," and *Cetiosaurus*, meaning "whale lizard," in the same year.

1850 Gideon Mantell named *Pelorosaurus*, or "monstrous lizard."

1856 Joseph Leidy (1823–1891) named five dinosaurs in one year, the first being *Deinodon*, or "terrible tooth."

DID YOU KNOW? The carnosaur *Tyrannosaurus rex* was the largest land-based carnivore ever to have walked the Earth, at 46 ft (14 m) long!

LAST SEEN ALIVE

AUROCHS 1627 This giant wild ox was last recorded in central Europe, after the need for more farmland in western Europe pushed its habitat eastward. The creature was extensively hunted, and the last died in Jaktorow Forest in Poland.

AEPYORNIS 1649 Also known as the "elephant bird," the 10-ft (3-m) wingless creature was once a native of the island of Madagascar.

DODO 1681 Unable to fly and easy to tame, the dodo (meaning "stupid" in Portuguese) was extensively collected by Europeans who discovered it in 1768. British naturalist Benjamin Harry saw the last dodo alive on the island of Mauritius, in the Indian Ocean, in 1681.

STELLER'S SEA COW 1768 This large marine mammal, one of the creatures that gave rise to the legend of the mermaid, was hunted to extinction.

PASSENGER PIGEON 1914 The last passenger pigeon, Martha, died at age 29 at the Cincinnati Zoo.

LARGEST DINOSAURS EVER DISCOVERED

YEAR	NAME	DIET	WEIGHT		LENGTH	
			TONS	TONNES	FT	M
1985	*Seismosaurus*	Plants	55–88	56–89	98–119	30–36
1972	*Supersaurus*	Plants	55	56	80–100	24–30
1929	*Antarctosaurus*	Plants	44–55	45–56	60–98	18–30
1890	*Barosaurus*	Plants	Uncertain		75–90	23–27.5

DID YOU KNOW? The dinosaur *Barosaurus* was named "heavy lizard" by US paleontologist Othniel C. Marsh in 1890. Archaeologists have found its remains in both North America and Africa, proving the existence of a land link between the two continents in Jurassic times, some 205–140 million years ago.

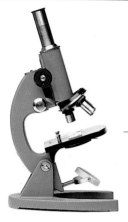

SCIENCE

SCIENCE FACTS

MILESTONES OF SCIENCE

c.400 BC Greek philosophers Epicurus and Democritus suggest that matter is made of particles called atoms.

c.350 BC Aristotle's study and classification of living things dominates scientific thinking for centuries.

c.260 BC Greek scientist Archimedes (287–212 BC) devises the principles of mechanics and invents many devices.

c.2 BC Early chemists attempt to turn metals to gold.

1638 Galileo Galilei (1564–1642) founds mechanics and is the first to use a telescope to explore the planets.

1661 Robert Boyle (1627–1691) uses the theory of moving particles to explain chemical reactions.

1661 Isaac Newton (1642–1727) develops laws of motion and gravitation.

1779 Italian physicist Alexander Volta (1745–1827) invents the battery.

1803 British chemist and physicist John Dalton (1766–1844) proposes modern atomic theory, developing Greek thought.

1869 Dmitri Mendeleyev (1834–1907) devises the periodic table of the elements.

1888 German physicist Heinrich Hertz (1857–1894) creates radio waves.

1905 Albert Einstein (1879–1955) writes his relativity theories.

1938 Enrico Fermi (1901–1954) builds a nuclear reactor.

1960 Laser is invented by Theodore Maiman (b.1927).

FAMOUS SCIENTISTS

ISAAC NEWTON (1642–1727) Developed three laws of motion, a law of gravitation, and made discoveries in light and maths.

HENRY CAVENDISH (1731–1810) Discovered hydrogen in 1766.

WILLIAM HERSCHEL (1738–1822) Discovered infra-red waves in 1800. He also discovered Uranus and many stars.

ANTOINE LAVOISIER (1743–1794) Named oxygen in 1779. Named some of the components of air and water.

HUMPHREY DAVY (1778–1829) Discovered potassium, sodium, magnesium, barium, calcium, and strontium during 1807–1808.

JAMES JOULE (1818–1889) In 1843, he formulated the relationship between heat, power, and work.

LOUIS PASTEUR (1822–1895) Pioneered a rabies vaccine and the pasteurization process.

JOSEPH LISTER (1827– 1912) First to use carbolic acid as an antiseptic.

MAX PLANCK (1858–1947) Proposed his quantum theory in 1900, stating that energy consists of small units called "quanta."

MARIE CURIE (1867–1934) Pioneer of research into radioactivity. She also discovered the elements polonium and radium.

ALBERT EINSTEIN (1879–1955) Published the special and general theories of relativity, which form the basis of our ideas about the Universe.

ALEXANDER FLEMING (1881–1955) Discovered penicillin in 1928. It was first used in World War II.

FIELDS OF SCIENCE

ASTRONOMY The study of the nature and movement of the objects in the Universe: planets, moons, comets, asteroids, stars, and galaxies.

BIOLOGY The study of plants and animals and how they grow, feed, reproduce, and evolve.

CHEMISTRY The study of the basic substances, or elements, that are found in the Universe, and how they combine to form complex substances called compounds.

COSMOLOGY The study of the structure and origin of the Universe.

ECOLOGY The study of the relationships between organisms and their environment.

ELECTRONICS A science that deals with electrical signals.

GENETICS The study of the genes in the human body and the way that characteristics are inherited.

GEOLOGY The study of the shape and structure of the Earth and its physical features.

MATHEMATICS The study of numbers, shapes, and quantities.

MEDICINE The study of the illnesses and diseases that affect the human body and the search for nonsurgical prevention, relief, and cures.

METEOROLOGY The study of the weather and the Earth's atmosphere.

PHYSICS Investigates energy and matter, the material from which everything is made.

PHYSIOLOGY The study of how living organisms and their parts work.

TECHNOLOGY The science in which scientific discoveries are put to practical use.

MATTER FACTS

Lowest melting point Since Mercury melts at -38°F (-38.9°C), it is liquid at room temperature. Mercury is used in thermometers because it expands as it is heated.

Highest melting point The temperature must be 6,606°F (3,652°C) before carbon will melt – two-thirds as hot as the sun's surface.

Rarest elements Astatine is the rarest element on Earth; rhodium is the scarcest metal in the world – just 2.9 tons (3 tonnes) are mined every year.

Heaviest metal A 13-in³ (33-cm³) cube of osmium weighs 1,411 lb (640 kg) – equivalent to ten people each weighing 141 lb (64 kg), or a small car!

!DID YOU KNOW? At 32°F (0°C) water becomes solid (ice). Above 212°F (100°C) it turns to gas (steam).

NEWTON'S LAWS OF MOTION

In 1661, this English physicist developed three laws describing motion:

First law An object will remain still or continue to travel at the same velocity unless a force acts on it.

Second law The acceleration of an object depends upon its mass and the amount of force acting on it.

Third law When two forces act on each other, they experience equal forces in opposite directions.

ATOMIC TERMS

Atom The smallest part of an element that can exist. Its nucleus contains protons and neutrons, surrounded by electrons. Everything is made of atoms.

Element A substance in its purest form – it cannot be broken down any further.

Electron A particle with a negative electric charge. Found in all atoms.

Neutron A particle in the nucleus of an atom that has no electric charge.

Proton A particle in the nucleus of an atom with a positive charge.

Nucleus This is the center of an atom, and contains protons and neutrons.

Atomic number The number of protons in the nucleus of an atom.

Atomic mass The mass of an atom in relation to that of a carbon-12 atom.

!DID YOU KNOW? A proton is about 2,000 times heavier than an electron!

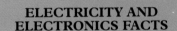

ELECTRICITY AND ELECTRONICS FACTS

Electricity The name comes from the Greek word *elektron*, meaning "amber." The Greeks noticed that when amber was rubbed with a cloth, static electricity made small objects stick to it.

Amazing microchips In 1950, nine million transistors would have covered eight football fields. By 1994, this many transistors could be fitted into a single microchip the size of a fingernail!

Electronics in your life Everyday equipment that relies on electronics to work includes calculators, car controls, cameras, washing machines, medical scanners, mobile telephones, radar systems, and computers.

Fiber-optic cables These very fine cables carry more data than copper ones, transmitting information in light pulses.

!AMAZING FACT! Computer performance has increased by a factor of one million between 1950 and 1990!

ACIDS AND ALKALIS

The acid or alkali (or base) content of a substance is measured in pH (potential Hydrogen) on a scale of 0–14. Acids dissolve in water to form sharp-tasting solutions, like lemon juice. Alkalis dissolve in water to form soapy solutions.

Substance		pH
Hydrochloric acid	(Acid)	0
Car battery acid		1.0
Lemon juice		2.4
Apple		3.0
Vinegar		4.0
Rainwater		5.6
Milk		6.6
Pure water	(Neutral)	7.0
Human blood		7.4
Seawater		7–8
Baking soda		8.5
Ammonia		12.0
Caustic soda	(Alkali)	14.0

SOUND LEVELS

The decibel (dB) measures sound. Every 10 dB is a tenfold increase in intensity.

Sound	dB
Silence	0
Rustle of leaves	10
Normal conversation, soft music	30
Quiet countryside, ticking watch	40
Restaurant, office	50–60
Busy traffic, loud television	70
Inside car, subway train	80
Very loud snore	88
Roaring lion	90
Lawnmower, chainsaw, blender	100
Powerful rock music	100
Rocket taking off	130

COLORS OF THE SPECTRUM

Red • Orange • Yellow • Green • Blue Indigo • Violet

!MEMORY TIP! Imagine the name ROY G. BIV.

THE ELEMENTS

! WHAT'S AN ATOMIC NUMBER? Every element has a specific atomic number, which is the number of protons in the nucleus of one atom of the element.

ELEMENT	SYMBOL	ATOMIC NUMBER	DISCOVERER	COUNTRY	DATE	DESCRIPTION AND USES
Actinium	Ac	89	André Debierne	France	1899	Soft, silvery radioactive metal: nuclear research
Aluminum	Al	13	Hans Christian Oersted	Denmark	1825	Light silvery metal: aircraft, cars, drink cans, foil
Americium	Am	95	Glen Seaborg & team	US	1945	Silvery radioactive metal: radiography
Antimony	Sb	51	Unknown	Unknown	c.1600 BC	Silvery metal: batteries, machine bearings
Argon	Ar	18	W. Ramsay/Baron Rayleigh	UK	1894	Colorless gas: used in metal-making, lamps
Arsenic	As	33	Albertus Magnus	Germany	c.1250	Gray poisonous metal: alloys, pesticides, glassmaking
Astatine	At	85	D. R. Corson & team	US	1940	Radioactive nonmetal: no practical uses
Barium	Ba	56	Sir Humphry Davy	UK	1808	Soft, silvery white metal: clinical body imaging
Berkelium	Bk	97	Glen Seaborg & team	US	1949	Silvery radioactive metal: nuclear research
Beryllium	Be	4	F. Wöhler/A. A. Bussy	Germany/France	1828	Soft, silvery white metal: alloys for tools
Bismuth	Bi	83	Unknown	Unknown	c.1500	Silvery metal: electronics, chemicals, cosmetics
Bohrium	Bh	107	Peter Armbruster & team	Germany	1981	Radioactive metal: no practical uses
Boron	B	5	Sir Humphry Davy	UK	1808	Dark powder: glass, detergents, fireproofing
Bromine	Br	35	A. Balard/C. Löwig	France/Germany	1826	Red liquid: fuel additives, pesticides, photography
Cadmium	Cd	48	Friedrich Stromeyer	Germany	1817	Silvery metal: batteries
Calcium	Ca	20	Sir Humphry Davy	UK	1808	Soft, silvery white metal: water treating, cement
Californium	Cf	98	Glen Seaborg & team	US	1950	Silvery radioactive metal: cancer treatment, mining
Carbon	C	6	Unknown	Unknown	Ancient	Various forms (graphite, diamonds, coal): many uses
Cerium	Ce	58	Wilhelm Hisinger & team	Sweden	1803	Gray metal: alloys, glass, ceramics, lighter flints
Cesium	Cs	55	Gustav Kirchhoff	Germany	1860	Gold metal: glass, radiation equipment
Chlorine	Cl	17	Carl Scheele	Sweden	1774	Gray-yellow gas: purifying water
Chromium	Cr	24	Nicolas-Louis Vauquelin	France	1797	Hard blue-white metal: chrome plating
Cobalt	Co	27	Georg Brandt	Sweden	1735–39	Silvery blue metal: magnets, ceramics, paints
Copper	Cu	29	Unknown	Unknown	c.5000 BC	Reddish metal: electrical wires, pipes, coins
Curium	Cm	96	Glen Seaborg & team	US	1944	Silvery radioactive metal: no common uses
Dubnium	Db	105	Russian/US teams	Russia/US	1970	Radioactive metal: no common uses
Dysprosium	Dy	66	Paul de Boisbaudran	France	1886	Silvery metal: alloys and magnets
Einsteinium	Es	99	Albert Ghiorso & team	US	1952	Radioactive metal: no practical uses
Erbium	Er	68	Carl Mosander	Sweden	1842	Silvery metal: glass and alloys
Europium	Eu	63	Eugène Demarcay	France	1901	Soft, silvery metal: minor uses in alloys
Fermium	Fm	100	Albert Ghiorso & team	US	1953	Radioactive metal: no practical uses
Fluorine	F	9	Henri Moissan	France	1886	Pale yellow gas: metal-making, drugs
Francium	Fr	87	Marguerite Perey	France	1939	Radioactive metal: no common uses
Gadolinium	Gd	64	Jean de Marignac	Switzerland	1880	Soft, silvery metal: alloys used in electronics
Gallium	Ga	31	Paul de Boisbaudran	France	1875	Soft, silvery metal: electronics
Germanium	Ge	32	Clemens Winkler	Germany	1886	Silvery metal: electronics and glass
Gold	Au	79	Unknown	Unknown	c.3000 BC	Shiny yellow metal: jewelry
Hafnium	Hf	72	Dirk Coster & team	Denmark	1923	Silvery metal: nuclear industry, alloys, ceramics
Hassium	Hs	108	Peter Armbruster & team	Germany	1984	Radioactive metal: no practical uses
Helium	He	2	W. Ramsay & team	UK	1895	Light colorless gas: balloons and diving
Holmium	Ho	67	Per Cleve & team	Sweden	1878	Silvery metal: magnetic equipment
Hydrogen	H	1	Henry Cavendish	UK	1766	Lightest gas: was used in balloons, now chemicals
Indium	In	49	F. Reich/H. Richter	Germany	1863	Silvery metal: electronics
Iodine	I	53	Bernard Courtois	France	1811	Black solid: medicines, dyes, photography
Iridium	Ir	77	Smithson Tennant	UK	1804	Hard silvery metal: alloys, spark plugs
Iron	Fe	26	Unknown	Unknown	c.2500 BC	Silvery metal: has many uses, as steel
Krypton	Kr	36	W. Ramsay/M. Travers	UK	1898	Colorless gas: no practical uses
Lanthanum	La	57	Carl Mosander	Sweden	1839	Soft, silvery white metal: optical glass, flints
Lawrencium	Lr	103	Albert Ghiorso & team	US	1961	Radioactive metal: no practical uses
Lead	Pb	82	Unknown	Unknown	c.1000 BC	Soft gray metal: batteries, solder, glass
Lithium	Li	3	Johann Arfvedson	Sweden	1817	Light metal: alloys, greases, batteries
Lutetium	Lu	71	Georges Urbain	France	1907	Hard metal: used only in chemical research
Magnesium	Mg	12	Sir Humphry Davy	UK	1808	Silvery white metal: alloys, fireworks, electrical uses
Manganese	Mn	25	Johan Gahn	Sweden	1774	Brittle silvery metal: steel, ceramics, fertilizers
Meiterium	Mt	109	Peter Armbruster & team	Germany	1982	Radioactive metal: no practical uses

THE RAREST METAL IS RHODIUM – JUST 2.9 TONS (3 TONNES) ARE PRODUCED EACH YEAR

Element	Symbol	Atomic Number	Discoverer	Country	Date	Description and Uses
Mendelevium	Md	101	Glen Seaborg & team	US	1955	Radioactive metal: no practical uses
Mercury	Hg	80	Unknown	Unknown	c.1500 BC	Liquid silvery metal: thermometers, street lights
Molybdenum	Mo	42	Carl Scheele	Sweden	1778	Silvery metal: alloys and electrical uses
Neodymium	Nd	60	Carl Auer	Austria	1885	Silvery white metal: lasers, magnets, glass
Neon	Ne	10	W. Ramsay/M. Travers	UK	1898	Colorless gas: neon lighting
Neptunium	Np	93	E. McMillan/P. Abelson	US	1940	Silvery radioactive metal: nuclear research
Nickel	Ni	28	Axel Cronstedt	Sweden	1751	Silvery white metal: alloys, coins, metal-plating
Niobium	Nb	41	Charles Hatchett	UK	1801	Silvery metal: stainless steel
Nitrogen	N	7	Daniel Rutherford	UK	1772	Colorless gas: fertilizers, explosives, plastics
Nobelium	No	102	Albert Ghiorso & team	US	1958	Radioactive metal: no practical uses
Osmium	Os	76	Smithson Tennant	UK	1804	Heavy silvery metal: alloys and catalysts
Oxygen	O	8	J. Priestley/C. Scheele	UK/Sweden	1774	Colorless gas: medicine, chemicals, steel-making
Palladium	Pd	46	William Wollaston	UK	1803	Silvery white metal: catalysts
Phosphorus	P	15	Hennig Brand	Germany	1669	White and red versions: fertilizers, foods, detergents
Platinum	Pt	78	Julius Caesar Scalgier	Italy	1557	Silvery white metal: jewelry, cancer drugs, catalysts
Plutonium	Pu	94	Glen Seaborg & team	US	1940	Silvery radioactive metal: nuclear weapons and fuel
Polonium	Po	84	Pierre & Marie Curie	France	1898	Silvery radioactive metal: nuclear research, satellites
Potassium	K	19	Sir Humphry Davy	UK	1807	Soft white metal: fertilizers, chemicals, glass
Praseodymium	Pr	59	Carl Auer	Austria	1885	Soft, silvery metal: magnets, protective glass
Promethium	Pm	61	J. A. Marinsky & team	US	1945	Radioactive metal: miniature batteries
Protactinium	Pa	91	O. Hahn/F. Soddy & team	Germany/UK	1917	Silvery radioactive metal: no practical uses
Radium	Ra	88	Pierre & Marie Curie	France	1898	Soft, silvery radioactive metal: once used for cancer
Radon	Rn	86	Friedrich Dorn	Germany	1900	Colorless radioactive gas: sometimes used for cancer
Rhenium	Re	75	Walter Noddack & team	Germany	1925	Silvery metal: aero engines, lightbulbs, catalysts
Rhodium	Rh	45	William Wollaston	UK	1803	Hard silvery metal: catalysts
Rubidium	Rb	37	R. Bunsen/G. Kirschoff	Germany	1861	Soft white metal: no practical uses
Ruthenium	Ru	44	Karl Klaus	Russia	1844	Silvery metal: alloys, catalysts
Rutherfordium	Rf	104	Russian/US teams	Russia/US	1969	Radioactive metal: no practical uses
Samarium	Sm	62	Paul de Boisbaudran	France	1879	Silvery white metal: glass, catalysts, electronics
Scandium	Sc	21	Lars Nilson	Sweden	1879	Soft, silvery white metal: powerful lights
Seaborgium	Sg	106	Albert Ghiorso & team	US	1974	Radioactive metal: no practical uses
Selenium	Se	34	Jöns Berzelius	Sweden	1817	Silvery metal/red powder: photocopiers
Silicon	Si	14	Jöns Berzelius	Sweden	1823	Blue-gray crystals: semiconductors, alloys
Silver	Ag	47	Unknown	Unknown	c.3000 BC	Soft metal: silverware, jewelry, photography
Sodium	Na	11	Sir Humphry Davy	UK	1807	Soft, silvery white metal: industrial/nuclear processes
Strontium	Sr	38	A. Crawford	UK	1790	Silvery white metal: glass for computer screens
Sulfur	S	16	Unknown	Unknown	Ancient	Yellow powder (and other forms): chemicals
Tantalum	Ta	73	Anders Ekberg	Sweden	1802	Shiny silver metal: electronics, cutting tools
Technetium	Tc	43	C. Perrier/E. Segrè	Italy	1937	Radioactive metal: no practical uses
Tellurium	Te	52	Franz Müller	Romania	1782	Silvery white semimetal: alloys, electronics
Terbium	Tb	65	Carl Mosander	Sweden	1843	Silvery metal: electronics, lasers
Thallium	Tl	81	Sir William Crookes	UK	1861	Soft, silvery white metal: glassmaking
Thorium	Th	90	Jöns Berzelius	Sweden	1828	Silvery radioactive metal: nuclear industry, gas mantles
Thulium	Tm	69	Per Cleve	Sweden	1879	Silvery metal: X-ray machines
Tin	Sn	50	Unknown	Unknown	c.2100 BC	Soft, silvery white metal: tinplate, alloys
Titanium	Ti	22	William Gregor	UK	1791	Hard silvery metal: alloys, hip replacement joints
Tungsten	W	74	Fausto & Juan de Elhuyar	Spain	1783	Silvery white metal: alloys, cutting tools, light bulbs
Ununbium	Uub	112	Peter Armbruster & team	Germany	1996	Radioactive metal: no practical uses
Ununnilium	Uun	110	Peter Armbruster & team	Germany	1994	Radioactive metal: no practical uses
Unununium	Uuu	111	Peter Armbruster & team	Germany	1994	Radioactive metal: no practical uses
Uranium	U	92	Martin Klaproth	Germany	1789	Silvery radioactive metal: nuclear fuel and weapons
Vanadium	V	23	Nils Selfström	Sweden	1830	Silvery metal: alloys
Xenon	Xe	54	W. Ramsay/M. Travers	UK	1898	Colorless gas: few practical uses
Ytterbium	Yb	70	Jean de Marignac	Switzerland	1878	Soft, silvery white metal: stress gauges, few other uses
Yttrium	Y	39	Johan Gadolin	Finland	1794	Soft, silvery white metal: TV screens, X-rays, alloys
Zinc	Zn	30	Andreas Marggraf	Germany	1746	Bluish white metal: galvanizing, batteries, in brass
Zirconium	Zr	40	Martin Klaproth	Germany	1789	Hard silvery metal: alloys, nuclear reactors

DID YOU KNOW? Besides the 112 elements listed here, there are another six unnamed elements – numbers 113–118 – that exist theoretically, but have not yet been synthesized.

DID YOU KNOW? The elements are often arranged as a periodic table. The first person to set them out in this way was Russian chemist Dmitri Mendeleyev (1834–1907).

47

MATHEMATICS

MATHEMATICAL SYMBOLS

SYMBOL	MEANING	SYMBOL	MEANING
+	Plus or positive	<	Less than
-	Minus or negative	≤	Equal or less than
±	Plus or minus, positive or negative	≥	Equal or greater than
x	Multiplied by	~	Of the order of, similar to
÷ or /	Divided by	√	Square root
%	Percent	Σ	Sum of
=	Equal to	π	Pi
≠	Not equal to	°	Degree
>	Greater than	∞	Infinity

FAMOUS MATHEMATICIANS

PYTHAGORAS The Greek mathematician Pythagoras (c.580–500 BC) is remembered for his theories on trigonometry. His most-used theorem is named after him.

EUCLID One of the founders of geometry, the Greek theorist Euclid (c.300 BC) wrote a 13-volume book, *The Elements*, in which he detailed the main geometric shapes.

NAPIER Scotsman John Napier (1550–1617) is best known for inventing logarithms. Many mathematicians have used logarithms to devise new theories.

NEWTON Famous for his laws of motion and gravitation, Isaac Newton (1642–1727) made discoveries in math and physics.

REGULAR SOLIDS

POLYHEDRON Solid shape that has polygons as faces.

TETRAHEDRON Solid shape that has four equal triangles as faces.

CUBE Cubes have six equal square faces. Every angle is a right angle.

OCTAHEDRON Polyhedron with eight triangles as faces.

DODECAHEDRON Solid with 12 regular faces.

ALL THE PRIME NUMBERS UNDER 1,000

2	3	5	7	11	13	17	19
23	29	31	37	41	43	47	53
59	61	67	71	73	79	83	89
97	101	103	107	109	113	127	131
37	139	149	151	157	163	167	173
179	181	191	193	197	199	211	223
227	229	233	239	241	251	257	263
269	271	277	281	283	293	307	311
313	317	331	337	347	349	353	359
367	373	379	383	389	397	401	409
419	421	431	433	439	443	449	457
461	463	467	479	487	491	499	503
509	521	523	541	547	557	563	569
571	577	587	593	599	601	607	613
617	619	631	641	643	647	653	659
661	673	677	683	691	701	709	719
727	733	739	743	751	757	761	769
773	787	797	809	811	821	823	827
829	839	853	857	859	863	877	881
883	887	907	911	919	929	937	941
947	953	967	971	977	983	991	997

TRY THIS YOURSELF! Prime numbers can be divided only by themselves and 1. All, except the number 2, are odd numbers. Try dividing a few of these by other numbers and see for yourself!

TYPES OF NUMBERS

FRACTION Amounts expressed as one number divided by another are called fractions. If a cake is halved, each piece is equivalent to the whole, or 1, divided by 2. This is written as ½, one-half.

POWER Useful when dealing with very large or small numbers, powers show how many times a number is multiplied or divided by itself to give a larger or smaller number. For example, 10 multiplied by itself 5 times is 10 to the power of 5, or 10^5.

LOGARITHMS Invented in 1616, logarithms, or logs, are used to simplify complicated math problems. They show the number of times to multiply a number to get another larger number. For example, the log of raising 10 to 1,000 is 3, because 10 x 10 x 10 = 1,000.

PERCENTAGES Literally meaning "for each hundred," percent can be used to write down fractions. As a percentage, ½ becomes 50 percent (50%), or $^{50}/_{100}$.

SCIENTIFIC NOTATION When writing out very large or small numbers, scientific notation is helpful. It uses powers of 10, for example, 0.75 is 7.5 x 10^{-1}.

NUMBERS ONE TO TEN IN SIX LANGUAGES

ENGLISH	CHINESE	SPANISH	GERMAN	ITALIAN	FRENCH
one	一	uno	ein	uno	un
two	二	dos	zwei	due	deux
three	三	tres	drei	tre	trois
four	四	cuatro	vier	quattro	quatre
five	五	cinco	fünf	cinque	cinq
six	六	seis	sechs	sei	six
seven	七	siete	sieben	sette	sept
eight	八	ocho	acht	otto	huit
nine	九	nueve	neun	nove	neuf
ten	十	diez	zehn	dieci	dix

TIMES TABLES

	1	2	3	4	5	6	7	8	9	10
1	1	2	3	4	5	6	7	8	9	10
2	2	4	6	8	10	12	14	16	18	20
3	3	6	9	12	15	18	21	24	27	30
4	4	8	12	16	20	24	28	32	36	40
5	5	10	15	20	25	30	35	40	45	50
6	6	12	18	24	30	36	42	48	54	60
7	7	14	21	28	35	42	49	56	63	70
8	8	16	24	32	40	48	56	64	72	80
9	9	18	27	36	45	54	63	72	81	90
10	10	20	30	40	50	60	70	80	90	100

CIRCLE TERMS

ARC Part of a curve.

CIRCUMFERENCE The total distance around the edge of a circle.

CHORD A straight line joining any two points on the circumference.

DIAMETER A line from one side of circle to another, through the center.

PI The ratio of the circumference of a circle to its diameter. It is approximately equal to 3.14159 and is the same for all circles.

RADIUS (*pl.* radii) The distance from the center of a circle to the edge.

SECTOR A slice of a circle between two radii.

FAMOUS EQUATIONS

$e=mc^2$ Einstein's theory of relativity explains that the energy something uses can be calculated by multiplying its mass (*m*) by the speed of light (*c*) squared.

$a=\pi r^2$ The area of a circle can be found by multiplying pi by the circle's radius squared.

$a^2=b^2+c^2$ Pythagoras' Theorem states that in a right-angled triangle, the squares of the two sides adjacent to the right angle add up to the square of the longest side (hypotenuse).

REGULAR POLYGONS

POLYGON	NUMBER OF SIDES
Triangle	3
Square	4
Pentagon	5
Hexagon	6
Heptagon	7
Octagon	8
Nonagon	9
Decagon	10
Undecagon	11
Duodecagon (or dodecagon)	12

A figure enclosed by straight lines is a polygon. In a regular polygon, all sides are of equal lengths and its internal angles are the same. They will fit within a circle, all their points touching the edge.

ROMAN NUMERALS

ROMAN	ARABIC
I	1
II	2
III	3
IV	4
V	5
VI	6
VII	7
VIII	8
IX	9
X	10
XX	20
XXX	30
XL	40
L	50
LX	60
LXX	70
LXXX	80
XC	90
C	100
CC	200
CCC	300
CCCC	400
D	500
DC	600
DCC	700
DCCC	800
CM	900
M	1,000
MCMXCIX	1,999
MM	2,000

Roman numerals are "constructed" from seven letters (I, V, X, L, C, D, M). Small digits appearing before larger ones are subtracted from them. 90, XC, is made from X (10) subtracted from C (100). Small digits appearing after them are added. This can lead to very long strings of numbers!

BIG AND LITTLE NUMBERS

PREFIX	SYMBOL	POWER	NAME	VALUE
peta-	P	10^{15}	quadrillion	1,000,000,000,000,000
tera-	T	10^{12}	trillion	1,000,000,000,000
giga-	G	10^{9}	billion	1,000,000,000
mega-	M	10^{6}	million	1,000,000
kilo-	k	10^{3}	thousand	1,000
hecto-	h	10^{2}	hundred	100
deca-	da	10^{1}	ten	10
—	—	10^{0}	one	1
deci-	d	10^{-1}	tenth	0.1
centi-	c	10^{-2}	hundredth	0.01
milli-	m	10^{-3}	thousandth	0.001
micro-	μ	10^{-6}	millionth	0.000,001
nano-	n	10^{-9}	billionth	0.000,000,001
pico-	p	10^{-12}	trillionth	0.000,000,000,001
femto-	f	10^{-15}	quadrillionth	0.000,000,000,000,001

This chart shows short ways of writing very large or small numbers, using powers. Prefixes are the names of amounts, but are not always exact. For example, in computers, one "megabyte" is 1,048,576 bytes!

WEIGHTS and MEASURES

ANCIENT MEASUREMENTS

CUBIT In ancient Egypt, the cubit was measured as the distance from the tip of the forefinger to the elbow.

FOOT A foot is the average length of an adult foot. In ancient times it was equal to 11.5 in (29 cm), but today it is always 12 in (30 cm).

HAND A hand was approximately equal to 5 in (12.5 cm) and was officially the width of the hand, with all five digits together. A modern hand, used for measuring horses, is 4 in (10.2 cm) and is the width of only four digits.

SPAN A span was the distance between the tip of the little finger and thumb with the hand stretched out – approximately 9 in (23 cm).

YARD The yard, equal to 3 ft (91 cm), is the length of a man's belt. In the 1100s King Henry I of England standardized the yard as the distance from the thumb of his outstretched arm to his nose.

MILE The Roman *mille*, a thousand, was based on 1,000 paces of a marching army, and was shorter than a modern mile. A pace was equal to two steps – about 5 ft (1.5 m).

POUND The modern imperial pound comes from the Roman weight *libra pondo*. This is why the abbreviation for pound is "lb."

MEASURING INSTRUMENTS

INSTRUMENT	WHAT IT MEASURES
Anemometer	Wind
Barometer	Air pressure
Calendar	Days and months
Clock	Hours, minutes, seconds
Hygrometer	Specific gravity
Protractor	Angles
Ruler	Length
Scales	Weight
Seismometer	Earthquakes
Speedometer	Vehicle speed
Thermometer	Temperature
Voltmeter	Electricity

❗ DID YOU KNOW?
The division of hours into 60 minutes, and minutes into 60 seconds, is based on the ancient Babylonian sexagesimal measurement system, which divides everything into 60.

STANDARD MEASUREMENTS

In order to ensure that everyone means the same thing when stating measurements, certain basic units have very precisely defined standards, as these examples illustrate.

KILOGRAM The worldwide standard kilogram measure is a cylinder made of the metals iridium and platinum, which is kept under carefully controlled conditions at the International Bureau of Weights and Measures at Sèvres, France.

METER One meter was originally calculated as one 10-millionth of a quarter of the circumference of the Earth. Today, a meter is calculated as the distance light travels in a vacuum in 1/299792458th of a second.

SECOND One second is defined as "the duration of 9,192,631,770 periods of the radiation corresponding to the transition between the two hyperfine levels of the ground state of the cesium–133 atom"!

❗ DID YOU KNOW?
The first standard system of weights arose when traders needed to measure their goods.

ASSYRIAN LION WEIGHT

❗ DID YOU KNOW?
The origins of some imperial units can be found in early civilizations of the Near and Middle East. In ancient Assyria, weights were made for the King Shalmaneser.

THE SEVEN BASE SI UNITS

The seven base units SI (Système Internationale d'Unites, or International System of Units) is the standard system of units for scientists throughout the world.

QUANTITY	UNIT	SYMBOL
Mass	Kilogram	kg
Length	Meter	m
Time	Second	s
Electric current	Ampere	A
Temperature	Kelvin	K
Luminous intensity	Candela	cd
Amount of substance	Mole	mole

UNITS OF VOLUME

1 cubic mm (mm³)	
1 cubic centimeter (cc³)	1.000 mm³
1 cubic meter (m³)	1,000,000 cm³
1 cubic kilometer (km³)	1,000,000,000 m³
1 liter (l)	1,000 cm³
1 cubic inch (in³)	
1 cubic foot (ft³)	1,728 in³
1 cubic yard (yd³)	27 ft³
1 fluid oz (fl oz)	
1 pint (pt)	20 fl oz
1 gallon (gal)	8 pt

UNITS OF AREA

1 square millimeter (mm²)	
1 square centimeter (cm²)	100 mm²
1 square meter (m²)	10,000 cm²
1 hectare	10,000 m²
1 square kilometer (km²)	1,000,000 m²
1 square inch (in²)	
1 square foot (ft²)	144 in²
1 square yard (yd²)	9 ft²
1 acre	4,480 yd²
1 square mile (mile²)	640 acres

SPECIAL MEASUREMENTS

CARAT Gems, such as diamonds, are weighed in carats. The word comes from the tiny carob bean, which is remarkable for its consistent weight of 0.007 oz (0.2 g).

CHAIN The chain was once a 100-link chain measuring 66 ft (20.12 m) long. To this day, a cricket pitch is one chain long.

FATHOM A measure of depth used at sea, a fathom is the distance a man's arms stretch when paying out a rope – 6 ft (1.83 m).

KNOT Speed at sea is measured in knots – once the time a ship took to travel along a piece of knotted rope. A knot is now 1 nautical mph. A nautical mile is 6,076.11549 ft in the US, and 6,082.66 ft in the UK.

POINT Used by printers, the point size is the height of a letter such as an x: one point is equal to 0.013889 in (0.3528 mm). The point size of this text is 9.25.

MEASUREMENT SYSTEMS

People have been dividing things into units for thousands of years. Here are four basic systems that have been used. You may recognize some of them.

BINARY Hindus in India divide things into two, such as halves, quarters, eighths, and sixteenths.

DECIMAL China was the first country to use a decimal system, which divides things into tenths.

DUODECIMAL The Romans used units of 12 – which is why there are 12 months in a year, 12 in a dozen, and 12 inches in a foot.

SEXAGESIMAL The Babylonians used units of 60, still used to measure time.

UNITS OF WEIGHT

1 gram (g)	
1 kilogram (kg)	1,000 g
1 tonne	1,000 kg
1 ounce (oz)	
1 pound (lb)	16 oz
1 stone	14 lb
1 hundredweight	112 lb
1 long (ton)	2,240 lb
1 US short ton	2,000 lb

UNITS OF LENGTH

1 millimeter (mm)	
1 centimeter (cm)	10 mm
1 meter (m)	100 cm
1 kilometer (km)	1,000 m
1 inch (in)	
1 foot (ft)	12 in
1 yard (yd)	3 ft
1 mile	1,760 yd

TRICK QUESTION!

Which is heavier – a pound of feathers or a pound of gold? Most people think they weigh the same, but gold is measured in troy pounds, which contain only 12 oz (373 g), whereas a pound of feathers contains 16 oz (454 g). So, strange as it may seem, the feathers are in fact heavier!

MEASUREMENTS NAMED AFTER PEOPLE

MEASUREMENT	USED TO MEASURE	NAMED AFTER
Ampere	Electrical current	André-Marie Ampère (French, 1775–1836)
Angstrom	Light	Anders Jonas Ångstrom (Swedish, 1814–1874)
Celsius	Temperature	Anders Celsius (Swedish, 1701–1744)
Fahrenheit	Temperature	Gabriel Fahrenheit (German, 1686–1736)
Hertz	Frequency	Heinrich Rudolf Hertz (German, 1857–1894)
Joule	Energy	James Prescott Joule (British, 1818–1889)
Kelvin	Temperature	Lord Kelvin (British, 1824–1907)
Mach number	Speed of sound	Ernst Mach (Austrian, 1838–1916)
Ohm	Electrical resistance	Georg Simon Ohm (German, 1787–1854)
Volt	Electrical current	Alessandro Volta (Italian, 1745–1827)
Watt	Power	James Watt (British, 1736–1819)

MEASUREMENT CONVERSIONS

LENGTH CONVERSION

FROM	TO	MULTIPLY BY
Inches (in)	Centimeters (cm)	2.5400
Feet (ft)	Meters (m)	0.3048
Yards (yd)	Meters (m)	0.9144
Miles (mi)	Kilometers (km)	1.6093
Centimeters (cm)	Inches (in)	0.3937
Meters (m)	Feet (ft)	3.2808
Meters (m)	Yards	1.0936
Kilometers (km)	Miles	0.6214

TEMPERATURE

FROM	TO	MULTIPLY BY
Fahrenheit (°F)	Celsius (°C)	−32 x 5 ÷ 9
Celsius (°C)	Fahrenheit (°F)	x 9 ÷ 5 + 32

VOLUME CONVERSION

FROM	TO	MULTIPLY BY
Cubic inches (in³)	Cubic centimeters (cc)	16.3871
Cubic feet (ft³)	Cubic meters (m³)	0.0283
Cubic yards (yd³)	Cubic meters (m³)	1.3080
Cubic miles (mi³)	Cubic kilometers (km³)	4.1682
Pints	Liters (l)	0.5683
US gallons (gal)	Liters (l)	3.7853
Cubic centimeters (cc)	Cubic inches (in³)	0.0610
Cubic meters (m³)	Cubic feet (ft³)	35.3147
Cubic meters (m³)	Cubic yards (yd³)	0.7646
Cubic kilometers (km³)	Cubic miles (ml³)	0.2399
Liters (l)	Pints	1.7598
Liters (l)	US gallons (gal)	0.2642
Liters (l)	Gallons (gal)	0.2200
UK gallons (gal)	Liters (l)	4.5461

SPEED CONVERSION

FROM	TO	MULTIPLY BY
Feet per second (ft/s)	Meters per second (m/s)	0.3048
Miles per hour (mph)	Kilometers per hour (km/h)	1.609
Meters per second (m/s)	Feet per second (ft/s)	3.2808
Kilometers per hour (km/h)	Miles per hour (mph)	0.6214

MASS AND WEIGHT CONVERSION

FROM	TO	MULTIPLY BY
Ounces (oz)	Grams (g)	28.3495
Grams (g)	Ounces (oz)	0.0353
Pounds (lb)	Kilograms (kg)	0.4536
Kilograms (kg)	Pounds (lb)	2.2046
Stones	Kilograms (kg)	6.3503
Kilograms (kg)	Stones	0.1575
Hundredweight (cwt)	Kilograms (kg)	50.8024
Kilograms (kg)	Hundredweight (cwt)	0.0197
US (short) tons	UK tonnes	0.9072
UK tonnes	US (short) tons	1.1023
Tons (long)	Tonnes	1.0160
Tonnes	Tons (long)	0.9842

AREA CONVERSION

FROM	TO	MULTIPLY BY
Square inches (in²)	Square centimeters (cm²)	6.4516
Square feet (ft²)	Square meters (m²)	0.0929
Square yards (yd²)	Square meters (m²)	0.8361
Square miles (mi²)	Square kilometers (km²)	2.5900
Acres	Hectares	0.4047
Square centimeters (cm²)	Square inches (in²)	0.1550
Square meters (m²)	Square feet (ft²)	10.7639
Square meters (m²)	Square yards (yd²)	1.1960
Square kilometers (km²)	Square miles (mi²)	0.3861
Hectares	Acres	2.4711

FRACTIONS, DECIMALS, AND PERCENTAGES

TO CONVERT A FRACTION INTO A DECIMAL Divide 1 by the lower number of the fraction and then multiply the answer by the top number, e.g. ⅜ = 1 ÷ 8 x 3 = 0.375

TO CONVERT A DECIMAL NUMBER INTO A PERCENTAGE Multiply the decimal number by 100, e.g. 0.375 x 100 = 37.5%

TO CONVERT A PERCENTAGE INTO A FRACTION Make a fraction by putting the percentage over 100, then see if there is a number that will divide exactly into both the top and bottom numbers of the fraction, e.g. 37.5% = ³⁷·⁵/₁₀₀. If you divide 37.5 and 100 by 2.5, you get ¹⁵/₄₀. Then divide 15 and 40 by 5 to get ⅜. Sometimes, it will be impossible to simplify a fraction, e.g. ⁴¹/₁₀₀ – there is no number that will divide exactly into both 41 and 100.

COOKING MEASURES AND CONVERSIONS

OBJECT	IMPERIAL	METRIC
1 thimble	30 drops	2.5 ml
60 drops/1 teaspoon	1 teaspoon/1 dram	5 ml
1 dessert spoon	2 drams	10 ml
1 tablespoon	4 drams	20 ml
1 wine glass	2 fl oz	100 ml
1 tea cup	5 fl oz (1 gill)	200 ml
1 mug	10 fl oz (½ pint)	400 ml
1 US cup	8 fl oz	227 ml
1 US pint	16 fl oz	504 ml

QUICK CHECK HEIGHT CHART

FT	IN	M
3	8	1.12
3	9	1.14
3	10	1.17
3	11	1.19
4	-	1.22
4	1	1.24
4	2	1.27
4	3	1.30
4	4	1.32
4	5	1.35
4	6	1.37
4	7	1.40
4	8	1.42
4	9	1.45
4	10	1.47
4	11	1.50
5	-	1.52
5	1	1.55
5	2	1.57
5	3	1.60
5	4	1.62
5	5	1.65
5	6	1.68
5	7	1.70
5	8	1.73
5	9	1.75
5	10	1.77
5	11	1.80
6	-	1.83

QUICK CHECK WEIGHT CHART

LB	KG	STONES	LB
57	26	4	1
62	28	4	6
66	30	4	10
71	32	5	1
75	34	5	5
79	36	5	9
84	38	6	-
88	40	6	4
93	42	6	9
97	44	6	13
101	46	7	3
106	48	7	8
110	50	7	12
115	52	8	3
119	54	8	7
124	56	8	11
128	58	9	2
132	60	9	6
137	62	9	11
141	64	10	1
146	66	10	6
150	68	10	10
154	70	11	-
159	72	11	5
163	74	11	9
168	76	12	-
172	78	12	4
176	80	12	8
181	82	12	13

QUICK TEMPERATURE CONVERSIONS

FAHRENHEIT	CELSIUS	KELVIN
320	160	433
302	150	423
284	140	413
266	130	403
248	120	393
230	110	383
211	100	373
194	90	363
176	80	353
158	70	343
140	60	333
122	50	323
104	40	313
86	30	303
68	20	293
50	10	283
32	0	273
14	-10	263
-4	-20	253
-22	-30	-243
-40	-40	233
-58	-50	223

DID YOU KNOW? The Kelvin scale is also known as the absolute temperature scale, and is often used in science. To convert degrees Celsius into kelvins, add 273.16.

OVEN TEMPERATURES

TEMPERATURE °F	°C	RATING
250	120	Slow
275	140	–
300	150	–
325	170	–
350	180	Moderate
375	190	–
400	200	Hot
425	220	–
450	230	Very hot
500	260	–

KIDS' SHOE SIZES

US AND CANADA	WORLD	UK
0	15	00
1	16	½
1½	17	1
2½	18	2
3½	19	3
4	20	3½
4	21	4½
5½	22	5
6½	23	6
7½	24	7
8	25	7½
9	26	8½
9½	27	9
10½	28	10
11½	29	11
12	30	11½
13	31	12
13½	32	13
1½	33	13½

ADULT SHOE SIZES

US AND CANADA	EUROPE	UK
2	34	1½
4	35	2½
4½	36	3
5½	37	4
6½ / 5½★	38	5
7 / 6★	39	5½
8 / 7★	40	6½
8½ / 7½★	41	7
9½ / 8½★	42	8
10½ / 9½★	43	9
10★	44	9½
10½★	45	10
11½★	46	11
12★	47	11½

US men's and women's sizes differ. Men's sizes are marked by an asterisk.

MEASURING TIME

TIME CAPSULES TELL OUR STORY

Cleopatra's Needle is an Egyptian obelisk made about 3,400 years ago. It was brought to London in 1878. The time capsule placed beneath it, a sealed urn, includes:

PRINTED MATTER London map, Bibles, magazine article describing how the Needle was brought to England, newspapers, translation of Needle's hieroglyphics

IMAGES Portait of Queen Victoria, portraits of 12 of Britain's prettiest women

OBJECTS Iron ropes, submarine cables, baby bottle, scale model of the obelisk and a piece of granite from it, British currency, toys, 2-ft (60-cm) ruler, hairpins, cigars, razor, hydraulic jack

The *Voyager* spacecraft was launched by the US in 1978, and is still in space. On board, a time capsule in the form of a 12-in (30-cm) copper disk tells our story to extraterrestrials. It includes:

IMAGES Earth, DNA, family, Great Wall of China, Monument Valley, snowflake, animals, Taj Mahal, X ray of a hand, radio telescope

SOUNDS Rain, wind, surf, volcano, fire, earthquake, footsteps, heartbeat, laughter, kiss between a mother and child, Saturn-5 lift-off, spoken greetings in 55 languages

MUSIC Song from Zaire, excerpt from *The Magic Flute*, sounds of Louis Armstrong, Navajo chant, Peruvian panpipes, Indian raga

NAMES OF THE MONTHS

The names of the months in English, and many other languages, come from the Latin language.

JANUARY The first month is named after Janus, Roman god of beginnings.

FEBRUARY *Februa* was a purification festival that took place in late winter.

MARCH Named after Mars, god of war.

APRIL The month when plants open – from *aperire* meaning "to open."

MAY Probably named after Maia, the goddess of growth and fertility.

JUNE Named either after a Roman family name *Junius*, meaning young, or after the goddess Juno.

JULY Named in 44 BC by Mark Antony in honor of Julius Caesar.

AUGUST Named in honor of Emperor Augustus in 8 BC.

SEPTEMBER From *septem*, "seven," the Roman calendar's seventh month.

OCTOBER The eighth month in the Roman calendar, from *octo*, "eight."

NOVEMBER The ninth month in the Roman calendar, from *novem*, "nine."

DECEMBER The tenth month in the Roman calendar, from *decem*, "ten."

WORLD CALENDARS

GREGORIAN

The Gregorian calendar, named after Pope Gregory XIII who introduced it in 1582, is the most widely used today. It is based on the time it takes for the Earth to circle the Sun (365.2425 days). The calendar has 365 days – the extra 0.2425 days are made up every four years by adding an extra day to make a leap year. The Gregorian calendar is just one day off in every 3,300 years.

Month	Days
January	31
February	28/29
March	31
April	30
May	31
June	30
July	31
August	31
September	30
October	31
November	30
December	31

JEWISH

The Jewish calendar is based on the Moon's cycle. A "common," nonleap year has 353, 354, or 355 days divided into 12 months. A leap year has 383, 384, or 385 days and 13 months. In a leap year, which falls in years 3, 6, 8, 11, 14, 17, and 19 of a 19-year cycle, Adar has 30 days; it is followed by Adar II with 29 or 30 days. The three year lengths are called "minimal," "regular," and "full."

Month	Days
Tishri	30
Heshvan	29/30
Kislev	30/29
Tevet	29
Shevat	30
Adar	29
Nisan	30
Iyar	29
Sivan	30
Tammuz	29
Av	30
Elul	29

ISLAMIC

The Islamic calendar is based on the Moon's cycle beginning with the year of the *Hejirah* (AD 622) when Muhammad traveled from Mecca to Medina. It runs in cycles of 30 years, of which years 2, 5, 7, 10, 13, 16, 21, 24, 26, and 29 are leap years. A year consists of 12 months of 29 or 30 days. Common years have 354 days, leap years 355. In a leap year the extra day is added at the end of the 12th month.

Month	Days
Muharram	30
Safar	29
Rabi'a I	30
Rabi'a II	29
Jumada I	30
Jumada II	29
Rajab	30
Sha'ban	29
Ramadan	30
Shawwal	29
Dhu al-Q'adah	30
Dhu al-Hijjah	29/30

TIMELINE OF MEASURING TIME

c.1500 BC Egyptians use sundials. The Sun's shadow moves round a dial marked with hours.

c.AD 890 Clock candles appear in England.

1335 First mechanical clock is erected in Milan, Italy. Their popularity spreads through Europe.

1364 First domestic clocks made by Italian Giovanni Dondi (1318–1389).

1657 Dutch physicist Christiaan Huygens (1629–1695) builds the first pendulum clock.

1800s American Eli Tery (1772–1852) develops cheaper clocks in the US.

c.1900 First wristwatches introduced.

1929 American Warren Morrison invents the quartz clock.

1948 The atomic clock is developed in the US.

1970s–1990s Digital watches become popular.

HOW LONG DOES IT TAKE?

EXAMPLE	SECONDS
Light to travel 12 in (30 cm) in air	0.000,000,001
A flash of lightning	0.000,001
Sound to travel 12 in (30 cm) in air	0.001
Olympic sprinter to run 3ft 3 in (1 m)	0.1
Quartz in a watch to vibrate 32,768 times	1
A snail to move 33 ft (10 m)	1,000
11.5 days to pass	1,000,000
Saturn to orbit the Sun	1,000,000,000

MEMORY TIP! Remember how many days in each month with this rhyme: "30 days has September, April, June, and November. All the rest have 31, excepting February alone, which has 28 days clear, with 29 in each leap year."

WORLD CALENDARS

INDIAN

India has several principal calendars. In 1957 the calendar known as the Saka era was declared the national calendar, to run concurrently with the Gregorian calendar. The Saka era dates from March 3, AD 78, in the Gregorian calendar. It is based on the solar year, which is the time taken for the Earth to orbit the Sun, and begins with the spring equinox. The 365 days (366 in a leap year) are divided into 12 months. In a leap year, the extra day is always added to the first month, Caitra.

MONTH	DAYS	EQUIVALENT GREGORIAN DATE
Caitra	30/31	March 22
Vaisakha	31	April 21
Jyaistha	31	May 22
Asadha	31	June 22
Sravana	31	July 23
Bhadra	31	August 23
Asvina	30	September 23
Kartika	30	October 23
Agrahayana	30	November 22
Pausa	30	December 22
Magha	30	January 21
Phalguna	30	February 20

CHINESE

The ancient Chinese calendar is based on a lunar year of 12 months of alternately 29 and 30 days. To keep the calendar in step with the Gregorian calendar, extra months are inserted. The months of the Chinese calendar are numbered and given one of the 12 animal names that are usually attached to years and hours in the Chinese calendar. The Chinese New Year always falls on the first new Moon to occur between January 21 and February 19. Chinese years are grouped in cycles of 60. Each year is named after one of 12 animals.

NUMBER	NAME	ANIMAL	DAYS
1	Zzi	Rat	29
2	Chou	Ox	30
3	Yin	Tiger	29
4	Mao	Hare	30
5	Chen	Dragon	29
6	Si	Snake	30
7	Wu	Horse	29
8	Wei	Sheep	30
9	Shen	Monkey	29
10	You	Fowl	30
11	Xu	Dog	29
12	Hai	Pig	30

TIME PERIODS

PERIOD	DURATION
Nanosecond	0.000,000,1 second
Millisecond	0.001 second
Second	¹⁄₆₀ minute
Minute	60 seconds
Hour	60 minutes
Day	24 hours
Week	7 days
Fortnight	2 weeks
Month	28, 29, 30, or 31 days, depending on calendar, month, and year
Trimester	3 months
Lunar month	29.53059 days
Year	12 months, 52 weeks, or 365 days
Leap year	366 days
Biennium	2 years
Triennium	3 years
Quadrennium, Olympiad	4 years
Lustrum, half-decade	5 years
Decade	10 years
Half-century	50 years
Century	100 years
Half-millennium	500 years
Millennium	1,000 years

INVENTIONS

INVENTIONS BEFORE THEIR TIME

1662 BUS French mathematician Blaise Pascal (1623–1662) adapted a horse-drawn coach to help transport the poor in and out of Paris. The first real omnibuses were not invented until 1847.

1760 ROLLER SKATES Belgian instrument maker Joseph Merlin made a grand entrance to a masquerade in London on roller skates of his own design – playing a violin! Out of control, he crashed, destroying a valuable mirror. Steerable roller skates were not invented until 1863.

1783 PARACHUTE Italian artist Leonardo da Vinci sketched the first parachute design, but there is no evidence that he attempted to use a full-sized version. The first ripcord parachute was not used until 1908.

1880 BABY INCUBATOR In this year, a Frenchman called Budin invented a crude type of baby incubator, which consisted of a wooden cabinet heated by pans of hot water, for premature or weak babies. A more sophisticated incubator was introduced by Frenchman Dr Alexandre Lion in 1891.

1925 IN-FLIGHT MOVIES During an Imperial Airways flight from London to Paris, a silent film was shown. In-flight movies did not become part of regular service until 1961.

DID YOU KNOW? The gramophone was invented in 1888 by German-born American Emile Berliner (1851–1921).

"SOMEONE HAD TO INVENT IT" – EVERYDAY INVENTIONS AND THEIR INVENTORS

DATE	INVENTION	INVENTOR	LOCATION
1792	Pencil	Jacques-Nicolas Conté	France
1882	Electric iron	Henry W. Seely	US
1888	Kodak camera	George Eastman	US
1891	Swiss army knife	Karl Elsener	Switzerland
1903	Safety razor	King Camp Gillette	US
1906	Electric washing machine	Alva J. Fisher	US
1924	Frozen food	Clarence Birdseye	US
1926	Aerosol spray	Erik Rotheim	Norway
1927	Pop-up toaster	Charles Strite	US
1945	Microwave oven	Percy LeBaron Spencer	US
1948	Velcro	Georges de Mestral	Switzerland
1955	Transistor radio	Sony	Japan
1979	Compact disc player	Sony, Philips Co	Japan, Netherlands

FIRST US WOMEN PATENTEES

Patents are legal documents that stop anyone from copying an inventor's idea. The first women to apply for patents were:

PATENTEE	PATENT	DATE
Mary Kies	Straw weaving with silk or thread	May 5, 1809
Mary Brush	Corset	July 21, 1815
Sophia Usher	Carbonated liquid	September 11, 1819
Julia Planton	Foot stove	November 4, 1822
Lucy Burnap	Weaving grass hats	February 16, 1823
Diana H. Tuttle	Accelerating spinning-wheel heads	May 17, 1824

INVENTIONS NAMED AFTER THEIR INVENTORS

INVENTION	DESCRIPTION	DATE	NAMED AFTER	LIVED	COUNTRY
Biro	Ballpoint pen	1938	László Joszef Biró	1900–1985	Hungary
Braille	Raised dot type for blind people	1837	Louis Braille	1809–1852	France
Bunsen burner	Gas heater used in laboratories	1855	Robert Wilhelm Bunsen	1811–1899	Germany
Dolby stereo	Sound recording noise reducer	1966	Ray Milton Dolby	b.1933	US
Ferris wheel	Fairground attraction	1893	George Washington Gale Ferris	1859–1896	US
Mackintosh	Waterproof material (raincoat)	1823	Charles Macintosh	1760–1843	UK
Plimsoll line	Line on ship to show load level	1876	Samuel Plimsoll	1824–1898	UK

BIZARRE INVENTIONS

FIRE ESCAPE PARACHUTE American Benjamin B. Oppenheimer invented this safety gadget in 1879. If you should find yourself trapped in a blazing building, you attach the parachute to your head, put on the cushioned shoes, and jump out of the window!

SELF-RAISING HAT When the wearer of the hat patented by James C. Boyle of the US in 1896 tilts his or her head forward, a clockwork motor spins it around and replaces it!

EYEGLASSES FOR CHICKENS Patented in 1903, American Andrew Jackson Jr.'s eyeglasses did not aid his chickens' eyesight, but were designed to protect their eyes from the pecks of other chickens.

CHOCOLATE RECORDS Invented in 1903 by German company Gebrüder Stollwerck for chocoholics everywhere. Once you have played the record you can eat it!

BABY BOTTOM PATTER Californian Thomas V. Zelenka patented this device in 1971. Attached to the side of the crib, an electric motor operates a rod at the end of which a gloved hand pats the baby's bottom. Getting baby off to sleep has never been so easy!

COUGHING CIGARETTE PACKAGE Designed by Lewis R. Toppel of the US in 1972, the package produces a hacking noise when opened – a reminder of the dangers of smoking.

LEONARDO DA VINCI'S INVENTIONS

Italian genius Leonardo da Vinci (1452–1519) is hailed as one of the world's greatest inventors. He made plans for countless machines, most of which were never built. They include:

Air conditioner • Alarm clock • Ball-bearings • Clock • Compass • Crane Diving suit and bell • Flying machine Gas mask • Gears • Giant catapults Helicopter • Lifebelt • Mechanical musical instruments • Mileometer Multibarreled machine gun One-person battleship • Parachute Pedometer • Revolving stage • Screw-making machine • Eyeglasses • Steam engine • Tank • Telescope • Water turbine

YOUNG INVENTORS

HORATIO ADAMS In 1870, 16-year-old American schoolboy Adams assisted his father in experiments with chicle, the sap of a Mexican tree, and invented chewing gum!

LOUIS BRAILLE In 1837, at the age of 15, Braille, from France, invented raised-dot writing that enabled blind people to read for the first time.

CHESTER GREENWOOD In 1873, 15 year-old Chester Greenwood, from the US, invented earmuffs.

WALTER LINES British schoolboy Lines invented the scooter when he was 15 in 1897. He later founded Triang Toys, once Britain's leading toy manufacturer.

CHARLES BABBAGE Englishman Babbage was 19 when he first thought of the idea of the mechanical computer in 1834.

INVENTORS OF 20TH-CENTURY TOYS AND GAMES

YEAR	TOY/GAME	INVENTOR	COUNTRY
1900	Plasticine	William Harbutt	UK
1903	Teddy bear	Margarete Steiff	Germany
1913	Crossword puzzle	Arthur Wynne	US
1921	Pogo stick	George B. Hansburg	US
1929	Yo-yo	Donald F. Duncan	US
1946	Slinky spring	Richard James	US
1948	Frisbee	Fred Morrisson	US
1958	Skateboard	Bill & Mark Richards	US
1980	Rollerblades	Scott & Brennan Olsen	US

EDISON'S INVENTIONS

American inventor Thomas Alva Edison (1849–1931) started work as a newspaper boy at the age of 12. By the end of his long working life, he had registered 1,093 patents – more than anybody else has ever done to this day.

1869	Electric vote recorder (his first patent)
1870	Stock quotation printer (ticker tape machine)
1874	Duplex telegraphy (transmitting multiple messages)
1876	Mimeograph (copying machine)
1878	Phonograph (sound recording)
1879	Incandescent light bulb
1879	Carbon-resistance telephone transmitter
1889	Kinetoscope (motion picture device)
1890	Talking dolls
1890	Electric car motor

DID YOU KNOW? American inventor Thomas Edison and British inventor Joseph Swan both invented the screw-in light bulb in about 1880.

IMPOSSIBLE INVENTIONS

Inflatable dartboard • Waterproof teabag One-way elevator • Nonslip ice-skates Blank dice • Fish scuba apparatus

COMMUNICATIONS

MAIL PER PERSON PER YEAR

The average daily outgoing mail for the tiny population of Vatican City appears to be 26 letters per person! In fact, the mail is mostly letters from the headquarters of the Roman Catholic Church.

COUNTRY	LETTERS MAILED PER PERSON
Vatican City	9,545
US	689
Liechtenstein	573
Norway	525
Sweden	503
Netherlands	420
France	416
Finland	379
Canada	360
Denmark	335
Belgium	329
Austria	322

COMMUNICATIONS MILESTONES

1793 Frenchman Claude Chappe invents semaphore, a way of sending messages using arm movements.

1845 Samuel Morse (US) builds the first telegraph line.

1876 Telephones are invented by Alexander Graham Bell (US).

1901 Guglielmo Marconi astounds the world by transmitting a radio signal across the Atlantic Ocean, from the UK to Canada.

1945 ENIAC, the first automatic computer, is built in the US.

1962 First satellite telephone calls.

1981 First IBM personal computers using MS-DOS become available.

1985 First CD-ROMs appear.

1990s E-mail becomes widely used.

1994 Introduction of RISC (reduced instruction set computing) allows faster microchips to improve quality of multimedia images.

FIRST PLACES TO ISSUE POSTAGE STAMPS

PLACE OF ISSUE	YEAR OF ISSUE
Great Britain	1840
New York City	1842
Zurich, Switzerland	1843
Brazil	1843
Geneva, Switzerland	1843
Basle, Switzerland	1845
US	1847
Mauritius	1847
Bermuda	1848

The first adhesive postage stamps were the Penny Blacks which went on sale on May 1, 1840, in Great Britain. The first national stamps in the US were the 5-cent Benjamin Franklin and the 10-cent George Washington, issued in 1847.

PHONETIC ALPHABET

A	Alpha
B	Bravo
C	Charlie
D	Delta
E	Echo
F	Foxtrot
G	Golf
H	Hotel
I	India
J	Juliette
K	Kilo
L	Lima
M	Mike
N	November
O	Oscar
P	Papa
Q	Quebec
R	Romeo
S	Sierra
T	Tango
U	Uniform
V	Victor
W	Whisky
X	X-ray
Y	Yankee
Z	Zulu

DID YOU KNOW? "Mayday" is an international signal used as a distress call. The word is derived from the French phrase *M'aidez*, which means "Help me!"

TRY IT YOURSELF! You don't need to type http:// when you visit a web site – just the part of the URL beginning with "www" is enough!

COMMUNICATION FACTS

SPEEDY SORTING A mail-sorting machine can handle about 36,000 letters an hour!

GOOD TO TALK More than 4,000,000,000 messages are sent by e-mail in North America alone every year.

MOST MAIL The US Postal Service handles 170 billion letters every year.

WALK AND TALK Mobile telephones were first thought of in the US in the 1940s, but they did not appear for 30 years.

FLYING HIGH Airmail was first used in 1919, to transport letters quickly between the UK and France.

BEAMING DOWN High in the sky, communications satellites receive signals and beam them down to a receiver elsewhere in the world. In 1962, *Telstar 1* rebroadcast the first TV image.

WHO'S ON THE TELEPHONE?

COUNTRY	NUMBER OF LINES
US	169,100,000
Japan	62,680,000
China	54,100,000
Germany	45,800,000
France	32,580,000
UK	30,630,000
Russia	25,900,000
Italy	25,210,000
South Korea	19,650,000
Canada	16,500,000

DID YOU KNOW? The telephone network in China has grown rapidly from 6,596,000 lines in 1987 to eight times as many within just ten years!

COUNTRIES WITH THE MOST INTERNET USERS

COUNTRY	PERCENTAGE OF POPULATION	INTERNET USERS
US	23.00	62,000,000
Japan	7.00	8,840,000
Canada	27.00	8,000,000
UK	10.00	6,000,000
Germany	7.00	5,800,000
Sweden	22.00	1,900,000
India	0.16	1,500,000
Norway	32.00	1,400,000
Taiwan	6.00	1,260,000
Australia	7.00	1,210,000

CHILDREN'S INTERNET SITES

BERIT'S BEST SITES FOR CHILDREN
http://db.cochran.com/li_toc:theoPage.db

CHILDREN'S SEARCH ENGINES
www.internets.com/children.htm

GREAT SITES!
www.ala.org/parentspage/greatsites/

INTERESTING PLACES FOR KIDS
www.starport.com/places/forKids

KIDS' CORNER
http://kids.ot.com/

DID YOU KNOW?

Telephones have not always come in neat, rectangular shapes. This candlestick model from the 1930s was one of the first to allow the caller to dial without using the operator.

INTERNET ABBREVIATIONS

ABBREVIATION	WHAT IT STANDS FOR	WHAT IT MEANS
ASCII	American Standard Code for Information Interchange	Basic or "plain" text. E-mail messages are sent in ASCII.
BBS	Bulletin Board System	A system where people leave messages on electronic bulletin boards to be read by other users.
bps	Bits Per Second	The speed a modem can send and receive data.
DNS	Domain Name Service	The system by which a name (such as an e-mail address or a URL) is converted into a series of numbers.
e-mail	Electronic mail	The way in which messages can be sent and received by computer.
FAQ	Frequently Asked Questions	The questions most asked – reading them will save time and help you navigate the site.
FTP	File Transfer Protocol	A way of moving files between two Internet sites, used less now than in the early years of the Internet.
HTML	HyperText Markup Language	A way of coding text so that words appearing on Internet sites in styles such as underlined or bold can be linked to take you to another site.
http	HyperText Transfer Protocol	Most web page locations begin with "http://", which tells the computers how to connect with each other.
IMO	In My Opinion	One of many abbreviations used by people to save time when they send messages, especially to newsgroups.
IRC	Internet Relay Chat	A system for many users to have discussions over the Internet via IRC channels.
ISDN	Integrated Services Digital Network	A fast way of transferring data over telephone lines.
ISP	Internet Service Provider	Allows you to access the Internet. You connect to it every time you log on to the Internet.
JPEG	Joint Photographic Experts Group	A type of illustration file.
LAN	Local Area Network	Computers connected over a limited area, such as within a university or a business.
MIME	Multipurpose Internet Mail Extensions	A coding method by which nontext files can be sent with Internet mail messages.
Modem	MOdulator, DEModulator	The device that enables you to connect your computer to another computer, via a phone or cable line.
TCP/IP	Transmission Control Protocol/Internet Protocol	The software that lets your computer use the Internet.
URL	Uniform Resource Locator	The Internet "address" of a site.
www	World Wide Web	Often used to describe the Internet itself, it is the system by which all Internet sites can be accessed from anywhere in the world.

BUILDINGS

TALLEST APARTMENT BUILDINGS

BUILDING	LOCATION	YEAR	NO. OF STORIES	HEIGHT FT	M
Lake Point Tower	Chicago	1968	70	645	197
Central Park Place	New York City	1988	56	628	191
Olympic Tower	New York City	1976	51	620	189
May Road Apartments	Hong Kong	1993	58	590	180
Marina City Apartments	Chicago	1968	61	588	179

LONG FLIGHTS OF STAIRS

LOCATION	COUNTRY	STEPS
Niesenbahn funicular railway, Spiez	Switzerland	11,674
T'ai Chan Temple	China	6,600
Mår Power Station	Norway	3,875
Aura Power Station	Norway	3,715
CN Tower, Toronto	Canada	3,642
Ostankino Tower, Moscow	Russia	3,544
World Trade Center, New York	US	3,140
Empire State Building, New York	US	2,908

LARGEST SPORTS STADIUMS

STADIUM	LOCATION	CAPACITY
Strahov Stadium	Prague, Czech Republic	240,000
Maracaña Municipal Stadium	Rio de Janeiro, Brazil	205,000
Rungnado Stadium	Pyongyang, South Korea	150,000
Estadio Maghalaes Pinto	Belo Horizonte, Brazil	125,000
Estadio Morumbi	São Paulo, Brazil	120,000
Stadio da Luz	Lisbon, Portugal	120,000
Senayan Main Stadium	Jakarta, Indonesia	120,000
Yuba Bharati Krirangan	Calcutta, India	120,000
Estadio Castelão	Fortaleza, Brazil	119,000
Estadio Arrudão	Recife, Brazil	115,000
Estadio Azteca	Mexico City, Mexico	115,000
Nou Camp	Barcelona, Spain	115,000

DID YOU KNOW? The New Orleans Superdome is the largest indoor stadium, with a capacity of 97,365 – only a little smaller than the Stadium for the 2000 Olympic Games in Sydney, Australia, which can seat 110,000 people.

TALLEST CHIMNEYS

CHIMNEY	HEIGHT FT	M
Ekibastuz power station, Kazakhstan	1,377	420
International Nickel Company, Canada	1,250	381
Pennsylvania Electric Company, US	1,216	371
Kennecott Copper Corporation, US	1,215	370
Ohio Power Company, US	1,206	368
Zasavje power station, Yugoslavia	1,181	360
Empresa Nacional de Electricidad SA, Spain	1,169	356
Appalachian Power Company, US	1,103	336
Indiana & Michigan Electric Company, US	1,037	316

HIGH BUILDINGS YOU CAN VISIT

The chance to go up and look out over vast distances is a feature of buildings the world over. The Eiffel Tower in Paris, France is 900 ft (274 m) high. It was built between 1887 and 1889 and remained the highest viewing platform for 42 years, until the Empire State Building opened. From the 1930s onward, US observatories dominated the world, but have steadily lost ground to Asian buildings, with the KL Tower, Kuala Lumpur, recently joining the list.

BUILDING	OBSERVATORY	LOCATION	YEAR	HEIGHT FT	M
CN Tower	Space deck	Toronto, Canada	1975	1,465	447
World Trade Center	Roof top Tower B	New York	1973	1,360	415
Sears Tower	103rd floor	Chicago	1974	1,353	412
Empire State Building	102nd floor Outdoor observatory	New York	1931	1,250 1,050	381 320
Ostankino Tower	5th floor turret	Moscow, Russia	1967	1,181	360
Oriental Pearl	VIP Observation level	Shanghai, China	1995	1,148	350
Jin Mao Building	88th floor	Shanghai, China	1997	1,115	340
John Hancock Center	94th floor	Chicago	1968	1,030	314
Sky Central Plaza	90th floor	Guanghzhou, China	1996	1,016	310
KL Tower	Revolving restaurant	Kuala Lumpur, Malaysia	1995	925	282

LARGEST BUILDINGS

LARGEST AQUARIUM The Living Seas Aquarium in EPCOT Center, Florida, is filled with 50,000,000 pints (23,660,000 liters) of water – enough to fill nearly 300,000 baths!

LARGEST FACTORY The Boeing aircraft main assembly plant, in Everett, Washington, measured 196,476,000 ft³ (5,564,200 m³) when it was built in 1968. It has since expanded to 472,000,000 ft³ (13,400,000 m³).

LARGEST CINEMA The Radio City Music Hall in New York City can hold 5,874 people.

LARGEST OPERA HOUSE New York's Metropolitan Opera House has a total seating capacity of 4,065.

LARGEST ROMAN STADIUM The Circus Maximus, in Rome, built in the first century BC, had a track measuring 2,000 ft (610 m) long and 600 ft (183 m) wide. It is said to have drawn crowds of 250,000 spectators!

LARGEST MONUMENT The pyramid Quetzalcóatl at Cholula de Rivadabia, Mexico, was built by the Aztecs, who held power in Mexico between the 14th and 16th centuries. The pyramid has an estimated volume of 4,300,000 yd³ (3,300,000 m³) – bigger than Egypt's Great Pyramid, which has a volume of 9,300,000 ft³ (2,400,000 m³).

LARGEST SHOPPING CENTER West Edmonton Mall, in Alberta, Canada, has 11 department stores and 800 shops that cover an areas as large as 90 football fields!

LARGEST CASTLE Built in about AD 850, Prague Castle, in the Czech Republic, covers an area of 20 acres (8 hectares).

A CENTURY OF TALL BUILDINGS

BUILDING	LOCATION	YEAR	STORIES	HEIGHT FT	M
Auditorium Building	Chicago	1889	15	270	82
Masonic Temple Building demolished 1939	Chicago	1891	20	274	84
American Surety Building (now Bank of Tokyo)	New York	1895	21	306	90
Saint Paul Building	New York	1899	16	310	94
Park Row Building	New York	1899	29	386	118
City Hall	Philadelphia	1901	7	511	155
Singer Building (demolished 1970)	New York	1908	41	656	200
Metropolitan Life	New York	1909	50	700	212
Woolworth Building	New York	1913	57	792	241
40 Wall Street	New York	1929	71	927	282
Chrysler Building	New York	1930	77	1,046	319
Empire State Building	New York	1931	102	1,250	381
World Trade Center, New York Tower A	New York	1972	110	1,368	417
Sears Tower	Chicago	1974	110	1,454	443
Petronas Towers	Kuala Lumpur, Malaysia	1996	96	1,482	452
Shanghai World Finance Centre	Shanghai, China	Expected 2001	95	1,508	460

TALL PLACES OF WORSHIP

PLACE OF WORSHIP	LOCATION	YEAR BUILT	FT	M
Rouen Cathedral I	Rouen, France	1520	512	156
St. Nicholas Church	Hamburg, Germany	1847	475	145
Rouen Cathedral II	Rouen, France	1876	485	148
Cologne Cathedral	Cologne, Germany	1880	513	156
Ulm Cathedral	Ulm, Germany	1890	528	161
Chicago Methodist Temple	Chicago	1924	568	173

CITIES WITH MOST SKYSCRAPERS

CITY	SKYSCRAPERS
New York City	140
Chicago	68
Hong Kong, China	36
Houston	36
Kuala Lumpur, Malaysia	25

The term "skyscraper" technically describes all habitable buildings with a height of more than 500 ft (152 m).

SEVEN WONDERS OF THE ANCIENT WORLD

STRUCTURE	LOCATION	DATE	BUILDERS
Pyramids of Egypt	Egypt	2575–2465 BC	Ancient Egyptians
Hanging Gardens of Babylon	Iraq	605–562 BC	Ancient Babylonians
Temple of Diana at Ephesus	Turkey	550 BC	Ancient Turks
Statue of Zeus by Phidias at Olympia	Greece	c.447 BC	Ancient Greeks
Mausoleum at Halicarnassus	Turkey	350 BC	Ancient Greeks
Pharos of Alexandria	Greece	297 BC	Ancient Greeks
Colossus of Rhodes	Greece	c.280 BC	Ancient Greeks

BRIDGES, TUNNELS, and DAMS

DID YOU KNOW? Built in 1964, the Glen Canyon Dam on the Colorado River, Arizona, is 710 ft (216 m) high and 1,558 ft (475 m) long. It holds back 8 miles³ (33 km³) of water!

DEADLY DAMS

INDIA The Machu Dam, India, burst on August 9, 1979, flooding the town of Morvi. The death toll was officially 1,000, but may have been as high as 5,000.

US On May 31, 1889, a large earth dam burst at Johnstown, Pennsylvania. It released nearly 20 million tons (20.3 million tonnes) of water that engulfed the town, causing about 2,200 deaths. Incredibly, a 5-month-old baby was rescued alive after floating 75 miles (121 km) downstream on the floor of its wrecked home.

ITALY On October 9, 1963, a landslide into the reservoir resulted in the overflowing of the Vaiont Dam, causing a flood that killed more than 2,000 people.

FRANCE The Malpasset Dam, Fréjus, collapsed on December 3, 1959, and a 15-ft (4.5-m) wave poured into the town, drowning 419.

CHINA During July 1981, the Yangtze River, China, overflowed. Blocked by the Gezhou Dam, vast areas flooded, leaving 753 dead.

DAM FACTS

WHAT IS A DAM? A dam is built to divert or store water.

OLDEST KNOWN DAM The Sadd-el-Kafara dam in Egypt was built from rock and earth in about 3000 BC.

LARGEST DAM Canada's Syncrude Tailings dam has a capacity of 706,000,000 ft³ (540,000,000 m³).

LONGEST SEA DAM Afsluitdijk, Netherlands, is 38.8 miles (62.5 km) long and is built in two sections.

TUNNEL FACTS

UNDERWATER TUNNEL Connecting the Japanese islands of Honshu and Hokkaido, the Seikan tunnel is 33.46 miles (53.85 km) long, of which 14.4 miles (23.3 km) lie 328 ft (100 m) below the sea bed.

ROAD TUNNEL Switzerland's St. Gotthard tunnel runs for 10 miles (16 km) in the Alps.

WATER TUNNEL New York's West Delaware tunnel, which supplies the city with water, is 105 miles (169 km) long.

WORLD'S HIGHEST DAMS

DAM	RIVER	COUNTRY	BUILT	HEIGHT FT	M
Rogun	Vakhsh	Russia	Unfinished	1,099	335
Nurek	Vakhsh	Tajikstan	1980	984	300
Grand Dixence	Dixence	Switzerland	1961	935	285
Inguri	Inguri	Georgia	1980	892	272
Vaiont	Piave	Italy	1961	869	265
Chicoasén	Grijalva	Mexico	Unfinished	856	261
Tehri	Bhagirathi	India	Unfinished	856	261
Kishau	Tons	India	Unfinished	830	253
Ertan	Yangtze	China	Unfinished	804	245

LONGEST RAIL TUNNELS

TUNNEL	COUNTRY	BUILT	MILES	KM
Alp Transit Link	Switzerland	Unfinished	35.42	57.00
Seikan	Japan	1988	33.46	53.85
Channel Tunnel	France, UK	1994	31.03	49.94
Moscow Metro (Medvedkovo–Belyaevo)	Russia	1979	19.08	30.70
London Underground (Northern Line)	UK	1939	17.30	27.84
Daishimizu	Japan	1982	13.81	22.23
Simplon II	Italy, Switzerland	1922	12.32	19.82

LONGEST ROAD TUNNELS

TUNNEL	BUILT	MILES	KM
St. Gotthard, Switzerland	1980	10.1	16.3
Arlberg, Austria	1978	8.7	14.0
Fréjus, France/Italy	1980	8.0	12.9
Pinglin Highway, Taiwan	Unfinished	8.0	12.9
Mont-Blanc, France/Italy	1965	7.2	11.6
Gudvangen, Norway	1992	7.1	11.4
Leirfjord, Norway	Unfinished	6.9	11.1
Kan-Etsu, Japan	1991	6.8	11.0
Kan-Etsu, Japan	1985	6.8	10.9
Gran Sasso, Italy	1984	6.3	10.2

BRIDGE TYPES

BEAM The simplest, oldest, and weakest type, a beam bridge is supported at each end and may need to be strengthened underneath.

ARCH Built of stone, steel, or concrete, an arch bridge is supported by a keystone in the center of each arch.

STEEL ARCH Similar to an arch bridge, a steel arch is supported by tension on the piers on either shore.

CANTILEVER This type has two long arms held in place at the ends by anchors that balance the force. Some swing to let ships through.

TRESTLE Supported with diagonal struts or legs, trestle bridges often carry trains across valleys.

PONTOON A floating bridge – often temporary – used to replace damaged bridges.

SUSPENSION These very long, strong bridges are supported by steel cables from towers on the banks.

BASCULE The center of a bascule bridge opens like a drawbridge to allow tall ships to pass through.

CABLE-STAYED Cables from towers support the deck of a cable-stayed bridge.

GIRDER A girder bridge is like a beam bridge, but uses strong steel girders.

FAMOUS BRIDGES

BRIDGE OF SIGHS, ITALY Linking Venice's Doge's Palace with the city jail, prisoners sentenced to death traveled over it; its name comes from their sighs of despair.

LONDON BRIDGE, UK The replacement for the wooden medieval bridge was dismantled, stone by stone, in 1970 and moved to Arizona in the US.

SYDNEY HARBOUR BRIDGE, AUSTRALIA Built in 1932 to carry road and rail, Sydney Harbour Bridge is 160 ft (49 m) wide.

GOLDEN GATE BRIDGE, US San Francisco's Golden Gate was designed for motor vehicles with trains on a deck below – but it has only ever carried road traffic.

LONGEST CABLE-STAYED BRIDGES

BRIDGE	LOCATION	BUILT	MAIN SPAN FT	M
Pont de Normandie	Le Havre, France	1994	2,808	856
Qunghzhou Minjiang	Fozhou, China	1996	1,985	605
Yangpu	Shanghai, China	1993	1,975	602
Meiko-Chuo	Nagoya, Japan	1997	1,936	590
Xupu	Shanghai, China	1997	1,936	590
Skarnsundet	Trondheim Fjord, Norway	1991	1,739	530
Ikuchi	Onomichi-Imabari, Japan	1994	1,608	490
Higashi-Kobe	Kobe, Japan	1992	1,591	485
Ying Kau	Hong Kong, China	1997	1,558	475
Seohae Grand	Asan Man, South Korea	1997	1,542	470

ENGINEERING EXTREMES

STRONG SUSPENSION The Akashi-Kaikyo bridge, Japan, completed in 1998, is the longest suspension bridge, measuring 6,529 ft (1,990 m). It can withstand winds of 180 mph (290 km/h) and earthquakes up to 8.5 on the Richter scale.

LOST LIVES Switzerland's St. Gotthard Tunnel, completed in 1882, was the costliest in human lives: 310 workers were killed and 877 injured.

TAKING TIME The concrete used for the Boulder Dam, in the US, renamed Hoover in 1947 after the president, is still not fully set after over 60 years!

DID YOU KNOW? A novice engineer designed San Francisco's Golden Gate.

SHIPS and BOATS

TOP SHIPPING COUNTRIES

COUNTRY	SHIPS	GROSS TONNAGE
Panama	6,188	91,128,000,000
Liberia	1,697	60,058,000,000
Bahamas	1,221	25,523,000,000
Greece	1,641	25,288,000,000
Cyprus	1,650	23,653,000,000

WHAT'S TONNAGE? A ship's gross tonnage is its weight when empty. Its deadweight tonnage is its laden weight, which includes cargo and crew. Tonnage is measured in British tons and never converted into metric tons.

WATER SPEED RECORD MILESTONES

The first high-speed motor boats were invented in the early years of the 20th century. It was not until Garfield Wood set his 1928 record that speeds were officially measured as the average of two runs (just as with the land speed record).

PILOT	NATIONALITY	BOAT	YEAR	SPEED MPH	SPEED KM/H
Garfield Wood	US	*Miss America VII*	1928	92.83	149.40
Sir Henry Segrave	UK	*Miss England II*	1930	98.76	158.94
Sir Malcolm Campbell	UK	*Bluebird K4*	1939	141.74	228.10
Stan C. Sayers	US	*Slo-Mo-Shun IV*	1952	178.50	287.26
Donald Campbell	UK	*Bluebird K7*	1964	276.30	444.66
Kenneth Warby*	Australia	*Spirit of Australia*	1978	319.63	514.39

* Current world record-holder

FASTEST SPEEDS ON AND UNDER THE WATER

ROWING EIGHT The Oxford and Cambridge Boat Race speed record is 15.09 mph (24.28 km/h), achieved by the Oxford Crew in 1984.

SAILBOARD The record is 51.39 mph (82.70 km/h), achieved in France by Frenchman Thierry Bielak in 1993.

HOVERCRAFT In 1980, a US Navy Bell SES-1008 experimental vehicle achieved a speed of 105.6 mph (170 km/h).

YACHT The Australian trifoil *Yellow Pages Endeavour* reached 53.57 mph (86.21 km/h) in Australia in 1993.

SUBMARINE (SUBMERGED) Russian *Alfa* class submarines are believed to attain 51.8 mph (83.4 km/h), and US Navy *Los Angeles* class 46 mph (74 km/h), but the precise figures are military secrets.

WORST OIL TANKER SPILLS OF ALL TIME

In addition to the six major oil spills listed here, it is estimated that an average of 1,968,400 tons (2,000,000 tonnes) of oil are spilled into the world's seas every year. Oil spills cause major environmental damage to sea and bird life and shorelines.

TANKER	LOCATION	DATE	APPROXIMATE SPILLAGE TONS	TONNES
Atlantic Empress and *Aegean Captain*	Trinidad	1979	295,260	300,000
Castillio de Bellver	Cape Town, South Africa	1983	250,971	255,000
Olympic Bravery	Ushant, France	1976	246,050	250,000
Showa-Maru	Malacca, Malaya	1975	233,255	237,000
Amoco Cadiz	Finistère, France	1978	219,476	223,000
Odyssey	Atlantic Ocean, off Canada	1988	137,788	140,000

DID YOU KNOW? Although the grounding of the *Exxon Valdez* in Prince William Sound, Alaska, on March 24, 1989, ranks outside the worst oil spills, at about 34,450 tons (35,000 tonnes), it resulted in major environmental damage, with many fish, marine mammals, and birds killed.

WORLD'S BUSIEST PORTS

Port (Country)	Goods handled per year in millions of tons	tonnes
Rotterdam (Netherlands)	345	350
Singapore (Singapore)	285	290
Chiba (Japan)	171	174
Kobe (Japan)	168	171
Hong Kong (China)	145	147

BIGGEST SHIPS THROUGH HISTORY

Original name of ship	Launched	Gross tonnage
Great Western	1838	1,340
Himalaya	1853	4,690
Lusitania	1907	31,550
Mauretania	1907	31,938
Titanic	1912	46,232
Vaterland	1914	54,282
Bismarck	1922	56,621
Normandie	1935	79,301
Queen Mary	1936	80,774
Grand Princess	1998	104,000
RCCL Eagle 1	1999	142,000

DID YOU KNOW? The *RCCL Eagle 1* is almost 106 times bigger than the *Great Western*!

FAMOUS SAILORS

CHRISTOPER COLUMBUS (1451–1506) Italian sailor, famed for his voyage to America in 1492.

SIR FRANCIS DRAKE (c.1540–1596) First Englishman to sail around the globe, in 1588 Drake also defeated the Spanish Armada.

CAPTAIN JAMES COOK (1728–1779) British seaman who explored the Australian coast and South Seas.

LARGEST OIL TANKERS

Ship	Year built	Country	Gross tonnage	Deadweight tonnage
Jahre Viking	1979	Japan	260,851	564,763
Sea Giant	1979	France	261,862	555,051
Kapetan Giannis	1977	Japan	247,160	516,895
Kapetan Michalis	1977	Japan	247,160	516,423
Sea World	1978	Sweden	237,768	491,120
Nissei Maru	1975	Japan	238,517	238,517

WORLD'S LONGEST CRUISE SHIPS

Ship	Year built	Country	Length ft	m
Norway	1961	France	1,035.0	315.5
RCCL Eagle 1	1999	Finland	1,014.0	309.0
RCCL Eagle 2	2000	Finland	1,014.0	309.0
United States	1952	US	990.0	301.7
Disney Magic	1998	Italy	964.5	294.0
Disney Wonder	1998	Italy	964.5	294.0

FAMOUS SHIPWRECKS

MARY ROSE A Tudor galleon, which sank in 1545, was found in 1968, and raised in 1982. It is exhibited in Portsmouth, UK.

WASA A Swedish warship that capsized in Stockholm harbor in 1628. The ship and its treasures were recovered from the sea bed in 1961.

TITANIC This great liner sank in 1912, with the loss of 1,500 lives. The wreck was discovered and explored in 1986.

EMPRESS OF IRELAND The ship sank after a collision in the St. Lawrence River, Canada, 1914, killing 1,012. Divers have since visited the wreck.

ANDREA DORIA The *Andrea Doria* sank after colliding off the US coast in 1956.

FAMOUS MARINE DISASTERS

WORLD WAR II LINER Up to 7,800 people were killed in 1945 when the German liner *Wilhelm Gustloff*, laden with refugees, was torpedoed off the Polish coast by a Soviet submarine.

SPANISH ARMADA In 1588, a three-month naval conflict off the British coast between Britain and Spain destroyed the Spanish fleet (Armada), killing 4,000.

FERRY DISASTER The *Dona Paz* sank in the Philippines in 1987 after being hit by an oil tanker. The official death toll was 3,000 but may be as high as 4,386.

STEAMBOAT EXPLOSION In 1865, a boiler explosion destroyed a Mississippi River steamboat, the *Sultana*, killing 1,547. Although the death toll may be an underestimate, it is the US's worst marine accident.

ROAD TRAVEL

ON THE BUSES

FIRST DOUBLE DECKER Horse-drawn double decker buses were first seen on the streets of London, UK, in 1857. Gasoline-engined buses were first used in Germany in 1895, and in Bradford, UK, in 1897.

LONGEST BUS ROUTE A bus travels 6,003 miles (9,660 km) from Venezuela to Argentina.

BIGGEST BUS The articulated Super City Train Buses used in the Democratic Republic of Congo (formerly Zaire) measure 105 ft 8 in (32.2 m) in length. They can carry 110 seated passengers and 140 standing in the first part, and 60 seated passengers and 40 standing in the second.

AMAZING CARS

HEAVIEST A Lincoln Continental limousine, built in 1968 in the US, weighed 5.9 tons (5.35 tonnes). More than half of its weight was protective armor plating!

SMALLEST The *Peel* is one of the smallest cars ever built, at only 4.4 ft (1.34 m) long. It has no reverse gear.

MOST LUXURIOUS A Rolls-Royce Phantom 1 made in 1927 had an interior upholstered in silk tapestry.

FASTEST SOLAR In 1988, General Motors' solar-powered *Sunraycer* reached 48.71 mph (78.4 km/h) on sunlight alone. Its special panels convert sunlight into electrical energy.

DID YOU KNOW? There are about 60,000 taxis in Mexico City, Mexico.

DID YOU KNOW? During its peak production years, over half the new cars in the world were Model T Fords.

BEST-SELLING CARS

BEETLEMANIA Sales of the Volkswagen Beetle, first manufactured in Germany in 1937, now exceed 21,220,000, making it the most-produced model of all time.

LONG-RUNNER The British Morgan 4/4 sports car has been made continuously since 1935.

MODEL CAR Production of the Model T Ford began in the US in 1908 and ended in 1927, by which time 16,536,075 had been built. The Model T was the first to be assembled on a production line.

BIGGEST MANUFACTURER The General Motors Corporation, US, produced a total of 9,297,395 vehicles in 1978, more than any other company before or since that time.

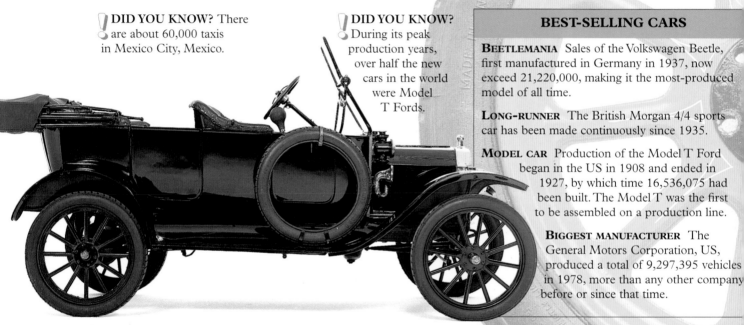

LAND SPEED RECORD MILESTONES

DRIVER	COUNTRY	VEHICLE	DATE	LOCATION	RECORD SPEED	
					MPH	KM/H
Barney Oldfield	US	*Benz Blitzen*	March 16, 1910	Daytona, FL	131.28	211.27
Tommy Milton	US	*Duesenberg*	April 27, 1920	Daytona, FL	156.03	251.11
Henry Segrave	UK	*Golden Arrow*	March 11, 1929	Daytona, FL	231.45	372.48
John Cobb	UK	*Railton Mobil Special*	September 16, 1947	Bonneville Flats, UT	394.196	634.396
Donald Campbell	UK	*Bluebird*	July 17, 1964	Lake Eyre, Australia	403.100	648.730
Art Arfons	US	*Green Monster*	November 7, 1965	Bonneville Flats, UT	576.553	927.870
Craig Breedlove	US	*Spirit of America Sonic 1*	November 15, 1965	Bonneville Flats, UT	600.601	966.574
Gary Gabelich	US	*The Blue Flame*	October 23, 1970	Bonneville Flats, UT	622.407	1,001.667
Richard Noble	UK	*Thrust 2*	October 4, 1983	Black Rock, NV	633.468	1,019.237

COUNTRIES WITH MOST CAR-OWNERS

COUNTRY	CARS	COMMERCIAL VEHICLES	TOTAL
US	147,171,000	48,298,000	195,469,000
Japan	42,678,430	22,333,042	65,011,472
Germany	39,917,577	2,960,334	42,877,911
Italy	29,800,000	2,777,500	32,577,500
France	24,900,000	5,140,000	30,040,000
UK	23,831,906	3,604,972	27,436,878
Russia	13,549,000	9,856,000	23,405,000

FIRST ON THE ROAD

FIRST CAR In 1886, German engineer Karl Benz exhibited a three-wheeled gas-fueled two-seater called the "Motorwagen." It could go up to 8 mph (13 km/h).

FIRST ELECTRIC TRAM Launched in 1901, electric trams took their power from overhead cables, carried no fuel, and did not pollute the streets.

FIRST TRUCK Benz produced the first diesel-powered truck in 1923. It became commercially available the following year. Diesel engines are more powerful, run on cheaper fuel, and allow more distance to be covered per tank than gas engines.

FIRST FIRE ENGINE The first practical fire engine appeared in 1731, in Philadelphia, where a hand-operated pump was used to put out fires instead of a chain of water-filled buckets. It was mounted on wheels.

FIRST METERED TAXI Arguments between taxi drivers and passengers over fares were all too common, so the first metered cabs took to Germany's roads in 1896. The idea spread quickly.

ROAD RECORDS

MOST ROADS Probably not surprisingly, the US has a network of roads about 3,904,721 miles (6,284,039 km) long. It is followed by India, with roads stretching 1,342,000 miles (2,159,740 km).

BUSIEST ROAD In the rush hour, 25,500 vehicles crawl along a 1 mile (1.5 km) stretch of Interstate 405 in Los Angeles, California.

LONGEST ROAD The Pan-American Highway runs 15,000 miles (24,140 km) through the US to Brazil.

HIGHEST ROAD In places, the road between Tibet and Xinjiang in China lies 18,480 ft (5,633 m) above sea level.

WIDEST ROAD The six-lane Monumental Axis in Brasília, Brazil, measures 820 ft (250 m) – the widest road in the world!

FIRST EXPRESS WAY In 1921, the first *Autobahn* (expressway) was opened in Berlin, Germany.

DID YOU KNOW? In the early days of motoring, Italians drove on the left in towns and on the right in the countryside!

ROAD DISASTERS

AFGHANISTAN, NOVEMBER 3, 1982 Following a collision with a Soviet army truck, a gasoline tanker exploded in the 1.7-mile (2.7-km) Salang Tunnel. Some authorities put the death toll from the explosion, fire, and fumes as high as 3,000.

COLOMBIA, AUGUST 7, 1956 About 1,200 people were killed when seven army ammunition trucks exploded in Cali, destroying eight city blocks. This included a barracks of 500 sleeping soldiers.

NEPAL, NOVEMBER 23, 1974 About 148 Hindu pilgrims were killed when a suspension bridge over the River Mahahali collapsed.

AMAZING VEHICLES

LONGEST LIMOUSINE A limousine built by Jay Ohrberg of California measures 100 ft (30.5 m) and has 26 wheels. It is so long that it has to be hinged in the middle to enable it to turn corners!

BIGGEST FIRE ENGINES Fire engines made by the Oshkosh Truck Corporation of Wisconsin, for use at airports, have eight wheels, 860-horsepower engines, and weigh 59 tons (60 tonnes).

DID YOU KNOW? One American limousine is equipped with a swimming pool and helicopter landing pad!

BIGGEST TIRES The largest road vehicle tires are 12 ft 6 in (3.82 m) in diameter, and are made by the Bridgestone Corporation, Japan, for giant dump trucks.

LARGEST LAND VEHICLES The Crawler-Transporters used to move Space Shuttles are 20 ft (6.1 m) high, 114 ft (34.7 m) wide, and 131 ft (40 m) deep. Each weighs 6 million lb (2.7 million kg) unloaded.

BIGGEST DUMP TRUCK The General Motors Terex Titan 33-19 mine truck, first made in 1974, is able to carry 312.5 tons (317.5 tonnes).

AMAZING FACT! The first (and last!) "motorized orange" car was made during the 1970s! It had the engine of a mini and a specially built chassis. The bizarre orange vehicle was manufactured by a firm that sold fruit.

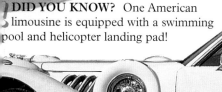

BIKES and MOTORCYCLES

BICYCLE TIMELINE

1790 CÉLÉRIFÈRE This wooden, hobby-horse-like machine is built by the French Count de Sivrac.

1817 HOBBY HORSE This early ancestor of the bicycle, made by Baron Karl von Drais, has no brakes or pedals.

1839 PEDAL-POWERED BICYCLE Built by Scottish blacksmith Kirkpatrick Macmillan, this bicycle is not a success.

DID YOU KNOW? Kirkpatrick Macmillan, inventor of the pedal-driven cycle, is also the first to be fined for a cycling offense. In 1842, a Scottish police court fines him for riding on the footpath and knocking down a child.

1861 VÉLOCIPÈDE Frenchman Ernest Michaux builds a bicycle with pedals at the front.

1870 ORDINARY, OR PENNY-FARTHING The big front wheel enables the bicycle to travel farther for each turn of the pedals.

1885 "ROVER" SAFETY BICYCLE Produced in England by J. K. Starley, this bicycle is the first to have two equal-sized wheels, the rear one driven by a chain from the pedals.

1888 PNEUMATIC TYRES Scotsman John B. Dunlop reinvents air-filled, pneumatic tires for his son's bicycle.

1903 FIRST TOUR DE FRANCE CYCLE RACE

1961 MOULTON This small-wheeled bicycle is the first new design for 50 years.

1981 MOUNTAIN BIKES The first all-terrain mountain bike is made by Charles Kelly and Gary Fisher of the US.

1983 BMX Bikes designed for rough terrain and tricks.

1990s RECUMBENT BICYCLES Propelled from an almost lying position, these unusual bicycles, with the pedals at the front, reach greater speeds than ordinary bicycles.

BICYCLES MADE FOR TWO – OR MORE

TANDEM The first successful tandems (bicycles for two) became popular in 1886. They were first made in the UK.

TENDEM This bicycle made for ten riders, first appeared in Massachusetts in 1924. The riders claim to have reached a speed of 60 mph (96.6 km/h).

QUINDEM A group of five US soldiers living in the UK in the 1940s built an unusual five-seater "quindem" so that they could all travel together.

MOTORIZED TANDEM Built in France, 1939, this vehicle had 2-in (5-cm) balloon tires and five chains for motor and pedal drives. The exhaust discharged onto the feet of the front driver.

FIREMAN'S DUAL TANDEM A rare team of British firefighters in the early 20th century rushed to fires on two tandems secured side by side. A pump in between was operated by pedaling.

CYCLING SAFETY TIPS

- Always wear a helmet to protect your head.

- Wear brightly colored or fluorescent clothes so you can be seen clearly.

- Yield to pedestrians when you are riding on bike trails and paths.

- Keep to bike trails and paths and do not damage crops or plants or disturb livestock or wildlife.

- Always attach lights to your bicycle when you ride in the dark.

- Check to see what other vehicles are doing, then signal your intentions clearly to traffic.

- Ride past parked cars with caution, and beware of a car door suddenly opening into your path.

- Seek out quiet routes away from heavy, fast-moving traffic.

- Obey all traffic signals and lights, and learn the highway codes.

- Try to think ahead! Anticipating the actions of others on the road and pavement could help you avoid an accident.

BICYCLES FOR FUN

AMPHIBIOUS BICYCLE In 1914, H. G. Belbin invented an amphibious bicycle with a float on either side that could be used on land or water without alteration. It was propelled in water by a screw propeller driven by a long cycle chain.

BICYCLES ON RAILS In the early 20th century, a special two-seater "rail cycle" was invented for inspecting the track in northern Britain. It was made of two adapted bicycles held parallel with each other by iron rods.

WATER CYCLE E. M. Yareed from India developed a homemade water cycle. It consisted of an ordinary bicycle without the tires, equipped with a steering wheel, seat, and three floats.

ICE-CYCLE Freddie Chapman, Britain's ice-skating champion in 1928, built an ice-cycle with just a rear wheel for propulsion and a blade in front and behind.

BED-CYCLE Canadian bicycle expert Charles Steilauf gave his wife the chance to sleep until the last minute on her way to work by fitting wheels, pedals, gears, and handlebars to her bed.

MUSICAL BICYCLES The Belgian army once added elbow rests to the bicycles ridden by their regimental bands, so that they could play their instruments while riding!

DID YOU KNOW? The fastest speed on a bicycle is 152.3 mph (245.08 km/h), achieved by American John Howard in 1985.

MOTORCYCLE TIMELINE

1867 STEAM-DRIVEN VELOCIPEDE
Frenchman L. G. Perreaux creates the first motorcycle when he fits a steam engine to Michaux's *velocipède*.

1885 DAIMLER MOTORCYCLE Gottlieb Daimler makes a motorcycle by fitting his internal combustion engine to a wooden-wheeled bicycle.

1901 STANDARD MOTORCYCLE
The French Werner brothers design a motorcycle with the engine and the pedals in the same place. This design becomes standard.

1904 HARLEY-DAVIDSON US motorcycling manufacturer Harley-Davidson goes into production, with the *Silent Gray Fellow*.

1907 FIRST TT RACE
The abbreviation TT stands for "Tourist Trophy." The first TT race is held in the Isle of Man, UK.

1959 BONNEVILLE This high-performance motorcycle is probably Triumph's most famous model.

1968 HONDA SUPERBIKE The development of multicylindered engines produces fast, smooth-running, reliable bikes, such as Honda's CB750.

1990s COMPUTERIZED MOTORCYCLE The engine of BMW's R1100 is managed by sophisticated electronics.

WACKY MOTORCYCLE RECORDS

SMALLEST MOTORBIKE A tiny motorbike was made with a front wheel diameter of 0.75 in (1.9 cm). It was ridden for 3 ft 4 in (1 m).

LONGEST RAMP JUMP In 1991, Doug Danger from the US jumped 251 ft (76.5 m) on a Honda CR 500.

LONGEST MOTORBIKE Designed and built by American Gregg Reid, the longest street-legal motorbike stretched for 15 ft (4.57 m).

LONGEST WHEELIE Yauyuki Kudo of Japan rode nonstop on the back wheel for 205.75 miles (331 km) in 1991.

DID YOU KNOW?
The Honda CB750, which went on sale in 1968, has a top speed of 120 mph (190 km/h).

HONDA SUPERBIKE

FIRST HOLDERS OF THE MOTORCYCLE SPEED RECORD

In 1920, the Fédération Internationale Motorcycliste (International Motorcycling Federation) became the first organization to officially ratify motorcycle speed records.

RIDER	MOTORCYCLE	LOCATION	YEAR	MPH	KM/H
Ernest Walker	994 cc Indian	Daytona Beach, FL	1920	104.19	167.67
Claude F. Temple	996 cc British Azani	Brooklands, UK	1923	108.48	174.58
Herbert Le Vack	867 cc Brough Superior	Arpajon, France	1924	118.05	191.59
Claude F. Temple	996 cc OEC Temple	Arpajon, France	1926	119.05	191.58
Oliver M. Baldwin	996 cc Zenith JAP	Arpajon, France	1928	124.62	200.56

FASTEST MOTORCYCLES

MODEL	SPEED	
	MPH	KM/H
Bimota SB6R	180	290
Honda CBR1100XX *Blackbird*	177	285
Bimota YB11	175	282
Kawasaki ZZ-R1100	174	280
Kawasaki Ninja ZX-9RR	174	280
Yamaha YZF-R1	173	278
Kawasaki Ninja ZX-7RR	169	272
Kawasaki Ninja ZX-6R	168	270
Honda CBR900RR *Fireblade*	167	269

LATEST HOLDERS OF THE MOTORCYCLE SPEED RECORD

All the records listed here were achieved at the Bonneville Salt Flats, US. To break a Fédération Internationale Motorcycliste record, the motorcycle has to cover a measured distance, making two runs within one hour, and taking the average of the two. US Motorcycling Association records require a turnround within two hours.

RIDER	MOTORCYCLE	YEAR	MPH	KM/H
Calvin Rayborn	1,480 cc Harley-Davidson	1970	254.99	410.37
Calvin Rayborn	1,480 cc Harley-Davidson	1970	264.96	426.40
Donald A. Vesco	1,496 cc Yamaha Silver Bird	1975	302.93	487.50
Donald A. Vesco	Twin 1,016 cc Kawasaki Lightning Bolt	1978	318.60	512.73
Dave Campos	Twin 91 cu in/1,491 cc Ruxton Harley-Davidson Easyriders	1990	322.15	518.45

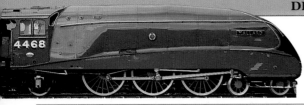

RAIL TRAVEL

FASTEST RAIL JOURNEYS

JOURNEY	LOCOMOTIVE	DISTANCE		SPEED	
		MILES	KM	MPH	KM/H
Hiroshima-Kokura, Japan	*Nozomi* 503/508	119.3	192.0	162.7	261.8
Lille-Roissy, France	TGV 538/9	126.4	203.4	158.0	254.3
Madrid-Seville, Spain	*AVE* 9616/9617	292.4	470.5	129.9	209.1
Würzburg-Fulda, Germany	ICE	57.9	93.2	124.0	199.7
London-York, UK	*Scottish Pullman*	188.5	303.3	112.0	180.2
Hässleholm-Alvesta, Sweden	X2000	60.9	98.0	104.4	168.0
Rome-Florence, Italy	10 Pendolini	162.2	261.0	102.5	164.9

BUSIEST RAIL NETWORKS

COUNTRY	PASSENGERS PER YEAR	
	PER MILE	PER KM
Japan	246,269,000,000	396,332,000,000
China	219,965,000,000	354,700,000,000
India	198,500,000,000	319,400,000,000
Russia	119,200,000,000	191,900,000,000
Ukraine	47,200,000,000	75,900,000,000
France	36,276,000,000	58,380,000,000
Germany	36,041,000,000	58,003,000,000

RAIL FIRSTS

FIRST WORKING STEAM LOCOMOTIVE In 1804, Richard Trevithick, of Cornwall, UK, built a steam locomotive that could haul coal wagons and 70 men.

FIRST TO PROVE STEAM WORKED In 1829, English engineers Henry Booth and Robert Stephenson built *Rocket*, heralding the age of steam trains.

FIRST TO SERVE MEALS The Baltimore and Ohio Railroad in the US began serving food on its trains in 1853.

FIRST UNDERGROUND TRAINS The first underground trains ran in 1863, beneath the bustling streets of London.

FIRST ELECTRIC TRAIN The first electric trains ran in Germany in 1881.

FIRST DIESEL LOCOMOTIVE Dr. Rudolph Diesel, a German engineer, demonstrated the first working diesel engine in 1893, and built the first reliable locomotive in 1897.

FIRST DRIVERLESS TRAIN A computer-operated train first ran in France in 1983!

FIRST RAILROADS

In their early years, some of the railroads listed offered only limited services over short distances, but their opening dates mark the generally accepted beginning of each country's railroad system.

COUNTRY	FIRST ESTABLISHED RAILROAD
UK	September 27, 1825
France	November 7, 1829
USA	May 24, 1830
Ireland	December 17, 1834
Belgium	May 5, 1835
Germany	December 7, 1835
Canada	July 21, 1836

LONGEST RAIL NETWORKS

COUNTRY	TOTAL RAIL LENGTH	
	MILES	KM
US	149,129	240,000
Russia	95,691	154,000
Canada	43,605	70,176
India	38,812	62,462
China	36,287	58,399
Germany	27,319	43,966
Australia	23,962	38,563

AMAZING FACT! The rail network of the US could stretch around the Earth almost six times over!

SHORTEST RAIL NETWORK! The Vatican City has just 2,789 ft (850 m) of track.

RAIL DISASTERS

FIRST FATALITY At the opening of the Liverpool and Manchester Railway, UK, in 1830, Member of Parliament William Huskisson was knocked down and killed.

WORST DISASTER On June 6, 1981, an Indian train plunged off a bridge when the driver braked to avoid hitting a cow. Officially, 268 bodies were recovered, but it is claimed that the train was so overcrowded that the actual figure was in excess of 800.

WORST SUBWAY DISASTER On October 28, 1995, a subway train in Azerbaijan, Asia, caught fire during the evening rush hour, killing more than 300 people.

DID YOU KNOW? Train toilets were first installed in the 1850s.

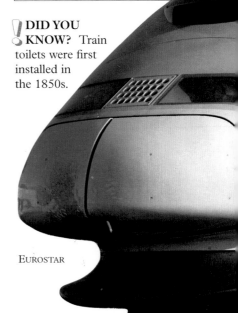

EUROSTAR

BUSIEST UNDERGROUND RAIL SYSTEMS

CITY	YEAR OPENED	TOTAL LENGTH MILES	KM	NUMBER OF STATIONS	PASSENGERS PER YEAR
Moscow, Russia	1935	152	244	150	3,183,900,000
Tokyo, Japan (TRTA)	1927	105	169	154	2,112,700,000
Mexico City, Mexico	1969	111	178	154	1,422,600,000
Seoul, Korea	1974	83	133	112	1,354,000,000
Paris, France	1900	125	201	372	1,170,000,000
New York, NY	1904	247	398	469	1,100,000,000
Osaka, Japan	1933	66	106	99	988,600,000
St. Petersburg, Russia	1955	57	92	50	850,000,000
Hong Kong, China	1979	269	43	38	804,000,000

! **AMAZING FACT!** New York's bustling Grand Central Terminal is the world's largest, with 44 platforms. Half a million people pass through the station every day.

OLDEST UNDERGROUND RAILROAD SYSTEMS

CITY	OPENED
London, UK	1863
Budapest, Hungary	1896
Glasgow, UK	1896
Boston, MA	1897
Paris, France	1900
Wuppertal, Germany	1901
Athens, Greece	1901
Berlin, Germany	1902
New York, NY	1904
Philadelphia, PA	1907
Hamburg, Germany	1912

RAILROAD RECORDS

HEAVIEST TRAIN *Challenger*, built in 1942, ran on the Union Pacific Railroad, and weighed 486 tons (494 tonnes).

MOST POWERFUL DIESEL-ELECTRIC TRAIN When the Deltic Train was built in 1956, it was the fastest in the world. In 1987, a British Airways High Speed Train achieved 176.4 mph (283.9 km/h).

FASTEST TRAIN A record trip of 320 mph (515 km/h) was made by the French TGV in May 1990.

LONGEST PLATFORM The Washington-Monroe-Jackson platform in Chicago stretches 3,500 ft (1,067 m)!

FASTEST STEAM TRAIN In 1938, the *Mallard* made its most famous journey when it set the world speed record at 126 mph (203 km/h).

MOST LUXURIOUS South Africa's Blue Train has been described as "a five-star hotel on wheels." Introduced in 1939, it runs between Pretoria and Cape Town.

LONGEST JOURNEY A train on the Russian Trans-Siberian line runs continuously from Moscow to Vladivostok, a distance of 5,777 miles (9,297 km).

DID YOU KNOW? *Eurostar*, which runs through the Channel Tunnel, can run on different voltages.

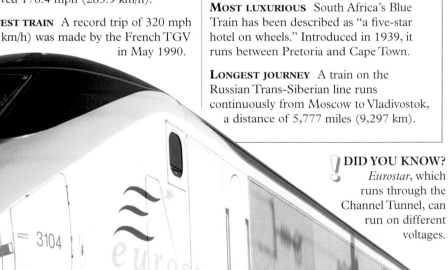

FAMOUS TRAINS

FLYING SCOTSMAN Built in 1923, the UK's *Flying Scotsman* took express passenger trains between London, England, and Edinburgh, Scotland. It continued in service until 1963.

BIG BOYS Built by the American Locomotive Company for the Union Pacific Railroad, these locomotives were in production between 1941 to 1944 and were among the largest ever built.

ORIENT EXPRESS This luxurious train was used by so many secret agents that it became known as the "Spies Express." It was introduced in 1883, and ran between London, Paris, Vienna, Budapest, and Constantinople (now Istanbul).

BULLET TRAIN Japan's high-speed, bullet-shaped train began running between Tokyo and Osaka in 1965. It is capable of speeds of up to 130 mph (210 km/h)!

FLYING HAMBURGER This speedy diesel train was introduced in Germany in 1933. It ran between Berlin and Hamburg at 100 mph (161 km/h).

HIAWATHA Introduced in 1935, in the US, this steam train traveled between Chicago and Minneapolis-St. Paul in five hours and five minutes.

PIONEERS of FLIGHT

FIRST BALLOON FLIGHTS

FIRST PASSENGERS The Montgolfier Brothers, Joseph and Etienne, were invited to demonstrate their balloon to Louis XVI at Versailles, France. On September 19, 1783, it took off with the very first air passengers: a sheep, a rooster, and a duck!

FIRST HUMANS TO FLY On November 21, 1783, François Laurent, Marquis d'Arlandes, and Jean-François Pilâtre de Rozier took off from the Bois de Boulogne, Paris, France, in a Montgolfier hot-air balloon. This first-ever manned flight covered a distance of about 5.5 miles (9 km) in 23 minutes, before landing near Gentilly.

FIRST SOLO On December 1, 1783, Jacques Alexandre César Charles and Nicholas-Louis Robert made the first-ever flight in a hydrogen balloon. They took off from the Tuileries, Paris, France, and traveled 27 miles (43 km) north to Nesle in about two hours. Charles then took off alone, becoming the first solo flier.

FIRST STOWAWAY On January 19, 1784, in Lyons, France, a man named Fontaine leaped into *La Flesselle*, a huge 131-ft (40-m) high Montgolfier hot-air balloon, as it was taking off. He shared the journey with pilot Pilâtre de Rozier, and Joseph Montgolfier, Prince Charles de Ligne, and the Comtes de La Porte d'Anglefort, de Dampierre, and de Laurencin.

FIRST FEMALE TO FLY On June 4, 1784, Elisabeth Thiblé, a French opera singer, became the first woman to fly in a balloon. She accompanied Monsieur Fleurant in his balloon *Le Gustava* in a flight from Lyons. The Marchioness de Montalembert and other aristocratic ladies had already ascended on May 20, 1784 – but in a tethered balloon.

FIRST TO CROSS THE CHANNEL, FIRST AMERICAN, AND FIRST AIRMAIL On January 7, 1785, Jean-Pierre Blanchard and Dr. John Jeffries (the first American to fly) achieved the first Channel crossing and carried the first airmail letter. As their balloon lost height, they had to reduce weight, so they threw everything overboard including their clothes!

EARLY FLYING DEATHS

FIRST TO DIE On June 15, 1785, Pilâtre de Rozier and Jules Romain were the first air fatalities near Boulogne, France, when their hydrogen balloon caught fire during an attempted Channel crossing.

ROBERT COCKING On July 24, 1837, pioneer parachutist Robert Cocking from Kent, UK, jumped from *Great Nassau Balloon*, but his parachute collapsed.

HENRI LETUR Parachutist Letur, from France, was injured when he fell from a balloon on June 27, 1854; he died eight days later.

VINCENT DE GROOF On July 9, 1874, the Belgian pioneer De Groof was killed when his ornithopter (a type of aircraft) crashed after being dropped from a balloon at Chelsea, UK.

FIRST ROCKET AND JET-POWERED AIRCRAFT

AIRCRAFT	COUNTRY	FIRST FLIGHT
Heinkel He 176★	Germany	June 1939
Heinkel He 178★	Germany	August 1939

> **DID YOU KNOW?** Prototypes of the rocket-powered Heinkels 176 and 178 first flew prior to World War II.

AIRCRAFT	COUNTRY	FIRST FLIGHT
DFS 194★	Germany	August 1940
Caproni-Campini N-1	Italy	August 1940
Heinkel He 280V-1	Germany	April 1941
Gloster E.28/39	UK	May 1941
Messerschmitt Me 163 Komet★	Germany	August 1941
Messerschmitt Me 262V-3	Germany	July 1942
Bell XP-59A Airacomet	US	October 1942
Gloster Meteor F Mk 1	UK	March 1943
Arado Ar234V-1 Blitz	Germany	June 1943

★ Rocket-powered

FIRST TO FLY IN HEAVIER-THAN-AIR AIRCRAFT

ORVILLE WRIGHT (1871–1948) On December 17, 1903, at Kitty Hawk, North Carolina, American inventor Orville Wright made the first-ever manned flight in his *Wright Flyer I*. It lasted 12 seconds, and covered a distance of 120 ft (37 m).

ALBERTO SANTOS-DUMONT (1873–1932) The Brazilian pilot set a European record of 21.2 seconds over 722 ft (220 m) on November 12, 1906. In the US in 1905, Wilbur Wright had flown over 24 miles (39 km).

HENRI FARMAN (1874–1958) On January 11, 1908, at Issy-les-Moulineaux, France, in his *Voisin-Farman I-bis*, Farman became the first European to fly for more than a minute and to cover more than 0.6 mile (1 km). Two days later, he flew the first kilometer circle in Europe. On March 28, 1908, Farman also became the first aircraft passenger when he flew with Delagrange at Issy.

LÉON DELAGRANGE (1873–1910) On November 5, 1907, at Issy-les-Moulineaux, France, Frenchman Delagrange flew his *Voisin-Delagrange I* for 40 seconds, covering 1,640 ft (500 m).

FIRST AND LAST FLIGHT

SPRUCE GOOSE This flying boat was built for $40 million by rich American flying enthusiast Howard Hughes (1905–1976). It had a wingspan of 320 ft (97.5 m) – just under twice that of a Boeing 747 Jumbo jet – making it the widest of all time. Weighing 179 tons (181 tonnes), it flew once, on November 2, 1947, with Hughes at the controls on its test flight off Long Beach Harbor, Los Angeles. The plane skimmed the surface of the water for only 3,000 ft (914 m).

FIRST TRANSATLANTIC FLIGHTS

FIRST TO "HOP" ACROSS Albert Cushing Read and his crew crossed the Atlantic from Newfoundland, Canada, to Lisbon, Portugal, in a series of hops, refueling at sea, between May 6–27, 1919. On May 31, their Navy/Curtiss flying boat NC-4 reached Plymouth, UK, having covered 4,717 miles (7,591 km)!

FIRST SOLO FLIGHT One of the most famous flights of all is that of Charles Lindbergh. Although he was actually the 92nd person to fly the Atlantic, he was the first to cross entirely alone. Lindbergh's epic journey took place on May 20–21, 1927, from Long Island, New York, to Paris, France, in the *Spirit of St. Louis*, a single-engined Ryan monoplane. Lindbergh covered a total distance of 3,610 miles (5,810 km) in a time of 33 hr 29.5 min.

FIRST AIRSHIP The British R-34 airship, flying from East Fortune, Scotland, to Roosevelt Field, New York, between July 2–6, 1919, was piloted by George Herbert Scott. It made the first Atlantic east-west crossing, and included the first ever transatlantic air stowaway, William Ballantyne. When it returned to Pulham, England, on July 13, it also became the first to complete a double crossing!

FIRST NONSTOP On June 15, 1919, British pilot John Alcock and navigator Arthur Whitten Brown achieved the first Atlantic nonstop flight. They flew from Newfoundland, Canada, to Galway, Ireland, in a twin Rolls-Royce-engined converted Vickers Vimy bomber, ditching in Derrygimla bog after 16 hours and 28 minutes!

FIRST TO CROSS THE ATLANTIC BY ACCIDENT! On July 11, 1938, US pilot Douglas Corrigan left New York to fly southwest for California. Instead he ended up in Dublin, Ireland. From then, he was known as "wrong way" Corrigan!

FIRST WOMAN TO FLY SOLO When American pilot Amelia Earhart (1898–1937) repeated Lindbergh's brave solo flight in 1932, she became the first woman to fly across the Atlantic Ocean. In 1937, in an attempt to fly around the world, she disappeared somewhere near New Guinea.

AMELIA EARHART

FLYING FAST

FIRST SPEED RECORD On May 20, 1909, Paul Tissander flew at 34.03 mph (54.77 km/h) in *Wright Flyer*.

FASTEST AIRCRAFT On October 3, 1967, William J. Knight (US) flew an X-15A-2 to 4,520 mph (7,274 km/h), or 6.7 times the speed of sound. The aircraft was air-launched, so it does not hold the official record.

FLYING HIGH

FIRST ALTITUDE RECORD Jean François Pilâtre de Rozier (France) rose 82 ft (25 m) in a tethered hot-air balloon in Paris on October 15, 1783.

HIGHEST AIRCRAFT The unofficial altitude record was set on August 22, 1963, when Joseph A. Walker (US) piloted an X-15 to 354,200 ft (107,960 m) – 67 miles (108 km) high.

ROUND-THE-WORLD FLIGHT MILESTONES

FIRST TO "HOP" AROUND THE WORLD American pilot teams Lowell H. Smith and Alva L. Harvey in the airplane *Douglas Chicago*, and Erik Nelson and John Harding, Jr., in *Douglas New Orleans*, were the first to fly around the world in a series of "hops" from one place to the next, refueling as they went. They made their trips between April 6 and September 28, 1924.

FIRST IN AN AIRSHIP Hugo Eckener and his crew circumnavigated the world in their airship *Graf Zeppelin*. They began their journey from Lakehurst, New Jersey, on April 8, 1929, and finished the trip on April 29 that year.

FIRST SOLO Wiley Post made history in a Lockheed Vega named *Winnie Mae*, between July 15 and 22, 1933. He began and finished his historic journey in New York.

FIRST NONSTOP (WITH REFUELING) From February 26 to March 2 1949, James Gallagher and his crew made the first nonstop trip around the world from Fort Worth, Texas, in *Lucky Lady II*. They refueled in midair.

FIRST WOMAN Between March 9 and April 17, 1964, Geraldine Mock became the first woman to fly solo around the world. She flew in *Spirit of Columbus*, named after the town from which she began her historic flight – Columbus, Ohio.

FIRST IN A HELICOPTER Beginning in Dallas, Texas, on September 1, 1982, H. Ross Perot, Jr., and Jay W. Coburn circled the world in a Bell 206L LongRanger II, *The Spirit of Texas*.

FIRST NONSTOP (WITHOUT REFUELING) American pilots Dick Rutan and Jeana Yeager successfully flew around the world without stopping, in their airplane *Voyager*. Their journey took place between December 14 and 23, 1986.

AIR TRAVEL

AIRLINES WITH MOST AIRCRAFT

AIRLINE	COUNTRY	AIRCRAFT IN SERVICE
American Airlines	US	665
Delta Airlines	US	566
United Airlines	US	564
US Airways	US	509
Northwest Airlines	US	366
Continental Airlines	US	307
Lufthansa	Germany	218
British Airways	UK	214
TWA	US	191
Air France	France	137
JAL	Japan	121
Qantas	Australia	86

DID YOU KNOW? The official name of the US President's aircraft is *Air Force One*. Two Boeing 747-200B aircraft are used for the President. Both are six stories high, and are equipped with 57 antennae, several antimissile devices, 4 computers, and 85 telephones!

AIRSHIP RECORDS

LE PETIT JOURNAL
LE SUPER-ZEPPELIN, LANCÉ PAR LES ALLEMANDS

FIRST AIRSHIP German Count Ferdinand von Zeppelin devised a 420-ft (128-m) airship called *LZ1* in 1900.

BIGGEST Germany's *Hindenburg* airship was 804 ft (245 m) long – more than 2.5 soccer fields laid end to end! It had a capacity of 2,354,033 yd³ (1,799,893 m³) and could carry 75 passengers and 25 crew members. The giant airship had a cruising speed of 78 mph (126 km/h). In 1937, the *Hindenburg* caught fire – a terrible disaster that was captured on film. The accident killed 35 people.

WORST AIRSHIP DISASTER On April 4, 1933, in a bad storm, the US Navy airship *Akron* crashed into the sea off the Atlantic coast of the US. As many as 73 people were killed, leaving only three survivors in the world's worst airship tragedy.

WHICH AIRCRAFT HAVE YOU FLOWN ON?

AIRCRAFT	APPROXIMATE NUMBER IN SERVICE
Boeing B-737	2,310
Douglas DC-9/MD-80	1,760
Boeing B-727	1,440
Boeing B-747	910
Airbus A-300/A-310	600
Boeing B-757	600
Boeing B-767	500
Airbus A-320	460
Douglas DC-10	300
Lockheed L-1011 TriStar	230

The list above includes turbo-jet airliners only. It excludes the airlines of China and the former Soviet republics.

AIRCRAFT RECORDS

FIRST AIRLINE SERVICE DELAG, the first airline, was established on October 16, 1909, to carry passengers between German cities by Zeppelin airships. Up to November 1913, more than 34,000 people had used the service.

FIRST ELECTRICALLY POWERED The Militky *MB-E1* took flight in Linz, Austria, on October 21, 1973.

HEAVIEST AIRCRAFT The Anatov An-225 *Mriya* (Dream) weighs 591 tons (600 tonnes)!

LARGEST PASSENGER AIRLINER The Boeing 747-400 has a wingspan of 213 ft (64.9 m) and can carry a total of 567 passengers.

SMALLEST AIRCRAFT Built in the US, *Bumble Bee II* had a wingspan of just 6 ft 3 in (1.9 m).

GREATEST GLIDE The world glider distance record is 308 miles (495 km), set by American Larry Tudor on July 1, 1994.

HIGHEST HELICOPTER The altitude record is 40,820 ft (12,442 m). It was set by Frenchman Jean Boulet, on June 21, 1972, in an Aérospatiale SA 315 Lama.

WORST AIR DISASTERS

TENERIFE, CANARY ISLANDS On March 27, 1977, a Pan Am Boeing 747 collided with a KLM Boeing 747 on the runway at Los Rodeos airport, after the KLM pilot took off without permission from the control tower. Both planes caught fire, killing a total of 583 people.

MOUNT OGURA, JAPAN On August 12, 1985, a JAL Boeing 747 on a domestic flight from Tokyo to Osaka crashed, killing 520. There were four survivors.

CHARKHI DADRIO, INDIA On November 12, 1996, a Saudi Airways Boeing 747 collided with a Kazakh Airlines Ilyushin IL-76 cargo aircraft on its descent and exploded, killing all 312 on the Boeing and 37 on the Ilyushin – 349 in total.

PARIS, FRANCE On March 3, 1974, a Turkish Airlines DC-10 crashed at Ermenonville, north of Paris, France, just after take-off for London, killing 346.

BIZARRE FLIGHT STORIES

FALLING IN LOVE On August 25, 1940, Arno Rudolphi and Ann Hayward were married in midair by the Reverend Homer Tomlinson as all three – and a small party of guests – parachuted toward Earth.

DOWN TO EARTH On January 26, 1972, following an aircraft explosion, stewardess Vesna Vulovic fell 33,300 ft (10,160 m). She landed in a snowdrift, with only a leg injury. The other 27 passengers and crew were killed.

BALLOONATIC In 1982, Larry Walters, California, attached 45 helium-filled weather balloons to his lawn chair and took off. He rose 16,000 ft (4,877 m), narrowly avoiding aircraft, then shot ten balloons, and sailed down. He was heavily fined.

POPULAR AIR SPORTS

BALLOONING Ballooning ascents in the 1780s made ballooning the first aerial sport. Gas ballooning is expensive and less common today, but hot-air ballooning has become increasingly popular since the 1960s.

SKYDIVING The first parachutists jumped from balloons 200 years ago. Skydiving as a sport began in the 1950s. BASE (Buildings, Antennae, Spans, Earth) jumping began in the US in the late 1970s. Parasailing leap from tall structures, such as cliffs or buildings. In parascending, parachutists are launched by being towed behind a vehicle, such as a boat.

GLIDING The first gliders, unpowered aircraft that need to be towed into the air by another aircraft, date from the 1850s. However, gliding did not become a popular sport until the 1920s.

HANGGLIDING AND PARAGLIDING Hanggliding, with rigid wings made from modern lightweight materials, has been popular with air-sport enthusiasts since the 1970s. In paragliding, a parachute-like canopy is used – the motorized versions of these are called microlights (also spelled "microlites" and "microlytes").

WING-WALKING Standing on the wings of an aircraft in flight – while securely strapped in place – has attracted enthusiasts since the early years of flying. Not surprisingly, this pastime, known as wing-walking, is an uncommon sport.

AUTOGYROS These are usually single-seaters, powered by a "pusher" propeller. Autogyros enable pilots to enjoy flying without the expense of larger aircraft.

BUSIEST INTERNATIONAL AIRPORTS

INTERNATIONAL AIRPORT	LOCATION	PASSENGERS PER YEAR
London Heathrow	London, UK	44,262,000
Frankfurt	Frankfurt, Germany	27,546,000
Charles de Gaulle	Paris, France	25,690,000
Hong Kong	Hong Kong	25,248,000
Schiphol	Amsterdam, Netherlands	22,943,000
New Tokyo International (Narita)	Tokyo, Japan	20,681,000
Singapore International	Singapore	20,203,000
London Gatwick	Gatwick, UK	19,417,000
J. F. Kennedy International	New York, NY	15,898,000
Bangkok	Bangkok, Thailand	13,747,000

DID YOU KNOW? The first microlights were flown in the mid-1970s, in the UK. They have a strong, fiberglass "tricycle" to hold the pilot and an average wingspan of 33 ft (10 m).

CONCORDE MILESTONES

WHAT IS THE CONCORDE? The Concorde is a supersonic aircraft that travels at 1,550 mph (2,494 km/h) – twice the speed of sound!

1955 The Concorde's "droop-snoot" nose is patented as early as 1955.

1963 On January 13, 1963, the Concorde is first named in a speech by President de Gaulle; the Anglo-French project is on the drawing board the following year.

DECEMBER 1967 The first prototype is shown in France at the Toulouse Air Show.

MARCH 1969 The first French flight takes place.

APRIL 1969 The first British flight takes place.

SEPTEMBER 1970 The Concorde's first landing at Heathrow, UK.

SEPTEMBER 1971 French Concorde flight test to South America.

DID YOU KNOW? The Concorde is the fastest passenger plane – it can fly from London to New York in three hours!

SEPTEMBER 1973 First landing in the US, at Dallas-Fort Worth.

JANUARY 1976 First scheduled flight, beginning Concorde's commercial service, from Paris to Rio de Janeiro in Brazil.

MAY 1976 The first scheduled flight to the US (Washington, D.C.) involves the simultaneous landing of a British and French Concorde.

APRIL 1989 During one of Concorde's flights from Christchurch, New Zealand, to Sydney, Australia, part of the craft's rudder falls off. Even so, the aircraft still manages to fly safely and without mishap at twice the speed of sound!

COUNTRIES

COUNTRIES and CONTINENTS

SMALLEST COUNTRIES

VATICAN CITY Situated in central Rome, this microstate covers an area measuring 0.17 sq mile (0.44 sq km). Although the Vatican had become part of unified Italy in the 19th century, it was recognized as a fully independent state by a treaty of February 11, 1929. Vatican City is the seat of the Catholic Church and holds a neutral stance in world affairs.

MONACO With an area of only 0.7 sq mile (1.81 sq km), Monaco is an independent principality that lies on the French and Italian border.

NAURU This tiny Pacific island has an area of just 8.2 sq miles (21.2 sq km), and is home to 11,000 people.

TUVALU A warm Pacific island, Tuvalu was a British colony until its independence in 1978. It has an area of 10 sq miles (26 sq km).

LONGEST COASTLINES

PLACES	LENGTH	
	MILES	KM
Canada	151,485	243,791
Indonesia	33,999	54,716
Greenland	27,394	44,087
Russia	23,396	37,653
Philippines	22,559	36,289
Japan	18,486	29,751
Australia	16,007	25,760
Norway	13,624	21,925
US	12,380	19,924
New Zealand	9,404	15,134
China	9,010	14,500
Greece	8,498	13,676

DID YOU KNOW? Monaco's coastline is only 2 miles (4 km) in total.

HIGHEST ESTIMATED POPULATION IN 2000

World population is constantly growing. The US Bureau of the Census estimates that the total world population will be 6,090,914,000 by the year 2000! Mexico will join the 100-million-plus club in 2000, with a population of 102,912,000!

COUNTRY	POPULATION
China	1,253,438,000
India	1,012,909,000
US	274,943,000
Indonesia	219,267,000
Brazil	169,545,000
Russia	147,938,000
Pakistan	141,145,000
Bangladesh	132,081,000
Japan	126,582,000

LARGEST COUNTRIES

COUNTRY	AREA	
	SQ MILES	SQ KM
Russia	6,592,812	17,075,400
Canada	3,849,646	9,970,537
China	3,705,408	9,596,961
US	3,539,224	9,166,600
Brazil	3,265,059	8,456,510
Australia	2,941,283	7,617,930
India	1,147,949	2,973,190
Argentina	1,056,636	2,736,690
Kazakhstan	1,049,156	2,717,300

DID YOU KNOW? Russia covers two continents – Europe in the west and Asia in the east – and is almost twice the size of the US!

CONTINENT FACTS

WHAT ARE THE CONTINENTS? The world's total land mass is divided into seven continents: Asia, Africa, North America, South America, Antarctica, Europe, and Australia.

WHICH IS THE LARGEST? Asia makes up 30 percent of the world's land mass and has the biggest population – 60 percent of the world's population.

WHICH HAS THE MOST COUNTRIES? Africa has the most countries, 53, and is also the warmest continent.

WHICH IS THE COLDEST? Antarctica is the coldest and least inhabited continent.

DID YOU KNOW? Australia is both a country and a continent!

COUNTRIES WITH MOST NEIGHBORS

CHINA Bordered by 15 other countries, China has more neighbors than any other country. They are Afghanistan, Burma, India, Kazakhstan, Kyrgyzstan, Laos, Macao, Mongolia, Bhutan, Nepal, North Korea, Pakistan, Russia, Tajikistan, and Vietnam.

RUSSIA The 14 countries of Azerbaijan, Belorussia, China, Estonia, Finland, Georgia, Kazakhstan, Latvia, Lithuania, Mongolia, North Korea, Norway, Poland, and Ukraine are all neighbors of Russia.

BRAZIL Nine countries share a border with Brazil: Argentina, Bolivia, Colombia, Guyana, Paraguay, Peru, Surinam, Uruguay, and Venezuela.

COUNTRY SYMBOLS

COUNTRY	SYMBOL
Canada	Maple leaf

DID YOU KNOW? Canada produces 75 percent of the world's maple syrup.

US	Bald eagle
Colombia	Orchid
Spain	Red carnation
Russia	Brown bear
India	Royal Bengal tiger
Japan	Cherry blossom
Denmark	Beech tree
South Africa	Blue crane
Greece	Olive branch
China	Dragon
Argentina	Ceibo (flower)
Bulgaria	Lion
England	Rose
Wales	Leek, dragon
Scotland	Thistle
Turkey	Tulip
Australia	Golden wattle flower
Ireland	Shamrock

DID YOU KNOW? The three leaves of Ireland's national emblem, the clover or shamrock, was used by Christians to represent the Holy Trinity; it was once an Arabian religious symbol too. A four-leaf clover is thought to bring luck!

COUNTRIES WITH NEW NAMES

USED TO BE	NOW NAMED	SINCE
British Honduras	Belize	1973
Ceylon	Sri Lanka	1972
Dahomey	Benin	1975
East Pakistan	Bangladesh	1971
French Somaliland	Djibouti	1977
Gold Coast	Ghana	1957
Mesopotamia	Iraq	1921
Siam	Thailand	1939
South West Africa	Namibia	1990
Southern Rhodesia	Zimbabwe	1980
Zaïre	Democratic Republic of Congo	1997

LANDLOCKED COUNTRIES

WHAT IS A LANDLOCKED COUNTRY? A landlocked country is one that is surrounded on all sides by land.

HOW MANY ARE THERE? There are more than 40 landlocked countries.

WHICH IS THE LARGEST? Kazakhstan covers an area of 1,049,156 sq miles (2,717,300 sq km). Mongolia follows in second place, with a total area of 604,250 sq miles (1,565,000 sq km). Hungary is Europe's largest landlocked state, at 35,919 sq miles (93,030 sq km).

WHICH IS THE SMALLEST? Europe also contains the world's smallest landlocked states. Andorra, Liechtenstein, Vatican City, and San Marino all have areas of less than 193 sq miles (500 sq km).

LONGEST FRONTIERS

This list represents the total length of each country's frontiers, or borders. It was compiled by adding together the lengths of individual land borders.

COUNTRY	TOTAL FRONTIER MILES	KM
China	13,759	22,143
Russia	12,514	20,139
Brazil	9,129	14,691
India	8,763	14,103
US	7,611	12,248
Kazakhstan	7,464	12,012
Congo (Zaïre)	6,382	10,271
Argentina	6,006	9,665
Canada	5,526	8,893

DID YOU KNOW? The border between Canada and the US is the world's longest frontier, stretching an incredible 3,987 miles (6,416 km)!

GREAT WALL OF CHINA

TIME ZONES

The Earth is divided into 24 time zones. Greenwich Mean Time (GMT) is the time in Greenwich, England, set at 0° longitude. Time advances by one hour for each 15° of longitude east of Greenwich.

TIME GMT	REGIONS
1200	UK, Iceland, Portugal
1300	Western Europe, W. Africa
1400	Southern and northern Europe, Africa
1500	Russia, Middle East
1600	Central Russia
1700	Russia, India, E. Europe
1800	Bangladesh, Burma, Bhutan
1900	Russia, Indonesia
2000	Russia, China, Australia
2100	Russia, Japan, Australia
2200	Russia, eastern Australia
2300	Micronesia
0000	South Pacific islands
0100	South Pacific islands
0200	None
0300	Alaska, western Canada
0400	Western Canada, western US
0500	Peru, Cuba, Panama
0600	Mexico, central US
0700	Eastern Canada, US
0800	Caribbean, Brazil, Chile
0900	Argentina, Greenland
1000	Atlantic islands
1100	Eastern Greenland

NATURAL BORDERS

RIVERS More than one-sixth of the borders between countries are formed by rivers. The River Danube borders many southeastern European countries, including Romania, Hungary, Croatia, Slovakia, Austria, Germany, and Bulgaria.

MOUNTAINS Ranges such as the Alps, Pyrenees, and Himalayas form natural country borders. The Andes, for example, divide Chile and Argentina.

LAKES The borders of countries that lie next to lakes are often fixed in the center of the lake. Lake Nyasa is shared between Malawi, Tanzania, and Mozambique.

INDEPENDENT COUNTRIES

COUNTRY	CAPITAL	AREA SQ MILES (SQ KM)	POPULATION 2000 (EST.)	GOVERNMENT	MAIN LANGUAGE(S)	MAJOR RELIGION(S)	CURRENCY
Afghanistan	Kabul	251,772 (652,090)	26,668,000	*Mujahideen* coalition	Dari, Pashtu	Muslim	Afghani
Albania	Tirana	10,579 (27,400)	3,427,000	Multiparty republic	Albanian	Muslim	Lek
Algeria	Algiers	919,590 (2,381,740)	31,788,000	Military regime	Arabic	Muslim	Dinar
Andorra	Andorra	181 (468)	73,000	Parliamentary democracy	Catalan	Christian	Fr. Franc Sp. peseta
Angola	Luanda	434,235 (1,124,670)	11,440,000	Multiparty rep.	Portuguese	Christian	Kwanza
Antigua & Barbuda	St. John's	170 (440)	68,000	Parliamentary democracy	English	Christian	E. Caribbean dollar
Argentina	Buenos Aires	1,156,636 (2,736,690)	36,202,000	Multiparty rep.	Spanish	Christian	Peso
Armenia	Yerevan	11,506 (29,800)	3,481,000	Multiparty rep.	Armenian	Christian	Dram
Australia	Canberra	2,941,283 (7,617,930)	18,950,000	Parliamentary democracy	English	Christian	Dollar
Austria	Vienna	31,942 (82,730)	8,108,000	Multiparty rep.	German	Christian	Schilling
Azerbaijan	Baku	33,436 (86,600)	7,902,000	Multiparty rep.	Azeri	Muslim	Manat
Bahamas	Nassau	3,864 (10,010)	269,000	Parliamentary democracy	English	Christian	Dollar
Bahrain	Manama	263 (680)	642,000	Absolute monarchy	Arabic	Muslim	Dinar
Bangladesh	Dhaka	51,703 (133,910)	132,081,000	Multiparty rep.	Bengali	Muslim	Taka
Barbados	Bridgetown	166 (430)	260,000	Parliamentary democracy	English	Christian	Dollar
Belgium	Brussels	12,672 (32,820)	10,144,000	Constitutional monarchy	Flemish, French	Christian	Franc
Belize	Belmopan	8,803 (22,800)	242,000	Parliamentary democracy	English	Christian	Franc
Belorussia	Minsk	80,154 (207,600)	10,545,000	Multiparty rep.	Belorussian	Christian	Rouble
Benin	Porto-Novo	42,710 (110,620)	6,517,000	Multiparty rep.	French	Traditional	Franc
Bhutan	Thimphu	18,147 (47,000)	1,996,000	Constitutional monarchy	Dzongkha	Buddhist	Ngultrum
Bolivia	La Paz; Sucre	418,683 (1,084,390)	7,680,000	Multiparty rep.	Spanish, Aymará, Quechua	Christian	Boliviano
Bosnia & Herzegovina	Sarajevo	19,741 (51,130)	2,618,000	Multiparty rep.	Serbo-Croat	Muslim, Christian	Dinar
Botswana	Gaborone	218,814 (566,730)	1,557,000	Multiparty rep.	English, Setswana	Trad., Christian	Pul
Brazil	Brasilia	3,265,059 (8,456,510)	169,545,000	Multiparty rep.	Portuguese	Christian	Real
Brunei	Bandar Seri Begawan	2,055 (5,270)	331,000	Absolute monarchy	Malay, English	Muslim	Dollar
Bulgaria	Sofia	42,683 (110,550)	8,769,000	Multiparty rep.	Bulgarian	Christian	Lev
Burkina	Ouaga-dougou	105,714 (273,800)	11,684,000	Multiparty rep.	French	Muslim	Franc
Burma	Rangoon	253,876 (657,540)	49,388,000	Military regime	Burmese	Buddhist, Christian	Kyat

DID YOU KNOW? The majority of the countires in the world are governed by a democracy. In most cases, it is a multiparty democracy in which citizens are given a choice between several parties to elect into office. Some countries have difficulties with this system; while they claim to be democratic, real power is held by the president.

COUNTRY	CAPITAL	AREA SQ MILES (SQ KM)	POPULATION 2000 (EST.)	GOVERNMENT	MAIN LANGUAGE(S)	MAJOR RELIGION(S)	CURRENCY
Burundi	Bujumbura	9,903 (25,650)	6,493,000	Multiparty rep.	French, Rundi	Christian	Franc
Cambodia	Phnom Penh	68,154 (176,520)	12,098,000	Constitutional monarchy	Khmer	Buddhist	Riel
Cameroon	Yaoundé	179,691 (465,400)	15,966,000	Multiparty rep.	English, French	Trad., Christian	Franc
Canada	Ottawa	3,560,217 (9,220,970)	29,989,000	Multiparty rep.	English, French	Christian	Dollar
Cape Verde	Praia	1,556 (4,050)	503,000	Multiparty rep.	Portuguese	Christian	Escudo
Central African Rep.	Bangui	240,530 (622,980)	3,539,000	Multiparty rep.	French	Christian	Franc
Chad	N'Djamena	486,177 (1,259,200)	7,760,000	Transitional	Arabic, French	Muslim	Franc
Chile	Santiago	289,112 (748,800)	14,996,000	Multiparty rep.	Spanish	Christian	Peso
China	Beijing	3,600,927 (9,326,410)	1,253,438,000	Single-party rep.	Mandarin Chinese	Trad., Buddhist	Yuan
Colombia	Bogotá	401,042 (1,038,700)	39,172,000	Multiparty rep.	Spanish	Christian	Peso
Comoros	Moroni	861 (2,230)	656,000	Islamic rep.	Arabic, French	Muslim	Franc
Congo	Brazzaville	131,855 (341,500)	2,750,000	Multiparty rep.	French	Trad., Christian	Franc
Costa Rica	San José	19,714 (51,060)	3,744,000	Multiparty rep.	Spanish	Christian	Colón
Croatia	Zagreb	21,829 (56,538)	5,044,000	Multiparty rep.	Serbo-Croat	Christian	Kuna
Cuba	Havana	42,803 (110,860)	11,272,000	Socialist rep.	Spanish	Christian	Peso
Cyprus	Nicosia	3,572 (9,251)	777,000	Multiparty rep.	Greek, Turkish	Christian	Pound
Czech Rep.	Prague	30,449 (78,864)	10,358,000	Multiparty rep.	Czech	Christian	Koruna
Dem. Rep. of Congo	Kinshasa	875,520 (2,267,600)	51,374,000	Constitutional monarchy	French	Christian	Zaïre
Denmark	Copenhagen	16,629 (43,070)	5,255,000	Constitutional monarchy	Danish	Christian	Krone
Djibouti	Djibouti	8,950 (23,180)	454,000	Single-party rep.	Arabic, French	Muslim	Franc
Dominica	Roseau	290 (750)	84,000	Multiparty rep.	English	Christian	Dollar
Dominican Republic	Santo Domingo	18,815 (48,730)	8,635,000	Multiparty rep.	Spanish	Christian	Peso
Ecuador	Quito	106,888 (276,840)	12,360,000	Multiparty rep.	Spanish	Christian	Sucre
Egypt	Cairo	384,343 (995,450)	68,437,000	Multiparty rep.	Arabic	Muslim	Pound
El Salvador	San Salvador	8,000 (20,720)	6,252,000	Multiparty rep.	Spanish	Christian	Cólon
Equatorial Guinea	Malabo	10,830 (28,050)	478,000	Multiparty rep.	Spanish	Christian	Franc
Eritrea	Asmara	36,170 (93,680)	4,537,000	Provisional military govt.	Arabic, English	Christian, Muslim	Ethiopian birr
Estonia	Tallinn	17,423 (45,125)	1,422,000	Multiparty rep.	Estonian	Christian	Kroon
Ethiopia	Addis Ababa	425,096 (1,101,000)	63,514,000	Multiparty rep.	Amharic	Christian, Muslim	Birr
Fiji	Suva	7,054 (18,270)	823,000	Multiparty rep.	English	Christian	Dollar
Finland	Helsinki	117,610 (304,610)	5,153,000	Multiparty rep.	Finnish, Swedish	Christian	Markka
France	Paris	212,394 (551,100)	59,239,000	Multiparty rep.	French	Christian	Franc
Gabon	Libreville	99,486 (257,670)	1,244,000	Multiparty rep.	French	Christian	Franc

COUNTRY	CAPITAL	AREA SQ MILES (SQ KM)	POPULATION 2000 (EST.)	GOVERNMENT	MAIN LANGUAGE(S)	MAJOR RELIGION(S)	CURRENCY
Gambia, The	Banjul	3,861 (10,000)	1,154,000	Military regime	English	Muslim	Dalasi
Georgia	Tbilisi	26,911 (69,700)	5,132,000	Republic	Georgian	Christian	Lari
Germany	Bonn	134,910 (349,520)	85,684,000	Multiparty rep.	German	Christian	Deutsche Mark
Ghana	Accra	92,100 (238,540)	19,272,000	Multiparty rep.	English	Christian	Cedi
Greece	Athens	50,521 (130,850)	10,878,000	Multiparty rep.	Greek	Christian	Drachma
Grenada	St. George's	131 (340)	98,000	Parliamentary democracy	English	Christian	Dollar
Guatemala	Guatemala City	41,865 (108,430)	12,408,000	Multiparty rep.	Spanish	Christian	Quetzal
Guinea	Conakry	94,926 (245,860)	7,640,000	Multiparty rep.	French	Muslim	Franc
Guinea-Bissau	Bissau	10,857 (28,120)	1,263,000	Multiparty rep.	Portuguese	Traditional	Franc
Guyana	Georgetown	76,004 (196,850)	693,000	Multiparty rep.	English	Hindu, Christian	Dollar
Haiti	Port-au-Prince	10,641 (27,560)	7,223,000	Multiparty rep.	French	Christian	Gourde
Honduras	Tegucigalpa	43,201 (111,890)	6,192,000	Multiparty rep.	Spanish	Christian	Lempira
Hungary	Budapest	35,652 (93,040)	9,795,000	Multiparty rep.	Magyar	Christian	Forint
Iceland	Reykjavik	38,707 (100,250)	277,000	Constitutional republic	Icelandic	Christian	Króna
India	New Delhi	1,147,949 (2,973,190)	1,012,909,000	Multiparty rep.	Hindi, English	Hindu, Muslim, Christian	Rupee
Indonesia	Jakarta	699,447 (1,811,570)	219,267,000	Multiparty rep.	Indonesian Malay	Muslim, Christian	Rupiah
Iran	Teheran	631,660 (1,636,000)	71,879,000	Islamic republic	Farsi	Muslim	Rial
Iraq	Baghdad	168,869 (437,370)	24,731,000	Single-party rep.	Arabic	Muslim	Dinar
Ireland	Dublin	26,598 (68,890)	3,627,000	Multiparty rep.	Irish, English	Christian	Punt
Israel	Jerusalem	7,849 (20,330)	5,507,000	Multiparty rep.	Hebrew, Arabic	Jewish	Shekel
Italy	Rome	113,536 (294,060)	57,807,000	Multiparty rep.	Italian	Christian	Lira
Ivory Coast	Abidjan	122,780 (318,000)	16,172,000	Multiparty rep.	French	Muslim, Christian, trad.	Franc
Jamaica	Kingston	4,181 (10,830)	2,664,000	Parliamentary democracy	English	Christian	Dollar
Japan	Tokyo	145,374 (376,520)	126,582,000	Constitutional monarchy	Japanese	Shinto, Buddhist	Yen
Jordan	Amman	34,336 (88,930)	4,704,000	Constitutional monarchy	Arabic	Muslim	Dinar
Kazakhstan	Astana	1,049,150 (2,717,300)	16,943,000	Multiparty rep.	Kazakh	Muslim, Christian	Tenge
Kenya	Nairobi	218,907 (566,970)	30,490,000	Multiparty rep.	Swahili, English	Christian, trad.	Shilling
Kiribati	Tarawa	274 (710)	87,000	Multiparty rep.	English, Gilbertese	Christian	Dollar
Korea, North	Pyongyang	46,490 (120,410)	25,491,000	Single-party rep.	Korean	Traditional	Won
Korea, South	Seoul	38,120 (98,730)	47,351,000	Multiparty rep.	Korean	Buddhist, Christian	Won
Kuwait	Kuwait	6,880 (17,820)	2,420,000	Constitutional monarchy	Arabic	Muslim	Dinar
Kyrgyzstan	Bishkek	76,640 (198,500)	4,664,000	Multiparty rep.	Kyrgyz	Muslim	Som
Laos	Vientiane	89,112 (230,800)	5,557,000	Single-party rep.	Lao	Buddhist	Kip

COUNTRY	CAPITAL	AREA SQ MILES (SQ KM)	POPULATION 2000 (EST.)	GOVERNMENT	MAIN LANGUAGE(S)	MAJOR RELIGION(S)	CURRENCY
Latvia	Riga	24,938 (64,589)	2,380,000	Multiparty rep.	Latvian	Christian	Lats
Lebanon	Beirut	3,950 (10,230)	4,115,000	Multiparty rep.	Arabic	Muslim	Pound
Lesotho	Maseru	11,718 (30,350)	2,114,000	Constitutional monarchy	English, Sesotho	Christian	Loti
Liberia	Monrovia	37,189 (96,320)	3,048,000	Transitional	English	Christian	Dollar
Libya	Tripoli	679,358 (1,759,540)	6,294,000	Socialist state	Arabic	Muslim	Dinar
Liechtenstein	Vaduz	62 (160)	32,000	Constitutional monarchy	German	Christian	Franc
Lithuania	Vilnius	25,174 (65,200)	3,629,000	Multiparty rep.	Lithuanian	Christian	Litas
Luxembourg	Luxembourg	998 (2,585)	415,000	Parliamentary democracy	Luxemburgian	Christian	Franc
Macedonia	Skopje	9,929 (25,715)	2,152,000	Multiparty rep.	Macedonian	Christian	Dinar
Madagascar	Antana-narivo	224,533 (581,540)	15,295,000	Multiparty rep.	Malagasy, French	Traditional, Christian	Franc
Malawi	Lilongwe	45,745 (118,480)	10,011,000	Multiparty rep.	English, Chewa	Christian	Kwacha
Malaysia	Kuala Lumpur	126,853 (328,550)	21,610,000	Fed. constitu-tional monarchy	Malay	Muslim, trad., Buddhist	Dollar
Maldives	Male	116 (300)	310,000	Republic	Dhivehi	Muslim	Rufiyaa
Mali	Bamako	471,115 (1,220,190)	10,911,000	Multiparty rep.	French	Muslim	Franc
Malta	Valletta	124 (320)	382,000	Multiparty rep.	English, Maltese	Christian	Lira
Marshall Islands	Majuro	70 (181)	68,000	Republic	Marshallese	Christian	Dollar
Mauritania	Nouakchott	395,955 (1,025,520)	2,653,000	Multiparty rep.	Arabic	Muslim	Ouguiya
Mauritius	Port Louis	718 (1,860)	1,194,000	Multiparty rep.	English	Hindu, Christian	Rupee
Mexico	Mexico City	736,945 (1,908,690)	102,912,000	Multiparty rep.	Spanish	Christian	Peso
Micronesia	Palikir	271 (702)	133,000	Republic	English	Christian	Dollar
Moldavia	Chisinau	13,000 (33,700)	4,543,000	Multiparty rep.	Moldavian	Christian	Leu
Monaco	Monaco	0.75 (1.95)	32,000	Constitutional monarchy	French	Christian	Franc
Mongolia	Ulan Bator	604,247 (1,565,000)	2,655,000	Multiparty rep.	Khalkha	Buddhist	Tugrik
Morocco	Rabat	172,316 (446,300)	32,229,000	Constitutional monarchy	Arabic	Muslim	Dirham
Mozambique	Maputo	302,737 (784,090)	19,829,000	Multiparty rep.	Portuguese	Trad., Christian	Metical
Namibia	Windhoek	318,260 (824,290)	1,886,000	Multiparty rep.	Afrikaans, English	Christian	Dollar
Nauru	—	8.2 (21.2)	11,000	Parliamentary democracy	Nauruan, English	Christian	Dollar
Nepal	Kathmandu	52,818 (136,800)	24,364,000	Constitutional monarchy	Nepali	Hindu, Buddhist	Rupee
Netherlands	Amsterdam	13,097 (33,920)	15,801,000	Constitutional monarchy	Dutch	Christian	Guilder
New Zealand	Wellington	103,733 (268,670)	3,698,000	Constitutional monarchy	English, Maori	Christian	Dollar
Nicaragua	Managua	45,849 (118,759)	4,729,000	Multiparty rep.	Spanish	Christian	Córdoba
Niger	Niamey	489,073 (1,266,700)	10,260,000	Multiparty rep.	French	Muslim	Franc
Nigeria	Abuja	351,648 (910,770)	117,328,000	Military regime	English, Hausa	Muslim, trad., Christian	Naira
Norway	Oslo	118,467 (306,830)	4,387,000	Constitutional monarchy	Norwegian	Christian	Krone

COUNTRY	CAPITAL	AREA SQ MILES (SQ KM)	POPULATION 2000 (EST.)	GOVERNMENT	MAIN LANGUAGE(S)	MAJOR RELIGION(S)	CURRENCY
Oman	Muscat	82,030 (212,460)	2,512,000	Monarchy with council	Arabic	Muslim	Omani
Pakistan	Muslimabad	297,637 (770,880)	141,145,000	Multiparty rep.	Urdu	Muslim	Rupee
Palau	Koror	196 (508)	18,000	Multiparty rep.	English, Palauan	Christian	Dollar
Panama	Panama City	29,340 (75,990)	2,828,000	Multiparty rep.	Spanish	Christian	Balboa
Papua New Guinea	Port Moresby	178,849 (452,860)	4,812,000	Parliamentary democracy	English, Tok Pisin	Christian	Kina
Paraguay	Asunción	153,398 (397,300)	6,104,000	Multiparty rep.	Spanish	Christian	Guarani
Peru	Lima	494,208 (1,280,000)	26,198,000	Multiparty rep.	Spanish, Quechua	Christian	Sol
Philippines	Manila	115,123 (298,170)	80,961,000	Multiparty rep.	English, Pilipino	Christian	Peso
Poland	Warsaw	117,552 (304,460)	39,010,000	Multiparty rep.	Polish	Christian	Zloty
Portugal	Lisbon	35,502 (91,950)	9,906,000	Multiparty rep.	Portuguese	Christian	Escudo
Qatar	Doha	4,247 (11,000)	587,000	Absolute monarchy	Arabic	Muslim	Riyal
Romania	Bucharest	88,934 (230,340)	20,996,000	Multiparty rep.	Romanian	Christian	Leu
Russia	Moscow	6,592,812 (17,075,400)	147,950,000	Multiparty rep.	Russian	Christian	Rouble
Rwanda	Kigali	9,633 (24,940)	8,900,000	Multiparty rep.	Rwanda, French	Christian	Franc
St. Kitts & Nevis	Basseterre	139 (360)	43,000	Parliamentary democracy	English	Christian	Dollar
St. Lucia	Castries	239 (620)	165,000	Parliamentary democracy	English	Christian	Dollar
St. Vincent & Grenadines	Kingstown	131 (340)	121,000	Parliamentary democracy	English	Christian	Dollar
Samoa	Apia	1,097 (2,842)	235,000	Parliamentary state	English, Samoan	Christian	Tala
San Marino	San Marino	24 (61)	25,000	Multiparty rep.	Italian	Christian	Italian lira
São Tomé & Principe	São Tomé	371 (960)	159,000	Multiparty rep.	Portuguese	Christian	Dobra
Saudi Arabia	Riyadh	829,995 (2,149,690)	22,246,000	Absolute monarchy	Arabic	Muslim	Riyal
Senegal	Dakar	74,336 (192,530)	10,390,000	Multiparty rep.	French	Muslim	Franc
Seychelles	Victoria	104 (270)	80,000	Multiparty rep.	Seselwa	Christian	Rupee
Sierra Leone	Freetown	27,652 (71,620)	5,580,000	Military regime	English	Muslim, trad.,	Leone
Singapore	Singapore	236 (610)	3,620,000	Multiparty rep.	Chinese, English, Malay, Tamil	Buddhist	Dollar
Slovakia	Bratislava	18,933 (49,036)	5,472,000	Multiparty rep.	Slovak, Czech, Hungarian	Christian	Koruna
Slovenia	Ljubljana	7,820 (20,250)	1,937,000	Multiparty rep.	Slovene, Serbo-Croat	Christian	Tolar
Solomon Islands	Honiara	11,158 (28,900)	470,000	Parliamentary democracy	English	Christian	Dollar
Somalia	Mogadishu	242,216 (627,340)	10,880,000	Transitional	Somali	Muslim	Shilling
South Africa	Cape Town, Pretoria, Bloemfontein	471,443 (1,221,040)	44,462,000	Multiparty rep.	Afrikaans, English, Zulu	Christian	Rand
Spain	Madrid	192,834 (499,440)	38,658,000	Constitutional monarchy	Spanish	Christian	Peseta
Sri Lanka	Colombo	24,996 (64,740)	19,377,000	Multiparty rep.	Sinhala, Tamil, English	Buddhist, Hindu	Rupee

MONGOLIA IS THE WORLD'S EMPTIEST COUNTRY WITH 0.2 PEOPLE PER SQ MILE (0.6 PER SQ KM)

COUNTRY	CAPITAL	AREA SQ MILES (SQ KM)	POPULATION 2000 (EST.)	GOVERNMENT	MAIN LANGUAGE(S)	MAJOR RELIGION(S)	CURRENCY
Sudan	Khartoum	917,374 (2,376,000)	35,454,000	Military regime	Arabic	Muslim, trad.	Dinar
Surinam	Paramaribo	62,344 (161,470)	465,000	Multiparty rep.	Dutch	Hindu, Christian	Guilder
Swaziland	Mbabane	6,641 (17,200)	1,137,000	Executive monarchy	English, Swazi	Christian	Lilangeni
Sweden	Stockholm	158,926 (411,620)	8,994,000	Constitutional monarchy	Swedish	Christian	Krona
Switzerland	Bern	15,355 (39,770)	7,268,000	Federal rep.	French, German, Italian	Christian	Franc
Syria	Damascus	71,066 (184,060)	17,759,000	Single-party rep.	Arabic	Muslim	Pound
Taiwan	Taipei	12,456 (32,260)	22,214,000	Multiparty rep.	Mandarin Chinese	Traditional, Buddhist	Dollar
Tajikistan	Dushanbe	55,251 (143,100)	6,384,000	Single-party rep.	Tajik	Muslim	Rouble
Tanzania	Dar es Salaam	342,100 (886,040)	31,045,000	Single-party rep.	Swahili, English	Muslim, traditional	Shilling
Thailand	Bangkok	197,255 (510,890)	61,164,000	Constitutional monarchy	Thai	Buddhist	Baht
Togo	Lome	21,000 (54,390)	5,253,000	Multiparty rep.	French	Traditional	Franc
Tonga	Nukualofa	278 (720)	110,000	Constitutional monarchy	English, Tongan	Christian	Pa'anga
Trinidad & Tobago	Port-of-Spain	1,981 (5,130)	1,273,000	Multiparty rep.	English	Christian	Dollar
Tunisia	Tunis	59,984 (155,360)	9,671,000	Multiparty rep.	Arabic	Muslim	Dinar
Turkey	Ankara	297,154 (769,630)	66,618,000	Multiparty rep.	Turkish	Muslim	Lira
Turkmenistan	Ashgabat	188,455 (488,100)	4,466,000	Single-party rep.	Turkmenian	Muslim	Manat
Tuvalu	Funafuti	10 (26)	11,000	Constitutional monarchy	English	Christian	Dollar
Uganda	Kampala	77,046 (199,550)	21,891,000	Multiparty rep.	English	Christian	Shilling
Ukraine	Kiev	233,090 (603,700)	50,380,000	Multiparty rep.	Ukrainian	Christian	Hryvna
United Arab Emirates	Abu Dhabi	32,278 (83,600)	3,582,000	Federation of monarchs	Arabic	Muslim	Dirham
United Kingdom	London	93,282 (244,600)	58,894,000	Constitutional monarchy	English	Christian	Pound
United States	Washington, D.C.	3,539,224 (9,166,600)	276,621,000	Multiparty rep.	English	Christian	Dollar
Uruguay	Montevideo	67,494 (124,810)	3,333,000	Multiparty rep.	Spanish	Christian	Peso
Uzbekistan	Tashkent	172,741 (447,400)	25,245,000	Single-party rep.	Uzbek	Muslim	Sum
Vanuatu	Port-Vila	4,707 (12,190)	193,000	Multiparty rep.	Bislama, English, French	Christian	Vatu
Vatican City	—	0.17 (0.44)	750	Papal commission	Italian	Christian	Lira
Venezuela	Caracas	340,560 (882,050)	23,596,000	Multiparty rep.	Spanish	Christian	Bolívar
Vietnam	Hanoi	125,621 (325,360)	78,350,000	Single-party rep.	Vietnamese	Buddhist	Dông
Yemen	Sana	203,849 (527,970)	15,547,000	Multiparty rep.	Arabic	Muslim	Riyal
Yugoslavia	Belgrade	39,449 (102,173)	10,787,000	Multiparty rep.	Serbo-Croat	Christian	Dinar
Zambia	Lusaka	285,992 (740,720)	9,899,000	Multiparty rep.	English	Christian	Kwacha
Zimbabwe	Harare	149,293 (390,580)	11,777,000	Multiparty rep.	English	Christian	Dollar

DID YOU KNOW? About ten million people live in "dependent territories," ruled by either the UK, the US, France, Denmark, Norway, Portugal, New Zealand, or Australia.

DID YOU KNOW? The United Nations (UN) was established in 1945 to promote world peace and understanding. Nearly every country is now a member of the UN.

WORLD CITIES

WHAT IS A CITY?

CITY A large town: in some countries, a city has a special status – in the US, it is an urban area with its own government. In the UK, it may have been given a royal charter.

TOWN A densely populated area with a defined boundary and its own government.

VILLAGE A small group of houses and other buildings in a rural area.

HAMLET A small village or a cluster of houses in a country area. In the UK, a village is considered a hamlet if it does not have a church.

SETTLEMENT A small group of inhabited buildings.

DID YOU KNOW?
Rome, the capital city of Italy, is built on seven hills: Aventine, Caelian, Capitoline, Esquiline, Palatine, Quirinal, and Viminal.

HIGHEST TOWNS AND CITIES

CITY	COUNTRY	MOUNTAIN RANGE	HEIGHT FT	M
Wenchuan	China	Nyenchen Tangla	16,730	5,099
Potosí	Bolivia	Andes	13,045	3,976
Oruro	Bolivia	Andes	12,146	3,702
Lhasa	Tibet	Himalaya	12,087	3,684
La Paz	Bolivia	Andes	11,916	3,632
Cuzco	Peru	Andes	11,152	3,399

DID YOU KNOW?
Although Sucre is Bolivia's official capital city, the country is governed from La Paz, which also has capital status.

MOST POPULATED CITIES IN YEAR 2000

These figures are based on an international system that calculates city populations based on "urban agglomerations." This means that certain cities connect, and totals will differ from those based on actual city boundaries.

CITY	COUNTRY	POPULATION IN 2000
Tokyo-Yokohama	Japan	29,971,000
Mexico City	Mexico	27,872,000
São Paulo	Brazil	25,354,000
Seoul	South Korea	21,976,000
Bombay	India	15,357,000
New York	US	14,648,000

FASTEST-GROWING CITIES

CITY	COUNTRY	ANNUAL GROWTH RATE (%)
Tanjung Karang	Indonesia	6.52
Maputo	Mozambique	6.07
Esfahan	Iran	5.66
Kabul	Afghanistan	5.56
Conakry	Guinea	5.17
Nairobi	Kenya	5.16
Lagos	Nigeria	5.05
Dacca	Bangladesh	5.03
Luanda	Angola	4.99
Yaounde	Cameroon	4.94
Kampala	Uganda	4.87
Lusaka	Zambia	4.80
Peshawar	Pakistan	4.72
Bogor	Indonesia	4.65
Douala	Cameroon	4.65
Abidjan	Ivory Coast	4.56

AMAZING FACT! A city of one million people that grows by five percent in a year will have an extra 50,000 mouths to feed at the end of it!

LOST CITIES

ANGKOR, CAMBODIA Once the world's largest city, it covered 30 sq miles (78 sq km). Surrounded by a moat, it had a population of over 1,000,000. About AD 1100, it was abandoned and was not discovered by Westerners until 1861, when French naturalist Henri Mouhot stumbled upon it.

ATLANTIS Some people believe that the city and island of Atlantis perhaps in the Mediterranean, was destroyed by an earthquake and flooded almost 12,000 years ago. Its story remains a mystery.

CHICHÉN ITZÁ, MEXICO Once the center of the Mayan empire, the city, built in AD c.400, was abandoned in AD 1200.

CLIFF PALACE, COLORADO This Native American Indian city was built on a cliff side, but was abandoned during drought conditions in the 13th century. It remained unknown until 1888.

MACHU PICCHU, PERU The fortified Inca city built in the 15th century on top of a mountain was abandoned for centuries, but was rediscovered in 1911.

POMPEII, ITALY The Roman city was buried by volcanic ash when Mount Vesuvius erupted in AD 79. Excavations began in 1748, and many treasures have been found.

TROY, TURKEY Believed to exist only in Greek legend, the site of Troy was discovered in the 1870s.

UR, IRAQ Once a great city, Ur was abandoned in c.300 BC. It was excavated between 1922 and 1934.

ANCIENT CITIES

CAIRO, EGYPT Egypt's capital and Africa's largest city, Cairo has a population of 6,000,000. It has at least 1,000 mosques, and bustling bazaars (markets) sit alongside modern bars.

BEIJING, CHINA China's capital for 2,000 years, Beijing is built symmetrically in three rectangles, with the Forbidden City at its heart. It has many ancient temples.

SAMARKAND, UZBEKISTAN This ancient city includes buildings from the 14th century, and was once the center of the silk trade from China. Cotton and textiles are still the city's main industry.

TBILISI The city of Tbilisi, on the banks of the River Kura, has been Georgia's capital since the fifth century.

OLDEST CITIES

The following are the oldest cities on each continent that remain inhabited. Many equally old, or even older settlements on each continent have been abandoned.

CITY	COUNTRY	FIRST SETTLED
Gaziantep	Turkey, Asia	c.3650 BC
Zurich	Switzerland, Europe	c.3000 BC
Giza and Minya	Egypt, Africa	pre-2568 BC
Quito	Ecuador, South America	c.AD 1000
St. Augustine	Florida, US, North America	1565
Sydney	Australia	1788

The oldest inhabited settlements in what is now the US are the subject of much debate. Some sources give Tallahassee, Florida, as having been originally settled in 1539. This date relates only to the winter camp of the Spanish explorer Hernando de Soto (c.1500–1542) and his 600 companions.

ONE AND ONLY CITIES

CITY IN TWO CONTINENTS Istanbul, Turkey's largest city and main port, is the only city in the world to lie in two continents. It is split between Europe and Asia by a narrow channel of water called the Bosphorus.

CITY WITH NO CARS The ancient city of Venice, Italy, is built on water. The only way to get around is on foot or by boat.

NON-US CAPITAL CITY NAMED AFTER A US PRESIDENT Monrovia, the capital of Liberia, in Africa, was named after James Monroe, the fifth US president.

FIRST CITIES WITH MORE THAN ONE MILLION PEOPLE

CITY	COUNTRY	ONE MILLION BY THE YEAR
Rome	Italy	133 BC
Angkor	Cambodia	AD 900
Hangchow	China	1279
London	UK	1810
Paris	France	1850
Beijing	China	1860
Canton	China	1870
Berlin	Prussia	1875
New York	US	1875
Vienna	Austria	1880
Tokyo	Japan	1880
St. Petersburg	Russia	1880
Nanking	China	1885
Chicago	US	1887
Philadelphia	US	1888
Birmingham	UK	1900
Calcutta	India	1900
Boston	US	1900

DID YOU KNOW? Today, there are at least 300 cities in the world that have a population of one million or more inhabitants.

UNITED STATES of AMERICA

STATE	STATE NICKNAME	CAPITAL CITY	AREA SQ MILES (SQ KM)	POPULATION
Alabama	Cotton state, heart of Dixie	Montgomery	52,237 (135,293)	4,319,154
Alaska	America's last frontier	Juneau	615,230 (1,593,438)	609,311
Arizona	Grand Canyon state	Phoenix	114,006 (295,274)	4,554,966
Arkansas	Land of opportunity	Little Rock	53,182 (137,741)	2,522,819
California	Golden state	Sacramento	158,869 (411,469)	32,268,301
Colorado	Switzerland of America	Denver	104,100 (269,618)	3,892,644
Connecticut	Land of steady habits	Hartford	5,544 (4,359)	3,269,858
Delaware	First state, peach state	Dover	2,396 (6,206)	731,581
Florida	Sunshine state, alligator state	Tallahassee	59,928 (155,213)	14,653,945
Georgia	Goober state, cracker state	Atlanta	58,977 (152,750)	7,486,242
Hawaii	Aloha state, pineapple state	Honolulu	6,459 (16,729)	1,186,602
Idaho	Gem state	Boise	83,574 (216,456)	1,210,232
Illinois	Prairie state, Land of Lincoln	Springfield	57,918 (150,007)	11,895,849
Indiana	Hoosier state	Indianapolis	36,420 (94,327)	5,864,108
Iowa	Hawkeye state, corn state	Des Moines	56,276 (145,754)	2,852,423
Kansas	Sunflower state, cyclone state	Topeka	82,282 (213,109)	2,594,840
Kentucky	Bluegrass state, tobacco state	Frankfort	40,411 (104,664)	3,908,124
Louisiana	Pelican state, sugar state	Baton Rouge	49,651 (128,595)	4,351,769
Maine	Pine tree state	Augusta	33,741 (87,389)	1,242,051
Maryland	Free state, old line state	Annapolis	12,297 (31,849)	5,094,289
Massachusetts	Bay state, baked bean state	Boston	9,241 (23,934)	6,117,520
Michigan	Wolverine state, auto state	Lansing	58,527 (151,585)	9,773,892
Minnesota	North star state, land of 10,000 lakes	St. Paul	86,943 (225,181)	4,685,549
Mississippi	Magnolia state, eagle state	Jackson	48,286 (125,060)	2,730,501
Missouri	Show me state, bullion state	Jefferson City	69,709 (180,545)	5,402,058
Montana	Treasure state, stub toe state	Helena	147,046 (380,847)	878,810
Nebraska	Tree-planters state, antelope state	Lincoln	77,358 (200,356)	1,656,870
Nevada	Sagebrush state, battle-born state	Carson City	110,567 (286,367)	1,676,809
New Hampshire	Granite state	Concord	9,283 (24,043)	1,172,709
New Jersey	Garden state, clam state	Trenton	8,215 (21,277)	8,052,849
New Mexico	Cactus state, land of enchantment	Santa Fe	121,598 (314,937)	1,729,751
New York	Empire state	Albany	53,989 (139,831)	18,137,226
North Carolina	Tarheel state, old north state	Raleigh	52,672 (136,420)	7,425,183
North Dakota	Flickertail state, peace garden state	Bismarck	70,704 (183,123)	640,883
Ohio	Buckeye state	Columbus	44,828 (116,104)	11,186,331
Oklahoma	Sooner state, Boomer's paradise	Oklahoma City	69,903 (181,048)	3,317,091
Oregon	Beaver state, sunset state	Salem	97,132 (251,571)	3,243,487
Pennsylvania	Keystone state, Quaker state	Harrisburg	46,058 (119,290)	12,019,661
Rhode Island	Little Rhody, ocean state	Providence	1,231 (3,188)	987,429
South Carolina	Rice state, swamp state	Columbia	31,189 (80,779)	3,760,181
South Dakota	Coyote state, sunshine state	Pierre	77,121 (199,742)	737,973
Tennessee	Volunteer state, big bend state	Nashville	42,146 (109,158)	5,368,198
Texas	Lone star state, beef state	Austin	267,277 (692,244)	19,439,337
Utah	Beehive state, Mormon state	Salt Lake City	84,904 (219,900)	2,059,148
Vermont	Green mountain state	Montpelier	9,615 (24,903)	588,978
Virginia	Mother of presidents	Richmond	42,326 (109,624)	6,733,996
Washington	Evergreen state, Chinook state	Olympia	70,637 (182,949)	5,610,362
West Virginia	Mountain state, panhandle state	Charleston	24,231 (62,758)	1,815,787
Wisconsin	Badger state, copper state	Madison	65,499 (169,642)	5,169,677
Wyoming	Equality state, cowboy state	Cheyenne	97,818 (253,347)	479,743

DID YOU KNOW? Washington, District of Columbia, or D.C., is not state, but is the capital city of the US, from where the government rules. It has its own tree, the scarlet oak, a district flower, the American Beauty rose, and its own bird, the woodthrush. Washington, D.C., is home to 528,964 people, and covers an area of 68 sq miles (176 sq km).

NTERED UNION	MAIL CODE	STATE TREE	STATE FLOWER	STATE BIRD
ecember 14, 1819	AL	Longleaf yellow pine	Camellia	Yellowhammer
nuary 3, 1959	AK	Sitka spruce	Forget-me-not	Willow ptarmigan
ebruary 14, 1912	AZ	Paloverde (green-barked acacia)	Saguaro cactus blossom	Cactus wren
ne 15, 1836	AR	Pine	Apple blossom	Northern mockingbird
eptember 9, 1850	CA	California redwood	Golden poppy	California valley quail
ugust 1, 1876	CO	Colorado blue spruce	Rocky Mountain columbine	Lark bunting
nuary 9, 1788	CT	White oak	Mountain laurel	American robin
ecember 7, 1787	DE	American holly	Peach blossom	Blue hen (chicken)
March 3, 1845	FL	Cabbage palm	Orange blossom	Mockingbird
nuary 2, 1788	GE	Live oak	Cherokee rose	Brown thrasher
ugust 21, 1959	HI	Kukui (candlenut)	Yellow hibiscus	Nene (Hawaiian goose)
ly 3, 1890	ID	Western white pine	Mock orange	Mountain bluebird
ecember 3, 1818	IL	White oak	Native violet	Northern cardinal
ecember 11, 1816	IN	Tulip poplar	Peony	Northern cardinal
ecember 28, 1846	IA	Oak	Wild rose	Eastern goldfinch
nuary 29, 1861	KS	Cottonwood	Native sunflower	Western meadowlark
ne 1, 1792	KY	Coffee tree	Golden rod	Kentucky cardinal
pril 30, 1812	LA	Bald cypress	Southern magnolia	Eastern brown pelican
March 15, 1820	ME	Eastern white pine	White pine cone	Black-capped chickadee
pril 28, 1788	MD	White oak	Black-eyed Susan	Baltimore oriole
ebruary 6, 1788	MA	American elm	Mayflower	Chickadee
nuary 26, 1837	MI	White pine	Apple blossom	American robin
May 11, 1858	MN	Red (Norway) pine	Showy lady's slipper	Loon
ecember 10, 1817	MS	Evergreen magnolia	Magnolia	Northern mockingbird
ugust 10, 1821	MO	Dogwood	Hawthorn	Bluebird
ovember 8, 1889	MT	Ponderosa pine	Bitterroot	Western meadowlark
March 1, 1867	NE	Cottonwood	Golden rod	Western meadowlark
ctober 31, 1864	NV	Single-leaf pinyon	Sagebrush	Mountain bluebird
ne 21, 1788	NH	White birch	Lilac	Purple finch
ecember 18, 1787	NJ	Northern red oak	Purple violet	Eastern goldfinch
nuary 6, 1912	NM	Pinon (nut pine)	Yucca	Greater roadrunner
ly 26, 1788	NY	Sugar maple	Rose	Bluebird
ovember 21, 1789	NC	Longleaf pine	Dogwood	Northern cardinal
ovember 2, 1889	ND	American elm	Wild prairie rose	Western meadowlark
March 1, 1803	OH	Buckeye	Scarlet carnation	Northern cardinal
ovember 16, 1907	OK	Redbud	Mistletoe	Scissor-tailed flycatcher
ebruary 14, 1859	OR	Douglas fir	Oregon grape	Western meadowlark
ecember 12, 1787	PA	Hemlock	Mountain laurel	Ruffed grouse
May 29, 1790	RI	Red maple	Violet	Rhode Island red (chicken)
May 23, 1788	SC	Cabbage palm	Yellow jessamine	Carolina red
ovember 2, 1889	SD	Black Hills spruce	American pasque flower	Ring-necked pheasant
ne 1, 1796	TN	Tulip poplar	Iris	Mockingbird
ecember 29, 1845	TX	Pecan	Bluebonnet	Mockingbird
nuary 4, 1896	UT	Blue spruce	Sego lily	Seagull
March 4, 1791	VT	Sugar maple	Red clover	Hermit thrush
ne 25, 1788	VA	Flowering dogwood	Flowering dogwood	Northern cardinal
ovember 11, 1889	WA	Western hemlock	Coast rhododendron	Willow goldfinch
ne 20, 1863	WV	Sugar maple	Rhododendron	Northern cardinal
May 29, 1848	WI	Sugar maple	Wood violet	American robin
ly 10, 1890	WY	Cottonwood	Indian paintbrush	Meadowlark

PLACE NAMES

LONGEST ◆ PLACE NAMES

KRUNG THEP MAHANAKHON BOVORN RATANAKOSIN MAHINTHARAYUTTHAYA MAHADILOK POP NOPARATRATCHATHANI BURIROM UDOMRATCHANIVETMAHASATHAN AMORNPIMAN AVATARNSATHIT SAKKATHATTIYAVISNUKARMPRASIT The 167-letter full name of Bangkok, the capital of Thailand, is rarely used, but it is sometimes abbreviated to "Krung Thep," meaning "City of Angels."

TAUMATAWHAKATANGIHANGAKOAUAUOTAMATEAT URIPUKAKAPIKI-MAUNGAHORONUKUPOKAI WHEN UAKITANATAHU This is the 85-letter version of the Maori name of a hill in New Zealand. It translates as "The place where Tamatea, the man with the big knees, who slid, climbed, and swallowed mountains, known as land-eater, played on the flute to his loved one."

GORSAFAWDDACHA'IDRAIGODANHEDDOGLEDDOL LÔNPENRHYN-AREURDRAETHCEREDIGION A 67-letter name, which was invented by the Fairbourne Steam Railway, Gwynedd, North Wales, in order to gain publicity for the railway. It means "The Mawddach station and its dragon teeth at the Northern Penrhyn Road on the golden beach of Cardigan Bay."

CITY NICKNAMES

ATHENS OF THE NORTH Edinburgh, Scotland has been so-called since the 18th century, when, like Athens, Greece, the city became famous for its culture and architecture.

BRIDE OF THE SEA Traditionally, the ruler of Venice sailed into the Adriatic on Ascension Day, dropping a wedding ring into the sea as a symbol of Venice's status as a sea power.

CITY OF DAVID The city of Jerusalem, in Israel, is called the City of David in the Bible, after King David.

CITY OF LIGHT Paris, the capital of France, is notable for its colorful nightlife.

ETERNAL CITY This nickname describes the enduring quality of Rome's architecture.

BIG APPLE New York, New York, is so-called after a translation of "*manzana principal*," Spanish for the main apple orchard, or most important place.

SMOKE In the 19th century, the chimneys of thousands of homes and factories belched out so much soot and smoke that London was often shrouded in fog, hence its nickname.

THINGS NAMED AFTER PLACES

JEANS The word "jeans" comes from the name given to material once made in Genoa, *Gênes* in old French. The blue denim from which jeans are most often made was once a product of the city of Nîmes, or *de Nîmes*, in French.

BADMINTON The game of badminton, played with rackets and birdies, was invented in about 1870 at Badminton House, the home of the English Duke of Beaufort. It spread throughout the world, and in 1992 became an Olympic sport.

BAYONET A bayonet is a daggerlike steel weapon, attached to the muzzle of a gun and used for attacking an opponent in hand-to-hand combat. The weapon is named after Bayonne in France, where it was first made and used.

MARATHON In 490 BC, the news that the Athenians had defeated the Persians at the Battle of Marathon was carried by Pheidippides, a messenger, who ran nonstop to Athens. He died from exhaustion. At the first modern Olympics, held in Athens in 1896, runners covered the same 26-mile (42-km) route, and the marathon was born.

CITIES WITH NEW NAMES

USED TO BE CALLED	IS NOW CALLED
Batavia, Indonesia	Jakarta
Christiania/Kristiania, Norway	Oslo
Ciudad Trujillo, Dominican Republic	Santo Domingo
Constantinople, Turkey	Istanbul
Danzig, Poland	Gdansk
Kecho, Vietnam	Hanoi
Leningrad, USSR	St. Petersburg, Russia
Peiping, China	Beijing
Rangoon, Burma	Yangon
Saigon, Vietnam	Ho Chi Minh City
Salisbury, Rhodesia	Harare, Zimbabwe
Stalingrad, USSR	Volgograd, Russia

PLACES NAMED AFTER REAL PEOPLE

COLOMBIA Italian explorer Christopher Columbus (1451–1506) named the country of Colombia, one of the many places he visited during his four voyages to South America.

COOK ISLANDS These Pacific Ocean islands are named after British explorer Captain James Cook (1728–1779).

SAUDI ARABIA Abdul Aziz ibn-Saud (1882–1953) named the country that he ruled after himself.

UNITED STATES OF AMERICA The maps of famous Italian explorer Amerigo Vespucci (1451–1512) were so good that people referred to the area he charted as "Amerigo's Land," or "America."

WHAT DO YOU CALL A PERSON FROM...?

CITY	INHABITANT
Aberdeen, Scotland	Aberdonian
Brussels, Belgium	Bruxellois
Buffalo, US	Buffalonian
Calcutta, India	Calcuttan
Cambridge, UK	Cantabrigian
Chicago, US	Chicagoan
Dublin, Ireland	Dubliner
Dundee, Scotland	Dundonian
Glasgow, Scotland	Glaswegian
The Hague, Netherlands	Hagenaar
Hamburg, Germany	Hamburger
Los Angeles, US	Angeleno
Manchester, UK	Mancunian
Mosow, Russia	Muscovite
Oslo, Norway	Osloer
Paris, France	Parisian (m), Parisienne (f)
Tangier, Morocco	Tangerine
Troy, US	Trojan
Yucatán, Mexico	Yucatec
Zurich, Switzerland	Zurcher

DUPLICATE TOWNS

BIRMINGHAM There are places called Birmingham in Canada, the UK, and in three of the US states: Alabama, Iowa, and Michigan!

EGYPT The most famous place of this name is the African country, but there are also Egypts in Georgia, Mississippi, Texas, and Pennyslvania, and a village near Slough, UK.

HALIFAX The first Halifax is in Yorkshire, UK, but there is also a Halifax in Canada, at least three in the US, and two in Queensland, Australia.

KINGSTON Probably best-known for being Jamaica's capital, this is one of the most traveled names. There are three Australian Kingstons, and a Kingston Beach. Canada and New Zealand have also used the name, and there are five Kingstons in the UK, including a Kingston-upon-Thames and a Kingston-upon-Hull. There are at least 11 Kingstons in the US.

COUNTRIES WITH LONG OFFICIAL NAMES

OFFICIAL NAME	ENGLISH NAME	LETTERS
Al-Jamahiriyah al 'Arabiyah al Libiyah ash Sha'biyah al Ishtirakiyah	Libya	56
Al-Jumhuriyah al Jaza'iriyah ad Dimuqratiyah ash Sha'biyah	Algeria	49
United Kingdom of Great Britain and Northern Ireland	United Kingdom	45
Sri Lanka Prajathanthrika Samajavadi Janarajaya	Sri Lanka	43
Jumhuriyat al-Qumur al-Ittihadiyah al-Islamiyah	Comoros	41

SHORTEST NAMES

A	Danish village
E	Scottish river
L	American lake
O	English brook
Y	French village
AE	Scottish town
EA	Irish inlet
OA	Scottish town
TA	Irish town
UZ	American town

MISLEADING PLACE NAMES

BUENOS AIRES The name of the capital of Argentina means "good winds" – but not because the city has them. Part of the original full name included "Our Lady the Virgin Mary of Good Winds" – because sailors prayed that she grant favorable winds for their sailing ships.

SINGAPORE The name means "City of Lions," but none have ever been seen there.

CAPE OF GOOD HOPE The sea off southwest Africa was called Cabo Tormentoso, or "Cape of Storms," by sailor Bartolomeu Dias, who first sailed around it in 1488. The Portuguese king, John II, thought it would deter future explorers, so he renamed it Cabo da Bõa Esperança, or "Cape of Good Hope."

GREENLAND Some 85 percent of Greenland is not green, but icy white. It was named in AD 982 by Norse sailor Erik the Red, who wanted to encourage his countrymen to settle there.

NOME The Alaskan port was marked by a British mapmaker as "Name?" but his writing was bad, and his question is what it became!

PACIFIC When explorer Ferdinand Magellan crossed the Pacific (1520–1521), he named it "Mar Pacífico," meaning "calm sea." He was lucky – what we now call the Pacific Ocean can experience some of the world's stormiest weather.

PAGO PAGO Allegedly, the correct name of the Samoan port is "Pango Pango," but missionaries who were printing a newspaper there did not have not enough Ns when they printed the heading, so it became Pago Pago.

YUCATÁN According to one account, the Spanish explorer Hernando Cortez asked a local man what he called the Mexican peninsula. He replied "Yukatan," meaning "I don't understand you."

TRAVEL and TOURISM

NATIONAL PARKS

National parks are set up by governments to preserve areas of land, and the plants and wildlife it contains. Yellowstone National Park in the US, established in 1870, was the first.

GREAT BARRIER REEF, AUSTRALIA Situated off the Queensland coast, this reef extends across 84,956,418 acres (34,380,000 hectares). Founded as a national park in 1979, the reef supports many rare marine animals and plants.

GALÁPAGOS ISLANDS, ECUADOR These volcanic islands are home to a variety of birds, seals, and unique creatures, including giant turtles and iguanas. Founded in 1986, the park measures 19,744,089 acres (7,990,000 hectares).

WOOD BUFFALO, CANADA Founded in 1922, this 11,072,257-acre (4,480,700-hectare) area of forests, plains, and lakes has the largest herd of wild buffalo in the world. It preserves rare animals and birds, such as the whooping crane.

WRANGELL-ST. ELIAS, ALASKA The largest US national park, founded in 1978, this Alaskan wilderness covers 8,357,294 acres (3,382,014 hectares). It contains many glaciers and peaks of more than 16,000 ft (4,880 m), as well as wild animals.

SERENGETI, TANZANIA Founded in 1951, this 3,648,084-acre (1,476,300-hectare) park is home to many wild animals.

FAMOUS GRAVES

KARL MARX The originator of communism, Karl Marx died in London, England, in 1883, and is buried in the city's Highgate Cemetery.

JOHN F. KENNEDY
The popular US President, shot in the head as he was driven in a convertible car through Dallas, Texas, in 1963, is buried at Arlington National Cemetery.

ELVIS PRESLEY Rock singer Presley died in 1977, and was buried at his home, Graceland, Memphis, Tennessee. His grave is visited by thousands.

PRINCESS DIANA Killed in a car crash in Paris, France, in 1997, Diana's grave is on an island at Althorp House, Northamptonshire, England – her family home. It is not accessible to the public.

TOP AMUSEMENT AND THEME PARKS

PARK	LOCATION	ATTENDANCE (1997)
Tokyo Disneyland	Tokyo, Japan	17,368,000
Disneyland	Anaheim, California	17,000,000
Magic Kingdom at Walt Disney World	Lake Buena Vista, Florida	17,000,000
Disneyland Paris	Marne-la-Vallée, France	14,250,000
EPCOT at Walt Disney World	Lake Buena Vista, Florida	11,796,750
Disney-MGM Studios	Lake Buena Vista, Florida	10,473,750

TRAVELING TALES

Since ancient times, people have had to travel to survive – to graze their livestock, to trade, or to escape persecution. However, not all travel was a matter of life and death and many people traveled for pleasure and enlightenment.

TAKING THE WATERS The Romans placed great value on bathing, and settled in many places close to natural springs, developing cities as spas (the name comes from Spa in Belgium). It became fashionable to visit spas to "take the waters" – drinking and bathing as cures for various illnesses.

THE GRAND TOUR From the 18th century onward, taking the "Grand Tour" of the great European cities was regarded as part of a gentleman's or lady's education. The idea of sightseeing vacations – visiting buildings and art treasures – has grown from this.

COASTAL TOURISM The health benefits of sea bathing were first promoted in the mid-18th century, when seaside vacations were taken by the wealthy. This marked the start of the development of coastal resorts as tourist attractions.

EXHIBITIONS In the 19th and 20th centuries, major exhibitions in Europe and the US attracted millions people to the major cities of the world. Many people had never previously traveled beyond their own homes.

PILGRIMAGE The religion of Islam requires its followers to visit Mecca, in the west of Saudi Arabia – the birthplace of the prophet Muhammad. Millions of pilgrims a year flock to Mecca to visit the sacred Ka'ba shrine.

ANNUAL EVENTS Festivals such as the Lent carnival held in Rio de Janeiro, Brazil, are attended by vast numbers of people every year. In Rio, there are all-night street parties, live music, and a contest for the best costume and float.

THE PACKAGE TOUR In 1841, 570 people were taken by train from Leicester, England, to a park in Loughborough, for a day trip. This ten-mile journey, organized by Thomas Cook (1808–1892), was the first ever package tour. From this small beginning, Cook opened up travel for the masses, and developed one of the world's best-known travel companies.

THINGS TO SEE IN...

US	UK	FRANCE	CHINA	ITALY

US

STATUE OF LIBERTY A gift from the French to the American people in 1884, this statue stands on an island in New York harbor.

MOUNT RUSHMORE It took more than 14 years to carve the faces of four US presidents in the granite cliffs in South Dakota. Finished in 1941, the heads are 60 ft (18 m) tall.

SEARS TOWER The Sears Tower, in Chicago, is the tallest skyscraper in the US, at 1,453 ft (443 m). It has 110 stories, 100 elevators, and 16,000 windows!

UK

NELSON'S COLUMN This 165-ft (50-m) statue commemorates Admiral Lord Nelson, who beat Napoleon at the Battle of Trafalgar. It stands in Trafalgar Square, London.

CAERPHILLY CASTLE This castle was built in Wales in the 13th century by an English nobleman. Concentric walls (one wall inside another) and complex waterways make this one of the best-defended of all castles.

LOCH NESS This lake, near Inverness, Scotland, is home to the elusive Loch Ness monster, whose existence has been speculated for many years.

FRANCE

LASCAUX II Lascaux, southwest France, is the site of ancient caves, notable for their prehistoric paintings. Due to deterioration, they are closed to the public, but a reconstruction, Lascaux II, has been created close to the original site.

MUSÉE DU LOUVRE This museum, in Paris, contains important art collections, including Leonardo da Vinci's *Mona Lisa*.

NOTRE-DAME Standing on the site of a Roman temple, this cathedral in Paris was completed in about 1330.

CHINA

GREAT WALL Built over 2,000 years ago to protect China from invaders, this wall, found in the northeast, is 3,375 miles (5,400 km) long.

IMPERIAL PALACE This palace, in Bejing, dates from the 15th century, and houses a priceless collection of relics from various dynasties.

MAGAO CAVES These are hand-crafted Buddhist shrines, which date back to the second century AD. A national treasure, they are situated in Dunhuang, northwest China.

ITALY

COLOSSEUM This ancient open theater in Rome held fights, in which gladiators and wild beasts fought to the death.

LEANING TOWER OF PISA This 184.5-ft (56.2-m) marble bell tower was built about 700 years ago. It began to lean during its construction!

SANTA CROCE This Gothic church in Florence was built in the late 13th century. The tombs of many famous Florentines, including the sculptor Michelangelo, are found there.

TOP TOURIST COUNTRIES

In 1997, it was reckoned that about 613,488,000 people – almost one in ten of the world's population – traveled as tourists to another country. Of these, more than half visited the destinations listed here. Certain trends are emerging, such as the increasing popularity of countries like Poland, which was ranked 27th in the world in 1990, but is now the seventh most popular country to visit.

COUNTRY	% OF WORLD TRAVELERS	VISITORS PER YEAR
France	10.9	66,800,000
US	8.0	49,038,000
Spain	7.1	43,403,000
Italy	5.6	34,087,000
UK	4.2	25,960,000
China	3.9	23,770,000
Poland	3.2	19,514,000
Mexico	3.2	19,351,000
Canada	2.9	17,610,000
Czech Republic	2.8	17,400,000

AMAZING FACT! France's Eiffel Tower, a popular tourist attraction, has 1,652 steps up to the third level!

FAMOUS BEACHES

BONDI Situated in Sydney, Australia, Bondi is one of the best and most popular surfing beaches in the world.

TAHITI Surfing originated in the waves breaking on the beaches of this South Pacific island.

MALIBU A fashionable California surfing beach, Malibu is a popular place for many celebrities to live.

SKELETON COAST In Namibia, the Namib Desert joins the sea, creating one of the world's longest beaches – 1,200 miles (1,900 km) in length.

BLACKPOOL One of the world's most-visited beaches, Blackpool, UK, attracts some 7,500,000 people a year to attend tourist attractions on the coast.

CONEY ISLAND Situated in Brooklyn, New York, Coney Island's beach and amusements once attracted up to 50,000,000 visitors a year.

COPACABANA Found in Rio de Janeiro, Brazil, Copacabana is one of the world's most popular beach resorts.

VIRGINIA BEACH The world's largest pleasure beach at 28 miles (45 km) long, Virginia Beach is found in Virginia.

NATURAL WONDERS OF THE WORLD

ULURU This huge red sandstone boulder rises 1,143 ft (348 m) above the Australian desert, and is 1.5 miles (2.4 km) long. Its colors change from pink at dawn, to orange at midday, red at sunset, and lavender at night.

GRAND CANYON The Grand Canyon, in Arizona, was gouged out of rock by the Colorado River. It is 217 miles (349 km) long, up to 19 miles (30 km) wide, and 1 mile (1.6 km) deep. Its deepest point cuts through 2-billion-year-old rock.

ANGEL FALLS The Angel Falls in Venezuela are the tallest in the world, with a total drop of 3,212 ft (979 m), almost three times as high as the Empire State Building.

DEAD SEA This inland sea situated between Israel and Jordan lies 1,300 ft (400 m) below sea level, and is the lowest point on Earth. Its water is so salty that it allows people to float easily.

NORTHERN LIGHTS In the Arctic, on dark nights, colored lights known as Auroras can be seen in the sky. They are caused by electricity in the upper atmosphere, and are brightest in midwinter, when the sun never rises.

PEOPLE

HUMAN BODY

BODY SYSTEMS

RESPIRATORY SYSTEM The body needs a regular supply of oxygen. Air is filtered through the nose and mouth, and then passes into the lungs, where oxygen is absorbed into the blood through tiny air sacs called alveoli. Carbon dioxide is breathed out.

DIGESTIVE SYSTEM Food is broken down and processed in the digestive system. Nutrients are absorbed, and undigested waste is expelled.

SKELETAL SYSTEM The internal framework of the body, the skeleton has 206 bones. It keeps the body rigid and protects the delicate internal organs.

CARDIOVASCULAR SYSTEM The heart and blood vessels keep blood circulating around every part of the body and supply chemicals that regulate body processes.

NERVOUS SYSTEM The brain and the spinal cord make up the central nervous system (CNS), which carries messages to and from the brain, and coordinates the body's actions.

ENDOCRINE SYSTEM These glands release hormones that stimulate and coordinate processes within the body. For example, the pancreas produces insulin to regulate blood sugar levels.

DID YOU KNOW? The spinal column is made up of 33 bones called vertebrae. A human neck has the same number of vertebrae as a giraffe!

BRAIN FACTS

HEAVY HEAD An average brain weighs 3 lb (1.3 kg).

GRAY MATTER The gray matter, or cortex, of the brain is made up of nerve cell bodies. If the cortex was spread out flat, it would cover an office desk!

CELL MATES One brain cell connects to up to 25,000 others.

LEFT AND RIGHT The brain is made up of two halves: the right controls logic and speech, while the left nurtures creativity.

LARGEST ORGANS

ORGAN		AVERAGE WEIGHT	
		OZ	G
Skin		384.0	10,886
Liver		55.0	1,560
Brain	male	49.7	1,408
	female	44.6	1,263
Lungs	both	38.5	1,090
Heart	male	11.1	315
	female	9.3	265
Kidneys	both	10.2	290
Spleen		6.0	170
Pancreas		3.5	98

BODY NUMBERS

MUSCLES The body has 650 muscles to pull bones and enable movement. It takes 17 muscles to smile, and 42 to frown!

WATER Your body is 70 percent water.

NERVES Messages are sent to the brain, via nerves, at 224 mph (360 km/h). Neurons, which carry these messages, are the longest cells in the human body, and can measure 4 ft (1.2 m) long.

BLOOD Your body contains 9 pints (5 liters) of blood that travels along 62,000 miles (100,000 km) of blood vessels – equivalent to 2.5 times around the Equator.

TEMPERATURE The human body's normal temperature is 98.6°F (37°C).

THE FIVE SENSES

TOUCH The skin contains nerve endings that send messages to the brain and detect degrees of pressure, cold, warmth, and pain.

TASTE The tongue contains more than 10,000 taste buds that detect chemicals in food and drink. A baby is born with taste buds all over its mouth, but they slowly disappear. Taste buds are renewed weekly.

SMELL The nose detects smells by sensing chemicals in the air. You can identify 2,000–4,000 different smells. Smells are processed by the same part of the brain that deals with emotions and memories.

HEARING Sound vibrations trigger a chain of movements in the skull. Our ears can detect 1,500 different tones, 350 degrees of loudness, and can gauge the direction of a sound within three degrees.

SIGHT Light is detected by the eye and focused to form an image. Humans can detect a lighted candle 1 mile (1.6 km) away.

BODY NAMES AND THEIR MEANINGS

PART	MEANING
Appendix	To append, or add to
Auricle	Latin *auricula*, or external ear
Biceps (forearm muscle)	Latin *biceps*, meaning two heads
Canine (tooth)	Latin *canis*, meaning a dog
Clavicle (shoulder blade)	Latin *clavis*, meaning a key
Coccyx (tail bone)	Cuckoo – its triangular shape resembles a cuckoo's beak!
Cranium	Greek *kranion*, meaning skull
Fibula (calf bone)	Latin *figere*, to fasten
Follicle	Latin *folicula*, small bag
Incisor	Latin *incidere*, to cut
Liver	Greek *liparos*, fat
Mandible (lower jawbone)	Latin *mandibula*, jaw
Orbit (eye socket)	Latin *orbis*, a circle or orb
Pancreas	Greek *pan* (all) and *kreas* (flesh)
Pelvis (hip etc)	Basin (its shape)
Phalanges (finger bones)	Greek *phalaggion*, spider's web
Sacrum (base of spine)	Latin *os sacrum*, holy bone (used in sacrifices)
Triceps (forearm muscles)	Latin *triceps*, meaning three heads

LITTLE-USED NAMES FOR PARTS OF THE BODY

NAME	BODY PART
Axilla	The armpit
Canthus	Either corner of the eye
Cilia	The eyelashes
Columella	The part of the nose between the nostrils
Darwinian tubercule	A small lump found on the edges of some people's ears
Dorsum	The back of the tongue
Fossette	A dimple on the chin
Frenum	The muscle beneath the tongue
Gelasin	A dimple in the cheek
Hallux	The big toe
Lunula	The white half-moon shapes on the nails
Popliteal space	The area behind the knee
Sclera	The white of the eye

YOUR AMAZING BODY

BREATHING You take between 13 and 17 breaths per minute at rest, and up to 80 during exercise. If you take an average of 20 breaths a minute, you breathe 28,800 times a day!

ELEMENTS The human body contains many elements, including gold! In one human, there is enough carbon to fill 900 pencils and enough iron to make a 3-in (7.6-cm) nail. To make a 0.1-oz (3-g) 18-carat gold wedding ring, you would need the gold from 316 people, or to make a thermometer, you would need the mercury from the bodies of 40 people.

CELLS There are 50 trillion cells in your body, of which 3 billion die per minute. Most of them are replaced.

DIGESTION Your stomach produces up to 3.5 pints (2 liters) of hydrochloric acid daily and 500,000 cells are replaced every minute so acid cannot damage the stomach walls.

SNEEZES Your sneezes, a result of an irritation in the nasal passages, can travel at 99 mph (160 km/h)!

BRAIN Your brain contains about 15 billion cells. You can retain about seven facts at any one time in your short-term memory, but over the long-term your brain has to forget things to make room for new memories.

TASTE With 10,000 taste buds on your tongue, you can identify 500 different tastes.

VISION Some 10,000 colors can be detected by the human eye. Color blindness can affect 1 in 30 people, but as many as 1 in 12 men.

DID YOU KNOW? You are 0.4 in (1 cm) taller in the morning than the evening, because the cartilage in the spine compresses during the day.

LONGEST BONES IN THE BODY

BONE	AVERAGE LENGTH IN	CM
Femur (thighbone – upper leg)	19.88	50.50
Tibia (shinbone – inner lower leg)	16.94	43.03
Fibula (outer lower leg)	15.94	40.50
Humerus (upper arm)	14.35	36.46
Ulna (inner lower arm)	11.10	28.20
Radius (outer lower arm)	10.40	26.42
Seventh rib	9.45	24.00
Eighth rib	9.06	23.00
Innominate bone (hipbone – half pelvis)	7.28	18.00
Sternum (breastbone)	6.69	17.00

DID YOU KNOW? The bones in the female skeleton are usually 6 to 13 percent smaller than in that of the male, with the exception of the sternum, which is virtually identical. However, in childhood, girls grow much faster than boys!

AMAZING PEOPLE

WORLD'S TALLEST PEOPLE

NAME	DATES	COUNTRY	HEIGHT		
			FT	IN	CM
Robert Pershing Wadlow	1918–1940	US	8	11.1	272
John William Rogan	1871–1905	US	8	8.0	264
John F. Carroll	1932–1969	US	8	7.75	263.5
Väinö Myllyrinne	1909–1963	Finland	8	3.0	251.4
Bernard Coyne	1897–1921	US	8	2.0	248.9
Don Koehler	1925–1981	US	8	2.0	248.9

WORLD'S OLDEST PEOPLE

This list includes only those for whom there are accurate records.

NAME	DATES	COUNTRY	AGE	
			YEARS	DAYS
Jeanne Calment	1875–1997	France	122	164
Shigechiyo Izumi	1865–1986	Japan	120	237
Carrie White	1874–1991	US	116	88
Christian Mortensen	1882–1998	Denmark/US	115	252
Charlotte Hughes	1877–1993	UK	115	229

WORLD'S HEAVIEST PEOPLE

Precise weights of certain people have never been verified, but these are the main contenders for the list of "world's heaviest," based on records of peak weights (some later dieted and reduced their weights):

NAME	DATES	COUNTRY	MAXIMUM WEIGHT	
			LB	KG
Jon Minnoch	1941–83	US	1,400	635
Walter Hudson	1944–91	US	1,201	545
Rosalie Bradford	b.1943	US	1,199	544
Michael Walker	b.1934	US	1,186	538

FAMOUS LEFT-HANDED PEOPLE

Ludwig van Beethoven, composer • Julius Caesar, Roman emperor
Fidel Castro, Cuban president • Bill Clinton, US president
Leonardo da Vinci, artist • Albert Einstein, scientist • Elizabeth II,
British queen • Jimi Hendrix, guitarist • Michelangelo, painter
Wolfgang Amadeus Mozart, composer • Pablo Picasso, painter

!DID YOU KNOW? People called Kerr are more likely to be left-handed, because they descend from a Scottish clan which had so many left-handers that they built spiral staircases in their castles counterclockwise!

!DID YOU KNOW?
Your largest bone, the thighbone, or femur, is 150 times as long as your smallest bone, the stirrup bone, inside your ear.

HIGHEST MALE LIFE EXPECTANCY

Fifty years ago, most people died before the age of 50. Today, most survive well beyond that age. Global average life expectancy is now 64 years for men, 73.1 years in the US.

COUNTRY	LIFE EXPECTANC YEAR
Iceland	76.
Japan	76.
Sweden	75.
Greece	75.
Cyprus	74.
Australia	74.
Switzerland	74.
Israel	74.
Spain	74.
Netherlands	74.
Canada	74.2

HIGHEST FEMALE LIFE EXPECTANCY

Many women around the world live longer than men. The average life expectancy for women is now 67 years. 79.1 years in the US.

COUNTRY	LIFE EXPECTANCY YEARS
Japan	82.5
Switzerland	81.2
Sweden	81.1
France	80.8
Iceland	80.8
Canada	80.7
Australia	80.6
Italy	80.6
Spain	80.5
Netherlands	80.4
Norway	80.3
Greece	80.1

IN ONE DAY...

Your body sheds 36 million skin cells.

A man produces 300 million sperm cells.

173 billion red blood cells are created and destroyed.

Your heart beats 100,800 times.

You take 30,000 breaths a day.

10 billion white blood cells are made.

You blink 9,365 times.

Your kidneys filter 792 gallons (3,600 liters) of blood – equivalent to 45 baths!

100 hairs are lost and replaced.

Enough body heat is produced to power a light bulb for 1.5 days.

Your toenails grow 0.004 in (0.1 mm).

About 3 pints (1.7 liters) of urine is made.

Your mouth produces 1.8 pints (1 liter) of saliva.

Your stomach produces 3.5 pints (2 liters) of hydrochloric acid.

Your body expels an average of 3.5 pints (2 liters) of gas.

One teaspoonful of tears spills from your eyes – though crying empties out more.

AMAZING PEOPLE

LONGEST NAILS Shridar Chillal of Pune, India (b.1937) has not cut the nails on his left hand since 1952. By 1996, his nails measured 231 in (587 cm) in total.

LONGEST BEARD The 17 ft 6-in (5.33-m) beard of Norwegian-born US immigrant Hans Langseth (1846–1927) has been in the Smithsonian Institution, Washington D.C., since 1967.

LONGEST MOUSTACHE The moustache of Kalyan Ramji Sain of Sundargath, India, spans 11 ft 11.5 in (3.29 m)!

LONGEST HAIR Swami Pandarasannadhi, the religious leader of a monastery in Madras, India, had hair that was measured in 1949 at 26 ft (7.9 m).

MOST SNEEZES Donna Griffiths of Pershore, UK, sneezed for 978 days, starting on January 13, 1981.

MOST HICCUPS Charles Osbourne from Anthon, Iowa, hiccuped from 1922 to 1990.

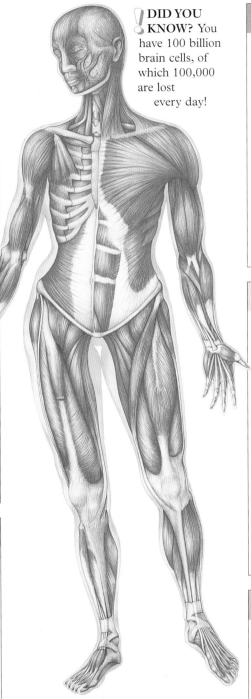

DID YOU KNOW? You have 100 billion brain cells, of which 100,000 are lost every day!

AMAZING BRAINS

MATH GENIUS In seconds, Zerah Colburn (1804–1840) from the US, correctly calculated how many seconds had elapsed since the birth of Christ!

INFANT PRODIGY By the age of four, Kim Ung-Yong of Korea (b.1963) could speak fluent Korean, English, Japanese, and German.

PHONE NUMBERS Gon Yang-ling of Harbin, China, has memorized more than 15,000 telephone numbers.

FAMOUS SHORT PEOPLE

NAME	OCCUPATION	HEIGHT FT IN	CM
Alexander Pope	English writer	4 6	137
Queen Victoria	British monarch	5 0	152
Dolly Parton	Country singer	5 0	152
Danny DeVito	US actor	5 0	152
Paul Simon	US singer	5 2	157
Yuri Gagarin	Soviet cosmonaut	5 3	160
Nikita Kruschev	Soviet leader	5 3	160
Michael J. Fox	US actor	5 4	162
Pablo Picasso	Spanish painter	5 4	162

DWARFS OF THE PAST

"COUNT" JOSEPH BORUWLASKI (1739–1837) Known as the Polish Dwarf, Boruwlaski was 3 ft 3 in (1 m) at his tallest. In 1782, he met English giant Patrick Cotter, whose knee was level with the top of the Count's head!

JEFFREY HUDSON (1619–1682) A court dwarf who once leaped out of a pie at a banquet for Charles I, Hudson was said to have grown to 3 ft 6 in (1.07 m).

"TOM THUMB" (1838–1883) US showman Phineas T. Barnum persuaded the parents of 4-year-old, 2-ft (0.6-m) tall Charles Stratton to exhibit him in a show. He was advertised as "General Tom Thumb, a dwarf eleven years of age, just arrived from England."

FEATS OF GREAT STRENGTH

WEIGHTY MOMENT Basque strongman Mielxto Saralegi holds the world record for lifting a block of stone onto his shoulder – 721 lb (327 kg) – the weight of five adults!

TAKING THE PLANE At Sydney Airport, Australia, on April 2, 1996, David Huxley pulled a Boeing 747-400 weighing 184 tons (187 tonnes), for 154.7 ft (79.5 m).

PULLING TEETH Robert Galstyan of Armenia dragged two Russian railroad cars weighing 215 tons (219 tonnes) a distance of 23 ft (7 m) using his teeth.

AHEAD OF TRAFFIC In 1972, Walter Cornelius pushed a bus 0.5 mile (0.8 km) with his head, at Peterborough, UK.

PUSH-UPS On January 12, 1985, British strongman Mick Gooch did 16 push-ups using one finger balanced on a coconut!

HEALTH and MEDICINE

ALTERNATIVE MEDICINE

Alternative therapies often aim to restore the body's state of balance, using natural methods or ingredients.

AROMATHERAPY A natural therapy in which oils extracted from plants are used in massage or bathing, or are inhaled.

YOGA A course of exercises designed to promote physical and mental health.

ALEXANDER TECHNIQUE This therapy aims to treat and prevent a range of disorders by improving posture.

NUTRIENTS

Nutrients are the essential elements for healthy eating. They include:

VITAMINS Aid the release of energy from glucose, and assist the body's growth and repair.

MINERALS Help growth and repair processes, the release of energy from nutrients, and help to form new tissues.

CARBOHYDRATES Compounds of carbon, hydrogen, and oxygen, such as starch and sugar, that provide the body with energy.

PROTEIN A substance needed by the body for growth and repair.

MEDICAL MYTHS

COLDS Colds are caused by cold temperatures.

HICCUPS Being given a scare cures hiccups.

HAIR Hair can turn white in a night.

STRENGTH Spinach makes you strong.

RIBS Men have one rib less than women.

BONES The "funny bone" on the elbow is a bone.

TAPEWORMS Tapeworms ingest food in the human intestine, which causes hunger.

VITAMIN C Large amounts of Vitamin C do not help to ward off colds.

EYESIGHT Carrots give you good eyesight, and help you see in the dark.

DID YOU KNOW? The medical myth that eating fish is good for your brain probably originated in the Middle Ages, when monks, who were noted for their literacy and intelligence, always ate fish on Fridays. The association of intelligence with the consumption of fish has persisted!

MOST COMMON CAUSES OF DEATH WORLDWIDE

CAUSE	APPROXIMATE DEATHS PER YEAR
Ischemic heart disease	7,200,000
Cancers	6,346,000
Cerebrovascular disease	4,600,000
Acute lower respiratory infection	3,905,000
Tuberculosis	3,000,000
Chronic obstructive pulmonary disease	2,888,000
Diarrhea, including dysentery	2,473,000

MOST EFFECTIVE FITNESS ACTIVITIES

These are the sports and activities recommended by fitness experts as the best means of acquiring all-around fitness, building stamina and strength, and increasing flexibility.

Swimming	Dancing
Cycling	Soccer
Rowing	Jogging
Gymnastics	Walking (brisk!)
Judo	

MEDICAL MILESTONES

c.460 BC First medical studies are made by Greek physician Hippocrates.

1543 Accurate medical drawings are done by Flemish doctor Andreas Vesalius.

1796 A vaccination against the deadly smallpox virus is pioneered by English doctor Edward Jenner.

1805 German Friedrich Sertürner discovers the painkiller morphine.

1816 First stethoscope is invented by French doctor René Laënnec.

1818 First blood transfusion is carried out by Thomas Blundell, in England.

1864 The Red Cross is founded by Swiss businessman Henri Dunant.

1895 German physicist William von Röntgen discovers the X ray.

1928 Penicillin is discovered by Scottish bacteriologist Alexander Fleming.

1954 First internal heart pacemaker is fitted in Stockholm, Sweden.

1967 First heart transplant is performed by South African surgeon Christiaan Barnard.

1978 The first test-tube baby, Louise Brown, is born in Britain.

1980s-1990s Laser surgery is used in eye operations and to remove cancer cells.

UNUSUAL PHOBIAS

Fear of	Phobia name
Ants	Myrmecophobia
Bathing	Ablutophobia
Beards	Pogonophobia
Chickens	Alektorophobia
Chins	Geniophobia
Dolls	Pediophobia
Flutes	Aulophobia
Frogs	Batrachophobia
Going to bed	Clinophobia
Knees	Genuphobia
Mirrors	Eisoptrophobia
Paper	Papyrophobia
Slime	Blennophobia
Teeth	Odontophobia

DISEASES NAMED AFTER REAL PEOPLE

Disease	Named after/dates	Nationality	Affects
Alzheimer's Disease	Alois Alzheimer (1864–1915)	German	brain
Bell's Palsy	Sir Charles Bell (1774–1842)	Scottish	face muscles
Crohn's Disease	Burrill Bernard Crohn (1884–1983)	American	digestion
Graves' Disease	Robert James Graves (1796–1853)	Irish	thyroid gland
Lou Gehrig's Disease	Henry Louis Gehrig (1903–1941)	American	nervous system
Hodgkin's Disease	Thomas Hodgkin (1798–1866)	British	lymph system
Ménière's Disease	Prosper Ménière (1799–1862)	French	ears
Parkinson's Disease	James Parkinson (1755–1824)	British	nervous system
Raynaud's Disease	A. G. Maurice Raynaud (1834–1881)	French	fingers and toes

DID YOU KNOW? The first stethoscope, invented in 1816, was made from a roll of paper!

HOME SAFETY TIPS

Do not use electrical equipment in the bathroom or near water.

Store dangerous items, such as household products containing chemicals, in a high cupboard, away from young children.

Keep saucepan handles turned inward so they do not hang over the work surface, and use the back burners of the stove first.

Run cold water into the bathtub first, and keep testing the temperature as you add the hot water.

Do not leave an iron on the floor to cool; put it in a place where it cannot be easily touched.

Every home and car should have a first-aid kit, containing items needed for emergency treatment.

MOST COMMON PHOBIAS

Object of phobia	Medical term
Spiders	Arachnephobia or arachnophobia
People and social situations	Anthropophobia or sociophobia
Flying	Aerophobia or aviatophobia
Open spaces	Agoraphobia, cenophobia, or kenophobia
Confined spaces	Claustrophobia, cleisiophobia, cleithrophobia, or clithrophobia
Vomiting	Emetophobia or emitophobia
Heights	Acrophobia, altophobia, hypsophobia, or hypsiphobia
Thunderstorms	Brontophobia or keraunophobia
Death	Necrophobia or thanatophobia
Cancer	Carcinomaphobia, carcinophobia, carcinomatophobia, or cancerophobia

MOST COMMON ALLERGENS

Food	Environmental
Nuts	House dust mite
Shellfish and seafood	Grass pollens
Milk	Tree pollens
Wheat	Cats
Eggs	Dogs
Fresh fruit	Horses
Fresh vegetables	Molds
Cheese	Birch pollen
Yeast	Weed pollen

ODD ACCIDENTS

PLAY ACTING While watching a production of *Hamlet* in Pittsburgh, Patricia Spahic received head wounds when Hamlet's dagger slipped out of his hand and flew into the audience.

WEIGHTY PROBLEM In 1836, a paddle steamer carrying a circus menagerie was shipwrecked off the US coast. Some of the sailors launched a raft, but were drowned when an elephant leaped onto it.

ANGLING FOR TROUBLE An angler on the Amazon accidentally struck a tree with his fishing rod, dislodging a nest of bees. To escape the bees, he jumped into the river – and was eaten by piranhas.

TOOTH TROUBLE In 1918, magician William Ellsworth Robinson was shot dead on stage in London, England, when a trick in which he appeared to catch bullets in his teeth went wrong.

STICKY END In 1919, 21 people were killed in Boston, when a tank containing 2 million gallons (9 million liters) of sticky molasses burst and flooded the city.

97

PEOPLE'S NAMES

> **DID YOU KNOW?** By the mid-1990s, Madonna was the biggest-selling female recording artist in the world.

FAMOUS PEOPLE KNOWN BY ONE NAME

NAME	REAL NAME
Cher	American singer Cherilyn Sarkasian, b.1946
Dion	American singer Dion DiMucci, b.1939
Donovan	British singer Donovan P. Leitch, b.1943
Fabian	American singer Fabian Forte, b.1943
Giles	British cartoonist Carl Giles, 1916–1995
Houdini	American escapologist Erich Weiss, 1874–1926
Liberace	American pianist Wladziu Valentino Liberace, 1919–1987
Lulu	British singer Marie McDonald McLaughlin, b.1948
Madonna	American singer Madonna Louise Ciccone, b.1958
Michelangelo	Italian painter Michelangelo Buonarroti, 1475–1564
Sade	Nigerian singer Helen Folasade Adu, b.1960
Sting	British singer Gordon Matthew Sumner, b.1951
Topol	Israeli actor Chaim Topol, b.1935
Vangelis	Greek composer Evangelos Papathanassious, b.1943

SANTA CLAUS NAMES

FATHER CHRISTMAS
England

BABBO NATALE
Italy

JUL EMANDED
Denmark

JULTOMTEN
Sweden

KRISS KRINGLE
Hungary

LE PERE NOEL
France

PAPA NOEL
Brazil

ST. NICHOLAS
Germany

SHEN TAN LAO JEN
China

UKKO
Finland

SINTER KLAUS
Holland

FAMOUS STAGE NAMES

MARILYN MONROE American film actress, who died in 1962. Her real name was Norma Jean Baker.

JOHN WAYNE American film actor, who died in 1979. His real name was Marion Morrison.

CLIFF RICHARD British singer and actor, whose real name is Harry Clive Webb.

ELTON JOHN British singer. His real name is Reginald Dwight.

WOODY ALLEN American film actor and director, whose real name is Allen Konigsberg.

MICHAEL CAINE British film actor. His real name is Maurice Micklewhite.

CARY GRANT American film actor, whose real name was Archibald Leach.

ANNE KLEIN American fashion designer, whose real name is Hannah Golofski.

WORLD'S MOST COMMON SURNAMES

COUNTRY	SURNAME
France	Martin
UK/US	Smith
Germany	Müller
Spain	Garcia
Netherlands	De Vries
Sweden	Johansson
Russia	Ivanov
Italy	Rossi
China	Li

> **DID YOU KNOW?** One of the longest surnames ever recorded is that of Major Tollemache-Tollemache de Orellana-Plantagenet-Tollemache-Tollemache (1858–1917), a British soldier.

ROYAL NICKNAMES

NICKNAME	REAL NAME
Alfonso the Fat (reigned 1212–1223)	Alfonso II, king of Portugal
Charles the Bald (reigned 840–877)	Charles I, king of France
Christian the Cruel (reigned 1513–1523)	Christian II of Denmark and Norway
Fulk the Surly (reigned 1068–1109)	Fulk IV, count of Anjou
Ivan the Terrible (reigned 1533–1584)	Ivan IV, tsar of Russia
Louis the Sluggard (reigned 986–987)	Louis V, king of France
Sebastian the Madman (reigned 1557–1578)	Sebastian of Portugal
Selim the Grim (reigned 1512–1520)	Selim I, Turkish sultan
William the Bad (reigned 1154–1166)	William I of Sicily

LONGEST NAMES

US Rhoshandiatellyneshiaunneveshenk Koyaanfsquatsiuty Williams was born in Texas in 1984.

FRANCE Louis George Maurice Adolph Roch Albert Abel Antonio Alexandre Noé Jean Lucien Daniel Eugène Joseph-le-Brun Josephe-Barême Thomas Thomas-Thc Pierre-Cerbon Pierre-Maurel Barthelemi Artus Alphonse Bertrand Dieudonne Emanuel Josue Vincent Luc Michel Jules-de-la-Plane Jules-Bazin Julio-César Jullien was a French composer (1812–1860).

HAWAII Dawn Lee of Honolulu, Hawaii, was born in 1967, and given a 94-letter middle name: Napaumahalaonaonekawehiwehionakuahiweanenawawakehoonkakehoaalekeeaonanainananiakeao'Hawaiikawao.

SAUDI ARABIA The full name of the Sultan of Brunei is Kebawah Duli Yang Maha Hulia Paduka Seri Baginda Sultan Dan Yang Dipertuan Sir Muda Hassanal Bolkiah Muizzaddin Waddaulah Ibni Duli Yang Teramat Mulia Paduka Seri Begawan Sultan Sir Muda Omar Ali Saifuddin Sa'adul Khairi Waddin.

ENGLAND Ann Pepper, born in Derby, England, in 1882, was given 25 first names: Ann Bertha Cecilia Diana Emily Fanny Gertrude Hypatia Inez Jane Kate Louisa Maud Nora Orphelia Quince Rebecca Starkey Teresa Ulysis Venus Winifred Xenophen Yetty Zeus Pepper.

DID YOU KNOW? You can legally change your name to be as long or strange as you like!

UNUSUAL NAMES FOR CELEBRITY CHILDREN

DANDELION Daughter of Keith Richard, a member of the group the Rolling Stones.

DWEEZIL AND MOON UNIT Children of Frank Zappa, singer.

FIFI TRIXIBELLE, PIXIE, AND PEACHES Children of Paula Yates, UK television personality, and Bob Geldof, British musician.

LARK SONG Daughter of Mia Farrow, actress, and André Previn, conductor.

ZOWIE Child of David Bowie, singer.

BETTY KITTEN Daughter of Jonathon Ross, UK television personality, and his wife, Jane Goldman.

NAMES FOR COLLECTORS

NAME	COLLECTS
Philographist	Autographs
Plangonologist	Dolls
Bibliosphilist	Books
Conchologist	Shells
Numismatist	Coins
Philatelist	Stamps
Deltiologist	Postcards
Copoclephilist	Key rings
Archtophilist	Teddy bears

DID YOU KNOW? Teddy bears get their name from US President Theodore "Teddy" Roosevelt, who, on a hunting trip, refused to shoot a bear cub.

POP GROUP NAME ORIGINS

ABBA The group members' first names are Agnetha, Benny, Björn, and Annifried. The initials form the name Abba.

BEE GEES The Brothers Gibb.

DURAN DURAN The name of a mad scientist in the film *Barbarella*.

R.E.M R.E.M stands for Rapid Eye Movement, a psychological term describing the dream state during sleep.

SIMPLY RED The group's singer Mick Hucknall has red hair.

ONCE UPON A TIME... FAIRYTALE NAMES

ALADDIN A young boy who rubs a magic lamp, releasing a genie.

SNOW WHITE Named for her fair complexion, Snow White is deemed the fairest in the land by a magical mirror.

SEVEN DWARFS Dopey, Bashful, Sleepy, Grumpy, Happy, Doc, and Sneezy are Snow White's companions.

CINDERELLA Made to do household chores by her cruel stepsisters, Cinderella eventually marries a prince.

RED RIDING HOOD Dressed in a red cape, Red Riding Hood goes to visit her grandmother, but meets a wolf on the way.

RAPUNZEL Locked in a tower, the princess Rapunzel's hair grew so long that a prince was able to use it as a rope to climb up and rescue her.

GOLDILOCKS A golden haired girl who encountered a family of bears after she had eaten their porridge.

PINOCCHIO A wooden puppet whose nose grew longer every time he told a lie.

HANSEL AND GRETEL A brother and sister who find a house made of candy and gingerbread.

DID YOU KNOW? One of the main characters in the book *Peter Pan*, by James Barrie, is called Wendy, a name which had never been used prior to the book's publication!

RULERS and LEADERS

RULING SYSTEMS

COMMUNISM Communists believe that everyone should eventually be equal, but until that time, the government should hold all the wealth of the country and share it fairly among the people. In communist countries, the Communist Party controls the government, the army, the civil service, economy, education, and the media.

DEMOCRACY Within a democracy, all persons have the right to play a part in the government of their country. Today, most democracy is representative, which means that the people elect representatives to make decisions on their behalf.

MONARCHY In a monarchy, a king or queen rules the country. Today, only a few monarchs, such as the king of Saudi Arabia, have real power, but four centuries ago in Europe, kings and queens made all the laws and collected the taxes.

PRESIDENCY In a republic such as the US, three branches of government share power: the president leads the members of the executive branch in deciding the government's policy; members of the legislature make the laws; and the judges, who are appointed by the executive branch, interpret the law.

FIRST TEN ROMAN EMPERORS

EMPEROR	BORN	ACCEDED	DIED	FATE
Julius Caesar	July 12, 100 BC	48 BC	March 15, 44 BC	Assassinated
Augustus	September 23, 63 BC	27 BC	August 19, AD 14	Died
Tiberius	November 16, 42 BC	AD 14	March 16, AD 37	Died
Caligula	August 31, AD 12	AD 37	January 24, AD 41	Assassinated
Claudius	August 1, AD 10	AD 41	October 13, AD 54	Assassinated
Nero	December 15, AD 37	AD 54	June 9, AD 68	Suicide
Galba	December 24, AD 3	AD 68	January 15, AD 69	Assassinated
Otho	April 28, AD 32	AD 69	April 16, AD 69	Suicide
Vitellius	September 24, AD 15	AD 69	December 22, AD 69	Assassinated
Vespasian	November 18, AD 9	AD 69	June 23, AD 79	Died

WORLD'S LONGEST-REIGNING MONARCHS

MONARCH	COUNTRY	REIGN	AGE AT ACCESSION	REIGN YEARS
Louis XIV	France	1643–1715	5	72
John II	Liechtenstein	1858–1929	18	71
Franz-Josef	Austria–Hungary	1848–1916	18	67
Victoria	Great Britain	1837–1901	18	63
Hirohito	Japan	1926–1989	25	62
Kangxi	China	1662–1722	8	61
Qianlong	China	1736–1796	25	60
George III	Great Britain	1760–1820	22	59
Louis XV	France	1715–1774	5	59

REIGNS OF BRITAIN'S MONARCHS

SAXON KINGS: Edward the Confessor (1042–1066) • Harold II (1066)

NORMAN KINGS: William I (1066–1087) William II (1087–1100) • Henry I (1100–1135)

BLOIS KING: Stephen (1135–1154)

PLANTAGENETS: Henry II (1154–1189) Richard I (1189–1199) • John (1199–1216) Henry III (1216–1272) • Edward I (1272–1307) Edward II (1307–1327) • Edward III (1327–1377) • Richard II (1377–1399) Henry IV (1399–1413) • Henry V (1413–1422) Henry VI (1422–1461)

YORK: Edward IV (1461–1470)

LANCASTER: Henry VI (1470–1471)

YORK: Edward IV (1471–1483) • Edward V (1483) • Richard III (1483–1485)

TUDOR: Henry VII (1485–1509) • Henry VIII (1509–1547) • Edward VI (1547–1553) Jane (1553) • Mary I (1553–1558) Elizabeth I (1558–1603)

STUART: James I (1603–1625) • Charles I (1625–1649)

COMMONWEALTH: Council of State (1649–1653) • Oliver Cromwell (1653–1658) Richard Cromwell (1658–1659)

STUART: Charles II (1660–1685) • James II (1685–1688) • Mary II (1689–1694) • William III and Mary II (1689–1694) • William III (alone) (1694–1702) • Anne (1702–1714)

HANOVER: George I (1714–1727) • George II (1727–1760) • George III (1760–1820) George IV (1820–1830) • William IV (1830–1837) • Victoria (1837–1901)

SAXE-COBURG: Edward VII (1901–1910)

WINDSOR: George V (1910–1936) Edward VIII (1936) • George VI (1936–1952) • Elizabeth II (1952–)

DID YOU KNOW? The Crown Jewels of the British royal family have been housed under tight security in the Jewel House of the Tower of London, London, UK, since the early 14th century. They include the regalia used in the coronations of British monarchs since that of Charles II in 1660.

ROYAL TITLES

KING/QUEEN The ruler of a monarchy: that is, the chief authority over a country and people. Kings and queens were once thought to receive their power directly from God.

RAJAH A king or prince in India.

EMPEROR/EMPRESS The sovereign or supreme ruler of an entire empire, such as the Roman Empire.

PHARAOH An Egyptian king was referred to as the pharaoh. This name derives from the word *per-ao*, meaning "great house," and referred to the palace where the king lived.

SULTAN The ruler or sovereign of an Islamic country, such as Turkey.

TSAR An emperor or king. A former emperor of Russia.

DID YOU KNOW? After his release from prison in 1990, Nelson Mandela began the long task of modernizing and stabilizing South Africa.

FAMOUS WORLD LEADERS

CHAIRMAN MAO Born Mao Zedong (1893–1976), he set up the Chinese Communist Party in 1921, which took power in China in 1949. He founded the People's Republic of China in the same year, and was its first leader.

LENIN Vladimir Lenin (1870–1924) was the leader of the Social Democratic Party. In 1917, he led a revolution that overthrew the tyrannical tsarist rulers of Russia. He then set up the world's first communist regime in the country.

CASTRO In 1959, Fidel Castro (b.1927), a Cuban lawyer, led a revolution against Cuba's dictator, President Batista. Castro became head of government, and Cuba became a communist state.

MANDELA Nelson Mandela (b.1918) was the leader of the African National Congress (ANC), a political party and black rights group, which was banned in 1960. In 1964, he was imprisoned for life, but was finally released in 1990. Mandela became the first black president of South Africa in 1994.

FIRST WOMEN PRIME MINISTERS AND PRESIDENTS

NAME	COUNTRY	DATES
Sirimavo Bandaranaike (PM)	Ceylon (Sri Lanka)	1960–1965 1970–1977
Indira Gandhi (PM)	India	1966–1977 1980–1984
Golda Meir (PM)	Israel	1969–1974
María Estella Peron (President)	Argentina	1974–1976
Elisabeth Domitien (PM)	Central African Republic	1975–
Margaret Thatcher (PM)	UK	1979–1990
Dr. Maria de Lurdes Pintassilgo (PM)	Portugal	1979–
Vigdís Finnbogadóttir (President)	Iceland	1980–1996

ALL THE PRESIDENTS OF THE US

NO.	NAME	PARTY	OFFICE
1	George Washington	Federalist	1789
2	John Adams	Federalist	1797
3	Thomas Jefferson	Dem-Rep	1801
4	James Madison	Dem-Rep	1809
5	James Monroe	Dem-Rep	1817
6	John Quincy Adams	Dem-Rep	1825
7	Andrew Jackson	Democrat	1829
8	Martin Van Buren	Democrat	1837
9	William Henry Harrison	Whig	1841
10	John Tyler	Whig	1841
11	James Knox Polk	Democrat	1845
12	Zachary Taylor	Whig	1849
13	Millard Fillmore	Whig	1850
14	Franklin Pierce	Democrat	1853
15	James Buchanan	Democrat	1857
16	Abraham Lincoln	Republican	1861
17	Andrew Johnson	Democrat	1865
18	Ulysses Simpson Grant	Republican	1869
19	Rutherford Birchard Hayes	Republican	1877
20	James Abram Garfield	Republican	1881
21	Chester Alan Arthur	Republican	1881
22	Grover Cleveland	Democrat	1885
23	Benjamin Harrison	Republican	1889
24	Grover Cleveland	Democrat	1893
25	William McKinley	Republican	1897
26	Theodore Roosevelt	Republican	1901
27	William Howard Taft	Republican	1909
28	Woodrow Wilson	Democrat	1913
29	Warren Gamaliel Harding	Republican	1921
30	Calvin Coolidge	Republican	1923
31	Herbert Clark Hoover	Republican	1929
32	Franklin Delano Roosevelt	Democrat	1933
33	Harry S. Truman	Democrat	1945
34	Dwight David Eisenhower	Republican	1953
35	John Fitzgerald Kennedy	Democrat	1961
36	Lyndon Baines Johnson	Democrat	1963
37	Richard Milhous Nixon	Republican	1969
38	Gerald Rudolph Ford	Republican	1974
39	Jimmy Carter	Democrat	1977
40	Ronald Reagan	Republican	1981
41	George Bush	Republican	1989
42	Bill Clinton	Democrat	1993

HUMAN ACHIEVEMENTS

POLE POSITIONS

THE FIRST TO REACH THE NORTH POLE? Dispute continues as to which – if either – of two men was the first to reach the North Pole: American adventurer Frederick Albert Cook (1865–1940) announced that he had attained his goal, accompanied by two Inuit, on April 21, 1908, but his claim appears to have little foundation, since he is known to have committed other fraudulent actions. It is more likely that American Robert Edwin Peary (1856–1920) and his African-American companion Matthew Alexander Henson (1866–1955), accompanied by four Inuit, were first at the Pole on April 6, 1909. If Peary's claim is valid, Henson also becomes the first African-American person to reach the Pole.

THE FIRST TO FLY OVER THE POLES IN AN AIRPLANE Two Americans, Lieutenant Commander (later Admiral) Richard Evelyn Byrd (1888–1957), who was team-leader and navigator, and pilot Floyd Bennett (1890–1928) traversed the North Pole on May 9, 1926. Their aircraft was a three-engined Fokker F.VIII-3m, named *Josephine Ford* after the granddaughter of automobile magnate Henry Ford, who sponsored the exploit with John D. Rockefeller. On November 29, 1929, Byrd also became the first to fly over the South Pole.

THE FIRST TO FLY OVER THE NORTH POLE IN AN AIRSHIP A team of 16 led by Roald Amundsen (1872–1928), the Norwegian explorer who first reached the South Pole in 1911, flew across the North Pole on May 12, 1926 in the Italian-built airship *Norge*. Amundsen and his companion Oscar Wisting, who was with him at the South Pole, became the first people to see both Poles.

THE FIRST TO LAND AT THE NORTH POLE IN AN AIRCRAFT A Soviet team comprising Pavel Afanaseyevich Geordiyenko, Mikhail Yemel'yenovich Ostrekin, Pavel Kononovich Sen'ko, and Mikhail Mikhaylovich Somov arrived at and departed from the Pole by air on April 23, 1948. The first US landing at the Pole was that of Lieutenant Colonel William Pershing Benedict, with ten Air Force officials and scientists on May 3, 1952. In the same year, the Scandinavian airline SAS became the first to fly scheduled flights over the Pole.

FIRST TO GO OVER NIAGARA FALLS AND SURVIVE

NAME	DATE	VESSEL
Annie Edison Taylor	October 24, 1901	Barrel
Bobby Leach	July 25, 1911	Steel barrel
Jean Lussier	July 4, 1928	Rubber ball attached to oxygen cylinders
William Fitzgerald (aka Nathan Boya)	July 15, 1961	Rubber ball

FIRST CROSS-CHANNEL SWIMMERS

SWIMMER	COUNTRY	TIME HR:MIN	DATE
Matthew Webb	UK	21:45	August 24–25, 1875
Thomas Burgess	UK	22:35	September 5–6, 1911
Henry Sullivan	US	26:50	August 5–6, 1923
Enrico Tiraboschi	Italy	16:33	August 12, 1923
Charles Toth	US	16:58	September 8–9, 1923

FAMOUS DISABLED ACHIEVERS

SARAH BERNHARDT (1844–1923) Despite having her leg amputated in 1915 after a fall, this French tragic actress was determined to continue with her acting career.

DAVID BLUNKETT (b.1947) The British Minister of Education is blind and attends parliamentary sessions accompanied by his guide dog.

STEPHEN HAWKING (b.1942) This celebrated UK physicist, who suffers from motor-neurone disease, is confined to a wheelchair and speaks with the aid of a voice synthesizer.

HELEN KELLER (1880–1968) Although she was blind, deaf, and dumb, American author Helen Keller campaigned for rights for the handicapped.

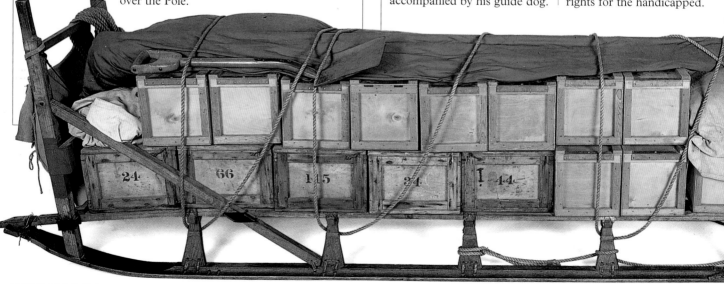

FIRST EUROPEANS TO LAND IN THE AMERICAS

EXPLORER	COUNTRY	DISCOVERY/ EXPLORATION	YEAR
Christopher Columbus	Italy	West Indies	1492
John Cabot	Italy/ England	Nova Scotia/ Newfoundland	1497
Alonso de Hojeda	Spain	Brazil	1499
Vicente Yañez Pinzón	Spain	Amazon	1500
Pedro Alvarez Cabral	Portugal	Brazil	1500
Gaspar Corte Real	Portugal	Labrador	1500
Rodrigo de Bastidas	Spain	Central America	1501
Vasco Nuñez de Balboa	Spain	Panama	1513
Juan Ponce de León	Spain	Florida	1513
Juan Díaz de Solís	Spain	Río de la Plata	1515

YOUNG ACHIEVERS

YOUNGEST BRITISH MONARCH
Henry VI was born on December 6, 1421, and became king of England on September 1, 1422, at the age of eight months.

YOUNGEST PATENT HOLDER ON INVENTIONS John J. Stone-Parker received a US Patent in 1989 when he was four years old, for an attachment to stop ice from slipping out of a glass.

YOUNGEST ARTIST TO EXHIBIT AT UK'S ROYAL ACADEMY Lewis Lyons' painting *Trees and Monkeys* was shown on April 29, 1967, a day before his fifth birthday.

YOUNGEST PUBLISHED AUTHOR
Allen Welsh Dulles (1893–1969) had his book *The Boer War: A History* published in 1902, when he was eight. Dulles later became the director of the Central Intelligence Agency (CIA).

DID YOU KNOW? A team of 12 husky dogs can pull a loaded sledge weighing 0.49 ton (0.5 tonne).

LADIES FIRST

PARACHUTIST
Jean Genevieve Garnerin was the first female parachutist. She parachuted from a hotair balloon in Paris, in 1799.

NOBEL PRIZE WINNER
In 1903, Marie Curie of Poland shared the Nobel Prize for physics for her work on radioactivity.

POLICEWOMAN
Alice Stebbins Wells became the first ever policewoman, in Los Angeles in 1910.

CLIMBER Junko Tabei from Japan was the first woman to reach the top of Everest. She achieved this in 1975.

SAILOR In 1969, American Sharon Adams became the first woman to sail across the Pacific single-handed.

EDITOR In 1762, Anna Maria Smart became the first female editor in the UK when she edited the *Reading Mercury*. In the US, Ann Franklin became editor of the *Newport Mercury* in the same year.

AROUND-THE-WORLD FIRSTS

AROUND THE WORLD
Juan Sebastian de Elcano, and his crew of 17 on board *Vittoria*, sailed around the world from Spain, returning to Italy on September 6, 1522. The expedition was originally led by Ferdinand Magellan, but he was murdered in the Philippines, April 27, 1521.

AROUND THE WORLD IN LESS THAN 80 DAYS
US journalist "Nellie Bly" (Elizabeth Cochrane) set out to beat the fictitious "record" established in Jules Verne's novel, *Around the World in 80 Days*. She traveled from New York, and returned on January 25, 1890 – a record circumnavigation of 72 days, 6 hours, 11 minutes, and 14 seconds.

SOLO AROUND THE WORLD
In 1895, US sea captain Joshua Slocum (1844–1910) set out from Boston in *Spray*, an oyster boat he had built himself, returning three years later. He financed his trip by giving lectures along the way. Surprisingly, Slocum was unable to swim!

DID YOU KNOW? Sun rays shining on Arctic snow can cause temporary blindness.

DID YOU KNOW? Deaths on Everest are on the increase. The sheer volume of people now climbing the mountain means that more and more people are coming to untimely ends.

FIRST MOUNTAINEERS TO CLIMB EVEREST

MOUNTAINEER	COUNTRY	DATE
Edmund Hillary	New Zealand	May 29, 1953
Tenzing Norgay	Nepal	May 29, 1953
Jürg Marmet	Switzerland	May 23, 1956
Ernst Schmied	Switzerland	May 23, 1956
Hans-Rudolf von Gunten	Switzerland	May 24, 1956
Adolf Reist	Switzerland	May 24, 1956
Wang Fu-chou	China	May 25, 1960
Chu Ying-hua	China	May 25, 1960
Konbu	Tibet	May 25, 1960
Nawang Gombu	India	May 1, 1963
James Whittaker	US	May 1, 1963

Nawang Gombu and James Whittaker arrived at Everest's summit at the same time – neither wishing to deny the other the privilege of being first, they ascended the last stretch side by side.

INDUSTRY

THE WORLD of WORK

! **DID YOU KNOW?** The first plow was called an ard.

COUNTRIES WITH THE MOST WORKERS

As defined by the International Labor Organization, the "labor force" includes people between the ages of 15 and 64 who are currently employed and those who are also unemployed.

COUNTRY	LABOR FORCE
China	709,000,000
India	398,000,000
US	133,000,000
Indonesia	89,000,000
Russia	77,000,000
Brazil	71,000,000
Japan	66,000,000
Bangladesh	60,000,000
Pakistan	46,000,000
Nigeria	44,000,000
Germany	40,000,000

MOST HOLIDAYS

COUNTRY	AVERAGE NO. OF DAYS OFF PER YEAR
Austria	30
Belgium	30
Finland	25
France	25
Norway	25

MOST STRESSFUL JOBS

The following jobs are considered the most stressful. Most of them involve a high level of responsibility.

- Firefighter
- Race car driver
- Astronaut
- Surgeon
- National Football League player
- Police officer
- Highway patrol officer
- Air traffic controller

LEAST STRESSFUL JOBS

- Musical instrument repairer
- Industrial machine repairer
- Medical records technician
- Pharmacist
- Software engineer
- Typist, word processor
- Librarian
- Janitor
- Bookkeeper
- Forklift operator

ANIMALS AT WORK

Many animals work with people, helping with tasks that make use of their special skills.

DOGS Often described as "man's best friend," dogs are chosen to work with people in many jobs, ranging from guiding the blind and assisting the police, to pulling sleds, rounding up sheep, and even sniffing for drugs.

CAMELS These strong animals are chosen to carry people and goods across the desert because they can go for long periods without rest or water.

ELEPHANTS The strength of Asian elephants is put to good use in tropical forests where they haul logs.

DANGEROUS JOBS

Life insurance companies base their premiums on statistics according to the likelihood of people being involved in an accident at work. These are the most dangerous jobs:

- Formula One driver
- Bomb disposal officer
- Test pilot
- Special forces soldier
- Circus performer
- Film stuntman/woman
- Commercial diver
- Oil rig worker
- Scaffolder
- Fisherman/woman
- Miner
- Dockworker
- Merchant Navy
- Electric linesman

20TH-CENTURY ENTREPRENEURS

NAME	BUSINESS
Sochiro Honda (1906–1991)	Motorcycles and cars
William Hewlett (b.1913) and David Packard (1912–1996)	Computers
Akio Morita (b.1921)	Sony electronic products
Sir Terence Conran (b.1931)	Retail shops, restaurants
Sir Clive Sinclair (b.1940)	Electronic products
Anita Roddick (b.1942)	Eco-friendly body products
Alan Sugar (b.1947)	Amstrad electronic products
Richard Branson (b.1950)	*Virgin* records, airline, trains
Bill Gates (b.1955)	Computer software
Steve Jobs (b.1955)	Apple computers

DID YOU KNOW?
The largest food company the world is Nestlé. s top-selling product is it Kat – about 400 are ten every second!

COUNTRIES WITH MOST FARMERS

This list is compiled by the United Nations and is based on the number of people that depend on agriculture for their livelihood, even if they do not own land of their own.

COUNTRY	PERCENT FARMING
Bhutan	93.9
Nepal	93.3
Burkina	92.4
Rwanda	91.2
Burundi	90.7
Niger	89.2
Mali	89.2
Ethiopia	85.3
Guinea Bissau	84.1
Uganda	83.1
Tanzania	81.6

AMAZING FACT!
Although most people in Bhutan are farmers, only three percent of its land can actually be cultivated.

DID YOU KNOW?
When farmers grow only enough food to support themselves and their families, it is called subsistence farming.

UK COMPANIES WITH MOST EMPLOYEES

This list includes only companies with shares on the Stock Exchange. Government, and other organizations, are also major employers – the National Health Service, for example, employs about a million people.

COMPANY	EMPLOYEES
British Telecom	129,600
BTR	115,805
HSBC Holdings	109,298
Compass Group	107,843
Rentokil Initial	107,767
J. Sainsbury	102,544
Tesco	98,440
Lonrho	93,497

DID YOU KNOW?
Indian Railways employs 1,602,000 people – 18 percent of the country's population!

PROFESSIONS THAT WALK THE MOST

This list is based on a survey conducted in the US by footwear manufacturer Dr. Scholl's, and the American Podiatry Association. These figures are averages, and certain individuals may walk much more or less than these suggest.

PROFESSION	AVERAGE WALKED PER YEAR	
	MILES	KM
Police officer	1,632	2,626
Mail carrier	1,056	1,699
TV reporter	1,008	1,622
Nurse	942	1,516
Doctor	840	1,352
Retail clerk	804	1,294
Secretary	792	1,275
Actor	776	1,249
Public relations executive	666	1,072
Real estate agent	622	1,001

US COMPANIES WITH MOST EMPLOYEES

COMPANY	EMPLOYEES
Wal-Mart Stores	825,000
General Motors	608,000
Ford Motor	363,892
United Parcel Service	331,000
Sears Roebuck	296,000
Columbia/HCA Healthcare	285,000
General Electric	276,000
IBM	269,465
J. C. Penney	260,000
Kmart	258,000
Boeing	239,000
McDonalds	237,000
Kroger	212,000
Marriot International	195,000
United Technologies	180,100
Lockheed Martin	173,000
Philip Morris	152,000
Aramark	150,000
Motorola	150,000
Dayton Hudson	149,500
Safeway	147,000
Bell Atlantic	141,000

PRESIDENTS' PREVIOUS JOBS

PRESIDENT	OCCUPATION
Ronald Reagan	Actor
George Bush	Oilman
Jimmy Carter	Peanut farmer
Harry Truman	Haberdasher
Theodore Roosevelt	Rancher
George Washington	Surveyor, planter

MOST PHYSICALLY DEMANDING JOBS

Firefighter • Laborer

Farmer • Lumberjack

Cowboy • Construction worker

Ironworker • Garbage collector

Miner • Athlete

Stuntman/woman • Acrobat

MONEY and WEALTH

MONEY FIRSTS

COINS The first coins were staters, minted in Lydia (now Turkey), from 680 to 645 BC. Their value depended on their weight.

BANKNOTES Paper money was invented by the Chinese in the tenth century.

CREDIT CARD The Diners Club card issued in the US in 1950 was the first credit card. It enabled the first 200 members to eat on credit at 27 New York restaurants.

RICHEST PEOPLE IN THE WORLD – EXCLUDING RULERS

NAME	COUNTRY	SOURCE	WORTH (US $)
William H. Gates III	US	Computer software	51,000,000,000
Walton Family	US	Stores	48,000,000,000
Warren E. Buffett	US	Investments	33,000,000,000
Paul Gardner Allen	US	Computer software	21,000,000,000
Kenneth Thomson	Canada	Newspapers	14,400,000,000
Jay A. and Robert Pritzker	US	Finance	13,500,000,000
Mars family	US	Inheritance	13,500,000,000
Lee Shau Kee	China	Property	12,700,000,000
Albrecht family	Germany	Stores	11,700,000,000
Steven A. Ballmer	US	Computer software	10,700,000,000
Mulliez family	France	Stores	10,300,000,000
Michael Dell	US	Computers	10,000,000,000
Li Ka-Shing	China	Property	10,000,000,000

POOREST COUNTRIES

Gross Domestic Product (GDP) is the total value of a country's goods and services, produced annually within the country. Dividing a country's GDP by its population can indicate how "rich" it is.

COUNTRY	GDP PER HEAD (US $)
Sudan	36
São Tomé & Principe	49
Mozambique	77

RICHEST COUNTRIES

COUNTRY	GDP PER HEAD (US $)
Liechtenstein	42,416
Switzerland	42,416
Japan	41,718

❗ DID YOU KNOW?
A lack of raw materials in Switzerland led to the development of specialized high-tech industries, bringing the country great wealth.

COUNTRIES WITH THE MOST GOLD

COUNTRY	GOLD RESERVES, 1998		
	TROY OUNCES	TONS	TONNES
US	261,710,000	8,011	8,140
Germany	95,180,000	2,913	2,960
Switzerland	83,280,000	2,549	2,590
France	81,890,000	2,507	2,547
Italy	66,670,000	2,040	2,073
Netherlands	27,070,000	828	841
Japan	24,230,000	741	753
UK	18,420,000	563	572
Portugal	16,070,000	491	499

WORLD'S HIGHEST-EARNING ACTORS AND ACTRESSES

ACTOR	COUNTRY	RECENT WORK	INCOME 1996–1997 US $
Arnold Schwarzenegger	Austria/US	*Batman and Robin*	74,000,000
Harrison Ford	US	*Air Force One*	72,000,000
Tim Allen	US	*Home Improvement* (TV)	66,000,000
John Travolta	US	*Michael, Face Off*	61,000,000
Mel Gibson	Australia	*Ransom, Conspiracy Theory*	59,000,000
Roseanne	US	*Roseanne* (TV)	55,000,000
Jim Carrey	US	*The Truman Show*	53,000,000
Robin Williams	US	*Flubber, Good Will Hunting*	50,000,000
Eddie Murphy	US	*The Nutty Professor, The Metro*	49,000,000
Kevin Costner	US	*Tin Cup, The Postman*	42,000,000

HISTORIC TREASURES MADE OF GOLD

BUDDHA The world's largest single gold object is a 15th-century statue of Buddha in Bangkok, Thailand. It is 10 ft (3 m) high and weighs 5.4 tons (5.5 tonnes).

TUTANKHAMUN'S TOMB In 1923, British archaeologist Howard Carter discovered the tomb of 14th-century-BC pharaoh Tutankhamun. The treasures included a gold mask inside a solid gold coffin, weighing 243 lb (110 kg).

SALT CELLAR An elaborate salt cellar was crafted in gold by Italian Benvenuto Cellini (1500–1571).

RICHEST RULERS IN THE WORLD

Name	Country	In power since	Estimated wealth (US $)
Sultan Hassanal Bolkiah	Brunei	1967	38,000,000,000
King Fahd Bin Abdulaziz Alsaud	Saudi Arabia	1982	20,000,000,000
Sheikh Jaber Al-Ahmed Al-Jaber Al-Sabah	Kuwait	1977	15,000,000,000
Sheikh Zayed Bin Sultan Al Nahyan	United Arab Emirates	1966	10,000,000,000
President Saddam Hussein	Iraq	1979	5,000,000,000
Queen Beatrix	Netherlands	1980	4,700,000,000
Prime Minister Rafik Al-Hariri	Lebanon	1992	3,000,000,000
King Bhumibol	Thailand	1946	1,800,000,000

HIGHEST-EARNING CELEBRITIES

Name	Occupation	Income 1996–1997 US $
Steven Spielberg	Film producer/director	313,000,000
George Lucas	Film producer/director	241,000,000
Oprah Winfrey	TV host/producer	201,000,000
Michael Crichton	Novelist/screenwriter	102,000,000
Jerry Seinfeld	Actor/comedian	94,000,000
David Copperfield	Magician	85,000,000
Stephen King	Novelist/screenwriter	84,300,000
Arnold Schwarzenegger	Actor	74,000,000
John Grisham	Novelist/screenwriter	66,000,000
Celine Dion	Singer	65,000,000
Siegfried and Roy	Magicians	58,000,000
Michael Jackson	Singer	55,000,000
Michael Flatley	Dancer	54,000,000
Spice Girls	Singers	47,000,000
U2	Band	40,000,000

FAMOUS MISERS

HETTY GREEN (1834–1916) Hetty Green was the daughter of a US shipping and whaling magnate. Despite her great wealth, she lived in cheap boardinghouses, on a diet of porridge.

J. PAUL GETTY (1892–1976) One of the 20th century's richest men, US oil magnate Getty made his guests pay for telephone calls by installing coin-operated telephones in the bedrooms of his mansion in Surrey, England.

MONEY FACTS

LARGEST COINS The Swedish ten-daler copper coins of 1644 weighed 43 lb 7 oz (19.71 kg).

SMALLEST COINS The Nepal silver quarter-jawa of c.1740 weighed 0.00007 oz (0.002g). You would need 231,700 coins to make 1 lb, or 500,000 to weigh 1 kg.

LARGEST BANKNOTES Chinese 14th-century one-guan notes measured 9 × 13 in (22.8 × 33 cm).

SMALLEST BANK NOTES The Romanian ten-bani notes of 1917 had a printed area of just 1.6 × 1.5 in (27.5 × 38 mm).

MOST MINTED In 1997, a total of 12,194,723,000 coins were minted in the US.

MILLIONAIRES OF THE PAST

CORNELIUS VANDERBILT (1794–1877) Steamship owner and once richest man in the US.

ANDREW CARNEGIE (1835–1918) Scottish-born US steel millionaire.

JOHN DAVISON ROCKEFELLER (1835–1937) US oil millionaire.

HENRY FORD (1863–1947) A US auto industry magnate.

HOWARD HUGHES (1905–1976) US aviator and airline owner.

A MILLION DOLLARS

WEIGHT ON YOUR SHOULDERS $1 million in $1 bills would weigh exactly 1 ton (1 tonne), and if you put them in a pile, it would be 361 ft (110 m) high – as tall as 60 adults standing on each other's shoulders! If you had $1 million in $100 bills, it would weigh only 22 lb (10 kg), so you'd be able to carry it. However, if you had $1 million in one-cent coins – 100 million of them – it would weigh 246 tons (250 tonnes).

WHO WANTS TO BE A MILLIONAIRE? The first reference to "millionaire" appears in *Vivian Grey*, a novel written in 1826 by British author Benjamin Disraeli: "Were I the son of a millionaire, or a noble, I might have all."

SAVING A MILLION If you earned $100 a week, it would take 192 years to earn $1 million – and that's before taxes!

DID YOU KNOW? In 1864, American John Washington Steel inherited more than $1 million. He spent the entire inheritance in one year.

FOOD PRODUCTION

TOP FARMING COUNTRIES

COUNTRY	AGRICULTURAL AREA (HECTARES)		
	CROPS	PASTURE	TOTAL
China	96,554,000	400,000,000	496,554,000
Australia	46,877,000	415,885,000	462,762,000
US	187,776,000	239,172,000	426,948,000
Brazil	61,350,000	185,500,000	246,850,000
Russia	133,929,000	83,100,000	217,029,000
India	169,700,000	11,770,000	181,470,000
Argentina	27,200,000	142,100,000	169,300,000
Mongolia	1,396,000	124,600,000	125,996,000
Mexico	24,720,000	74,499,000	99,219,000
South Africa	1,317,000	81,378,000	82,695,000

DID YOU KNOW? The total area of agricultural land used for cultivating crops worldwide is 3,562,271,040 acres (1,441,573,000 hectares). There are 8,296,767,672 acres (3,357,520,000 hectares) of pasture land.

FISHY FOOD

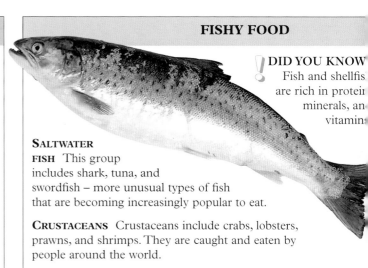

DID YOU KNOW
Fish and shellfis[h] are rich in protei[n], minerals, an[d] vitamin[s]

SALTWATER FISH This group includes shark, tuna, and swordfish – more unusual types of fish that are becoming increasingly popular to eat.

CRUSTACEANS Crustaceans include crabs, lobsters, prawns, and shrimps. They are caught and eaten by people around the world.

SUSHI Sushi is a traditional Japanese dish of raw or lightly cooked fish, often marinated, and served with rice.

SHELLFISH Shellfish, such as mussels, oysters, and scallops, have hard shells, inside of which is a soft, edible body. Most shellfish are eaten cooked – except oysters, which are swallowed raw!

BIGGEST FOODS EVER MADE

BIGGEST PIZZA On December 8, 1990, staff at the Norwood Hypermarket, Norwood, South Africa, produced a pizza that measured 122 ft 8 in (37.4 m) in diameter!

BIGGEST CHEESE In his *Natural History*, Roman historian Pliny the Elder (AD 23–79) describes a 1,000-lb (454-kg) cheese that was made in the Italian town of Luni. The current record holder is a monster Cheddar made in 1995 in Quebec, Canada, by Loblaws Supermarkets and Agropur Dairies. It weighed 57,508 lb (26,085 kg)!

BIGGEST COOKIE The world's largest cookie was a chocolate chip cookie baked by Cookie Time of Christchurch, New Zealand, on April 2, 1996. It contained 2.46 tons (2.5 tonnes) of chocolate, had a diameter of 81.8 ft (24.9 m), and covered an area of 5, 241.5 sq ft (486.95 sq m) – almost twice the size of a tennis court!

LIVESTOCK POPULATIONS

BEEF India has almost 200 million cows, more than any other country.

PIGS Denmark has twice as many pigs as humans – more than 11 million, with a human population of just over five million.

HENS China has the most chickens of any country – more than three billion. The US has half this number – equal to six chickens for every human inhabitant.

FOODS AND DRINKS NAMED AFTER PLACES

FOOD	FROM
Stilton cheese	Stilton, UK
Cantaloupe	Cantaluppi, Ital[y]
Champagne	Champagn[e] region of Franc[e]
Currants	Corinth, Greec[e]
Frankfurter	Frankfurt, German[y]
Madeira (wine, cake)	Madeira, Portuga[l]
Mayonnaise	Mahón, Spai[n]
Tangerines	Tangier, Morocc[o]
Port	Oporto, Portuga[l]

TOP FRUIT CROPS

CROP	COUNTRIES	WORLD PRODUCTION	
		TONS	TONNES
Oranges	Brazil, US, Mexico	62,781,724	63,789,600
Bananas	India, Brazil, Ecuador	58,120,898	59,053,950
Grapes	Italy, France, US	57,190,760	58,108,880
Apples	China, US, Turkey	55,136,232	56,021,370
Watermelons	China, Turkey, US	45,702,813	46,436,510
Mangoes	India, China, Mexico	23,275,956	23,649,620
Pears	China, US, Spain	13,219,597	13,431,820
Pineapples	Thailand, Brazil, Philippines	12,853,898	13,060,250
Peaches	China, US, Italy	10,738,636	10,911,030
Lemons and limes	Mexico, India, Argentina	8,644,882	8,783,664

TOP VEGETABLE CROPS

CROP	COUNTRIES	WORLD PRODUCTION	
		TONS	TONNES
Sugar cane	Brazil, India, China	1,231,580,638	1,251,352,000
Wheat	China, India, US	599,226,430	608,846,200
Corn	US, China, Brazil	577,649,321	586,922,700
Rice	China, India, Indonesia	561,885,685	570,906,000
Potatoes	China, Russia, US	286,797,652	291,401,800
Sugar beet	France, Germany, US	260,366,665	264,546,500
Barley	Russia, Canada, Germany	154,029,367	156,502,100
Tomatoes	China, US, Turkey	87,333,578	88,735,600
Legumes	India, UK, Kenya	55,493,625	56,384,500
Oats	Russia, Canada, US	30,746,555	31,240,150
Carrots	China, US, Russia	17,551,374	17,873,090

DID YOU KNOW? About 15 million burgers are consumed every day in the US!

BANANA FACTS

WHAT IS A BANANA?
Botanically, the banana is a herb. The name comes from Portuguese, but is adapted from African words.

HOW DO THEY GROW?
Bananas grow upside down on a bush.

WHICH COUNTRY GROWS MOST?
India grows more bananas than any other country in the world, producing almost 9.8 million tons (10 million tonnes) a year.

HOW MANY ARE EATEN?
Worldwide, nearly 59.1 million tons (60 million tonnes) of bananas are eaten every year.

WHEN WERE THEY INVENTED?

Popcorn	3,000 BC
Croissants	1683
Potato chips	1853
Chewing gum	1875
Coca-Cola	1885
Corn flakes	1894
Chop suey	1896
Pepsi-Cola	1898
Hamburger	1902
Ice cream cone	1904
Instant coffee	1909
Frozen food	1923
Fish sticks	1929

POTATO FACTS

GOING UNDERGROUND We eat only the potato tuber, which grows underground. The fruits and leaves of the potato plant, which grow above ground, are poisonous.

POTATO MYTHS Through the ages, potatoes have been blamed for causing everything from love to leprosy. At one time, the Scots refused to eat them because they were not mentioned in the Bible! In the Andes, the Incas thought the potato made childbirth easier, and also used it to treat injuries.

A SNACK IS BORN Potato chips were invented by a North American Indian named George Crum, in the mid-19th century.

FOOD and EATING

CRUISE SHIP SHOPPING LIST

On an average 14-day cruise, the 1,975 passengers and 760 crew members of the luxurious ocean liner *Oriana* will eat 116,550 meals. The shopping list for the huge amount of food and drink required on the journey is as follows:

Fresh fruit and vegetables	61,729 lb (28,000 kg)
Potatoes	39,683 lb (18,000 kg)
Meat	32,187 lb (14,600 kg)
Flour	18,739 lb (8,500 kg)
Poultry and game	15,212 lb (6,900 kg)
Fats and cheese	10,141 lb (4,600 kg)
Fish	8,157 lb (3,700 kg)
Bacon	7,716 lb (3,500 kg)
Sugar	4,189 lb (1,900 kg)
Shellfish	3,748 lb (1,700 kg)
Coffee	1,433 lb (650 kg)
Milk	2,310 gallons (10,500 liters)
Ice cream	880 gallons (4,000 liters)
Fresh eggs	5,100
Champagne and white wine	2,600 bottles
Red wine	1,200 bottles
Whiskey	352 gallons (1,600 liters)
Spirits	264 gallons (1,200 liters)
Cognac	88 gallons (400 liters)
Beer	33,000 cans
Mixers	28,000 bottles

DID YOU KNOW? A meringue made with fruits and cream was named in honor of the Russian ballerina Anna Pavlova (1885–1931) during a tour of Australia and New Zealand. In Australia, its name is often shortened to a "pav."

PAVLOVA

STRANGE APPETITES

MAN OF IRON An inquest into the death of British farmer Frederick Edwards in 1933 found 1 live revolver bullet, 200 nails, 36 staples, 3 penknives, and 43 phonograph needles in his stomach.

MONSIEUR MANGETOUT Frenchman Michel Lotito (b.1950), whose stage name is "Monsieur Mangetout" (Mr Eat-All), has eaten: 15 shopping carts, 7 TV sets, 1 waterbed, 1 coffin, 1 pair of skis, 18 bicycles ("the chain is the tastiest part"), 1 robot, 1 computer, 1 Cessna light aircraft, and numerous razor blades!

HUNGRY WRITER The French author Honoré de Balzac (1799–1850) frequently consumed 100 oysters, 12 lamb cutlets, a duck, and a couple of partridges in one sitting.

DISHES NAMED AFTER PEOPLE

APPLE CHARLOTTE French master chef Marie Antonin Carême (1784–1833) created this dessert while employed by the English Prince Regent. He named it Charlotte after the Prince's daughter.

MELBA TOAST AND PÊCHE MELBA The Australian opera singer Dame Nellie Melba (1861–1931) had several dishes named after her, including Pêche Melba. Melba Toast was created at London's Savoy Hotel, where she was staying.

SANDWICH The first sandwich was created when John Montagu, fourth Earl of Sandwich (1718–1792), allegedly asked for roast beef between slices of bread so that he could continue a marathon card game uninterrupted.

TOP SUGAR EATERS

COUNTRY	CONSUMPTION PER HEAD PER YEAR		
	LB	OZ	KG
Swaziland	448	10	203.5
Singapore	181	14	82.5
Fiji	173	12	78.8

DID YOU KNOW? Danish people consume 37 lb (17 kg) of sweets and chocolate per head per year!

TOP FISH EATERS

COUNTRY	CONSUMPTION PER HEAD PER YEAR		
	LB	OZ	KG
Denmark	100	8	45.6
Portugal	87	12	39.8
Japan	82	0	37.2

DID YOU KNOW? Fish is a good source of protein and is healthier and lower in calories than red meat.

TOP MEAT EATERS

COUNTRY	CONSUMPTION PER HEAD PER YEAR		
	LB	OZ	KG
US	257	11	16.9
Australia	229	5	104.0
New Zealand	222	3	100.8

DID YOU KNOW? India has one-fifth of the world's cattle, but many Indians don't eat beef due to religious beliefs.

EXTRAORDINARY FEASTS

MUSICAL PIE The highlight of a four-day French banquet given in 1454 by Philip, Duke of Burgundy, came when a huge pie was brought into the room. The lid of the pie was raised to reveal an orchestra of 28 musicians playing within!

CRAZY CUSTARD CAPER During a large banquet held in 1521 at Dover Castle, in the south of England, a court jester amused the guests by leaping into a gigantic bowl of custard!

DEATHLY DINNER In about 1820, the eccentric French culinary expert Grimod de la Reynière staged one of the most macabre meals of all time – in the Paris mortuary. Coffins were placed behind each diner's seat, and 300 spectators observed the bizarre event from the mortuary gallery.

DIZZY DINNER On October 23, 1843, just before the statue of Lord Nelson was hauled to the top of Nelson's Column in Trafalgar Square, London, 14 men ate rump steak on the plinth, 167 ft (51 m) above the ground!

INSIDE A DINOSAUR On New Year's Eve 1853, Professor Richard Owen, later head of the Natural History Department of the British Museum, hosted a banquet inside the framework of a model of the dinosaur *Iguanodon*!

ON HORSEBACK At Sherry's elegant restaurant in New York on March 28, 1903, 36 formally attired gentlemen sat down to dinner on horseback! Their horses were brought to the ballroom by elevator and the floor was laid with turf. Pheasant was served in nosebags, and the champagne in rubber buckets!

THE GREATEST BANQUET

A manuscript said to have been found in the Tower of London, England, is the shopping list for a banquet to end all banquets. Organized in York by the Earl of Warwick to commemorate the installation of his brother George as the Archbishop of York in 1465, it was prepared by 62 cooks, backed up by 515 kitchen helpers, and served to the guests by 1,000 waiters. Imagine going to the supermarket to buy all this!

5,000 Woodcocks	300 Pigs
4,000 Pigeons	300 Hogs
4,000 Rabbits	300 Capons
4,000 Ducks	300 Quarters of wheat
4,000 Bucks, does, and roebucks	(1 quarter = 10.3 ft^3/ 291,000 cm^3)
4,000 Cold custards	300 Tuns of ale
4,000 Cold venison pasties (meat pies)	(1 tun = 210 gallons/935.8 liters)
3,000 Calves	200 Rees (a bird)
2,000 Chickens	200 Cranes
2,000 Hot custards	200 Kids (goats)
1004 Wethers (rams)	204 Bitterns
1,000 Dishes of jellies	200 Pheasants
1,000 Eggets (perhaps a small egg)	155 Hot venison pasties (meat pies)
500 Partridges	100 Peacocks
400 Plovers	100 Curlews
400 Hernsies (young herons)	100 Quails
400 Tarts	104 Tuns of wine
300 Pikes (fish)	10 Fat oxen
300 Breams (fish)	8 Seals
	6 Wild bulls
	4 Porpoises
	1 Pipe of spiced wine (1 pipe = 105 gallons/477.3 liters)

GIANT FROG RECIPES

Dr. Albert Broel, who described himself as the "originator of canned frog legs," provides a list of over 50 tasty recipes for giant frogs in his strange book, *Frog Raising for Pleasure and Profit* (1950). Don't try these at home!

Fried Frog Legs

Giant Frog Sandwich Spread

Giant Bullfrog Cream Broth

Deviled Giant Bullfrog Meat

American Giant Bullfrog Cocktail

Giant Bullfrog Mince Meat

Jellied Giant Bullfrogs

Chinese-style Bullfrog and Rice

Bullfrog Chop Suey

Escalloped Bullfrog with Celery

Giant Bullfrog Omelette

Stuffed Egg with Giant Bullfrog

Baked Apples Stuffed with Frog Meat

Stuffed Baked Tomatoes with Bullfrogs

Giant Bullfrog Fondue

French Toasted Giant Bullfrog Special

DID YOU KNOW? A South African bullfrog can be in (90 cm) length – longer than your arm!

THE EARTH'S RICHES

MOST-EXTRACTED MINERALS PER YEAR

MINERAL	MILLIONS OF	
	TONS	TONNES
Iron ore	973.1	988.8
Salt	181.9	184.9
Aluminum ore (bauxite)	109.3	111
Potash	20.01	20.34
Magnesite	14.46	14.7
Chromium	9.773	9.930
Copper ore	9.372	9.522
Manganese	6.889	7.000
Zinc ore	6.786	6.895
Lead ore	2.721	2.764
Nickel ore	0.789	0.802
Tin ore	0.167	0.169
Molybdenum	0.111	0.113
Uranium	0.035	0.039
Tungsten	0.031	0.032
Cobalt ore	0.027	0.028
Vanadium	0.022	0.023
Silver	0.013	0.014
Mercury	0.003	0.003
Gold	0.002	0.002

TOP GOLD PRODUCERS

COUNTRY	PRODUCTION	
	TONS	TONNES
South Africa	468.8	495
US	324	329
Australia	284	289
Canada	161	164
China	142	145
Russia	123	130
Indonesia	91	92
Uzbekistan	70	71
Peru	64	65
Brazil	63	64

DEEPEST DRILLINGS THROUGHOUT HISTORY

YEAR	DRILLING	LOCATION	DEPTH	
			FT	M
150 BC	Szechuan	China	2,000	610
1886	Schladebach	Germany	5,735	1,748
1928	Big Lake	Texas	8,523	2,598
1949	Sublette County	Wyoming	20,521	6,255
1958	Pecos County	Texas	25,340	7,727
1972	Beckham County	Oklahoma	30,050	9,159

DID YOU KNOW? In the 15th century, the amethyst was believed to have many unusual power including the ability to cure drunkenness!

CRUDE OIL PRODUCTS

Detergents • Drugs • Dye
Fertilizers • Oil • Paints
Gasoline • Plastic • Tires

DEEPEST MINES THROUGH HISTORY

YEAR	MINE	DEPTH	
		FT	M
1835	Kitzbühel copper mine, Austria	2,764	842
1875	St. Vojtech mine, Czechoslovakia	3,280	1,000
1919	Ooregum gold mine, Kolar, India	5,419	1,652
1934	Robinson Deep gold mine, South Africa	8,400	2,560
1938	Crown Mines, South Africa	8,530	2,600
1939	Champion Reef Mines, South Africa	8,604	2,622
1953	East Rand Proprietary Mine, South Africa	9,288	2,831
1959	East Rand Proprietary Mine, South Africa	11,246	3,428
1977	Western Deep Levels gold mine, South Africa	11,749	3,581

DID YOU KNOW? It is believed that the world's deepest mine, the Western Deep Levels gold mine, Carletonville, South Africa, will reach 12,600 ft (3,841 m) by the year 2004. Mining engineers need long elevator shafts, and the temperature at such depths is 131°F (55°C), which means people cannot work unless the air is chilled.

TOP TIMBER-PRODUCING COUNTRIES

COUNTRY	ANNUAL PRODUCTION	
	CUBIC FT	CUBIC M
US	17,491,533,000	495,305,00
China	11,051,973,000	312,957,00
India	10,747,631,000	304,339,00
Brazil	7,782,047,000	220,363,00
Indonesia	7,090,638,000	200,784,50
Canada	6,654,414,000	188,432,00
Nigeria	4,036,855,000	114,311,00
Russia	3,399,037,000	96,250,00
Sweden	1,992,595,000	56,424,00
Ethiopia	1,742,945,000	49,354,70
Dem. Rep. of Congo	1,715,410,000	48,575,00

TOP OIL PRODUCERS

Despite its huge output, the US produces less than half the 2,246,133 tons (2,282,192 tonnes) of oil it consumes per day. This is equivalent to more than 2.95 tons (3 tonnes) per person per year, consumed directly through consumption of heating fuel, motor fuel, or indirectly through consumption of electricity produced by processes such as oil-fired power stations.

COUNTRY	PRODUCTION 1996	
	TONS	TONNES
Saudi Arabia	422,024,960	428,800,000
US	376,850,180	382,900,000
Russia	296,342,620	301,100,000
Iran	180,895,960	183,800,000
Mexico	161,015,120	163,600,000

TOP COAL PRODUCERS

COUNTRY	ANNUAL PRODUCTION	
	TONS	TONNES
China	1,328,670,000	1,350,000,000
US	948,965,640	964,200,000
India	303,133,600	308,000,000
Russia	250,971,000	255,000,000
Australia	246,050,000	250,000,000
Germany	231,385,420	235,100,000
South Africa	203,729,400	207,000,000
Poland	195,855,8000	199,000,00
Czech Republic	80,212,300	81,500,000
Kazakhstan	75,389,720	76,600,000

DID YOU KNOW?

Apple-green chrysoprase, a form of chalcedony, has been used in jewelry since pre-Roman times.

DIAMOND FACTS

WEIGH IT UP The weight of diamonds is measured in carats. The word derives from the carob bean, which is remarkable for its consistent weight of 0.0007 oz (0.2 g). There are approximately 142 carats to the ounce.

ROUGH DIAMONDS Fewer than 1,000 rough diamonds weighing more than 100 carats have ever been recorded.

BIBLICAL GEM The first recorded reference to diamonds occurs in the Bible: Exodus 28.18 and 39.11 describe how a diamond is mounted on a priest's breastplate.

CARBON COPY In 1796, Smithson Tennant (1761–1815), a British scientist, was the first to show that diamonds are composed of carbon. The diamond is the only gem composed of a single element.

FAMOUS DIAMONDS

CULLINAN DIAMOND The Cullinan diamond measured 5 in (2.5 cm) across and weighs 3,106 carats, almost 1 lb 6 oz (0.621 kg), making it the largest diamond ever. It was found at the Premier Mine in South Africa, probably in 1905, although there is some debate about the circumstances of its discovery. The Cullinan has been cut, resulting in 105 separate diamonds, the most important of which are now among the British Crown Jewels. They include the Star of Africa, a pear shape of 530.20 carats, which is mounted in the Queen's Sceptre. This is the largest cut diamond in the world.

HOPE DIAMOND The Hope, a 45.52-carat blue diamond, is America's most famous diamond, which was presented to the Smithsonian Institution, Washington D.C., by Harry Winston in 1947. Its fame rests on the legend that it is an "unlucky" jewel and that it has been responsible for some 20 deaths.

JUBILEE DIAMOND The 245.35-carat Jubilee is regarded as the world's most perfectly cut diamond. It can be balanced on the culet point (the flat face at the bottom), which is less than 0.07 in (2 mm) in diameter.

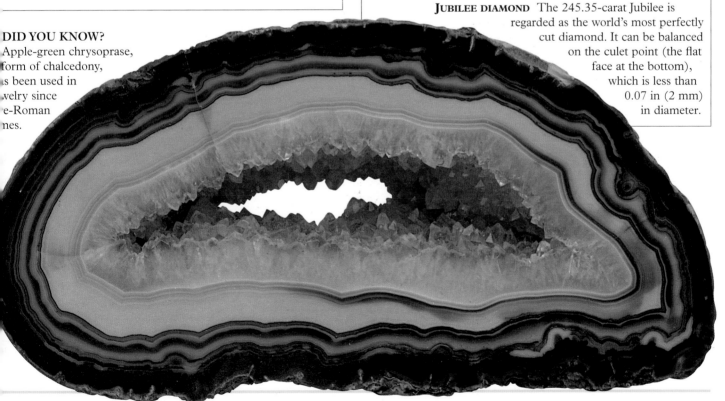

ENERGY

COUNTRIES MAKING HYDROELECTRICITY

COUNTRY	PRODUCTION (% OF WORLD TOTAL)
Canada	13.9
US	13.2
Brazil	10.4
China	7.3
Russia	6.1
Norway	4.1
Japan	3.4
India	2.8
France	2.7
Venezuela	2.1

NUCLEAR REACTORS

Some 442 nuclear power stations are in operation worldwide.

COUNTRY	REACTORS
US	110
France	57
Japan	53
UK	35
Russia	29
Canada	21
Germany	20
Ukraine	16
Sweden	12
South Korea	11

POWER CONSUMPTION OF ELECTRICAL ITEMS

DID YOU KNOW? One day's hydroelectricity for the world could power a 100W lightbulb for 2.7 million years!

APPLIANCE	WATTS (PER YEAR)
Heater	3,000
Electric kettle	2,000
Photocopier	1,500
Iron	1,450
Vacuum cleaner	1,300
Toaster	850
Microwave oven	750
Halogen security light	500
Hair dryer	500
Food mixer	460
Power drill	250
Computer (CPU without monitor)	175
Stereo	150
Lightbulb	100
Television	100
Freezer	83
VCR	32
Electric razor	4.5

ENERGY SOURCES TIMELINE

c.100 BC Romans use coal as fuel.

c.650 BC Persians use windmills to harness wind power.

1712 Thomas Newcomen manufactures the first steam engine.

1799 Alessandro Volta invents the battery from a stack of copper and zinc plates.

1818 First geothermal installation, utilizing jets of natural steam, is set up by Frenchman F. de Larderel.

1881 First electricity-generating power plant opens at Surrey, UK.

1891 First hydroelectric power station is built near Frankfurt, Germany.

1951 First nuclear power station opens in Idaho, US, producing electricity generated by an experimental breeder reactor.

1954 Solar batteries are developed for commercial use by American scientists.

1960 First solar thermal power plant is built in Turkmenistan.

1966 First tidal power station opens in France.

DID YOU KNOW? The world produces 8,858 million tons (9 million tonnes) of oil every day.

NUCLEAR ENERGY TIMELINE

1905 German-American physicist Albert Einstein demonstrates that mass can be converted into energy.

1919 New Zealand-English physicist Ernest Rutherford splits the nucleus of a nitrogen atom.

1939 German chemists Otto Hahn and Fritz Strassman discover nuclear fission.

1942 First nuclear reactor is built by Italian-American physicist Enrico Fermi.

1951 First nuclear power station to produce electricity starts in the US.

1956 First commercial nuclear power station begins operation in the UK.

1991 First controlled nuclear fusion, at JET (Joint European Torus) in the UK.

WORLD'S TOP ENERGY CONSUMERS

These figures show millions of tons (tonnes) of oil equivalent.

COUNTRY	OIL		GAS		COAL		NUCLEAR		HYDROELECTRIC		TOTAL	
	TONS	TONNES	TONS	TONNES	TONS	TONNES	TONS	TONNES	TONS	TONNES	TONS	TONNES
US	819.8	833.0	560.2	569.2	508.0	516.0	180.4	183.3	28.3	28.8	2,096.6	2,130.3
China	169.8	172.5	15.6	15.9	655.5	666.0	3.6	3.7	15.6	15.9	860.2	874.0
Russia	126.0	128.0	312.0	317.0	117.1	119.0	27.7	28.1	13.0	13.2	595.7	605.3
Japan	265.6	269.9	58.6	59.5	86.9	88.3	75.6	76.8	7.3	7.4	494.0	501.9
Germany	135.2	137.4	74.0	75.2	87.5	88.9	41.0	41.7	1.7	1.8	340.0	345.0
India	77.5	78.7	19.2	19.5	138.1	140.3	2.06	2.1	5.9	6.0	242.7	246.6
France	89.6	91.0	28.5	29.0	14.5	14.7	101.2	102.8	5.9	6.0	240.0	243.5
UK	82.4	83.7	75.5	76.7	44.2	44.9	24.1	24.5	0.295	0.3	226.5	230.1

THE WORLD'S ENERGY SOURCES

Industry, transportation, and homes need energy to power everything from furnaces to televisions. Much of this energy is produced by burning fossil fuels like oil, but supplies of these are running out, so renewable energy sources, such as solar power, are becoming increasingly important.

SOURCE	OBTAINED BY	POWER PRODUCED BY	%
Oil	Mining	Burning	39.7
Coal, peat, etc	Mining	Burning	27.2
Natural gas	Mining	Burning	23.2
Nuclear	Mining	Chemical reaction	7.0
Hydroelectric	Water	Turbines	2.5
Geothermal and wind	Hot gases and wind	Turbines	0.4

ENERGY RECORDS

LARGEST SOLAR PLANT
The Harper Lake Site in the Mohave Desert, California, has two 80-megawatt plants.

LARGEST WIND GENERATOR The largest generator is the Boeing Mod-5B at Oahu, Hawaii. It has 320-ft (97.5-m) rotors, and produces 3,200 kilowatts (kW) at a wind speed of 32 mph (51 km/h).

TIDAL POWER The first and largest tidal power station is the Usine Marmémotrice de la Rance, Brittany, France, opened in 1966. It can produce 544 million kW a year – enough to supply power to 120,000 households.

LARGEST OIL PRODUCER Saudi Arabia produces 8,965,000 barrels of oil every day.

LARGEST ELECTRICITY GENERATOR The turbo-generator at Lithuania's Ignalina atomic power station has a capacity of 1,450 megawatts.

SOURCES OF RENEWABLE ENERGY

WIND Wind turbines generate electricity at "wind farms," many of which were established during the 1980s. By the middle of the 21st century, scientists hope that wind power will provide over ten percent of the world's electricity.

SUN Solar energy can be converted into electricity in special cells, which are used to power calculators, among other things. Heat from the Sun can also be used for heating water in hot countries.

WATER Tidal power is made at barriers built across estuaries. As the tide rises or falls, water is kept at a high or low level inside the barrier. When this level differs by about 10 ft (3 m), water flows through huge turbines, creating power which is in turn used to make electricity.

HYDROELECTRIC This type of power is generated at dams and waterfalls. Falling water drives turbines, which create electricity. Around seven percent of the world's energy is provided by hydroelectricity.

DID YOU KNOW? The total amount of sunshine that falls on roads in the US in one year contains twice as much energy as all the coal and oil used around the world in the same amount of time!

ENVIRONMENT

BIGGEST PAPER CONSUMERS

The amount of paper consumed in total per year compared with the amount consumed per person depends on different factors, such as how industrialized a country is. For example, Germany has a high total annual paper consumption, but consumption per individual member of the population is lower than in other countries. The United Nations has predicted that by the year 2010, the US's total demand will have reached 858 lb (389 kg) for each member of the 291,290,000 population projected for that year.

COUNTRY	PER PERSON		TOTAL CONSUMPTION	
	LB	KG	TONS	TONNES
US	679	308	76,277,468	77,502,000
Sweden	659	299	2,533,331	2,574,000
Denmark	571	259	1,315,875	1,337,000
Japan	518	235	28,631,362	29,091,000
Belgium/ Luxembourg	500	227	2,307,949	2,345,000
Netherlands	487	221	3,269,514	3,322,000
Finland	485	220	1,085,572	1,103,000
Switzerland	474	215	1,432,011	1,455,000
Germany	459	208	16,366,262	16,629,000
Canada	456	207	5,494,788	5,583,000

DID YOU KNOW? The average US citizen "consumes" five times his or her own weight in paper annually!

ENVIRONMENTAL DISASTERS

NUCLEAR DISASTER In 1986, a reactor at Chernobyl, Ukraine, exploded. It killed 31 people, and sent tons of radioactive material into the atmosphere. Thousands of people were affected by radioactive contamination.

CHEMICAL SPILLS Waste mercury released into Minamata Bay, Japan, in 1952, caused thousands of people to develop paralysis and mental disease.

OIL SPILLS In 1989, the *Exxon Valdez* tanker ran aground in Alaska, and dispersed 34,450 tons (35,000 tonnes) of oil, which covered the shoreline and killed wildlife.

GARBAGE MOUNTAIN At Georgswerder, Germany, 196,200,000 cubic yards (150 million cubic meters) of waste form a landfill site 131 ft (40 m) high.

WATER CONTAMINATION Waste from industry, farming, and sewage can badly contamine the water supply. One of the most polluted rivers is the Huang He in China: a quart contains 0.085 oz of suspended solids (a liter contains 2.42 g).

GLOBAL WARMING High levels of carbon dioxide gas (CO_2) in the Earth's atmosphere are causing global temperatures to rise, leading to altered climate zones.

TOP CARBON DIOXIDE EMITTERS

COUNTRY	EMISSIONS	
	TONS	TONNES
United Arab Emirates	30.29	30.78
US	19.11	19.42
Singapore	18.75	19.05
Norway	16.58	16.85
Australia	15.87	16.12
Canada	14.43	14.66
Saudi Arabia	13.70	13.92
Kazakhstan	12.98	13.19
Trinidad and Tobago	12.98	13.19
Russia	11.90	12.09

Carbon dioxide (CO_2) emissions derive mainly from the burning of fossil fuels, such as oil and coal; cement manufacturing; and gas flaring. In the latter half of the 20th century growing industrialization has resulted in large increases in carbon output, which is seriously affecting world climate. Today, most countries actively monitor CO_2 output.

TOP WASTE PRODUCERS

COUNTRY	DOMESTIC WASTE PER HEAD PER YEAR	
	LB	KG
US	1,609	730
Australia	1,521	690
Canada	1,455	660
Finland	1,367	620
Iceland	1,235	560
Norway	1,124	510
Netherlands	1,102	500
Luxembourg	1,080	490
France	1,036	470
Denmark	1,014	460

DOMESTIC WASTE

ITEM	MINIMUM TIME TO DECOMPOSE
Apple core	20 days
Plastic	100 years
Glass	4,000 years

DID YOU KNOW? Each year, the average family throws away 270 glass bottles and jars, and 110 lb (50 kg) of plastic.

THE MOST COMMON TYPES OF LITTER

Chewing gum • Cigarette butts Matches • Bits of paper • Candy wrappers • Glass fragments Plastic fragments • Aluminum foil Chewing gum wrappers • Tickets

TOP WATER USERS

This list gives the volume of water used per person per year.

COUNTRY	GALLONS	LITERS
US	1,609	730
Australia	1,521	690
Canada	1,455	660

ENVIRONMENTAL CONCERNS

In 1997, MORI, a British market research organization, carried out a survey of almost 2,000 adults, asking them which conservation and environmental issues concerned them most. Pollution is clearly the primary concern, including air pollution, industrial pollution, and especially pollution caused by traffic. When considering the environment, most people think about issues that affect them directly, such as air quality. World issues such as deforestation, global warming, and destruction are not so important to them.

Air pollution

Exhaust fumes from cars and trucks

Too much traffic

Pollution of rivers, streams, and water

Pollution of seas; waste disposal at sea

Litter in streets and countryside

Pollution of beaches and coastline

Nuclear waste

Dumping of toxic and chemical waste

Destruction of the rainforests; deforestation

Animal testing

Increase in asthma rates from pollution

Loss of the greenbelt; overbuilding

Destruction of the ozone layer

Preservation of wildlife; protection of the countryside

Animal welfare

Lack of water; sufficient water to meet everyone's needs

Waste disposal

Crop spraying; use of insecticides

HOW TO SAVE WATER

STOP DRIPS A dripping faucet can waste about 19.8 gallons (90 liters) of water a week. It is worth checking and replacing worn washers.

QUICK SHOWERS Take a five-minute shower a day instead of a bath – it uses a third of the water.

USE WHAT YOU NEED Fill your kettle with just enough water for your needs, but don't fill it up every time you boil water. This will also reduce fuel bills.

SWITCH OFF Turn off the faucet when brushing your teeth. Leaving it running wastes almost 1.98 gallons (9 liters) a minute.

WAYS YOU CAN HELP

- Read or watch television programs about environmental issues.

- Take bottles, glass, paper, or cans for recycling. You can also recycle clothes and books.

- Volunteer your help to environmental charities.

- Select environmentally friendly products, and use recycled paper.

- Request information from an environmental organization, or join one.

- Visit or write a letter to your senator or representative about an environmental issue.

- Walk or bike to school instead of being driven.

- Turn off lights and other electrical appliances when not in use.

- Turn down the central heating by one degree: this will save ten percent of the energy used to heat your home.

- When ordinary lightbulbs are burned out, replace them with energy-efficient, compact fluorescent light bulbs. These lightbulbs will last much longer.

DEFORESTING COUNTRIES

AREA LOST 1990–1995

This list shows the area of forest lost in key countries between 1990 and 1995. The total global loss of tropical forest during this period was 217,552 sq miles (563,460 sq km), an area about four times the size of California.

COUNTRY	AREA LOST MILES	KM
Brazil	9,861	25,540
Indonesia	4,185	10,840
Dem. Rep. of the Congo	2,857	7,400
Bolivia	2,243	5,810
Mexico	1,961	5,080
Venezuela	1,942	5,030
Malaysia	1,544	4,000
Burma	1,494	3,870
Sudan	1,363	3,530
Thailand	1,270	3,290
Paraguay	1,263	3,270
Tanzania	1,247	3,230
Zambia	1,019	2,640
Colombia	1,012	2,620
Philippines	1,012	2,620
Angola	915	2,370
Peru	838	2,170
Ecuador	730	1,890
Cambodia	633	1,640

PERCENTAGE LOST

While Brazil tops the list of countries with the highest area of forest loss, because Brazil has so much rainforest its rate of deforestation is only 0.5 percent. Other countries are losing a much higher proportion of their total forest cover, as the following list shows:

COUNTRY	PERCENTAGE LOST PER YEAR
Lebanon	7.8
Jamaica	7.2
Afghanistan	6.8
Comoros	5.6
Philippines	3.5
Haiti	3.4
El Salvador	3.3
Costa Rica	3.0
Sierra Leone	3.0
Pakistan	2.9
Bahamas	2.6
Paraguay	2.6
Thailand	2.6
Jordan	2.5
Nicaragua	2.5
Malaysia	2.4
Honduras	2.3
Syria	2.2
Panama	2.1

TOP RECYCLABLE PRODUCTS

WATER Water can be recycled by watering plants with dirty dishwater.

PAPER Paper forms half of all garbage! Recycling reduces the need to fell trees, and decreases pollution caused by bleaching wood pulp.

GLASS This forms one-tenth of all household garbage. It can be recycled easily by crushing and melting.

ALUMINUM This is often used to make drink cans. Recycling reduces energy usage by 95 percent and pollution by 97 percent.

PLASTIC The wide range of different kinds of plastics available makes recycling hard. Some plastic products are graded at the time of manufacture to make sorting and recycling easier.

WORLD BELIEFS

RELIGIONS of the WORLD

TOP WORLD RELIGIONS

RELIGION	FOLLOWERS	MAIN AREAS PRACTICED
Christianity	1,965,993,000	Europe, Americas, Australasia
Islam	1,179,326,000	Asia, Africa
Hinduism	767,424,000	India
Buddhism	356,875,000	Asia
Native religions	244,164,000	Africa, Australasia, Americas, Southeast Asia
New religions	99,191,000	Asia
Sikhism	22,874,000	India
Judaism	15,050,000	North America, Asia

DID YOU KNOW? There are 146,406,000 atheists in the world. Atheists deny the existence of any kind of god.

NOBLE TRUTHS OF BUDDHISM

Buddhists believe in the Four Noble Truths, or holy principles, which summarize the Buddha's view of the world and humanity.

DUKKHA All forms of existence are subject to suffering.

SAMUDAYA The craving, or search, for pleasure is the source of suffering.

NIRVANA It is possible to be free from these cravings by achieving a state of peace and contentment called nirvana.

THE EIGHTFOLD PATH The way to nirvana is through the Eightfold Path of Buddhism.

THE FIVE PILLARS OF ISLAM

Islamic life is based on a set of rules called the Five Pillars of Islam. Muslims believe that by following these rules, they will reach heaven.

SHAHADAH The affirmation of faith in Islam: "There is no god but God, and Muhammad is the messenger of God."

SALAT Prayers five times a day, in the direction of the Ka'ba, the sacred shrine at the center of the mosque at Mecca.

SAWM The daily fast between daylight and dusk that is performed throughout the month of Ramadan.

ZAKAT Almsgiving, which entails contributing usually one-fortieth of the annual income for the poor and needy.

THE HAJJ The pilgrimage to Mecca in the 12th Islamic month, which all healthy Muslims should try to make at least once in their lifetime.

DID YOU KNOW? All able-bodied Muslims are required to defend Islam, whenever it is threatened in the lesser Jihad, or Holy War.

JEWISH RULES AND RITUALS

CIRCUMCISION Baby boys are circumcised eight days after birth.

SABBATH The weekly day of rest – from dusk on Friday until after dark on Saturday – commemorates the way God rested after the creation.

FOOD Jews eat only food that is *kosher*, or fit to eat. Animals must have been slaughtered according to specific rules.

ADULTHOOD At the age of 13, boys become *Bar Mitzvah* – adult members of Jewish life. There is a similar ceremony for girls, which is known as *Bat Mitzvah*.

SYNAGOGUE Jews visit the synagogue to pray on the Sabbath day (Saturday).

THE FIVE Ks OF SIKHISM

To prove their deep commitment to Sikhism, the Khalsa, or Pure Ones, must wear or carry five items.

KESH Hair must remain uncut and in a turban.

KANGHA The comb is a symbol of cleanliness.

KACHH An undergarment that is practical in battle and a symbol of chastity.

KIRPAN The dagger symbolizes resistance of evil.

KARA The steel bangle is a symbol of allegiance to God.

HINDU GODS AND GODDESSES

Hindus have many gods. Most important is the Triad of Vishnu, Shiva, and Brahma, and the unifying spirit of Brahman.

GOD	ROLE
Agni	God of fire
Brahma	The Creator
Durga	Warrior goddess
Ganesh	Elephant-headed god of luck
Indra	God of rain and thunder
Kali	Goddess of destruction
Lakshmi	Goddess of wealth and fortune
Mahadevi	The Great Goddess
Shiva	The Destroyer
Skanda	God of armies and battles
Sarasvati	Goddess of arts and music
Vishnu	The Preserver

SIKH GURUS

NAME	DATES
Nanak	1469–1539
Angad	1539–1552
Amar Das	1552–1574
Ram Das Sodhi	1574–1581
Arjun Mal	1581–1606
Hargobind	1606–1644
Har Rai	1644–1661
Hari Krishen	1661–1664
Tegh Bahadur	1664–1675
Gobind Rai	1675–1708

DID YOU KNOW?

Gobind Rai was a child when he became Guru. He introduced the name Singh ("lion") for his followers, and such rules as not cutting the hair.

OTHER WORLD FAITH FACTS

BAHA'I FAITH Based on the worship of one God, the Baha'i faith was founded in Persia (now Iran) in the 19th century by Baha'u'lla (1817–1892).

CONFUCIANISM Based on following the *Tao* (The Way), not a god, Confucianism teaches the wisdom of living a balanced life in harmony with nature.

JAINISM Based on nonviolence and rebirth, Jainism was founded in India in the sixth century BC by Mahavira (c.540–468 BC). Most Jains live in India.

TAOISM Taoism, which began in China in about the fourth century, has many popular gods. Taoists live in China and the Far East. It is symbolized by *yin* and *yang*, the balance of existence.

SHINTOISM Based on the worship of gods of nature, Shintoism started in Japan in the eighth century BC. Followers worship alone.

ZOROASTRIANISM Founded in Persia (now Iran) in c.1000 BC, Zoroastrianism is based on the balance of good and evil. Zoroaster was the major prophet. Most followers live in India and Iran.

KEY RELIGIOUS LEADERS

JESUS CHRIST – CHRISTIANITY Jesus, the son of God, was born in Bethelehem, now in modern Israel, in c.4 BC. From the age of 30, he began to preach and heal the sick. A few years later he was tried and executed by the Roman authorities in Jerusalem.

MUHAMMAD – ISLAM The Islamic faith is based on belief in one God, Allah. The most important messenger of Allah is Muhammad, the last and greatest of the 26 Islamic prophets, who was born in Mecca in c.AD 570.

SIDDHARTHA GAUTAMA – BUDDHISM The Buddhist religion is based on the teachings of Siddhartha Gautama, who was born in India c.563 BC. Brought up as a prince, he left his home, aged 29, giving up his riches, to lead a life of meditation and preaching. He was named Buddha, which means "the enlightened one."

GURU NANAK – SIKHISM The Sikh religion was founded by Guru Nanak, who was born in 1469 in the Punjab region of north India and Pakistan. It has now spread to North America and the UK.

JUDAISM Abraham was the first leader of the Hebrews. He was born in Ur, in present-day Iraq, in about 2000 BC.

HINDU BELIEFS

CASTE SYSTEM Hinduism divides people up into four groups, or varnas. These broad divisions are also split into smaller castes, or jatis. Traditionally, people would not mix with castes lower than their own, but today there is more social flexibility.

REINCARNATION Hindus believe in a cycle of death and rebirth – when we die, our souls live on in another person, animal, or plant. The Hindu goal is to live such a good life that the soul breaks this cycle and becomes part of Brahman.

HOLY RIVER Hindus consider the River Ganges in northern India to be sacred. The waters are believed to wash away sin. The ashes of the dead are often scattered there.

SACRED COW Hindus respect all animals, especially cows, as sacred beings. Feeding a cow is considered an act of worship.

FOOD Most Hindus are vegetarians.

SACRED MOUNTAINS

ARARAT, TURKEY In Christian tradition, it was on the peak of this mountain that Noah's Ark came to rest after the Flood.

ATHOS, GREECE The Holy Mountain of the Greek Orthodox religion is occupied by monasteries, forbidden to women, and even to female animals.

EVEREST, TIBET Everest is known to Tibetans as Chomolungma, or "Goddess Mother of the World."

MOUNT OF OLIVES, JERUSALEM A holy site for Jews and Christians alike; the Garden of Gethsemane, on the Mount of Olives, is where Christ was buried after the crucifixion.

OLYMPUS, GREECE The home of Zeus and other important gods of ancient Greece.

SINAI, ISRAEL The place where the Christian and Jewish God gave Moses the Ten Commandments.

RELIGIOUS BOOKS

RELIGION	BOOK
Christianity	Bible
Islam	Koran
Buddhism	Pali Canon (three books)
Judaism	Torah
Hinduism	Vedas (four books)
Sikhism	Guru Granth Sahib

119

WORLD FESTIVALS

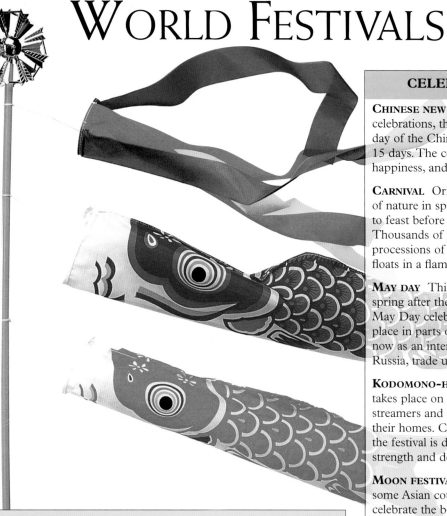

CELEBRATIONS AROUND THE WORLD

CHINESE NEW YEAR One of the world's most colorful celebrations, the Chinese New Year festival starts on the first day of the Chinese calendar, usually in February, and lasts for 15 days. The celebrations are based on bringing luck, health, happiness, and wealth throughout the coming year.

CARNIVAL Originally pagan festivals that celebrated the rebirth of nature in spring, carnivals later became seen as the last chance to feast before Lent, the Christian period of abstinence. Thousands of people line city streets around the world to watch processions of performers in elaborate costumes and majestic floats in a flamboyant spectacle.

MAY DAY This ancient fertility festival marked the first day of spring after the long, harsh months of winter. The traditional May Day celebration of dancing round the maypole still takes place in parts of northern Europe, but May Day is better known now as an international public holiday to honor workers. In Russia, trade union parades take place.

KODOMONO-HI This Japanese festival, meaning Children's Day, takes place on May 5. Families with young boys fly colorful streamers and enormous kites, in the shape of carp fish, above their homes. Carp fish symbolize courage and persistence, and the festival is designed to teach young boys the importance of strength and determination.

MOON FESTIVAL On the 15th day of the eighth lunar month, some Asian countries take part in a mid-autumn festival to celebrate the beauty of the moon, which is brighter and whiter than at any other time of the year. Moon-viewing parties are held and traditional moon cakes eaten. Prayers are addressed to the moon for protection from storms and for a good harvest.

DAY OF THE DEAD During this festival, Mexicans pray to the souls of their dead relatives so that they will return to the land of the living for just one night. They build altars in their homes and in cemeteries, and decorate them with cooked foods, candles, sugar skulls, and colorful flowers to welcome back the dead.

THANKSGIVING This is one of the most important festivals in the US. It marks the early settlers' first harvest in 1621 when they gave thanks to God that they survived their first harsh winter. Each year, on the fourth Thursday in November, families gather for a Thanksgiving feast of turkey, cranberry sauce, and pumpkin pie.

HALLOWEEN This ancient Celtic festival takes place on October 31, when it was once believed that witches and spirits roamed the world. Children in Europe and North America dress up in disguises and, as night falls, go from door to door, asking "trick or treat?" Glowing pumpkins are made to ward off evil spirits.

CHRISTIAN FESTIVALS

ADVENT The Christian year begins on Advent Sunday – the fourth Sunday before Christmas. Advent means "coming" and the period is one of preparation for Christmas. Advent calendars and candles count off the days until Christmas Day.

CHRISTMAS Held on December 25, this is a celebration of the birth of Jesus Christ. The many Christmas customs include giving presents and cards, decorating Christmas trees, singing carols, and eating traditional meals with the family.

EPIPHANY Christmas ends with Epiphany, which commemorates the visit of the Three Wise Men to Bethlehem. In Spain and Italy, presents are exchanged.

LENT Beginning on Ash Wednesday, this is a 40-day period of preparation for Easter, recalling the 40 days Jesus spent fasting in the wilderness. It is a period of spiritual discipline and many Christians abstain from certain foods and luxuries.

EASTER This is the major festival in the Christian year. On Good Friday solemn prayers are held to commemorate the death of Jesus on the cross. Easter Sunday falls three days later, and is a celebration of his resurrection. Easter eggs are given out.

PENTECOST/WHITSUN This celebrates the day when God sent his Holy Spirit to the apostles, ten days after the ascension of Jesus. It marks the beginning of the Christian Church.

HINDU FESTIVALS

FESTIVAL	MEANING
Ramanavami	Birthday of Lord Rama
Rathayatra	Pilgrimage of the Chariot at Jaggannath
Jhulanayatra	Swinging the Lord Krishna
Rakshabandhana	Tying on Lucky Threads
Janamashtami	Birthday of Lord Krishna
Durga-puja	Homage to Goddess Durga
Navaratri	Festival of Nine Nights
Lakshmi-puja	Homage to Goddess Lakshmi
Diwali, Dipavali	New Year festival of Lights
Guru Nanak Janati	Birthday of Guru Nanak
Sarasvati-puja	Homage to Goddess Sarasvati
Maha-sivaratri	Great Night of Lord Shiva
Holi	Festival of Fire
Dolayatra	Swing Festival

DID YOU KNOW? Every year, millions of Hindus flock to the River Ganges, India. The waters are believed to wash away sin.

SIKH HOLY DAYS

The Sikh faith was founded by Guru Nanak in 1469 and is based on the worship of one God. There are three main holy days:

BAISAKHI New Year and formation of Khalsa.

DIWALI Release from prison of Guru Hargobind, the sixth guru.

GURU NANAK Birthday of the founder of Sikhism.

ISLAMIC FESTIVALS

Most Islamic festivals commemorate events in the life of the religion's founder, the Prophet Muhammad:

NEW YEAR'S DAY On this day in AD 622, Muhammad set out from Mecca to Medina. Gifts are exchanged.

BIRTHDAY OF MUHAMMAD This day is celebrated with processions and lectures on the life of Muhammad.

NIGHT OF ASCENT This is a celebration of the night when Muhammad was taken up to heaven.

RAMADAN During the month of Ramadan, Muslims do not eat or drink between sunrise and sunset.

NIGHT OF POWER To remember the first revelation of the Koran to Muhammad by angel Gabriel, Muslims pray at night.

FEAST OF BREAKING OF THE FAST To mark the end of Ramadan, Muslims give food to the poor, and exchange presents.

FESTIVAL OF SACRIFICE Taking place after the Mecca pilgrimage, a sheep is sacrificed and shared with the poor.

BUDDHIST FESTIVALS

WHEN CELEBRATED	FESTIVAL
Sakyamuni (or Wesak)	Birth of Siddhartha Gautama
Bodhi Day	Buddha's enlightenment
Parinirvana	Buddha's ascent from Earth
Phagguna	Origin of life cycle

DID YOU KNOW? In the Esala Perahera festival in Sri Lanka, Buddha's tooth is paraded in a casket on an elephant's back.

JEWISH FESTIVALS

ROSH HASHANAH (NEW YEAR) This is a time of quiet reflection and soul-searching. A ram's horn trumpet, or shofar, is blown as a call to make sinners repent.

YOM KIPPUR (DAY OF ATONEMENT) The most solemn event in the Jewish calendar. Jews spend the day praying, fasting, and seeking God's forgiveness.

SUKKOTH (FEAST OF TABERNACLES) A seven-day harvest festival during which families eat meals outside under booths called sukkahs. They commemorate the way God looked after the Israelites in the wilderness on their way to the Promised Land.

SIMCHAT TORAH (REJOICING OF THE LAW) During this celebration, the scrolls of the Law (or Torah) are paraded around the synagogue, followed by children singing and dancing.

HANUKKAH (FESTIVAL OF LIGHTS) An eight-day midwinter festival that is marked by the lighting of candles. Each is lit from the central candle on a candlestick called a menorah. This symbolizes a drop of oil that was used to light the reclaimed Temple of Jerusalem in 164 BC. Children receive presents, and games are played.

PURIM (FEAST OF LOTS) A thanksgiving celebrating Esther's victory over Haman, which prevented a Jewish massacre. During this festival parties are held in which masks and elaborate costumes are worn.

PESACH (PASSOVER) This week-long spring festival celebrates the Exodus of the Jews from Egypt, when the angel of death passed over the Israelites, sparing their lives. In place of ordinary bread, unleavened bread (matzoh) is eaten.

HOLOCAUST REMEMBRANCE DAY This day commemorates the mass murder of an estimated six million European Jews by the German Nazi regime during World War II.

ISRAEL INDEPENDENCE DAY This is a modern celebration, commemorating the creation of the political state of Israel as a homeland for the world's Jews in 1948.

SHAVUOTH (FEAST OF WEEKS) This festival celebrates God giving the Ten Commandments to Moses on Mount Sinai, and the offering of the first fruits. Synagogues are decorated with flowers and dairy foods are eaten.

DID YOU KNOW? The symbol of Islam is a star and a crescent moon.

DID YOU KNOW? The symbol of Judaism is the Star of David.

THE CHRISTIAN WORLD

EARLY CHRISTIAN TIMELINE

c.6–4 BC Jesus of Nazareth is born in Bethlehem.

c.27 John the Baptist baptizes Jesus, who begins three years of preaching and healing the sick.

c.AD 30 Jesus is crucified on a cross. Three days later he is raised from the dead (the Resurrection).

c.37 Saul of Tarsus is converted from Judaism to Christianity. He is now known as Paul.

c.41–65 Paul goes on journeys, spreading Christianity in the eastern Mediterranean, until he reaches Rome.

c.67 Paul is imprisoned and executed in Rome on the orders of Emperor Nero.

c.40–100 Despite persecution by the Romans, Christianity gradually spreads throughout the Roman Empire.

c.380 Christianity becomes the official Roman religion.

MAIN CHRISTIAN BELIEFS

GOD For Christians, God is the creator of the universe and life.

JESUS CHRIST Christians believe Jesus is the only Son of God, who has existed with God the Father from before time began.

JESUS' BIRTH Jesus was incarnated, or given human form when, by the power of the Holy Spirit, his human mother, the Virgin Mary, gave birth to him.

WHY JESUS WAS SENT Christ appeared to reconcile people with God, as human sin had broken the relationship with God.

CRUCIFIXION Through the death of Jesus upon the Cross at Calvary, God broke the power of sin and evil.

RESURRECTION When Jesus rose from the dead on the third day, God showed the triumph of life over death and gave the promise of everlasting life to people who believe in Jesus.

THE HOLY TRINITY Christians believe that God is one but has three co-equal "persons:" God the Father, God the Son (Jesus Christ), and God the Holy Spirit.

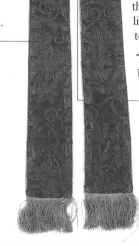

PATRON SAINTS

Christian saints are devout people who have lived – and often died – for the Christian cause. They often oversee a particular profession or circumstance.

PROFESSION/CIRCUMSTANCE	SAINT
Authors and journalists	Francis de Sales
Aviators	Joseph of Cupertino
Business people	Homobonus
Cab drivers	Fiacre
Children	Nicholas
Communications	Gabriel the Archangel
Desperate situations	Jude (and Rita of Cascia)
Possessed by devil	Gemma Galgani
Disabled	Giles
Doctors	Luke (and Cosmas and Damian)
Firefighters	Florian
Homes and families	Joseph
Lost articles	Antony of Padua
Nature and animals	Francis of Assisi
Office workers	Catherine of Siena
Race relations	Martin de Porres
Schools and universities	Thomas Aquinas
Sweethearts	Valentine

SYMBOLIC NUMBERS

NUMBER	MEANING
1	The one God
3	The Holy Trinity
7	God created the world in 7 days; 7 deadly sins
10	10 Commandments 10 Plagues of Egypt
12	12 days of Christmas 12 disciples 12 tribes of Israel
13	There were 13 at Jesus's fateful Last Supper
40	Moses' 40 days in the desert; the Flood lasted 40 days and 40 nights

LONGEST-SERVING POPES

The head of the Roman Catholic Church is the Pope, who traditionally lives in the Vatican in Rome. Popes are usually chosen from the ranks of cardinals, who are customarily men of advanced years. As a result, it is unusual for a pope to remain in office for more than 20 years.

POPE	TIME IN OFFICE	YEARS
Pius IX	1846–1878	31
Leo XIII	1878–1903	2?

AMAZING FACT! Leo XIII died aged 93, making him the oldest pope on this list.

Peter	c. 42–67	c. 2?
Pius VI	1775–1799	2?
Adrian I	772–795	2?
Pius VII	1800–1823	2?
Alexander III	1159–1181	2?
Sylvester	314–335	2?
Leo I	440–461	2?

DID YOU KNOW? The shortest-serving pope was Urban VII (d.1590), who held office for just 12 days before he died of malaria.

CHRISTIAN POPULATIONS

Christianity is the world's most widespread religion, with 1.6 billion Christians worldwide.

COUNTRY	POPULATION
US	224,457,000
Brazil	139,000,000
Mexico	86,210,000
Germany	67,170,000
Philippines	63,470,000
UK	51,060,000
Italy	47,690,000

SEVEN DEADLY SINS

Pride • Rage • Envy • Lust
Greed • Gluttony • Laziness

RELIGIOUS OBJECTS

ICON Painting of Christ or Mary.

CRUCIFIX Statuette of Christ crucified on the cross.

ROSARY BEADS A prayer is recited for each bead.

CHRISTIAN DENOMINATIONS

The Christian church is split into many denominations, but all are united in their belief in the life and teachings of Christ.

DENOMINATION	ADHERENTS
Roman Catholic	872,104,646
Slavonic Orthodox	92,523,987
United (including Lutheran/Reformed)	65,402,685
Pentecostal	58,999,862
Anglican	52,499,051
Baptist	50,321,923
Lutheran (excluding United)	44,899,837
Reformed (Presbyterian)	43,445,520
Methodist	31,718,508
Disciples (Restorationists)	8,783,192

DID YOU KNOW? At the Last Supper, Jesus broke bread and poured wine, which he blessed and shared with his disciples, saying that the bread was his body and the wine was his blood. At Eucharist, or mass, Christians partake ritually of the body and blood of Christ.

MODERN SAINTS AND MARTYRS

MOTHER TERESA (1910–1997) Born Agnes Gonxha Bojaxhiu, in Albania, Mother Teresa of Calcutta devoted her whole life to tending poor and dying children in India. She was awarded the Nobel Peace Prize in 1979, and is regarded by some to be a modern-day saint.

OSCAR ROMERO (1917–1980) Romero cared for the poor in El Salvador, where he alienated those who exploited them, and was murdered.

DIETRICH BONHOEFFER (1906–1945) A Lutheran theologian who opposed Hitler, Bonhoeffer sought to resolve the conflicts of World War II without bloodshed. He was executed for his stand in 1945.

MARTIN LUTHER KING, JR. (1929–1968) Champion of civil rights in the US, King was assassinated for a commitment born of his Christian faith.

JOSEPHINE BUTLER (1828–1907) Butler fought against exploitation of women and is remembered by the Church of England on December 30.

THE SEVEN SACRAMENTS

The most important Christian ceremonies are the sacred rites known as sacraments. The Roman Catholic and Orthodox Churches recognize seven sacraments.

BAPTISM The rite of entry into the Church; believers are cleansed in water.

CONFIRMATION After baptism, believers reaffirm their allegiance to the Church.

EUCHARIST, OR MASS Believers receive the bread and wine of the body of Christ.

PENANCE Believers turn to God to confess their sins.

EXTREME UNCTION Prayers, anointing with oil, or touch, help prepare the sick for death.

ORDINATION The ceremony in which the Church appoints people as priests and deacons.

MARRIAGE To Christians, marriage symbolizes the relationship of Christ with his Church.

SOME OF THE BIGGEST RELIGIOUS ORDERS

Monks, nuns, and friars are people who choose to live apart from the world as members of religious orders, some almost as ancient as Christianity.

JESUITS Founded in 1540 by St. Ignatius Loyola, the Jesuits are the biggest religious order. Today, there are about 33,000 Jesuit monks worldwide.

BENEDICTINES Founded in 1530 by St. Benedict, Benedictine monks pass their time in prayer, reading, and manual work. Today, there are about 9,000 Benedictine monks and more than 24,000 nuns.

CARMELITES Founded in 1451 and re-formed in 1562, the Carmelite nuns are a poor order. There are more than 24,000 Carmelite nuns today.

FRANCISCANS Founded in 1209 by St. Francis of Assisi, Franciscan friars live very frugally. There are still about 20,000 Franciscans worldwide.

THE BIBLE

SEVEN DAYS OF CREATION

1 On the first day, God created night and day, separating light from dark.

2 On the second day, God created the sky, which he called Heaven.

3 On the third day, God created land, dividing the waters into seas.

4 On the fourth day, God created the Sun, the Moon, and the stars.

5 On the fifth day, God created living creatures on the land and in the sea.

6 On the sixth day, God created a man and a woman.

7 On the seventh day, creation of the world was complete and God rested.

TEN PLAGUES OF EGYPT

In Exodus 7–13, Moses asks the pharaoh of Egypt to release the Israelites from slavery. When the king refuses, God strikes the country with a series of ten horrible disasters, which are known as the Ten Plagues of Egypt.

1 The Nile River turns to blood.

2 Frogs cover the land of Egypt.

3 Lice crawl over all men and women.

4 Swarms of flies attack people.

5 Disease strikes all livestock.

6 Boils afflict people and animals.

7 Hail and thunder damage crops.

8 The ground is covered by locusts.

9 Darkness lasts for three days.

10 All first-born children are slain.

THE TEN COMMANDMENTS

The set of rules or Commandments that God gave to Moses (Exodus 20) showed people how to live together in harmony.

1 You shall have no other gods before me.

2 You shall not make for yourself an idol.

3 You shall not misuse the name of the Lord your God.

4 Remember the Sabbath day by keeping it holy.

5 Honor your father and your mother.

6 You shall not murder.

7 You shall not commit adultery.

8 You shall not steal.

9 You shall not give false testimony against your neighbor.

10 You shall not covet... anything that belongs to your neighbor.

BIBLICAL SAYINGS

Some of our most familiar sayings and words come from the Bible. Here are a few you are sure to recognize, with their Bible references so you can look them up.

A MAN AFTER HIS OWN HEART
1 Samuel 13.14

ALL THINGS TO ALL MEN
1 Corinthians 9.22

APPLE OF YOUR EYE Psalms 17.8

BY THE SKIN OF YOUR TEETH Job 19.20

CRUMBS FROM THE RICH MAN'S TABLE Luke 16.21

PRIDE BEFORE A FALL Proverbs 16

SCAPEGOAT Leviticus 16

SEE EYE TO EYE Isaiah 52.8

SEPARATING THE SHEEP FROM THE GOATS Matthew 25.32

THE FOUR CORNERS OF THE EARTH Isaiah 11.12; Revelation 7.1

THE LEFT HAND DOESN'T KNOW WHAT THE RIGHT IS DOING Matthew 6.3

WOLF IN SHEEP'S CLOTHING Matthew 7.15

WHEELS WITHIN WHEELS Ezekiel 1.16, 10.10

ANIMALS MOST MENTIONED

ANIMAL	TESTAMENT		TOTAL
	OLD	NEW	
Sheep	155	45	200
Lamb	153	35	188
Lion	167	9	176
Ox	156	10	166
Ram	165	0	165
Horse	137	27	164
Bullock	152	0	152
Ass	142	8	150
Goat	131	7	138
Camel	56	6	62
Serpent	38	15	53
Kid	50	1	51
Calf	41	7	48
Dog	31	9	40
Dove	30	10	40
Eagle	30	4	34
Locust	24	4	28
Heifer	19	1	20
Owl	16	0	16

AMAZING FACT! There is no mention of cats or rats in the Bible!

OLD TESTAMENT LEADERS

LEADER (FOUND IN)	FAMOUS FOR
Abraham (Genesis 11–12)	First patriarch of the Israelite nation
Joseph (Genesis 41–46)	Protected Egypt from famine
Moses (Exodus 12–14)	Led the Israelites out of slavery
David (1 Samuel 17)	Defeated Goliath, the giant Philistine
Solomon (1 Kings 5–8)	Built a temple for worshipping God

GIFTS FROM THE MAGI

WISE MAN	GIFT
Melchior	Gold
Balthazar	Myrrh
Gaspar or Caspar	Frankincense

AMAZING FACT? In Matthew 2, the Bible says that Magi, or Wise Men, came from the east to Jerusalem, bearing gifts for the infant Jesus. However, contrary to belief, nowhere does it say how many Wise Men there were, nor does it mention their names.

PARABLES TOLD BY JESUS

A parable is a short story with a hidden message.

THE GOOD SAMARITAN (Luke 10) A Jewish man who has been attacked by thieves lay by the wayside. Two passing Jewish holy men ignored him, but a Samaritan helped him, even though Samaritans and Jews were sworn enemies.

THE SOWER (Mark 4) When a farmer sowed his seed, some was eaten by birds, and some fell on stones and was wasted. Only the seed that fell on good soil produced a thriving crop. Jesus is like the sower, but sows words rather than seeds.

THE GOOD SHEPHERD (Matthew 18) A shepherd had a flock of 100 sheep. When one strayed, he left his flock to find it.

THE PRODIGAL SON (Luke 15) The younger of two sons left home and wasted all his money. Poor, hungry, and repentant, the son returned home, and was welcomed by his father who instantly forgave him and welcomed him back with open arms.

THE BOOKS OF THE BIBLE

OLD TESTAMENT

Genesis • Exodus • Leviticus
Numbers • Deuteronomy
Joshua • Judges • Ruth
1 Samuel • 2 Samuel
1 Kings • 2 Kings
1 Chronicles • 2 Chronicles
Ezra • Nehemiah • Esther
Job • Psalms • Proverbs
Ecclesiastes • Song of
Solomon • Isaiah • Jeremiah
Lamentations • Ezekiel
Daniel • Hosea • Joel
Amos • Obadiah • Jonah
Micah • Nahum • Habakkuk
Zephaniah • Haggai
Zechariah • Malachi

NEW TESTAMENT

Matthew • Mark • Luke
John • Acts of the Apostles
Romans • 1 Corinthians
2 Corinthians • Galatians
Ephesians • Philippians
Colossians • 1 Thessalonians
2 Thessalonians • 1 Timothy
2 Timothy • Titus • Philemon
Hebrews • James • 1 Peter
2 Peter • 1 John • 2 John
3 John • Jude • Revelation

DID YOU KNOW? In the 15th century, when many people were not able to read, Bible stories, such as Noah's Ark (Genesis 6–7), were often depicted in stained-glass windows or in frescoes on church walls for everyone to see and enjoy.

JESUS' MIRACLES

MIRACLE	FOUND IN
Feeding the crowd with five loaves and two fish	Matthew 14
Walking on the waters of the lake	Matthew 14
Raising a child from the dead	Mark 5
Giving sight to a blind beggar	Luke 18
Turning water into wine	John 2
Calming the storm	Mark 4–5

DID YOU KNOW? The first book ever printed was a Latin version of the Bible in 1455. It was the work of the German inventor of moveable type, Johannes Gutenberg. Before then all Bibles were handwritten by monks.

TWELVE DISCIPLES OF JESUS

The disciples were the original followers of Jesus, who were chosen to teach people about Christianity. They were later joined by Paul and Matthias and, after the death of Jesus, became known as apostles, or messengers of Christ.

ANDREW, a fisherman from Galilee, he is said to have died on an x-shaped cross.

BARTHOLOMEW, or Nathanael, is thought to have become a missionary in Armenia and India.

JAMES THE GREATER was the brother of John and became one of Jesus' closest friends.

JAMES THE LESSER was the son of Alphaeus and probably shorter than the other disciple, James.

JOHN, known as John the Apostle, wrote one of the gospels in the New Testament.

JUDAS ISCARIOT betrayed Jesus to the Romans in return for 30 pieces of silver.

JUDAS, SON OF JAMES, was also known by the name of Thaddaeus.

MATTHEW, or Levi, was a tax collector before becoming a disciple of Jesus.

SIMON PETER was described by Jesus as "the rock" because of his solid faith.

PHILIP housed the Christian leader Paul on his visit to Caesarea in Judea.

SIMON THE ZEALOT is thought to have been a member of the fanatical Zealots.

THOMAS, or Doubting Thomas, refused to believe that Jesus had risen again.

MYTHS and LEGENDS

GREEK AND ROMAN GODS AND GODDESSES

GREEK	ROLE	ROMAN
Aphrodite	Goddess of love	Venus
Apollo	God of the arts and medicine	Apollo
Ares	God of war	Mars
Artemis	Goddess of hunting	Diana
Athene	Goddess of wisdom	Minerva
Demeter	Goddess of crops and soil fertility	Ceres
Dionysus	God of wine and revelry	Bacchus
Hephaestos	God of fire and craftsmanship	Vulcan
Hera	Goddess of marriage and childbirth	Juno
Hermes	God of travel, roads, trade	Mercury
Hestia	Goddess of the hearth and home	Vesta
Poseidon	God of the sea	Neptune
Zeus	Ruler of the gods	Jupiter

THE NINE MUSES

The Muses were daughters of the god Zeus and the Titan Mnemosyne. Originally they were deities associated with mountains and springs, but later they became goddesses of the arts and followers of the god Apollo.

MUSE	ART
Calliope	Poetry and eloquence
Clio	History
Erato	Love poetry
Euterpe	Poetry and flute-playing
Melpomene	Tragedy
Polyhymnia	Song and mime
Terpsichore	Dancing
Thalia	Poetry and comedy
Urania	Astronomy

LITTLE PEOPLE

ELVES, SPRITES, AND FAIRIES Often from mountainous areas, these mischievous folk cast spells and play tricks on humans, such as losing things and causing fights.

DWARFS Created from the maggots in the flesh of the first giant Ymir, dwarfs were wise. They lived underground and were skilled craftspeople.

LEPRECHAUNS Irish sprites, often depicted as little old men who will reveal the position of a pot of gold to anyone who can catch them.

MYTHICAL PLACES

ASGARD The fortified home of the Norse gods.

ATLANTIS An island, first mentioned by Greek philosopher Plato (427–347 BC), said to have sunk beneath the Atlantic Ocean.

AVALON The island where King Arthur is said to have gone at the end of his life.

EL DORADO An imaginary land of gold and riches that encouraged the Spanish to conquer South America.

NIFLHEIM The Norse realm of the dead.

SHANGRI-LA A paradise on earth, after the fictional Tibetan land of eternal youth in the novel *The Lost Horizon* (1933) by James Hilton.

UTOPIA A place of perfection as described in Sir Thomas More's *Utopia* (1516).

VALHALLA The home, in Asgard, of Norse warriors slain in battle.

HERAKLES' TWELVE LABORS

The king of Tiryns gave Greek hero Herakles twelve tasks, as penance for killing his own wife and children. Only when he succeeded in all of them would he be granted immortality.

1. Slay the Nemean lion
2. Kill the Lernean Hydra
3. Catch the Arcadian stag
4. Destroy the Erymanthian boar
5. Cleanse the Augean stables
6. Destroy the man-eating birds that lived by Lake Stymphalos
7. Capture the Cretan bull
8. Catch the horses of the Thracian Diomedes
9. Gain the beautiful girdle of Hippolyta, Queen of the Amazons
10. Capture the cattle that belonged to the three-bodied monster Geryon
11. Take the apples of the Hesperides
12. Capture Cerberus from Hades

HERAKLES AND THE ERYMANTHIAN BOAR

DID YOU KNOW? In Greek mythology, Herakle was the only human to be granted immortal

EGYPTIAN GODS AND GODDESSES

Anubis	Jackal-headed god of embalming
Bastet	Cat goddess
Geb	God of the sky
Hapy	God of Nile floods
Hathor	Cow goddess, guardian of women
Horus	Falcon-headed sky god
Isis	Divine mother, wife of Osiris
Khnum	Ram-headed creator
Neith	Mother goddess
Nut	Goddess of the sky
Osiris	God of underworld
Ptah	Creator god
Ra-Atum	Sun god
Sekhmet	Lion-headed goddess
Seth	God of storms
Shu	God of air
Tefnut	God of moisture
Thoth	Ibis-headed god

NORSE GODS AND GODDESSES

Balder	God of light
Bragi	God of poetry
Forseti	God of justice, son of Balder
Freyr	God of fertility
Freyja	Goddess of fertility
Frigg	Goddess of fertility
Hoder	Blind god
Hoenir	Silent god
Idun	Spring goddess
Loki	Trickster – part god and part giant
Njörd	God of the sea
Odin	Chief god
Skädi	Goddess of mountains
Thor	War god, Odin's son
Tyr	Sky god, son of Odin and Frigg
Vali	Odin's youngest son

! DID YOU KNOW?
According to Norse myth the world would end at the battle of Ragnarök.

MAYA AND AZTEC GODS

CHAC

MAYA

Kinich-Ahau	Sun god
Itzamna	Creator god
Ixchel	Fertility goddess
Tohil	God of fire
Ah Puch	God of death
Pauahtun	Thunder god
Hun Hunahpu	Corn god
Jaguar god	Fertility god
Chac	Rain god

AZTEC

Cinteotl	Corn god
Coatlicue	Earth goddess
Huehueotl	Fire god
Huitzilopochtli	War god
Ometeotl	Supreme creator
Quetzalcoatl	Wind god
Tezcatlipoca	Creator god
Tlaloc	Rain god
Xolotl	Coyote god

MYTHICAL MONSTERS

CENTAURS In Greek mythology, a creature with the lower body of a horse and the torso and head of a man.

VAMPIRE In Eastern European legend, a dark, undead creature, who wakes at dusk and feeds on human blood.

DRAGON A usually evil, fire-breathing, reptilian beast that often appears in European myths. Chinese dragons, however, are benevolent.

GORGONS Three monster sisters with wings, claws, and snakes for hair. One, Medusa, was killed by the hero Perseus.

SPHINX A mythical creature of ancient Greece and Egypt that had the body of a lion, a woman's head, and bird's wings.

HARPIES In Greek mythology the Harpies were birds with women's heads and sharp talons that preyed on people's souls.

MEDUSA

MINOTAUR A human-eating monster, part human, part bull, that lived on the Greek island of Crete.

MYTHICAL GIANTS

ANTAEUS A giant in Greek mythology, slain by Herakles. He was said to be 60 cubits – about 90 ft (27.4 m) – tall.

ATLAS In Greek mythology, the giant who supports the heavens. Mercator's book of maps (1595) shows him holding the world on his shoulders. Today, a collection of maps is known as an atlas.

CYCLOPES A race of giants, each with a single eye. According to Greek myth, they worked in the forge of the god Vulcan.

ENCELADUS In Greek legend, the most powerful of the hundred-armed giant sons of Uranus. Legend has it that the flames of the volcano Mount Etna are the breath of Enceladus.

GARGANTUA A giant in medieval legend. The word "gargantuan," meaning 'huge,' comes from his name.

GOLIATH The giant slain by David in the Bible. He was said to be 6 cubits and a span tall, or 9 ft 3 in (2.8 m).

ORION In Greek myth, a giant hunter, himself slain by Diana the huntress. The star constellation of Orion is named after him.

TITANS In Greek mythology, the race of giants who ruled the universe before Kronos, their leader, was overthrown by Zeus.

YMIR In Norse mythology, the first giant from whose body Odin and his brothers create the Universe.

PREDICTIONS <u>and the</u> UNEXPLAINED

! DID YOU KNOW?
The word "zodiac" is from a Greek word meaning "circle of life."

THE TWELVE SIGNS OF THE ZODIAC

ARIES The ram (March 21–April 20). Aries people are courageous, passionate, and kind, but can have a hot temper!

TAURUS The bull (April 21–May 21). Taurean people are practical and reliable, but with a stubborn streak!

GEMINI The twins (May 22–June 21). People born under this sign are versatile and quick-witted.

CANCER The crab (June 22–July 22). Cancerians are sensitive, home-loving, and protective.

LEO The lion (July 23–August 23). The typical Leo is faithful, generous, and dramatic!

VIRGO The virgin (August 24–September 22). Virgos are cautious, private, and practical.

LIBRA The scales (September 23–October 23). A Libran is diplomatic and fair.

SCORPIO The scorpion (October 24–November 22). Scorpios are intense, loyal, and private.

SAGITTARIUS The archer (November 23–December 21). A Sagittarian is honest and bold.

CAPRICORN The goat (December 22–January 20). Capricorns are cautious, disciplined, and hard-working.

AQUARIUS The water-bearer (January 21–February 18). Aquarians are independent and often opinionated!

PISCES The fishes (February 19–March 20). A Piscean is imaginative, intuitive, and can be changeable.

DREAM MEANINGS

FLYING Many people dream that they are flying. This can often mean that the dreamer, in waking life, desires freedom and wishes to cast off the problems and ties of the world below.

SWIMMING Water symbolizes the emotions, and these dreams could be an indication of your emotional well-being. Are you swimming confidently, or struggling, perhaps even drowning?

FORGETTING YOUR LINES Performing in a play and forgetting your lines is a classic anxiety dream that often indicates a lack of self-confidence or problems with communication.

TREES AND FLOWERS A tree might represent natural growth, strength, and stability. Dreams about flowers suggest a natural, healthy life, and sexuality.

GHOST STORIES

VANISHING HITCHHIKER A young girl is given a lift, but mysteriously vanishes during the journey. The baffled driver finds out that the girl died years before at the very spot where he picked her up. Different versions of this story exist all over the world.

ROMAN LEGION In 1953, an Englishman called Harry Martindale saw a ghostly legion of Roman soldiers marching through the cellar of the Treasurer's House in York, England. Their legs appeared to be chopped off at the knee, which may be because the old Roman road was below the cellar floor.

PREDICTIONS THAT WERE WRONG

"This telephone has too many shortcomings to be seriously considered as a means of communication." *Western Union internal memo, 1876*

"I think there is a world market for maybe five computers." *Thomas Watson, chairman of IBM, 1943*

"Rail travel at high speed is not possible, because passengers…would die of asphyxia [suffocation]." *Dr. Dionysius Lardner, Irish scientist, 1793–1859*

UNEXPLAINED MONSTERS

LOCH NESS MONSTER "Nessie," a huge dinosaur-like sea monster, is reputed to live in Loch Ness, UK.

YETI Also known as the Abominable Snowman, the Yeti is a hairy man-beast that is alleged to roam the Himalayas. Giant footprints are cited as proof.

BIG FOOT Sometimes called Sasquatch, this hairy, humanlike creature allegedly dwells in North America.

HOW TO PROTECT YOURSELF AGAINST A VAMPIRE

The legend of the vampire has terrified people across the world for centuries. Lurking in the shadows, waiting for nightfall and their next meal of human blood, they are reputed to possess superhuman strength, and can transform themselves into animals such as bats and wolves. Here are some ways to make sure you never get attacked by one!

RINGING BELLS These are supposed to drive away the undead.

BLACK DOGS Gypsies believe black dogs are the enemies of vampires – but, unfortunately, some experts believe they may act as vampires' assistants.

FISHNETS AND KNOTS Draping fishnets and knotted string around doorways or on graves distracts vampires, because they allegedly feel compelled to untangle them.

GARLIC The classic vampire deterrent is a bulb of garlic worn around the neck or rubbed around doors and windows. Today, eating garlic bread and chicken Kiev may be just as effective.

HOLY ARTICLES Items such as crosses, icons, holy water, and incense usually scare vampires away and may even stop them from returning to their graves. Holy water can be thrown at them or be sprinkled on their graves. Crosses painted with tar are said to be very effective – especially if the vampire gets stuck to them.

HOLLY OR JUNIPER Keeping branches of certain trees in the house will deter vampires; if you leave branches on the floor vampires may even trip over them in the dark.

MIRRORS Vampires are driven mad by mirrors hung on doors because they can't see their own reflections – which must make brushing their hair very difficult.

STEALING THEIR LEFT SOCK Effective only for certain species of vampire – and only if you dare get that close.

STAKES, KNIVES, AND PINS Plunging these weapons into the heart of a sleeping vampire is one way of disposing of him or her – but it must be done in a single blow and is extremely messy…

SUNLIGHT In many horror films, vampires dissolve into dust as soon as a sunbeam hits them. However, in the novel *Dracula*, Count Dracula manages to go out in daylight without any ill effects, so don't rely on this method.

WATER Vampires hate water, so if you have the chance, try to push your vampire into the bath!

MYSTERIOUS PLACES

PYRAMIDS Recent discoveries have deepened the mystery of the Pyramids of Giza in Egypt. Some people now believe the pyramids were deliberately aligned with the star belt of Orion.

ULURU Also known as Ayers Rock, Uluru has been sacred to the Aboriginal people in Australia for hundreds of years.

STONEHENGE Even today, nobody knows why or how this famous stone circle in southern England was built.

MACHU PICCHU High up in the Andean mountains of Peru, the Inca city of Machu Pichu remained hidden for centuries.

HOW TO MAKE A WISH

CANDLES A wish is supposed to come true if you make it when you blow out the candles on your birthday cake.

BONES If you pull part a chicken's "wishbone" with another person, and you pull away the longer piece, you can make a wish.

PUDDINGS The person who finds the sixpence (or any small coin wrapped in foil) in a Christmas pudding can make a wish.

UNEXPLAINED HAPPENINGS

SPONTANEOUS HUMAN COMBUSTION It is popularly believed that people may suddenly burst into flames for no apparent reason. The fire is so hot that the body is reduced to ashes.

DISAPPEARANCES Vanishing people, and even entire ships and aircraft, have been put down to such phenomena as the mysterious "Bermuda Triangle."

POLTERGEISTS One of the most violent of ghostly manifestations, these restless spirits allegedly move or throw furniture and objects around rooms.

WAYS OF PREDICTING THE FUTURE

Words ending in "-mancy" refer to types of divination, or ways of predicting the future by observing various natural and other phenomena. There are hundreds of methods, of which these are some of the most common – and strangest:

AILUROMANCY By observing the way a cat jumps.

ALEUROMANCY Using flour. The Chinese baked fortunes in dough – the fortune cookie is the well-known modern example.

ANTHOMANCY From flowers – we know this from the practice of removing petals from flowers and reciting, "She loves me, she loves me not!"

BIBLIOMANCY By opening a Bible, using the first passage one sees to predict the future.

CARTOMANCY By the dealing of playing cards.

CEROMANCY Observing the shapes produced by dropping melted wax into water.

CHEIROMANCY This is the art of telling a person's future by reading their palm.

CRYSTALLOMANCY By gazing into a crystal ball, a precious stone, or reflecting metal surface.

FOLIOMANCY By examining the pattern made by loose tea leaves left at the bottom of a cup.

OOMANCY Using eggs, for example, breaking them and observing the shapes produced.

ORNITHOMANCY By observing the flight of birds.

CRIME and WAR

LAW and DISORDER

PLACES WITH THE HIGHEST CRIME RATES

PLACE	REPORTED CRIMES PER 100,000 POPULATION
Surinam	17,819
St. Kitts and Nevis	15,468
Gibraltar	14,970
New Zealand	14,496
Sweden	13,750
Canada	13,297
US Virgin Islands	10,441
Denmark	10,399
Netherlands	10,181
Guam	10,080
England and Wales	9,395
Greenland	9,360
French Guiana	8,936
Bermuda	8,871
Botswana	8,758
Finland	8,388

An appearance in this list does not necessarily confirm these as the most crime-ridden places in the world, since the rate of reporting relates closely to people's confidence in local law enforcement authorities. Hence the rate of reported crimes in the US is 5,278 – not enough to make it onto this list.

AMAZING FACT! Togo has the lowest crime rate in the world, with just 11 reported crimes for every 100,000 of the population.

DID YOU KNOW? While imprisoned in Spain in 1597, Miguel de Cervantes began writing his classic novel *Don Quixote*.

TOP-GROSSING CRIME MOVIES

The Man in the Iron Mask (1998)

The Chamber (1996)

The Rock (1996)

Dead Man Walking (1995)

Fortress (1993)

Ernest Goes to Jail (1990)

Tango & Cash (1989)

The Running Man (1987)

Kiss of the Spider Woman (1985)

Escape from New York (1981)

Stir Crazy (1980)

Escape from Alcatraz (1979)

Midnight Express (1978)

Breakout (1975)

The Longest Yard (1974)

Papillon (1973)

Jailhouse Rock (1957)

THE LANGUAGE OF CRIMINALS

SLANG WORD	MEANING
Marks	Fingerprints
Dip	Pickpocket
Rat	Police informer
Five-O	Undercover cop
The blue people	Uniformed police
Doing time	Imprisonment
Inside	Prison
Wheelman	Getaway driver

WORLD'S CLUMSIEST CRIMINALS

WRITTEN ALL OVER HIS FACE Eugene "Butch" Flenough, Jr., of Texas was tracked down after a robbery at a pizza restaurant. As a disguise, he had worn a helmet printed with with "Butch" and "Eugene Flenough, Jr."

IT'S A HOLDUP Kevin Thompson, a 26-year-old man from New Jersey, was jailed for bank robbery after police found that his holdup note was written on his paycheck.

WEIGHED DOWN Two teenagers suspected of burglary were caught in Minnesota after attempting to swim away from pursuing police. Each was weighed down with about $25-worth of coins in his pocket.

CAUGHT RED-HANDED Cecelio Rodriguez and Armando Milian were arrested in Florida when police caught them breaking into a pawnshop. The burglars failed to hear the deafening burglar alarm over the noise of the powersaw they used to cut through the door.

SMUG THUG American John Cotle was imprisoned for burglary. The evidence against him were photographs of himself, posing with the stolen goods within hours of the burglary.

FICTIONAL DETECTIVES AND THEIR CREATORS

DETECTIVE	WRITER
Father Brown	G. K. Chesterton
Mike Hammer	Mickey Spillane
Sherlock Holmes	Arthur Conan Doyle
Inspector Maigret	Georges Simenon
Philip Marlowe	Raymond Chandler
Perry Mason	Erle Stanley Gardner
Hercule Poirot	Agatha Christie
Sam Spade	Dashiell Hammett
Lord Peter Wimsey	Dorothy L. Sayers

STRANGE LAWS

NO HANDLING OF THE PELICANS Under Section 23 of the London Royal and Other Parks and Gardens Regulations of 1977, "touching a pelican" is forbidden, unless written permission is first obtained.

NO SLURPING It is against the law to slurp soup in public in New Jersey.

NO CROAKING It is illegal for frogs to croak after 11pm in Memphis.

NO SNOWBALLS Snowballs must not be thrown at trees in Mount Pulaski, Illinois.

RED SWEATERS ONLY On Wimbledon Common, London, UK, "Every person playing golf is required to wear a red outer garment."

NO ATOM BOMBS Anyone detonating a nuclear weapon in Chico, California, risks a $500 fine.

NO SCRUFFINESS Your licence may be withdrawn if you are unwashed or badly dressed while driving in Athens, Greece.

NO FOREIGN RICE Japanese law states that rice grown in other countries can't be eaten.

NO ILLITERATE MARRIAGES To get married, Finnish people must be able to read.

FAMOUS THEFTS

CROWN JEWELS In 1671, disguised as a priest, Colonel Thomas Blood stole the jewels. He was pardoned by Charles I, who admired him.

MONA LISA Da Vinci's work was stolen in 1911 by Vicenzo Peruggia. He was caught trying to sell it.

GREAT TRAIN ROBBERY A gang stopped the Glasgow to London mail train in 1963 and stole £2.6 million.

PRISONER FACTS

FORGOTTEN PRISONER In 1786, Marie-Augustin was arrested for whistling at Queen Marie Antoinette. He remained imprisoned for 46 years.

LONGEST SENTENCE In Thailand in 1989, fraudster Chamoy Thipyaso was sentenced to 141,078 years.

LONGEST IN JAIL Paul Geidel, a US prisoner, was in prison for 68 years. He was released at the age of 85.

LITERARY FORGERIES

SHAKESPEARE'S LOST PLAYS As a boy, William Ireland (1777–1835) forged old texts which he claimed were by Shakespeare, including letters and the plays *Vortigern and Rowena* and *Henry II*.

HOWARD HUGHES' AUTOBIOGRAPHY In 1971, the American author Clifford Irving wrote what he claimed was the autobiography of the reclusive millionaire Howard Hughes and sold it to a US publisher. He received a 30-month jail sentence.

HITLER'S DIARIES In 1981, the German magazine *Stern* bought what they and various experts believed were Adolf Hitler's diaries. In 1983, they were exposed as forgeries by Konrad Kujau.

FAMOUS PRISONS

NEWGATE Once London's most notorious prison, Newgate Prison's famed inmates included Jack Sheppard, who escaped from it. Public hangings took place outside its gates, and it is featured in several Charles Dickens novels. The Central Criminal Court (Old Bailey) was built on the site.

DARTMOOR First used for prisoners of war during the Napoleonic Wars, Dartmoor, UK, has served as a high-security long-term prison ever since. Its remote location on a bleak Devon moor hinders any escape attempts by prisoners.

DEVIL'S ISLAND Off the coast of French Guiana, France's worst criminals and political prisoners, such as Alfred Dreyfus, were sent here in the period from 1852 to 1938. Henri Charrière, known as Papillon, is one of the few inmates ever to escape. Many prisoners died of disease on the island.

ALCATRAZ Known as "The Rock," an island in San Francisco Bay, California, Alcatraz was first used as a military prison. However, for 30 years up to 1963 it housed the country's most dangerous criminals, among them Al Capone. Robert Stroud, a bird expert who became famous as "The Birdman of Alcatraz," spent many years there.

SING-SING The New York prison, named after the Sin Sinck Indians who originally lived there, was built between 1825 and 1828. From 1891 onward, many murderers were electrocuted there.

THE WORLD'S MOST FAMOUS CRIMINALS

NED KELLY Kelly was an Australian outlaw who wore bullet-proof armor in shoot-outs with police. He was caught and hanged on November 11, 1880.

AL CAPONE Nicknamed "Scarface," gangland boss Capone controlled Chicago in the 1920s, and in 1929 was responsible for the St. Valentine's Day Massacre. He was jailed in 1931 (for tax evasion) and died, insane, in 1947.

JESSE JAMES James led a gang that robbed banks and trains and held up stagecoaches. He was shot dead in 1882.

BUTCH CASSIDY AND THE SUNDANCE KID Butch (real name Robert LeRoy Parker) and the Sundance Kid (Harry Longbaugh) were train robbers who some believed escaped to Bolivia.

DR. CRIPPEN American Harold Hawley Crippen (1862–1910) murdered his wife in London and fled to Canada with Ethel Le Neve disguised as a boy. The ship on which they traveled was contacted by radio (its first use in a criminal case), and Crippen was arrested and hanged.

BONNIE AND CLYDE Americans Bonnie Parker (1910–1934) and her partner Clyde Barrow (1909–1934) stole from banks, cafés, and gas stations. They were ambushed and shot by rangers.

LEE HARVEY OSWALD The assassin of US President John F. Kennedy was himself shot and killed by an assassin, Jack Ruby, on November 24, 1963.

CHARLES MANSON In 1969, with his followers, known as "The Family," Manson murdered six people in California, including actress Sharon Tate.

MURDER and PUNISHMENT

GRISLY EXECUTION METHODS

DROWNING During the Crusades (1096–1291), King Richard I ordered that any man found guilty of killing another should be tied to the victim's body and thrown into the sea. Later, in the 14th century, traitors were tied to stakes in the River Thames to drown at high tide.

BOILING ALIVE This punishment was introduced in England by Henry VIII in 1531, but abolished by his son Edward VI in 1547. In 1531, the Bishop of Rochester's cook, Richard Roose, was found guilty of poisoning guests at a banquet, and boiled to death in a large cauldron.

PRESSING Victims were chained to the ground and increasingly heavy weights put on their chests until they could not breathe.

WHEEL Victims were spread-eagled on a large wheel and repeatedly beaten until they died, "broken on the wheel." Used widely in Europe, it was not abolished in some countries until the early 19th century.

HAMMER A large mallet, or *mazzatello*, was used in Italy. Victims were struck until they died.

ELEPHANT In India in the 19th century, criminals had their heads placed on wooden blocks, where an elephant stamped on them.

MOST MURDERS PER YEAR

COUNTRY	MURDERS PER 100,000 POPULATION
Swaziland	87.8
Bahamas	52.6
Monaco	36.0
Philippines	30.1
Guatemala	27.4
Jamaica	20.9
Russia	19.9
Botswana	19.5

FAMOUS PEOPLE WHO LOST THEIR HEADS

JOHN THE BAPTIST According to legend, John the Baptist was beheaded at the request of Salome, daughter of Herodias, in 30 BC.

MARY, QUEEN OF SCOTS The English queen was executed on February 8, 1587, at Fotheringhay Castle, UK. The beheading was bungled, and the executioner dropped the queen's head when her wig fell off.

SIR WALTER RALEIGH This English adventurer was beheaded in 1618. His widow carried his embalmed head around for 30 years in a bag.

NICOLAS JACQUES PELLETIER A notorious French highwayman, Pelletier was the first to be sent to the guillotine, in Paris, on April 25, 1792.

LOUIS XVI The King of France was guillotined on January 21, 1793.

MARIE ANTOINETTE Queen of Louis XVI, Marie Antoinette was guillotined in October 1793.

EUGENE WEIDMANN The last public guillotine victim in France was executed at Versailles on June 17, 1939.

KING FAISAL King Faisal of Saudi Arabia was beheaded in 1975 for murdering his uncle.

THE CATO STREET CONSPIRATORS Five plotters were hanged on May 1, 1820, in London, UK. Their heads were then cut off and displayed to the public.

BURNED AT THE STAKE

JOAN OF ARC The famous French patriot Jeanne d'Arc led a battle against the English and turned French fortunes around. The French burned her in 1431 for witchcraft. She was later made a saint.

THOMAS CRANMER The Archbishop of Canterbury, and a Protestant martyr, he was burned at the stake in 1556.

GERMAN WITCHES Thousands of people, mostly women, were accused of witchcraft and burned in the 16th–18th centuries. As many as 100,000 were burned in Germany alone. In 1589, 133 died in a single day.

ELIZABETH GAUNT While Elizabeth Gaunt was burned at the stake for treason, at Tyburn, London, UK, on October 28, 1685, rainfall almost put out the fire. Some saw this as a sign that she was innocent.

CHRISTIAN MURPHY In 1789, a female member of a gang of coiners (people who forged coins) was strangled and then burned in London, UK. She was the last person burned in England – burning was abolished in 1790.

DID YOU KNOW?

The guillotine was proposed in 1789 by Dr. Joseph Guilloti[n] as a humane way of executing people.

EXECUTION MILESTONES

1241 Pirate William Marise is the first person in England to be hanged, drawn, and quartered.

1630 First recorded hanging in the US.

1686 Last witch, Alice Molland, hanged in the UK.

1705 John Smith, hanged at Tyburn, is reprieved and revived 15 minutes later. He becomes known thereafter as "half-hanged Smith."

1814 Beheading is abolished in England.

1831 John Any Bird Bell is executed at Maidstone, UK, aged 14, for murder.

1868 At the Old Bailey, London, UK, Michael Barrett is the last person to be publicly hanged in the UK.

1890 First electrocution, at Auburn Prison, New York.

1916 In Tennessee, Mary, an elephant, is hanged for murder.

1936 Last public execution takes place in the US.

1982 Charles Brooks is the first to be executed by lethal injection, in Texas.

MOST PROLIFIC PRE-20TH-CENTURY SERIAL KILLERS

BEHRAM Behram (or Buhram) was the leader of the Thugee cult in India, believed to be responsible for the deaths of up to 2,000,000 people. At his trial, Behram was found guilty of personally committing 931 murders between 1790 and 1830, mostly by ritual strangulation.

COUNTESS ERSZÉBET BÁTHORY Báthory (1560–1614), of Hungary, known as "Countess Dracula," allegedly murdered 300 to 650 girls in the belief that drinking their blood would prevent her from aging. She was arrested in 1611 and died alone in her castle.

MARY ANN COTTON Cotton, a former nurse, was hanged in the UK in 1873. In a 20-year period, she is believed to have killed 14 to 20 people.

! DID YOU KNOW? Jack the Ripper, a notorious murderer in 19th-century England, committed his crimes on weekends.

GILLES DE RAIS A French aristocrat, Gilles de Laval, Baron de Rais (1404–1440), allegedly dabbled in the occult and committed murders as sacrifices. He was accused of killing up to 200 children. He was strangled, and his body burned, in 1440.

HERMANN WEBSTER MUDGETT Also known as "H. H. Holmes," Mudgett, a former doctor, lured women to his Chicago home. Operating as a hotel, it was fully equipped for torturing, murdering, and dissecting victims. Mudgett disposed of the bodies in furnaces or in acid baths. He confessed to killing 27 people, but the remains of 200 victims were discovered in his house. He was hanged in May 1896.

MURDER COINCIDENCES

DELIBERATE OR COINCIDENCE? Sir Edmund Berry Godfrey, an English Member of Parliament, was murdered in 1678. His body was found at Greenberry Hill. Three men – called Green, Berry, and Hill – were executed for the crime.

BODY DOUBLE In 1900, King Umberto of Italy was dining in a restaurant when he discovered that the proprietor looked exactly like him. To his amazement, the king found that the restaurateur was also called Umberto, and that they had both been born in Turin on the same day in 1844. They both also married women called Margherita on the same day. Sensing an affinity with his "double," the king invited him to an athletics meeting the following day. As the king took his seat at the meeting, he was told that the other Umberto had been killed that morning in a mysterious shooting accident. As the king expressed his sorrow, an anarchist shot him dead.

MYSTERY PRESENCE Robert Todd Lincoln, son of Abraham, was present at Ford's Theater, Washington, D.C., in 1865, when his father was shot. He was on hand when President Garfield was shot in 1881, and in 1901, he was close to President William McKinley when he was shot.

WORST MASSACRES

331 BC Alexander the Great killed 10,000 Tyrians.

AD 390 Over 3,000 people were killed by Theodosius in Thessalonica, Greece.

1002 On St. Brice's Day, Ethelred II ordered the Danes in the UK to be killed.

1572 More than 50,000 Huguenots (French Protestants) were killed in the St. Bartholomew's Day Massacre.

1631 6,400 civilians were slaughtered by the German cavalry in Magdeburg, northern Germany.

1649 Oliver Cromwell's army massacred 2,000 people in Drogheda, Ireland.

1890 300 Sioux men, women, and children were murdered by 500 soldiers at Wounded Knee, South Dakota.

FAMOUS ASSASSINATION VICTIMS

JULIUS CAESAR Roman ruler, stabbed to death by conspirators in Rome, on the Ides of March (15th), in 44 BC.

SPENCER PERCEVAL The only British Prime Minister to be murdered, Perceval was killed by John Bellingham on May 11, 1812, in the House of Commons.

ABRAHAM LINCOLN The 16th US President was shot by John Wilkes Booth at Ford's Theater, Washington, D.C., on April 14, 1865. He died the following day.

GRIGORY RASPUTIN The "mad monk" of Russia was poisoned, shot, and drowned in 1916 for fear he would influence government.

JOHN F. KENNEDY The 35th President of the US was shot in the head and killed in Dallas, Texas, by Lee Harvey Oswald, on November 22, 1963.

MARTIN LUTHER KING, JR. This civil rights leader was shot in Memphis, by James Earl Ray, on April 4, 1968.

JOHN LENNON In 1980, the former Beatles musician was shot in New York by religious fanatic Mark Chapman.

YITZHAK RABIN The Israeli Prime Minister was shot dead in Jerusalem, Israel, on November 4, 1995.

FIRST TO ABOLISH CAPITAL PUNISHMENT

Capital punishment is when a criminal is put to death for a serious crime. Some of the countries listed here have since reinstated capital punishment.

COUNTRY	ABOLISHED
Russia	1826
Venezuela	1863
Portugal	1867
Brazil	1882
Costa Rica	1882
Ecuador	1897

WAR and BATTLES

MAJOR WARS

DATES	WAR
431–404 BC	Peloponnesian War
264–146 BC	Punic Wars
1096–1291	Crusades
1337–1453	Hundred Years War
1455–1485	Wars of the Roses
1618–1648	Thirty Years War
1642–1649	English Civil War
1701–1714	War of the Spanish Succession
1740–1748	War of the Austrian Succession
1756–1763	Seven Years War
1775–1783	American War of Independence
1792–1815	Napoleonic Wars
1812–1814	War of 1812
1846–1848	Mexican-American War
1853–1856	Crimean War
1861–1865	American Civil War
1870–1871	Franco-Prussian War
1894–1895	Chinese-Japanese War
1898	Spanish-American War
1880–1902	Boer Wars
1904–1905	Russo-Japanese War
1914–1918	World War I
1931–1933	Chinese-Japanese War
1936–1939	Spanish Civil War
1937–1945	Chinese-Japanese War
1939–1945	World War II
1950–1953	Korean War
1954–1975	Vietnam War
1982	Falklands War
1991	Gulf War
1991–1995	Bosnian War

DID YOU KNOW? The first records of the use of biological warfare date from the 1300s. Tartars, attacking a Crimean city, catapulted plague-ridden corpses over the walls, infecting inhabitants with the disease.

WEAPON MILESTONES

c.100,000 BC Neanderthal people use sharpened wooden spear points and simple stone axes.

c.1000 BC The iron sword evolves in southern and central Europe.

AD 1100 The mace and the crossbow become popular weapons of war.

1340–1400 Cannons are introduced into battles.

1836 American gunsmith Samuel Colt (1814–1862) develops the first effective revolver.

1890s Belt-fed machine guns are introduced, which allowed two people to fire at great speed.

1916 The first tank is used in war.

1945 The first atomic bomb, dropped on Hiroshima, Japan, changes the nature of warfare.

1980s Attack helicopters, armed with laser-guided missiles and machine guns, prove to be effective in battle.

DID YOU KNOW? During battles in past times, officers used to give up their swords as a sign of surrender.

UNCONVENTIONAL WEAPONS

CIRCULAR BATTLESHIP The brainchild of Vice-Admiral Popov of the Imperial Russian Navy, this bizarre vessel, named *Novgorod*, was launched in the Black Sea in 1873. Designed to spin like a top, and fire its large guns in any direction, it was unstable, and practically impossible to steer. It was taken out of service almost immediately!

HELMET GUN Patented by Albert B. Pratt of Vermont in 1916, the gun and its sights were attached to a helmet and the trigger fired by the wearer's mouth. A powerful strap held it in place – but may not have been sufficient to prevent the recoil from fatally injuring the wearer.

RIFLE TO SHOOT AROUND CORNERS During World War I, Jones Wister of Philadelphia patented a rifle with a curved barrel, so that soldiers could fire over the top of trenches without risking being shot themselves; a periscope took the place of sights.

HARD CHEESE During the 1865 war between Uruguay and Brazil, a Uruguayan ship ran out of cannon balls and fired stale Dutch cheeses – one of which dismasted an enemy vessel and killed two sailors.

COMBINED GUN AND PLOW Patented on June 17, 1862, by C. M. French and W. H. Fancher of New York, this unusual weapon was designed to be used by farmers who, if they were attacked while plowing, could quickly turn their implement into a powerful gun!

BOOMERANG BULLETS Patented in the US on October 4, 1870, by G. Hope of Kansas, boomerang bullets were designed to fire in a curved line – the only danger being that if they traveled in a complete circle, they could kill the person who fired them.

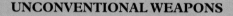

20TH-CENTURY WARS WITH MOST MILITARY FATALITIES

hese figures represent military historians' "best guesses," and
o not take into account the enormous death tolls among
vilian populations during the many wars of the 20th century.

AR	YEARS	MILITARY FATALITIES
orld War II	1939–1945	15,843,000
orld War I	1914–1918	8,545,800
orean War	1950–1953	1,893,100
hinese-Japanese War	1937–1945	1,000,000
afra-Nigeria Civil War	1967–1970	1,000,000
panish Civil War	1936–1939	611,000
etnam War	1954–1975	546,000
dia-Pakistan War	1947	200,000
SSR invasion of Afghanistan	1979–1989	200,000
an-Iraq War	1980–1988	200,000

DID YOU KNOW? War in the 20th century has killed
over 100 million people in total; 20 million since 1945.

GREAT NAVAL BATTLES

AEGOSOPOTAMI, 405 BC A flotilla of 80 Athenian triremes battled
with 170 Peloponnesian ships. The Athenians were conquered,
and the Peloponnesian War ended soon afterward.

MYLAE, 260 BC (PUNIC WARS) The battle at Mylae – the first of
three – saw a Roman victory over Carthage, North Africa.

LEPANTO, OCTOBER 7, 1571 (CYPRUS WAR) The Turkish fleet was
defeated by the Spanish. About 25,000 Turks were lost in 250 galleys.

SPANISH ARMADA, JULY 29, 1588 (ANGLO-SPANISH WAR) A fleet of
30 Spanish ships with 2,500 guns and 30,000 men set out to attack
England. Although outnumbered, the English fleet inflicted severe
damage with their guns, and the rest of the Spanish fleet was
destroyed by bad weather.

TRAFALGAR, OCTOBER 21, 1805 A sea battle between the British
fleet under Lord Nelson, and the French and Spanish. The British
won, but Lord Nelson was killed.

CORAL SEA, MAY 8, 1942 (WORLD WAR II) The US Navy fought
the Japanese in the first major battle using aircraft from carriers.

LEYTE GULF, OCTOBER 22–27, 1944 (WORLD WAR II) The US
defeated the Japanese, who lost three battleships, four aircraft
carriers, ten cruisers, and nine destroyers.

WORDS OF WAR

These common words all started out as military terms:

larm • Ambulance • Bachelor • Caddie/caddy • Canteen • Crusade • Field day
reelance • Garret • Gauntlet • Gremlin • Jeep • Kamikaze • Loophole
Magazine • Marathon • Picket • Pioneer • Slogan • Snorkel

DID YOU KNOW? During World War II, Japanese *kamikaze*
pilots would fly into Allied ships in planes packed with explosives,
elieving it an honor to die for their country. The word *kamikaze*
eans "divine wind" in Japanese.

FAMOUS WARRIOR GROUPS

IKINGS In the late eighth century,
ikings from present-day Denmark,
Norway, and Sweden began to leave
eir countries in search of treasure
o steal, or new lands to settle in.

RUSADERS Between the 11th and 13th
enturies, European Christians, known as
rusaders, organized armed expeditions
o regain Jerusalem, which had been
eized by the Saracens.

SAMURAI The Samurai were an
ristocratic class of warriors who first
ained power in Japan in the 12th century.

MONGOLS In the late 11th century, an
rmy in northeastern Asia, led by a
hieftain called Genghis Khan, invaded
China and Asia. The Mongols were skilled
ghters, and possessed powerful weapons.

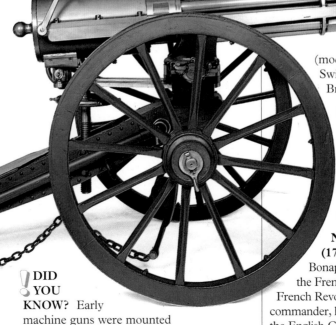

DID YOU KNOW? Early
machine guns were mounted
on carriages and looked like
conventional cannons.

GREAT MILITARY COMMANDERS

ALEXANDER THE GREAT (356–323 BC)
Alexander became king of Macedonia
when he was 20 years old. He was an
ambitious general, and conquered most
of the known world. His empire extended
from Asia Minor (now Turkey) to India.

**JULIUS CAESAR
(100–44 BC)** Caesar
became head of
the Roman
Republic in 49 BC.
He conquered Gaul
(modern France, Belgium and
Switzerland), and also invaded
Britain twice.

**HORATIO NELSON
(1758–1805)** The daring
Commander of the British
Royal Navy, Nelson
defeated the Spanish
and French at the Battle
of Trafalgar in 1805, but
died of serious wounds.

**NAPOLEON BONAPARTE
(1769–1821)** Corsican
Bonaparte restored the power of
the French government after the
French Revolution. A brilliant military
commander, he controlled Europe from
the English Channel to the Russian border.

WORLD WAR I

KEY EVENTS

JUNE 1914 The heir to the throne of Austria-Hungary, Archduke Franz Ferdinand, is assassinated. Serbia is blamed for the attack.

JULY 1914 Austria-Hungary invades Serbia in retaliation for Franz Ferdinand's death. Russia mobilizes troops to help Serbia.

AUGUST 1914 To help its ally Austria, Germany declares war on Russia and Russia's ally, France. Germany invades Belgium to get to France. Britain, pledged to protect Belgium's neutrality, declares war on Germany. Germany pushes back Britain at Mons, Belgium, and defeats Russia at Tannenberg.

APRIL 1915 The Germans use poisonous gas at the Battle of Ypres, Belgium. The Allies (Britain, France, and Russia) try to force Turkey out of the war by invading the Gallipoli peninsula.

MAY 1915 A German U-boat sinks British liner SS *Lusitania* killing 1,200. Italy joins the war to support the Allies.

FEBRUARY 1916 German forces try to capture the French fortress of Verdun in a ten-month battle.

JULY 1916 In the four-month battle of the Somme, France, tanks are used for the first time. Both sides suffer enormous losses.

APRIL 1917 US enters the war on the side of the Allies.

JULY 1917 More than 300,000 Allied troops die in the three-month battle of Passchendaele.

MARCH 1918 Germany and Russia make peace, while the German forces make advances on the Western Front.

AUGUST 1918 With US help, Allied troops succeed in breaking through crucial German lines.

OCTOBER 1918 Italy defeats Austria-Hungary, and Britain defeats Turkey. The Austria-Hungarians and Turks ask for peace.

NOVEMBER 1918 Germany and Allies sign an armistice. War ends.

JUNE 1919 Treaty of Versailles is signed. Germany is forced to pay reparations (damages). These were to become a major cause of World War II.

NEW WEAPONS

TANKS Able to cross rough ground and break through barbed wire defenses, tanks were first used in September 1916.

BOMBERS Zeppelin airships and multiengined aircraft capable of carrying heavy bombs were first used during World War I.

FLÉCHETTES These were steel darts, designed to be dropped from aircraft on the enemy beneath.

GASES Gases such as mustard gas, chlorine, and tear gas, were used to poison the enemy. Gas masks, designed to protect soldiers from gas attacks, quickly followed.

GIANT MORTARS "Big Bertha" is the best known of the giant guns built by the German armaments company Krupp.

MACHINE GUNS The water-cooled Browning machine gun, named after John Browning, its US inventor, was introduced in 1917. The aircraft machine gun also dates from World War I.

PERISCOPE RIFLES In 1915, an Australian soldier invented a rifle with periscopic sights that enabled its user to remain hidden

WAR AT SEA

SUBMARINE WARFARE
Submarines were used effectively as deadly weapons for the first time in World War I. They fired underwater missiles called torpedoes at enemy ships. In 1917, destroyers were built in the US. They were smaller and faster than battleships and were used mainly to protect other ships from enemy fire.

SINKING OF LUSITANIA
On its journey from the UK to the US, the British liner SS *Lusitania* was sunk by German torpedoes off the coast of Ireland on May 8, 1915. About 1,200 men, women, and children were drowned, 128 of whom were American. Some were close friends of the US President, Woodrow Wilson.

JUTLAND BATTLE In one of the most famous naval battles ever, fleets of British and German Dreadnought battleships fought at Jutland off the coast of Denmark, on May 31, 1916. Both side claimed to be victorious, bu while the German side was first to retreat, the British Navy suffered greater losses leaving a stalemate situation

MILITARY LOSSES

COUNTRY	KILLED
Germany	1,773,700
Russia	1,700,000
France	1,357,800
Austria-Hungary	1,200,000
British Empire	908,371
Italy	650,000
Romania	335,706
Turkey	325,000
US	116,516
Bulgaria	87,500
Serbia	45,000
Belgium	13,716
Portugal	7,222
Greece	5,000
Montenegro	3,000
Japan	320

FAMOUS AIR ACES

PILOT	COUNTRY	ENEMY DEATHS
Rittmeister Manfred von Richthofen ("The Red Baron")	Germany	80
Capitaine René Paul Fonck	France	75
Major Edward "Mick" Mannock	UK	73
Major William Avery Bishop	Canada	72
Major Raymond Collishaw	Canada	62

DID YOU KNOW? The term "air ace" describes a pilot who brought down more than five enemy aircraft.

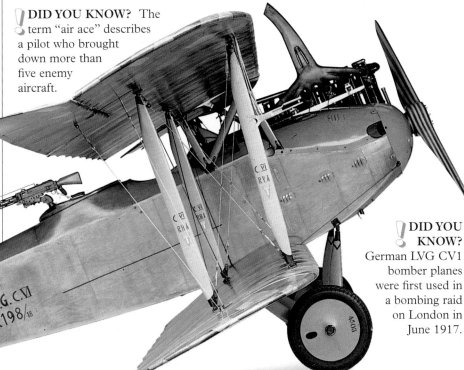

DID YOU KNOW? Romania had the highest death rate, losing 45 percent of its armed forces, while Japan lost just 0.04 percent of its 800,000-strong force. Only three Japanese were taken prisoner or reported missing.

DID YOU KNOW? German LVG CV1 bomber planes were first used in a bombing raid on London in June 1917.

DID YOU KNOW? The main role of reconnaissance fighter planes was to observe and photograph the enemy.

MOST TAKEN AS PRISONERS OF WAR

COUNTRY	CAPTURED
Russia	2,500,000
Austria-Hungary	2,200,000
Germany	1,152,800
Italy	600,000
France	537,000
Turkey	250,000
British Empire	191,652
Serbia	152,958
Romania	80,000
Belgium	34,659

BATTLES WITH MOST CASUALTIES

BATTLE	DATE	ESTIMATED CASUALTIES
Somme River I	July–November 1916	1,000,000
Verdun	February–December 1915	700,000
Gallipoli	April 1915–January 1916	500,000
Artois-Loos	September–October 1915	428,000
Somme River II	March 1918	300,000
Ypres I	October–November 1914	250,000

DID YOU KNOW? More soldiers were killed during the course of the four-month battle of the Somme, northwest France, than in any previous battle in history. Gunfire could be heard as far away as England. This battle saw the British army using tanks for the first time.

LARGEST ARMED FORCES

COUNTRY	COMBATANTS
Russia	12,000,000
Germany	11,000,000
British Empire	8,904,467
France	8,410,000
Austria-Hungary	7,800,000
Italy	5,615,000
US	4,355,000
Turkey	2,850,000
Bulgaria	1,200,000
Japan	800,000
Romania	750,000
Serbia	707,343

WORLD WAR II

KEY EVENTS

AUGUST 1934 Adolf Hitler becomes Führer (leader) of Germany.

APRIL 1938 Germany annexes Austria.

MARCH 1939 Germany occupies the whole of Czechoslovakia.

SEPTEMBER 1939 Germany invades Poland; Britain, France, Australia, and New Zealand declare war on Germany.

MAY 1940 Germany invades Belgium, the Netherlands, France, and the Channel Islands. British and French troops leave France via Dunkirk; Winston Churchill becomes Prime Minister of the UK.

JUNE 1940 Germany occupies Paris; Italy declares war on Britain and France.

SEPTEMBER 1940 The blitz – air raids on London – begins; Italy invades Egypt.

APRIL 1941 Germany invades Greece, Yugoslavia, and Russia.

DECEMBER 1941 Japan attacks Pearl Harbor; the US enters the war.

FEBRUARY 1943 Germany is defeated at Stalingrad, Russia.

JUNE 1944 British troops embark on France in the D-Day landings.

AUGUST 1944 The Allies liberate Paris.

APRIL 1945 The Allies liberate the concentration camps; US President Roosevelt dies and Truman takes over.

APRIL 1945 Mussolini is captured and hanged; the Allies take Venice.

APRIL 1945 Adolf Hitler commits suicide.

MAY 1945 The German forces surrender; VE (Victory in Europe) Day.

AUGUST 1945 Atomic bombs dropped on Hiroshima and Nagasaki; Japanese surrender; VJ (Victory over Japan) Day.

SEPTEMBER 1945 United Nations starts.

NOVEMBER 1945 The Nuremberg war crimes trials begin.

MILITARY LOSSES

This list covers the number of men who died on the battlefield. Untold millions of civilian war deaths should be added to these figures. Recent estimates have suggested an additional figure of up to 25,000,000 civilian deaths, as a result of Stalinist purges which began just before the outbreak of war.

COUNTRY	KILLED
USSR	13,600,000
Germany	3,300,000
China	1,324,516
Japan	1,140,429
British Empire	357,116
Romania	350,000
Poland	320,000
Yugoslavia	305,000
US	292,131
Italy	279,800
Total	21,268,992

DID YOU KNOW? The numbers killed in World War II have been the subject of intense argument for more than 50 years. The very high number of military casualties in the USSR in particular is hard to comprehend. Most authorities now believe that of the 30,000,000 Soviets who bore arms, there were 13,600,000 military deaths. This includes a total of approximately 7,800,000 battlefield deaths, plus up to 2,500,000 who died later of disease and wounds received in battle. Of the 5,800,000 who were taken prisoner, as many as 3,300,000, died in captivity.

DID YOU KNOW? Six million Jews are believed to have been killed by the German Nazi regime as part of an attempt by Hitler to rid Europe of all traces of Jewish life and culture.

LARGEST ARMED FORCES

COUNTRY	PERSONNEL
Former USSR	12,500,000
US	12,364,000
Germany	10,000,000
Japan	6,095,000
France	5,700,000
UK	4,683,000
Italy	4,500,000
China	3,800,000
India	2,150,000
Poland	1,000,000

WORLD WAR II SLANG

SLANG TERM	MEANING
Bought the farm (US)	Dead
Doughboy	US soldier
Gone for a Burton (UK)	Dead
Mae West	Lifejacket
Molotov cocktail	Antitank firebomb
Spit	Spitfire fighter plane
Write-off	Crashed aircraft

SEA BATTLES

PEARL HARBOR The Japanese attacked the US naval base of Pearl Harbor, in Hawaii, without warning on December 7, 1941. Five American battleships were sunk and 15 other vessels were also attacked. The US declared war on Japan immediately.

BISMARCK On May 27, 1941, the British sank the German ship *Bismarck* in the Atlantic, killing 1,000 crew.

PACIFIC BATTLES The US Navy gained two important successes against the Japanese in the Battle of the Coral Sea and the Battle of Midway, both in 1942. In the Battle of Midway, US torpedo bombers were used to disable and sink Japanese ships.

DECLARATIONS OF WAR

DECLARATION	DATE
UK on Germany	Sept. 3, 1939
Australia on Germany	Sept. 3, 1939
New Zealand on Germany	Sept. 3, 1939
France on Germany	Sept. 3, 1939
South Africa on Germany	Sept. 6, 1939
Canada on Germany	Sept. 9, 1939
Italy on UK and France	June 10, 1940
France on Italy	June 11, 1940
Japan on US, UK, Australia, Canada, New Zealand, and South Africa	Dec. 7, 1941
UK on Finland, Hungary, Romania	Dec. 7, 1941

WORLD WAR II BOMBING RAIDS

BATTLE OF BRITAIN
Hundreds of German bombers attacked the UK during the summer of 1940. Hermann Goering, commander of the German Luftwaffe, sent 1,000 planes across the channel daily to bomb the UK air bases.

BRITISH BLITZ In May 1941, 550 German planes dropped hundreds of explosive bombs over London, killing 1,436 people and starting 2,000 fires.

DRESDEN DESTRUCTION
In February 1945, Allied troops bombed the German city of Dresden for three nights, resulting in a death toll of nearly 100,000 and casualties numbering 400,000.

ATOMIC EXPLOSION
In a controversial attack, an American plane dropped an atomic bomb on the Japanese city of Hiroshima in August 1945. About 80,000 Japanese people were killed instantly.

NEW INVENTIONS

ATOM BOMBS Developed by US scientists and used at the end of the war.

BAILEY BRIDGES Invented by British engineer Donald Bailey, these were quick replacements for bridges that had been destroyed.

COMPUTERS The first programmable computer, *Colossus*, was used in the UK in 1943 to crack codes.

NYLON Invented just before the war, it was used for parachute cords.

TANKS OF WORLD WAR II

TANK	DATE	COUNTRY	WEIGHT		NUMBER
			TONS	TONNES	PRODUCED
M4A3 Sherman	1942	US	31	31.5	41,530

DID YOU KNOW? The tank named after US Civil War general William Tecumseh Sherman was used in large numbers by both US and British troops during World War II. It carried a crew of five and could cruise over a distance of 143 miles (230 km) at up to 25 mph (40 km/h).

T34 Model 42	1940	USSR	28.5	30.0	35,120
T34/85	1944	USSR	32.0	33.0	29,430
M3 General Stuart	1941	US	12.2	12.4	14,000
Valentine II	1941	UK	17.5	17.8	8,280
M3A1 Lee/Grant	1941	US	26.8	27.2	7,400
Churchill VII	1942	UK	40.0	40.5	5,640

DID YOU KNOW? During World War II, ordinary citizens had to make many adjustments to their lives. Scarce foods such as meat, eggs, and candy were rationed weekly. In Europe, children from the cities were often evacuated to safer homes in rural areas. City families slept in air-raid shelters and tried to blacken out all their windows, so bombers would not see any lights from the sky.

FAMOUS LEADERS

WINSTON CHURCHILL, UK (1874–1965)
Considered to be one of the greatest statesman, Churchill became British Prime Minister in 1940, leading the country through the war. Churchill was also a talented painter.

EMPEROR HIROHITO, JAPAN (1901–1989) As the ruler of his country during the war, many believed Hirohito should have been tried for crimes committed by Japanese troops.

BENITO MUSSOLINI, ITALY (1883–1945)
Mussolini led the National Fascist Party, and became dictator of Italy in 1922. He joined with Germany in 1940, but was defeated and executed in 1945.

ADOLF HITLER, GERMANY (1889–1945)
The leader of the Nazi party, Hitler became Germany's Chancellor in 1933. He began military action in Europe and a campaign to murder Jews.

FRANKLIN D. ROOSEVELT, US (1882–1945) The 32nd US President, Roosevelt brought the US into the war in 1941.

JOSEF STALIN, USSR (1879–1953)
Head of the Soviet Communist Party and Prime Minister during the war, Stalin was a ruthless man who killed many of his own people.

THE ARTS

LEARNING

OLDEST UNIVERSITIES

UNIVERSITY	COUNTRY	FOUNDED
Quaraouyine, Fez	Morocco	859
Al-Azhar, Cairo	Egypt	970
Parma	Italy	1064
Bologna	Italy	1088
Modena	Italy	1175
Paris	France	1200
Perugia	Italy	1200

WORLD'S LARGEST UNIVERSITIES

UNIVERSITY	COUNTRY	STUDENTS
Paris	France	308,904
Calcutta	India	300,000
Bombay	India	262,350
Mexico City	Mexico	261,693
Guadalajara	Mexico	214,986
Buenos Aires	Argentina	206,658
Rome	Italy	184,000

MOST STUDENTS

COUNTRY	UNIVERSIT STUDENT
US	8,529,13
India	4,425,24
China	3,170,93
Russia	2,587,51
Japan	2,311,61
Indonesia	1,889,40

AMAZING LIBRARIES

VATICAN LIBRARY The Vatican library in Vatican City has one of the world's largest and most valuable collections of early manuscripts and books. Founded in the mid-1400s, it is the central library of the Catholic church, and scholars from all over the world are permitted to use it.

BRITISH LIBRARY This library, in London, is one of the world's largest. It contains books and manuscripts, newspapers, maps, music, sound recordings, and stamps.

LIBRARY OF CONGRESS The largest library in the world is the United States Library of Congress in Washington, D.C. Founded in 1800, the library contains over 23,000,000 books and more than 100,000,000 cataloged items. It has 532 miles (856 km) of shelving and approximately 4,600 employees.

SILLY HOMEWORK EXCUSES

My dog ate my math book.

We had no paper at home.

It was too difficult.

We had a surprise visit from my grandparent/cousin/pen pal.

My ink ran out.

My sister/brother threw up on it.

My mom thought it was trash and threw it in the garbage can.

LONGEST SCHOOL YEARS

COUNTRY	SCHOOL YEA IN DAY
China	25
Japan	24
Korea	22
Israel	21
Germany	21
Russia	21
Switzerland	20
Netherlands	20

COUNTRIES WITH MOST SCHOOL CHILDREN

COUNTRY	PRIMARY SCHOOL CHILDREN	SECONDARY SCHOOL CHILDREN	TOTA
China	124,212,400	53,837,300	178,049,70
India	108,200,539	64,115,978	172,316,51
US	23,694,000	20,578,000	44,272,00
Indonesia	29,876,196	11,360,349	41,236,54
Pakistan	15,532,000	5,022,416	20,554,41
Mexico	14,574,202	7,264,650	21,818,85
Russia	7,849,000	13,732,000	21,581,00

PEOPLE WHO NEVER FINISHED SCHOOL

MARK TWAIN (1835–1910) Classic American novelist and humorist.

CHARLIE CHAPLIN (1889–1977) British silent film actor.

CHARLES DICKENS (1812–1870) British author.

THOMAS EDISON (1847–1931) Prolific American inventor.

CLAUDE MONET (1840–1926) French painter, began Impressionism.

COUNTRIES WITH MOST LIBRARIES

National literary traditions determine the ratio of libraries to population. The people of Japan, for example, do not customarily borrow books, and consequently the country has only 1,950 public libraries.

COUNTRY	LIBRARIES
Russia	96,177
UK	24,869
Ukraine	21,857
Kazakhstan	15,055
Germany	13,032
Poland	9,505
Belorussia	9,121
US	9,101
Czech Republic	7,986
Mexico	5,630
Spain	4,880
Bulgaria	4,879
Azerbaijan	4,647
Hungary	4,468
Georgia	3,929

DID YOU KNOW? In the 19th century, working people in the UK who did not have access to a library could borrow books from a horse-drawn mobile library.

DID YOU KNOW? Monet's painting of Rouen Cathedral typifies the Impressionist style.

TIPS FOR DOING WELL IN EXAMS

STAY CALM Try not to panic – you think more clearly when you're calm.

SLEEP WELL You won't perform well if you're tired. Get a good night's sleep the night before your exam.

FEED YOUR BRAIN Make sure you've had something to eat before the exam – your brain needs energy!

REMEMBER KEY WORDS When studying, make notes and break them down to key words – these will trigger your memory when you are in the exam. Some people use colors to aid memory.

PLAN A CELEBRATION Plan to do something you enjoy after your exam is over. You should feel more relaxed if you have something to look forward to!

TALK TO OTHERS You're not alone – thousands of people take exams every year. If you are really worried, talk to friends or family who have been in the same situation. They may offer good advice!

MOST ILLITERATE COUNTRIES

The United Nations defines an illiterate person as an adult who cannot, with understanding, both read and write a short, simple statement on their daily life.

COUNTRY	PERCENTAGE OF ILLITERACY
Nigeria	86.4
Burkina Faso	80.8
Nepal	72.5
Mali	69.0
Sierra Leone	68.6
Afghanistan	68.5
Senegal	66.9
Burundi	64.7

WORDS

HELLO AROUND THE WORLD

GREETING	LANGUAGE
Ahlan wasahlan	Arabic
Dobró útro	Bulgarian
Goddag	Danish
Hello	English
Hyvää päivää	Finnish
Bonjour	French
Garmardzobat	Georgian
Guten tag	German
Kalimera	Greek
Namaskar	Hindi
Gódan daginn	Icelandic
Buongiorno	Italian
Konnichiwa	Japanese
Nin hao	Mandarin
Go dag	Norwegian
Dzien dóbry	Polish
Bom dia	Portuguese
Zdravstvuyitye	Russian
Buenos días	Spanish
God dag	Swedish
Sawatdee	Thai
Iya gunler	Turkish
Assalm-u-alaikum	Urdu
Kunjani	Zulu

ONOMATOPOEIC WORDS

Onomatopoeic words are words that sound like the noise they describe. The best place to see these words is in comic strips.

Splash • Crack • Whoosh
Clang • Zoom • Zap
Crunch • Crackle • Pop
Whack • Wham • Boom
Whizz • Bang • Growl
Creak • Roar • Woof • Meow
Oink • Cock-a-doodle-doo
Slam • Snap • Gasp • Tap

ACRONYMS

Acronyms are sets of initials designed to be said as though they are words – they are thus not the same as abbreviations. The word acronym has itself been used only since 1943.

ACRONYM	MEANING
AIDS	**A**cquired **I**mmune **D**eficiency **S**yndrome
ASAP	**A**s **S**oon **A**s **P**ossible
AWOL	**A**bsent **W**ithout **L**eave (from the army, etc)
COBOL	**C**ommon **B**usiness **O**riented **L**anguage (computers)
DAT	**D**igital **A**udio **T**ape
FIFA	**F**édération **I**nternationale de **F**ootball **A**ssociation
GESTAPO	**G**eheime **Sta**ats-**P**olizei (Secret State-Police in Germany)
GULAG	**G**lavnoye **U**pravleniye Ispravitelno-Trudovykh **Lag**erei (Soviet labor camp)
LASER	**L**ight **A**mplification by **S**imulated **E**mission of **R**adiation
LEM	**L**unar **E**xcursion **M**odule
MAD	**M**utual **A**ssured **D**estruction (nuclear war term)
MASH	**M**obile **A**rmy **S**urgical **H**ospital
NASA	**N**ational **A**eronautics and **S**pace **A**dministration
NATO	**N**orth **A**tlantic **T**reaty **O**rganization
NIMBY	**N**ot **I**n **M**y **B**ack **Y**ard (used by protesters)
PLUTO	**P**ipe **L**ine **U**nder **T**he **O**cean
POW	**P**risoner **O**f **W**ar
RADAR	**Rad**io **a**nd **R**anging
SCUBA	**S**elf-**c**ontained **U**nderwater **B**reathing **A**pparatus
SHAPE	**S**upreme **H**eadquarters **A**llied **P**owers in **E**urope
TINA	**T**here **I**s **N**o **A**lternative (politics)
UFO	**U**nidentified **F**lying **O**bject
WASP	**W**hite **A**nglo-**S**axon **P**rotestant
WYSIWYG	**W**hat **Y**ou **S**ee **I**s **W**hat **Y**ou **G**et (computers)
YUPPIE	**Y**oung **U**rban **P**rofessional
ZIP	**Z**one **I**mprovement **P**lan (as in "zip code")

LONGEST WORDS AROUND THE WORLD

GERMAN Donaudampfschiffahrtselectrizitätenhauptbetriebs-werkbauunterbeamtengesellschaft – club for subordinate officials of the management of the Danube steamboat company, 80 letters.

ENGLISH Pneumonoultramicroscopicsilicovolcanoconiosis – a lung disease, 45 letters.

SPANISH Superextraordinarisimo – extraordinary, 22 letters.

TEN MOST COMMON ENGLISH WORDS

SPOKEN	WRITTEN
the	the
and	of
I	to
to	in
of	and
a	a
you	for
that	was
in	is
it	that

DID YOU KNOW?
English has about 1 million words – more than any other language.

MISLEADING WORDS

PANAMA HATS come from Ecuador – not Panama.

KOALA BEARS are not bears – they are marsupials.

GUINEA PIGS do not come from Guinea, and they are not pigs – they come from South America and are rodents.

LEAD PENCILS are not made from lead – they contain graphite, a type of carbon.

TURKEYS come from North America, not Turkey.

FIREFLIES are not flies – they are beetles.

BLINDWORMS are not sightless worms – they are legless lizards.

THE CANARY ISLANDS are named not after canaries but from *canes*, the Latin word for dogs that Roman invaders found there.

RICE PAPER is made not from rice but from the pith of a tree.

PEANUTS are a type of bean that grows underground – they are not true nuts at all.

HOMONYMS

Homonyms are words that sound the same when spoken but have different spellings and meanings.

WORD	WORD
accept (to take)	except (to exclude)
access (right of way)	excess (too much)
addition (something added)	edition (version of a book, etc)
aid (help)	aide (assistant)
altar (platform in church)	alter (to change)
aural (by ear)	oral (by mouth)
base (basis, foundation)	bass (a lower part in music)
bazaar (marketplace, fair)	bizarre (strange)
boy (a male child)	buoy (a floating object)
brake (to slow and stop)	break (to fracture, damage)
chord (musical tones)	cord (thin rope)
cite (to quote)	sight (power of seeing)
coarse (rude, rough)	course (series, route)
dual (of two, double)	duel (fight between two)
idle (inactive)	idol (image of a god)
miner (one who mines)	minor (underage person)
naval (of the navy)	navel (umbilicus, belly button)
pedal (foot lever)	peddle (to sell)
plane (airplane, to level)	plain (ordinary; open land)
precede (to go before)	proceed (to continue)
principal (chief, head person)	principle (rule)
reign (of a monarch)	rein (part of a horse's harness)
stationary (fixed)	stationery (paper supplies)
stile (steps over a wall or fence)	style (manner of doing things)
weather (state of atmosphere)	whether (if)

POPULAR SYNONYMS

Synonyms are different words that mean the same.

POLICE Fuzz, men in blue, cops, coppers, officers, the law

BATHROOM Can, toilet, ladies room, restroom, powder room, privy, latrine, commode, washroom

VOMIT Be sick, spew, throw up, puke, barf, upchuck

MONEY Bucks, cash, dinero, dough, bread, loot, currency, moolah, shekels, filthy lucre, scratch, pelf, green, kale

PALINDROMES

A palindrome is a word or a phrase that reads the same backward as well as forward.

MADAM I'M ADAM

POOR DAN IS IN A DROOP

ABLE WAS I ERE I SAW ELBA

RATS LIVE ON NO EVIL STAR

HANNAH

ANNA

NOT A TON

ROTOR

WORDS THAT CHANGED THEIR MEANINGS

The English language is constantly changing to accommodate new words and new meanings of old words. Some of the most surprising changes are those that have altered the original meaning of a word to such an extent that it is now used in a sense quite different from its original one – sometimes even meaning exactly the opposite!

ACCIDENT Until the 19th century, an accident was simply anything that happened, good or bad – hence we have such expressions as "by happy accident." Gradually, its meaning changed to mean something unexpected, and usually only refers to an unfortunate occurrence.

COMPANION This word was once used with contempt to imply an attendant or person of inferior social position – thus English writer William Shakespeare refers to a "scurvy companion." Only gradually did it come to mean "a person who accompanies, irrespective of status."

GIRL Amazingly, from the 13th century, a "girl" could mean any young person, whether female or male! To distinguish them, a female was sometimes known as a "gay girl," and a male as a "knave girl."

IDIOT An "idiot" was once the word used to describe an ordinary person; it became applied to a layman, as contrasted with a clergyman, and – since few people outside the church were educated – came to mean an uneducated person, and hence an ignorant or foolish one.

MANUFACTURE "Manufacture" means literally "handmade," but once mechanization was introduced into factories, it came to mean the opposite – "machine-made."

NAUGHTY In medieval times, "naughty" derived from "naught" and came to mean "having nothing," or "needy." Until the 17th century it meant "inferior," then "morally bad" – but gradually modified to suggest the minor misdemeanors of children, rather than serious criminal activities.

NICE The Latin word *nescius* meaning "ignorant," was the root of the English "nice," meaning "foolish." Gradually, in the 15th century it came to mean "coy" and in the 16th century "fastidious" – as in such expressions as "a nice distinction." By the 18th century, nice had come to mean "good" or "agreeable."

NOON "Noon" came from "nones," the ninth hour after sunrise, between midday and 3:00 PM, according to the time of year, a time reserved for praying in medieval monasteries. By the 12th century, prayers were recited earlier, so "noon" became midday.

QUILT A "quilt" was once the bedding under a person, from the Latin *culcita*, a mattress; by the 19th century, it had come to mean the covering on the sleeper.

SKIRT "Skirt" derives from the Old English word *scyrte* – which meant a "shirt." How the distinction between the two came about remains something of a mystery.

VILLAIN A "villain" was simply a farm laborer, and hence an uneducated person, long before it came to imply a dishonest one.

WORRY The original meaning of "worry" survives in the expression used to describe a dog attacking or "worrying" sheep; it formerly meant "to choke."

LANGUAGE

DID YOU KNOW? In silent Aboriginal hunting language, a closed hand slowly opening shows a kangaroo is near.

EUROPEAN LANGUAGES

Europe has nine official working languages. The percentage indicates the number of mother-tongue speakers:

German (22.1%) • English (17.5%) Italian (16.8%) • French (16.5%) Castilian Spanish (8.5%) • Dutch, including Flemish (5.9%) • Portuguese (3.1%) • Greek (3%) • Danish (1.5%)

DID YOU KNOW? Basque, which is spoken in southern France and northern Spain, is not related to any other language.

AMERICAN LANGUAGES

WHISTLE TALK The men of the native Mazateco people of Mexico can hold a conversation just by whistling.

FEWEST CONSONANTS Mohawk, an American Indian language, has only seven consonant sounds – English has 24!

NO FUTURE The Hopi people have no way of expressing the future or past and can indicate only how true a statement is to them. So instead of "he will walk" they say "I expect walking."

AUSTRALASIAN LANGUAGES

OFFICIAL PIDGIN In Papua New Guinea, Pidgin English has become an official national language. Known as Tok Pisin (talk pidgin) it is spoken by more than one million people and even used for road signs and newspapers.

SHORTEST ALPHABET Rotokas, from the Solomon Islands, has only 11 letters.

SPECIALIZED WORDS The people of the Pacific Solomon Islands have nine words for the ripening stages of the coconut.

ASIAN LANGUAGES

WRITE IT DOWN! China has six main languages, and many more dialects making it difficult for people from different regions to talk to each other. However, since all Chinese speakers share the same written language they can communicate in writing.

MOST VOWEL SOUNDS English has about 20 vowel sounds, but Sedang, a language spoken in Vietnam, has 50.

LEAST VOWELS, MOST CONSONANTS Many of the languages of the Caucasus mountains of southern Russia, such as Abhaz, have only one type of vowel, and more than 70 consonants, compared with the 24 in spoken English.

MOST COMPLEX SCRIPT Written Chinese has more than 50,000 signs, but only a few thousand are used.

LONGEST ALPHABET The language of Cambodia has 74 letters, compared with only 26 in English.

MADE-UP LANGUAGES

ESPERANTO Devised in 1887 by Lazarus Ludwig Zamenhof of Poland, this phonetic language with 28 letters is written as it sounds and has no irregular grammar rules. More than a million people have learned to speak it.

IDO This revised and simplified version of Esperanto was introduced in 1907.

VOLAPÜK Devised by German Johann Schleyer in 1879, Volapük was based on German.

INTERLINGUA A mix of Latin, English, French, and German, Interlingua was devised by Italian Giuseppe Peano in 1908. Interest was short-lived.

DID YOU KNOW? The official language of the people of Mongolia is called Khalka, and is spoken by Mongolia's population of 2.5 million.

MOST SPOKEN LANGUAGES

COUNTRY	MILLIONS OF SPEAKERS
Chinese (Mandarin)	1,034
English	500
Hindustani	478
Spanish	413
Russian	280
Arabic	230

ENGLISH SPEAKERS

COUNTRY	NUMBER OF SPEAKERS
US	228,770,000
UK	57,190,000
Canada	18,112,000
Australia	15,538,000
South Africa	3,800,000
Ireland	3,540,000
New Zealand	3,290,000

AFRICAN LANGUAGES

MANY TONGUES Africa is home to many hundreds of different peoples living in 53 countries and speaking more than 1,000 languages – an average of five different languages per country.

ONE COUNTRY, ONE LANGUAGE Somalia in East Africa is the only African country in which the entire population speaks the same language.

NOT IN WRITING The Berber people of North Africa have no written form of their language.

CLICK TALK Many African languages include a "click" sound that is pronounced at the same time as other sounds. Some southern African languages have as many as 15 different click consonants, including the sound made with the sides of the tongue to urge on a horse.

SPECIAL LANGUAGES

MORSE CODE In 1844, American Samuel Morse invented a means of communicating over long distances using a transmitter, a receiver, a single wire, and a code of dots and dashes. This is known as Morse code.

SIGN LANGUAGE People who cannot hear or speak can communicate through sign language. Signs may stand for whole words as well as individual letters. There are many different sign language systems around the world.

SEMAPHORE Until the early 1900s, ships would communicate by means of semaphore flag signals. Today, it remains a quick method of visual signaling and is still occasionally used for passing messages between ships sailing close to each other.

WAR LANGUAGE During World War II, US Marines outwitted the Japanese by using Navajo Indians to transmit radio messages in their native language.

MOTHER-IN-LAW LANGUAGE Some Australian Aboriginals have a special language for speaking to in-laws. In Djirbal, Queensland, the basic language is known as Guwa, but when a man wants to talk to his mother-in-law he speaks a language called Dyalnguy.

RHYMING SLANG Cockney rhyming slang probably began in the 19th century as a secret language among thieves in the East End of London. Typical examples are *apples and pears* (stairs), *plates of meat* (feet), *Scapa Flow* (go), *butcher's hook* (look), and *loaf of bread* (head). Often, only the first, non-rhyming half of the phrase is used so strangers cannot understand. Phrases such as "have a butcher's," "use your loaf," and "let's scarper" (from *Scapa Flow*) are now accepted as part of the English language.

BACK SLANG Children sometimes develop secret languages. In back slang they say words backward. The British word "yob" is back slang for "boy."

BODY LANGUAGE

The way you move your body can mean different things around the world:

FINGER POINTING In Hong Kong, to signal to a person, you reach out, palm down, and flutter your fingers. Only animals may be beckoned with a finger.

FEET In Pakistan, it is rude to show the soles of your feet or point a foot when you are sitting on the floor.

HEAD SHAKING In Sri Lanka, shaking your head means yes, and nodding it up and down means no.

TEETH In Japan, it is rude to show your teeth, so when Japanese women laugh they cover their mouth.

HANDS ON HIPS In Indonesia, talking with your hands on your hips is a sign of rudeness or anger.

BOOKS

KEY AUTHORS

AUTHOR	DATES	NATIONALITY	FAMOUS WORKS
Geoffrey Chaucer	1342–1400	English	*The Canterbury Tales*
John Milton	1608–1674	English	*Paradise Lost*
William Wordsworth	1770–1850	English	*Lyrical Ballads*
Jane Austen	1775–1817	English	*Pride and Prejudice*
Victor Hugo	1802–1885	French	*Les Misérables*
Herman Melville	1819–1891	American	*Moby Dick*
Fyodor Dostoyevsky	1821–1881	Russian	*Crime and Punishment*
Rabindranath Tagore	1861–1941	Indian	*Gitanjali*
James Joyce	1882–1941	Irish	*Ulysses*
Virginia Woolf	1882–1941	English	*To the Lighthouse*
Franz Kafka	1883–1924	Czechoslovakian	*Metamorphosis*
D. H. Lawrence	1885–1930	English	*Sons and Lovers*
William Faulkner	1897–1962	American	*The Sound and the Fury*
Günter Grass	b.1927	German	*The Tin Drum*
Toni Morrison	b.1931	American	*Beloved*

GREAT ANIMAL STORIES

BOOK	AUTHOR
Black Beauty	Anna Sewell
Animal Farm	George Orwell
Winnie the Pooh	A. A. Milne
The Wind in the Willows	Kenneth Graham
Peter Rabbit stories	Beatrix Potter
Charlotte's Web	E. B. White

TOP BOOK PRODUCERS

This list gives the total number of new titles, editions, and reprints in 1997.

COUNTRY	TITLES PUBLISHED
UK	101,504
China	73,923
Germany	62,277
US	49,276

ALL-TIME BEST-SELLERS

THE BIBLE No one really knows how many copies of the Bible have been printed, sold, or distributed. In 1992, the Bible Society estimated that six billion had been produced in more than 2,000 languages and dialects – equivalent to one for every person on Earth. Whatever the precise figure, it is the best-selling book of all time.

QUOTATIONS FROM THE WORKS OF MAO ZEDONG Chairman Mao's *Little Red Book* has sold 800 million, but could scarcely fail to become a best-seller: between the years 1966 and 1971 it was compulsory for every Chinese adult to own a copy.

AMERICAN SPELLING BOOK BY NOAH WEBSTER First published in 1783, this reference book by American wordsmith Noah Webster (1758–1843) – of *Webster's Dictionary* fame – remained a best-seller throughout the 19th century, selling about 100 million copies.

THE GUINNESS BOOK OF WORLD RECORDS First published in 1955 as *The Guinness Book of Records*, this book stands out as a modern publishing achievement. In the US alone 37 editions have been published since 1956, and there have been many foreign language editions. In all, it has sold about 80 million copies.

THE MCGUFFEY READERS Published from 1853, these US textbooks were compiled by William Holmes McGuffey (1800–1873), and sold 60 million copies.

CHILDREN'S BOOK ILLUSTRATORS

NAME	COUNTRY	WELL-KNOWN BOOKS
Quentin Blake (b.1934)	UK	Illustrations to Roald Dahl
Jean de Brunhoff (1899–1937)	France	*Babar* books
Tomie dePaola (b.1934)	US	*Strega Nona*
Clement Hurd (b.1908)	US	*Goodnight Moon*
Robert McCloskey (b.1914)	US	*Make Way for Ducklings*
Helen Oxenbury (b.1938)	UK	*Tom & Pippo* books
Beatrix Potter (1866–1943)	UK	*Peter Rabbit* books
Maurice Sendak (b.1928)	US	*Where the Wild Things Are*
Ernest Shepard (1879–1976)	UK	*The Wind in the Willows*
N. C. Wyeth (1882–1945)	US	*Robinson Crusoe*

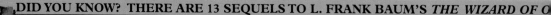

! DID YOU KNOW? The popular children's story *Alice in Wonderland* was translated into European languages soon after its publication in 1865. Today, it has been translated into almost every language in the world, even Esperanto.

BEST-SELLING CHILDREN'S AUTHORS

Author (dates)	Country	Example of work	Total sales
René Goscinny (1926–1977) Albert Uderzo (b.1927)	France	*Astérix the Gaul*	250,000,000
Hergé (Georges Rémi) (1907–1983)	Belgium	*Tintin*	150,000,000
Enid Blyton (1897–1968)	UK	*Noddy*	100,000,000
Dr. Seuss (Theodor Seuss Geisel) (1904–1991)	US	*The Cat in the Hat*	100,000,000
Beatrix Potter (1866–1943)	UK	*The Tale of Peter Rabbit*	50,000,000
Rev. W. Awdry (1911–1997)	UK	*Thomas the Tank Engine*	50,000,000
Mark Twain (Samuel Langhorne Clemens)(1835–1910)	US	*Adventures of Tom Sawyer*	40,000,000
Judy Blume (b.1938)	US	*Tales of a Fourth-Grade Nothing*	5,000,000

DID YOU KNOW? The total sales of Enid Blyton's works add up to more than 100,000,000, making her the best-selling English-language author of the 20th century.

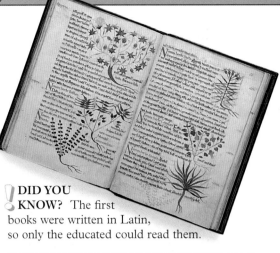

DID YOU KNOW? The first books were written in Latin, so only the educated could read them.

UNUSUAL BOOKS

Harnessing the Earthworm by Thomas J. Barrett, 1949

Wall-Paintings by Snake Charmers in Tanganyika by Hans Cory, 1953

Canadian National Egg Laying Contests by F. C. Elford & A. G. Taylor, 1924

Cluck! The True Story of Chickens in the Cinema by Jon-Stephen Fink, 1981

Scalping in America by George Frederici, 1906

Fish Who Answer the Telephone by Yury Petrovich Frolov, 1937

The Toothbrush: Its Use and Abuse by Isador Hirschfield, 1939

The Rhinoceros in Art by T. H. Clark, 1986

Why Bring That Up? A Guide To and From Seasickness by Joseph Franklin Montague, 1936

Frolic and Fun with Egg-Shells by Meredith Nugent, 1903

Little-known Sisters of Well-known Men by Sarah G. Pomeroy, 1912

The Dentist in Art by Jens Jorgen Pindborg and L. Marvitz, 1961

BOOKS BOUND NOT TO PLEASE

BOUND UP John Horwood, a murderer, was hanged on April 13, 1821. His skin was used to bind a book describing the dissection of his body by surgeon Richard Smith.

SKIN DEEP The Albert Memorial Library, Exeter, UK, possesses a copy of John Milton's *Poetical Works* (1830) bound in the skin of a murderer called George Cudmore.

ULTIMATE AUTOBIOGRAPHY The Boston Athenaeum, US, has a copy of James Allen's book, *Narrative of the Life of James Allen, alias George Walton, alias Jonas Pierce, alias James H. York, alias Burley Grove, the Highwayman, Being His Death-bed Confession to the Warden of the Massachusetts State Prison*, published in Boston, Massachusetts, in 1837, and bound in the author's own skin.

TYPES OF REFERENCE BOOKS

ALMANAC An annual calendar of dates and events, originally astronomical data, but now with useful statistical and other information.

ATLAS Book of maps. A road atlas is a book of maps used by travelers.

BILINGUAL DICTIONARY Dictionary that gives the translation of words and phrases to and from other languages, for example, a French-English, English-French dictionary.

CHRONOLOGY A dictionary of dated events.

DICTIONARY An alphabetical list of words and their meanings.

DIRECTORY An alphabetical list of names and addresses of people or organizations.

ENCYCLOPEDIA An information book, often in many volumes, with articles on subjects, usually arranged alphabetically.

GAZETTEER A geographical book that lists and describes countries, cities, and towns.

GLOSSARY List of words and phrases used in a particular field or subject.

MANUAL A subject-specific book that explains in detail how something works or how to do things. Usually includes diagrams.

PHRASEBOOK Book for travelers, with translations of words and phrases into and from a foreign language.

THESAURUS A book that organizes and groups words that have similar meanings.

TRAVEL GUIDE Book of information about a particular country or area.

YEARBOOK Annual reference book summarizing information about events of the previous year. Special yearbooks containing statistical information about a country, for example, are often called abstracts.

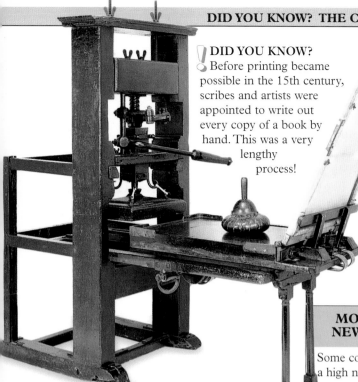

⚠ **DID YOU KNOW?**
Before printing became possible in the 15th century, scribes and artists were appointed to write out every copy of a book by hand. This was a very lengthy process!

THE PRESS

TOP-SELLING DAILY NEWSPAPERS

Some newspapers print two daily editions. In these cases, the morning figure has been used.

NEWSPAPER	COUNTRY	AVERAGE DAILY CIRCULATION
Yomiuri Shimbun	Japan	10,000,000
Asahi Shimbun	Japan	8,500,000
Sichuan Ribao	China	8,000,000
Bild-Zeitung	Germany	4,892,000
Mainichi Shimbun	Japan	4,500,000
The Sun	UK	3,767,941
Argumenty y Fakty	Russia	3,600,000
Nihon Keizai Shimbun	Japan	3,000,000
Chunichi Shimbun	Japan	2,900,000
Gongren Ribao	China	2,500,000
The Mirror	UK	2,321,608
The Daily Mail	UK	2,247,298
Renmin Ribao	China	2,150,000
Wall Street Journal	US	1,783,500
Wenhui Bao	China	1,700,000
USA Today	US	1,591,600
Trud	Russia	1,400,000
Daily Express	UK	1,199,392
The New York Times	US	1,091,100

MOST DAILY NEWSPAPERS

Some countries have a high number of daily newspapers, but as each serves a relatively small area they have only low circulations. In total, the US has 1,533 daily newspapers, but only four of them have daily sales of more than 1,000,000.

COUNTRY	NO. OF DAILY NEWSPAPERS
India	1,802
US	1,533
Germany	406
Turkey	400
Brazil	320
Mexico	310
Russia	292
Pakistan	223
Argentina	190
Greece	168
Japan	121
Canada	107
UK	103
Sweden	98
Czech Republic	90
Venezuela	89
Spain	85
Norway	83
France	80
Switzerland	79

NEWSPAPER MILESTONES

59 BC First handwritten newspapers are produced in Rome. Called *Acta diurna* (daily acts), they report on events of the day.

AD 618 Chinese civil servants in Peking circulate newsletter on court affairs.

1450s German Johannes Gutenberg (c.1398–1468) develops the first printing press using movable type.

1513 Newsbooks appear.

1615 First printed newpapers in Germany.

1645 The world's oldest continuously published weekly newspaper, the *Postock inrikes tidningar* appears in Sweden.

1703 Circulation begins of the Austrian *Wiener Zeitung*. It will become the world's oldest surviving daily newspaper.

1704 *The Boston Newsletter* is the first official newspaper in the US.

1815 The British newspaper *The Times* prints 5,000 copies per day.

1858 German P. J. Reuter (1816–1899) starts a foreign news agency.

1910–1920s American publisher Edward Scripps (1854–1926) pioneers ownership of popular working-class newspapers.

1962 First Sunday color supplement published in UK by *Sunday Times*.

1986 *Today* (UK) becomes first national daily printed in color.

UNUSUAL NEWSPAPERS

LARGEST On June 14, 1993, the Belgian newspaper *Het Volk* printed pages measuring 55.9 x 39.2 in (142 x 99.5 cm) – more than six times the area of an ordinary broadsheet.

HEAVIEST The Sunday edition of the *New York Times* for September 14, 1987, contained 1,612 pages and weighed 12 lb (5.4 kg).

SMALLEST The smallest regular publication is the *Daily Banner*, first published in 1876 in Oregon, which measures 3.75 x 3 in (9.5 x 7.6 cm).

WORST-SELLING In 1965, the London publisher of the *Commonwealth Sentinel* forgot to arrange distribution, and sold one copy of 50,000 printed.

MOST MISTAKES IN ONE STORY On August 22, 1978, *The Times* (London) contained 97 misprints in one story about the Pope. He was referred to throughout the article as "the Pop."

COMIC BOOK HEROES AND VILLAINS

CHARACTER	PUBLICATION	COUNTRY	DATE APPEARED
Tintin	*Le Vingtième Siècle*	Belgium	1929
Desperate Dan	*Dandy*	UK	1937
Superman	*Action Comics* No. 1	US	1938
Batman	*Detective Comics* No. 27	US	1939
The Human Torch	*Marvel Comics* No. 1	US	1939
Captain Marvel	*Whiz Comics* No. 1	US	1940
The Green Lantern	*All American Comics* No. 16	US	1940
The Flash	*Flash Comics* No. 1	US	1940
Catwoman	*Batman* No. 1	US	1940
The Joker	*Batman* No. 1	US	1940
Robin	*Detective Comics* No. 38	US	1940
The Spectre	*More Fun Comics* No. 52	US	1940
Wonder Woman	*All-Star Comics* No. 8	US	1941
Captain America	*Captain America Comics* No. 1	US	1941
The Penguin	*Detective Comics* No. 58	US	1941
Dennis the Menace	*Beano*	UK	1951
Astérix the Gaul	*Pilote*	France	1959
Supergirl	*Action Comics* No. 25	US	1959
Spiderman	*Amazing Fantasy* No. 15	US	1962
Silver Surfer	*Fantastic Four* No. 48	US	1965

TYPES OF NEWSPAPERS

BROADSHEET Newspaper with a large format, usually 24 x 15 in (61 x 38 cm).

FEATURE A non-news article.

HARD NEWS Up-to-the-minute news.

HEADLINE The phrase at the top of an article summarizing its subject.

LEADER Article giving opinion of the newspaper.

OBITUARY Biography of a famous person who has recently died.

POPULAR PRESS Newspapers aiming to provide lively news and entertainment for a mass readership.

QUALITY PRESS Newspapers aiming to provide serious news, information, and analysis.

SOFT NEWS Background news, or news that is not the latest.

TABLOID Newspaper with a smaller format – about half the size of broadsheets.

MAGAZINE FIRSTS

FIRST-EVER *Mercure Galant*, a gossip magazine, was first published in Paris in March 1672.

BRITISH MAGAZINE *The Gentleman's Journal*, a monthly magazine, was launched in January 1692, but ceased two years later.

WOMEN'S MAGAZINE *The Ladies' Mercury* was first published in London on June 27, 1693.

AMERICAN MAGAZINE Published in Philadelphia, *The American Magazine* probably began with the issue of February 13, 1741.

CHILDREN'S MAGAZINE *The Lilliputian Magazine* first appeared in June 1751 and ran for just over a year. It was published in London and had a page size of just 4 x 2.5 in (10 x 6 cm). The first in the US was the *Children's Magazine*, published in Hartford, Connecticut, in January 1789.

FASHION MAGAZINE The Paris magazine *Le Cabinet des Modes* was first published in 1785.

FIRST WITH A FREE RECORD The November 1955 issue of the US magazine *Pageant* contained a recording of Jaye P. Morgan singing *If You Don't Want My Love*.

MOST VALUABLE AMERICAN COMICS

ACTION COMICS NO. 1 Published in June 1938, the first issue of *Action Comics* marked the original appearance of Superman and is now worth $180,000.

DETECTIVE COMICS NO. 27 Issued in May 1939, the $160,000 *Detective Comics* is prized as the first comic book to feature Batman.

SUPERMAN NO. 1 The first comic book devoted to Superman, reprinting the original *Action Comics* story, was published in the summer of 1939. It is worth $125,000.

MARVEL COMICS NO. 1 The Human Torch and other heroes were first introduced in the $108,000 issue dated October 1939.

WHIZ COMICS NO. 1 First published in February 1940 – and confusingly numbered "2" – it was the first comic book to feature Captain Marvel. It is now worth $63,000.

BATMAN NO. 1 Published in Spring 1940, and now worth $62,000, *Batman* was the first comic devoted solely to Batman.

ALL AMERICAN COMICS NO. 16 The Green Lantern made his debut in the $60,000, July 1940 issue of *All American Comics*.

CAPTAIN AMERICA COMICS NO. 1 Published in March 1941, this was the original comic book in which Captain America appeared. Its value is estimated at $56,000.

FLASH COMICS NO. 1 Dated January 1940, and featuring The Flash, this issue is rare because it was produced in small numbers for publicity. It is worth about $55,000. The comic is also unique because the second issue was retitled *Whiz Comics*.

ART and ARTISTS

MOST EXPENSIVE AUCTIONED PHOTOGRAPHS

All these photographs were sold in US dollars, except the most expensive, which was sold in France for F. Fr 3,700,000.

FÉLIX TEYNARD (1817–1892) The Frenchman's photograph collection *Egypte et Nubie: Sites et monuments les plus intéressants pour l'étude de l'art et de l'histoire* (1858) was sold in 1990 by Laurin Guilloux Buffetaud Tailleur, in Paris, for the equivalent of $707,000.

EDWARD S. CURTIS (1868–1952) Curtis's collection *The North American Indian* (1907–1930) was sold in 1995 by Sotheby's, New York, for $662,500. It had previously been sold by Christie's for $464,500, and in 1992 for $396,000.

ALFRED STIEGLITZ (1864–1946) The world's most expensive single print, *Georgia O'Keeffe: A Portrait – Hands with Thimble* (1930) was sold in 1993 by Christie's, New York, for $398,500. A collection by the same artist, *Equivalents (21)*, taken in the 1920s, was sold in 1989 for $396,000.

FAMOUS ART GALLERIES

GALLERY	FOUNDED
Topkapi Palace Museum, Istanbul, Turkey	1454
Uffizi Gallery, Florence, Italy	1564
Louvre Museum, Paris, France	1500s
Hermitage Museum, St. Petersburg, Russia	1764
Kunsthistorisches Museum, Vienna, Austria	1781
Academy Gallery, Florence, Italy	1784
Prado Museum, Madrid, Spain	1819
National Gallery, London, UK	1824
Metropolitan Museum, New York	1870
National Gallery, Ottawa, Canada	1880
Tate Gallery, London, UK	1897

ART FAKES AND FORGERIES

Fakes are works done in the style of an artist; forgeries are copies of the original.

SITTING PRETTY The world's most valuable painting, Leonardo da Vinci's *Mona Lisa*, was stolen on August 21, 1911, by Vicenzo Peruggia, who strolled out of the Louvre with it under his arm. During the two years it was gone, forger Yves Chaudron painted six replicas, which he sold for $300,000 each.

WHAT A CORKER! In 1929, British writer Evelyn Waugh and a friend, Tom Mitford, invented a painter they called Bruno Hat. They held a successful exhibition of his works, which consisted of bits of cork stuck on canvas.

DUTCH DUPE Han van Meegeren (1889–1947), a Dutch painter, sold numerous fakes which he claimed were by Vermeer and other famous Dutch painters. He made a vast fortune.

THE THINKER BY AUGUSTE RODIN (1840–1917)

DID YOU KNOW? Painted by Leonardo da Vinci (1452–1519), the *Mona Lisa* was stolen from the Louvre, Paris, in 1911 and took two years to recover. Mona Lisa's eyes seem to follow you however you look at her.

ARTISTS' DEATHS

HENRI GAUDIER-BRZESKA This French sculptor was killed in battle at age 23.

VINCENT VAN GOGH The tempestuous Dutch painter attempted suicide many times, and finally shot himself at age 37.

MARK ROTHKO An American abstract painter, Rothko slashed his elbows in 1970.

ELIZABETH SIDDAL The talented artist and wife of painter and poet Dante Gabriel Rossetti died at age 32. Her coffin was dug up by Rossetti to retrieve the poems he had buried with her.

TALLEST STATUES

CHIEF CRAZY HORSE This 563-ft (172-m) high statue, in the Black Hills of South Dakota, was begun in 1948 by Korczak Ziolkowski and is being continued by his children.

BUDDHA The tallest Buddha statue is in Japan and measures 394 ft (120 m) high.

THE INDIAN ROPE TRICK Sculptor Calle Örnemark's statue is 337 ft (103 m) high and was built in Sweden.

KEY PAINTERS

ARTIST	DATES	NATIONALITY	FAMOUS WORKS
Leonardo da Vinci	1452–1519	Italian	*Mona Lisa*
Michelangelo	1475–1564	Italian	Sistine chapel ceiling
El Greco	1541–1614	Greek	*Burial of Count Orgaz*
Rembrandt van Rijn	1606–1669	Dutch	*The Night Watch*
Francisco Goya	1746–1828	Spanish	*Maja Nude/Clothed*
Sir John Millais	1829–1896	British	*Ophelia*
Edgar Degas	1834–1917	French	*The Rehearsal*
James Whistler	1834–1903	American	*Symphony in White*
Paul Cézanne	1839–1906	French	*Les Grandes Baigneuses*
Claude Monet	1840–1926	French	*Waterlilies*
Vincent van Gogh	1853–1890	Dutch	*Sunflowers*
Pablo Picasso	1881–1973	Spanish	*Self-portrait*
Salvador Dali	1904–1989	Spanish	*The Persistence of Memory*

WORLD'S LARGEST PAINTINGS

IL PARADISO Painted by Iacopo Tintoretto (1518–1594) and his son Domenico (1562–1635) in the Palazzo Ducale, Venice, Italy, this painting measures 23 x 72 ft (7 x 22 m).

INTERIOR OF WESTMINSTER ABBEY French painter Jean-Pierre Alaux's painting, *Interior of Westminster Abbey* in the Louvre, Paris, measures 62 x 131 ft (19 x 40 m).

THE TRIUMPH OF PEACE AND LIBERTY This painting by Sir James Thornhill (1676–1734) is the largest in the UK. It can be seen on the ceiling of the Royal Naval College, Greenwich, and measures 106 ft (32 m) by 51 ft (16 m) – almost twice the area of a tennis court!

PANORAMA OF THE MISSISSIPPI American self-taught artist, John Banvard (1815–1891) painted this from sketches made along the river. Measuring 12 ft (4 m) high and 5,000 ft (1,524 m) long, it was taken to England in 1848 but was later destroyed by fire.

THE BATTLE OF GETTYSBURG Completed in 1883 by Paul Dominique Philippoteaux, this painting is 70 ft (21 m) high and 410 ft (125 m) long.

MOST EXPENSIVE PAINTINGS EVER AUCTIONED

Picasso and van Gogh are notable for their entries in this list.

ARTIST/WORK/DATE SOLD	PRICE PAID
Vincent van Gogh, *Portrait of Dr Gachet*, Christie's, New York, May 15, 1990	$75,000,000
Pierre-Auguste Renoir, *Au Moulin de la Galette*, Sotheby's, New York, May 17, 1990	$71,000,000
Pablo Picasso, *Les noces de Pierrette*, Binoche et Godeau, Paris, November 30, 1989	F. Fr 315,000,000
Vincent van Gogh, *Irises* Sotheby's, New York, November 11, 1987	$49,000,000
Pablo Picasso, *Self Portrait: Yo Picasso*, Sotheby's, New York, May 9, 1989	$43,500,000

WESTERN ART STYLES

RENAISSANCE Means "rebirth" – art of the 15th and 16th centuries that replaced medieval styles and revived the art of the Greek and Roman period.

BAROQUE The ornate style first popular in Italy in the 17th and 18th century.

NEOCLASSICISM Style of the 18th century that models itself on Classical (Greek and Roman) art.

ROMANTICISM Late 18th- and early 19th-century style that explores emotion.

REALISM A 19th-century style that depicted real life.

PRERAPHAELITISM Invented in 1848, a short-lived but influential style founded in medieval history and mythology.

IMPRESSIONISM Developed in France and named in 1874, it has became one of the most appreciated art styles.

POSTIMPRESSIONISM A development from Impressionism, including the "Pointillism" (dot painting) of Seurat, and others.

ART NOUVEAU The flowing ornamental style of the late 19th and early 20th centuries.

SYMBOLISM An attempt by late 19th-century artists to link the real and the spiritual worlds in their work.

EXPRESSIONISM Early 20th-century style in which the emotions of the painter are powerfully expressed.

CUBISM The main abstract style (art that is not a direct representation of a subject), concerned with shape and color.

ART DECO The angular decorative style popular in the 1930s.

SURREALISM A style that emerged between World Wars I and II, in which dreams and fantasy are explored.

POP ART A style that began in the 1950s, using images from popular culture (films, comics, advertising, etc).

PERFORMANCE ART Dramatic art in which the artists themselves become involved.

ENVIRONMENTAL ART Art in which the landscape is decorated or altered.

ODD ARTY-FACTS

UPSIDE DOWN In 1961, it was discovered that Henri Matisse's painting, *Le Bateau (The Boat)*, in the Museum of Modern Art, New York, had been hanging upside-down for two months. None of the 116,000 visitors had noticed.

SWEET AND SOUR Spanish surrealist painter Salvador Dali pioneered "futurist" cooking, which included Herrings and Raspberry Jam, Sausage with Nougat, Pineapple with Sardines, and Cooked Salami immersed in Hot Black Coffee.

PRETTY PAUL Painter Paul Cézanne taught his parrot to say, "Paul Cézanne is a great painter!"

SUPER SPAM At Rhode Island College's first Spam Art Festival, the winning entry was *Spamhenge*, a spam model!

GREAT COLLECTIONS

COLLECTABLES

People collect items, small or large, for fun or because they have monetary value.

Animal objects • Antiques
Art • Autographs • Coasters
Cars • Coins • Comics
Costumes • Dolls • Erasers
Matchboxes • Militaria and
weapons • Pens • Personalia
(items that belonged to
famous people) • Postcards
Posters • Programs
Rocks and minerals • Shells
Sports equipment • Stamps
Teapots • Teddy bears • Toys

DID YOU KNOW? Stamps come in all shapes and sizes. Tonga has produced banana-shaped stamps; Norfolk Island has made them island-shaped; and Sri Lanka has issued triangular stamps!

DID YOU KNOW? Your stamp collection would become very valuable if you acquired an 1856 British Guiana One Cent, because only one was ever made. It was sold in 1980 for $850,000!

STRANGE MUSEUMS

BARBIE DOLL HALL OF FAME Palo Alto, California. A collection devoted to the children's doll Barbie and her accessories from 1959 to the present.

COCKROACH HALL OF FAME Plano, Texas. Record-breaking cockroaches, and insects dressed as famous people.

MUSEUM OF DOG COLLARS Leeds Castle, Maidstone, Kent, UK. A collection of dog collars, most of them dating from the Middle Ages.

FISHERMAN'S FRIEND MUSEUM Fleetwood, Lancashire, England. A museum devoted to the menthol and eucalyptus throat lozenge, invented in 1865.

MEDIEVAL CRIME MUSEUM Rothenburg, Germany. Medieval crime, punishment, and torture implements.

MUSEUM OF THE MOUSETRAP Bedwas, near Caerphilly, Wales, UK. A collection of more than 150 mousetraps from ancient Egypt to the present.

NUT MUSEUM Old Lyme, Connecticut. Nut carvings, 8-ft (2.4-m) long nutcrackers, and other nut-related exhibits.

POTTER'S MUSEUM OF CURIOSITY Jamaica Inn, Cornwall, England. Hundreds of stuffed kittens, rabbits, and other animals are clothed and arranged in various scenes, such as a tea party and a wedding.

WORLD'S SMALLEST MUSEUM Weslaco, Texas. A single room containing a collection of antique telephones.

PLAYING CARD MUSEUM Antwerp, Belgium. Traces the history of playing cards from the 15th century to the present, and contains some of the earliest cards and printing presses.

FREIAMT STRAW MUSEUM Wohlen, Switzerland. Celebrates the straw-braiding industry, at its height in the 18th and 19th centuries. Crafts produced during that period are on display.

APPLE AND PEAR MUSEUM Château Briqebec, France. Exhibits show traditional and modern methods of cider and apple and pear production.

TIPS FOR PRESERVING YOUR COLLECTION

STORE IT SAFELY Keep your collection away from food and drinks.

KEEP IT COOL Don't store comics, books, cards, or stickers in sunlight – they will fade!

LAY IT OUT Arrange your collection in boxes or books to keep it together and clean.

UNUSUAL THINGS SOLD AT AUCTIONS

EYE EYE A box of 300 glass eyes, sold at Christie's, London, on July 11, 1997, for £2,760.

SWEDISH SKULL The skull of the Swedish philosopher Emanuel Swedenborg, sold at Sotheby's, London, March 6, 1978, for £1,500, to the Stockholm Royal Academy of Science, which reunited it with the rest of his body, buried in Uppsala Cathedral.

FLEMING'S FUNGUS A dish containing a sample of penicillin mold prepared by Alexander Fleming in 1935 was sold by Christie's, London, on July 11, 1997, for £14,950.

WALKING TALL The pair of giant Doc Marten boots worn by Elton John in the film *Tommy* was sold at Sotheby's, London, on September 6, 1988, for £12,100.

IT'S ELECTRIFYING! An electric chair, sold by Bristol Auction Rooms, UK, was bought by the Science Museum, London, on September 10, 1997, for £4,800. Owned by artist Andy Warhol, it came from the Department of Penal Correction, California.

OLD SOCKS Socks worn by Emperor Napoleon sold at Sotheby's, London, May 15, 1996, for £2,990.

BURNED BREAD A burned loaf from the Great Fire of London, 1666, sold at Sotheby's, London, May 30, 1996, for £322.

ROYAL BRIEFS Queen Victoria's underpants sold for £253 at Sotheby's, London, in 1996.

BUYING A BRIDGE London Bridge sold for $2,460,000 in 1968 and was taken to Lake Havasu City, Arizona.

EXHIBITIONS THROUGH HISTORY

MARQUIS D'AVÉZE, 1798 A display of the wares made by the leading French porcelain manufacturers.

GREAT EXHIBITION, LONDON, 1851 A showpiece of the arts and industries of the world, with the Crystal Palace at its center, seen by more than 6,000,000 visitors.

PHILADELPHIA CENTENNIAL EXPOSITION, 1876 The first major show in the US, held in celebration of the 100th anniversary of the Declaration of Independence, was seen by more than 10,000,000 people.

CENTENNIAL EXPOSITION, PARIS, 1889 Commemorated 100 years since the French Revolution. The Eiffel Tower was built as a temporary exhibit. The exhibition drew a record crowd of 32,000,000.

WORLD'S COLUMBIAN EXPOSITION, 1893 This celebrated the 400th anniversary of Christopher Columbus' discovery of America. It attracted more than 21,400,000 visitors, many of whom witnessed electricity for the first time.

PARIS, 1878 The Trocadéro Palace was built for this major show, which was visited by about 16,000,000.

EXPOSITION INTERNATIONALE DES ARTS DECORATIFS ET INDUSTRIELS MODERNES, PARIS, 1925 This exhibition of art began the "Art Deco" style.

WORLD'S FAIR, 1939–1940 Held in Flushing Meadow Park, New York, the fair was visited by 34,000,000. It was repeated in 1964–1965.

FESTIVAL OF BRITAIN, LONDON, 1951 This celebration of postwar life attracted 8,500,000 visitors.

ANCIENT TREASURES

TUTANKHAMUN'S MASK This solid gold headpiece is inlaid with gemstones, and made in the image of the teenage king. It is one of the items discovered in the pharaoh's tomb in 1922.

NIKE OF SAMOTHRACE This Greek winged statue, on display at the Louvre, Paris, dates from 200 BC. It is thought to have been created to commemorate a naval victory.

VENUS DE MILO The figure depicted in this armless statue of the second century BC is the Greek goddess Aphrodite. The sculpture reflects the ideal classic face.

ROSETTA STONE The fragment of a monument, it is inscribed in three languages and helped translation of Egyptian hieroglyphics.

FAMOUS COLLECTIONS

QUEEN ELIZABETH II'S ROYAL COLLECTION The British monarch owns the largest private collection in the world, which contains more than 250,000 works, including 7,000 paintings.

MUSÉE NATIONAL PICASSO This French museum contains 251 paintings, 160 sculptures, 29 collages, 16 papiers collés, and more than 3,000 works on paper by the Spanish artist Picasso.

HERMITAGE MUSEUM Situated in St. Petersburg, Russia, it holds a vast collection, including 12,000 sculptures, 16,000 paintings, 600,000 drawings, and 266,000 examples of applied arts.

PRICELESS JEWELS ON SHOW

KOH-I-NOOR Meaning "mountain of light," this huge diamond is believed to bring bad luck to any male owner. Owned by Indian royalty for centuries, it was presented to Queen Victoria in 1850 and it is now part of the British Crown Jewels.

STAR OF AFRICA This jewel was split from the Cullinan diamond – the largest ever discovered. It is pear-shaped, weighs 530.2 carats, and fits into the head of the British monarch's scepter.

HOPE DIAMOND This deep-blue diamond weighs 44.5 carats and is believed to bring misfortune to its owners. It is part of the gem collection at the Smithsonian Institution, Washington, D.C.

PECULIAR EXHIBITS

ROCK-CRYSTAL SKULL Experts debate whether the large, translucent skull on display at the British Museum, UK, is the work of Mexican Aztec craftsmen or of more recent origin.

THE QUEEN'S DOLLS' HOUSE A scale model of a miniature 1920s royal residence is on display at Windsor Castle, UK. The dolls' house contains intricate furniture and ornaments and was built by a special team of skilled craftsmen.

MEGA MODEL The largest dinosaur ever displayed is the *Brachiosaurus* in Humboldt University Museum, Berlin, Germany. The specimen on display may have weighed 80 tons (78.8 tonnes) when alive.

ODD KING Found in Tutankhamun's tomb, no one knows who this statue is of.

MUSIC and INSTRUMENTS

NOTE VALUES

NOTE	VALUE
Breve	musical note equal to 8 beats
Semibreve	musical note equal to 4 beats
Minim	musical note equal to 2 beats
Crochet	musical note equal to 1 beat
Quaver	musical note equal to ½ beat
Semiquaver	musical note equal to ¼ beat
Demisemiquaver	musical note equal to ⅛ beat
Hemidemisemiquaver	musical note equal to ¹⁄₁₆ beat

MUSICAL TERMS

Written music traditionally uses Italian words to tell the musician how loud, soft, fast, or slow to play the piece.

TERM	ABBREVIATION	MEANING
adagio	–	slow and leisurely
allegro	–	fast and brisk
andante	–	moderately slow
crescendo	*cresc.*	gradual increase in volume
diminuendo	*dim.*	getting softer
forte	*f*	loud or strong
fortissimo	*ff*	very loud
leggero	–	lightly
mezzo-forte	*mf*	moderately loud
mezzo-piano	*mp*	moderately soft
pianissimo	*pp*	very soft
piano	*p*	soft
rallentando	*rall.*	slowing down
sforzando	*sf*	stress note or chord
staccato	–	short, separated notes

STRANGE MUSICAL INSTRUMENTS

ARPEGGIONE Briefly popular in the 1820s, the arpeggione resembled a guitar, and had six strings, but was as big as a cello and, like a cello, was played with a bow.

GLASS HARMONICA Glass bowls suspended in water were rotated by a treadle while the player rubbed the edges. Mozart composed several works for it. American statesman and inventor Benjamin Franklin devised a version called an "armonica."

CALLIOPE Invented in 1859 by an American named Arthur Dennis, the calliope was a steam-powered organ. It was so powerful that its sound could be heard 12 miles (20 km) away!

LUSTER CHANTANT This 19th-century instrument was invented by Frederick Kastner. Its name translates as "singing lamp," and it consisted of a keyboard connected to gas lamps, which made sounds while the brightness of the lights varied according to the notes played.

OLIPHANT A curved horn made from an elephant tusk.

PANOMONICO Invented by Karl Waezel of Vienna, Austria, the panomonico was a sort of mechanical one-man-band that played 379 instruments: 150 flutes, 150 flageolets, 50 oboes, 18 trumpets, 5 fanfares, 2 kettle drums, 1 triangle, and 3 large drums.

PANTALEON Invented by George Noel in 1767, the pantaleon had 270 strings, making it one of the largest and most complicated stringed instruments ever devised.

ROCK HARMONICON Joseph Richardson (1790–1855), a British mason, discovered that striking certain types of rock produced different notes, and invented an instrument called a "rock harmonicon." His sons played it on tours throughout Britain.

SERPENT Still occasionally seen in ancient music ensembles, the serpent is a twisting woodwind instrument, resembling a snake.

MUSICAL MEMORY TIPS

The five horizontal lines on which music is written is called the staff. The pitch of the staff – either treble (above middle C) or bass (below middle C) – is introduced by the treble or bass clef. Each line or space of the staff represents a different note. Here are some quick ways of remembering what each line and space means, always reading from bottom to top:

LINES ON THE TREBLE STAFF Remember **E**very **G**ood **B**oy **D**oes **F**ine, and you will never forget that these lines indicate the notes **E**, **G**, **B**, **D**, and **F**.

SPACES ON THE TREBLE STAFF This is simple. The spaces make the word **FACE** – the notes **F**, **A**, **C**, and **E**.

LINES ON THE BASS STAFF Remember **G**ood **B**oys **D**o **F**ine **A**lways for the notes **G**, **B**, **D**, **F**, and **A**.

SPACES ON THE BASS STAFF Remember **A**ll **C**ows **E**at **G**rass for the notes **A**, **C**, **E**, and **G**.

INSTRUMENTS OF THE ORCHESTRA

STRINGS

Stringed instruments produce their sound through the vibration of strings. They are normally played with a bow, but can be plucked. A harp is occasionally included in the strings section.

VIOLIN A violin has four strings tuned to G, D, A, and E. It is the highest pitched of the strings and usually carries the tune.

VIOLA Larger and deeper than a violin, the viola is tuned a fifth lower – C, G, D, and A.

CELLO The cello or violoncello evolved in the 16th century from an instrument called the violone. Its strings are tuned to C, G, D, and A, an octave lower than the viola. It is played resting on the ground between the performer's knees.

DOUBLE BASS The largest and deepest stringed instrument in the orchestra, tuned to E, A, D, and G, it also dates from the 16th century.

WOODWINDS

Woodwind instruments are either blown through a mouth hole, or played by means of a vibrating reed. The bigger the instrument, the lower its pitch.

FLUTE The side-blown flute, dating from the 12th century and improved in the early 19th, is the most familiar type of flute in the orchestra. A piccolo is a small flute dating from the early 18th century.

OBOE The oboe is a double-reeded woodwind developed from an old instrument called a shawn. It came into use in the orchestra in the 18th century.

CLARINET Developed from the chalumeau, the clarinet was introduced in the early 18th century.

BASSOON The bassoon, which dates from the 16th century but was introduced in the 18th century, produces the lowest woodwind notes.

BRASSES

Brass instruments are played by the action of valves and the position of the player's lips on the mouthpiece.

FRENCH HORN The French horn is so called because it is said to have developed from the French hunting horn. It was introduced to the orchestra in the late 17th century.

TRUMPET The descendant of an ancient instrument, the trumpet acquired valves in the early 19th century. Its relative the cornet is also sometimes included in the orchestra.

TROMBONE Derived from a medieval instrument called a sackbut, the trombone was first used in the orchestra in 1808, for a performance of Beethoven's Fifth Symphony in Vienna.

TUBA Most orchestras have just one tuba – a large valved 19th-century instrument that produces a deep sound.

PERCUSSION

Percussion instruments are played by being struck, rubbed, or shaken. They provide the rhythmic beat in an orchestra.

DRUMS The largest of the drum family is the bass drum, which can be operated by foot. Kettle drums are usually made of copper with a parchment skin. Strings on the underside of the smaller snare drum create a rattling sound.

TRIANGLE A small wire triangle that gives a tinkling sound.

CYMBALS Cymbals vary in size, but are clashed together, to make a clanging sound.

GLOCKENSPIEL A set of graduated steel bars set in a frame and hit with a hammer.

GONG Struck in the center, a gong makes an impressive noise.

TAMBOURINE Small cymbals set in a round frame make a sound when shaken.

WORLD'S LARGEST INSTRUMENTS

DOUBLE BASS Built by American Arthur K. Ferrisin in 1924, this giant instrument was 14 ft (4.26 m) long and weighed 1,301 lb (590 kg).

DRUMS The University of Texas Longhorn Band has a drum 25 ft (7.6 m) in circumference that has to be towed by a tractor. A drum with a circumference of 40 ft (12.5 m) was made by the Supreme Drum Co. of London in 1987.

LARGEST GUITAR In 1991, students in Jasonville, Indiana, made a scaled-up version of a Gibson guitar measuring 38 ft 2 in (11.63 m) long and weighing 1,865 lb (446 kg).

LARGEST ORGANS The 33,112-pipe Auditorium Organ in Atlantic City, New Jersey, was built in 1930. It is powered by a 365-horsepower blower and makes as much noise as 25 brass bands – making it also the world's loudest instrument. It is, however, only partly operational. The largest operational organ is the 30,067-pipe organ in the Wanamaker Department Store, Philadelphia. Passau Cathedral, Germany, houses the largest church organ built in 1928 with 16,000 pipes.

PIANO The largest is believed to be one weighing 1.25 tons (tonnes) and measuring 11 ft 8 in (3.55 m) long, built by Charles H. Challen of London in 1935.

TUBA John Philip Sousa, the American inventor of the Sousaphone, commissioned a 7-ft 6-in (2.3-m) tuba in 1896.

OUTSIZE ORCHESTRAS

Orchestras usually have about 90 musicians – but there is no limit!

1872 In Boston, Massachusetts on June 17, an 987-piece orchestra (including 400 first violinists), and a choir of 20,000 performed music by Johann Strauss.

1958 The Norwegian National Meeting of School Bands assembled 12,600 players at Trondheim, Norway.

1958 An orchestra of 2,023 musicians played on July 14, at Wolverhampton, UK.

RECORDING TIMELINE

1876 Alexander Graham Bell invents the microphone.

1877 Thomas Edison's makes the first recording of a human voice – "Mary had a little lamb" – on foil.

1887 Berliner invents the phonograph.

1898 Danish inventor Valdemar Poulson makes magnetic recordings of sound on to steel piano wire.

1904 First mass-produced double-sided discs sold in Germany.

1927 First coin-operated jukebox.

1930 Magnetic tape is used to record sound.

1931 Stereo recording introduced.

1948 First vinyl discs produced.

1964 Cassette tape becomes available.

1979 First Sony Walkman portable audio cassette players sold.

1982 First CDs sold.

CLASSICAL MUSIC

DID YOU KNOW? The first concertos were published in Italy around 1600.

CLASSICAL MUSIC TERMS

SYMPHONY Symphonies are pieces of music written for a full range of orchestral instruments. There is no dominant soloist.

CONCERTO In a concerto, a soloist is accompanied by an orchestra. A concerto orchestra usually has fewer brass and percussion instruments, which allows the soloist to be heard more clearly.

SONATA A musical composition in several movements.

FUGUE A musical composition with recurring themes.

MARCH A steady rhythmical piece composed to accompany a march.

WALTZ A piece of music in triple time, composed to accompany dancing couples.

MAZURKA Music to accompany a lively Polish dance. In moderately quick triple time.

POLKA Lively dance music, of Bohemian origin, in duple time, or two beats per measure.

MUSICAL ENSEMBLES

Groups range from duos, with two performers, to symphony orchestras which contain up to 120 or more.

DUO In a duo, one musician plays a brass, string, or wind instrument and the other a piano. Pieces for two players are called duets.

TRIO A group of three players is called a trio. A string trio uses a violin, viola, and cello. Piano trios are written for violin, cello, and piano.

QUARTET Four players together form a quartet. String quartets consist of two violins, a viola, and a cello.

QUINTET Five players make a quintet. Some quintets contain wind or brass instruments or instruments from different families.

CHOIR A group of singers. A mixed voice choir contains men and women, who sing four parts of the score.

DID YOU KNOW? A soloist is a musical artist who performs on his or her own. The word "soloist" was first used in 1864.

POPULAR OPERAS

An opera is a musical drama in which singers act out a story, accompanied by an orchestra. Most operas include passages of sung dialogue, known as recitative, solo songs called arias, and scenes with chorus.

TITLE	COMPOSER
Aïda	Giuseppe Verdi
Ariadne auf Naxos	Richard Strauss
Barber of Seville	Gioacchino Rossini
La Bohème	Giacomo Puccini
Carmen	Georges Bizet
Cosi Fan Tutte	Wolfgang Mozart
Dido and Aeneas	Henry Purcell
Don Giovanni	Wolfgang Mozart
Eugene Onegin	Peter Ilyich Tchaikovsky
Faust	Charles Gounod
Fidelio	Ludwig van Beethoven
Die Fledermaus	Johann Strauss
Götterdämmerung	Richard Wagner
Madama Butterfly	Giacomo Puccini
The Magic Flute	Wolfgang Mozart
Pagliacci	Ruggiero Leoncavallo
Peter Grimes	Benjamin Britten
Porgy and Bess	George Gershwin
Rigoletto	Giuseppe Verdi
Der Rosenkavalier	Richard Strauss
Tosca	Giacomo Puccini
La Traviata	Giuseppe Verdi

MOST PROLIFIC CLASSICAL COMPOSERS

COMPOSER	DATES	NATIONALITY	HOURS OF MUSIC
Franz Joseph Haydn	1732–1809	Austrian	340
George Frideric Handel	1685–1759	German	303
Wolfgang Amadeus Mozart	1756–1791	Austrian	202
Johann Sebastian Bach	1685–1750	German	175
Franz Schubert	1797–1828	German	134
Ludwig van Beethoven	1770–1827	German	120
Henry Purcell	1659–1695	English	116
Giuseppe Verdi	1813–1901	Italian	87
Anton Dvorák	1841–1904	Czech	79
Franz Liszt	1811–1886	Hungarian	76
Peter Ilyich Tchaikovsky	1840–1893	Russian	76

DID YOU KNOW? If the length of the composer's working life were to be included in the calculation of who is the most prolific, Schubert would be the overall winner: his 134 hours of music were composed in a career of only 18 years, which means he composed an average of 7 hours 27 minutes of music per year.

KEY CLASSICAL COMPOSERS

NAME	NATIONALITY	DATES	FAMOUS WORK
Antonio Vivaldi	Italian	1678–1741	*The Four Seasons*
Johann Sebastian Bach	German	1685–1750	*Brandenburg Concertos*
George Frideric Handel	German	1685–1759	*Messiah*
Franz Joseph Haydn	Austrian	1732–1809	*London Symphonies*
Wolfgang Amadeus Mozart	Austrian	1756–1791	*The Magic Flute*
Ludwig van Beethoven	German	1770–1827	*Pastoral Symphony*
Franz Schubert	Austrian	1797–1828	*Die Winterreise*
Hector Berlioz	French	1803–1869	*Symphonie Fantastique*
Felix Mendelssohn	German	1809–1847	*A Midsummer Night's Dream*
Frédéric Chopin	Polish	1810–1849	*Piano works*
Franz Liszt	Hungarian	1811–1886	*Les Préludes*
Richard Wagner	German	1813–1883	*The Flying Dutchman*
Giuseppe Verdi	Italian	1813–1901	*La Traviata*
Johann Strauss	Austrian	1825–1899	*Die Fledermaus*
Peter Ilyich Tchaikovsky	Russian	1840–1893	*Swan Lake*
Anton Dvorák	Czech	1841–1904	*Slavonic Dances*
Edward Elgar	English	1857–1934	*Enigma Variations*
Giacomo Puccini	Italian	1858–1924	*La Bohème*
Gustav Mahler	Austrian	1860–1911	*Resurrection Symphony*
Claude Debussy	French	1862–1918	*La Mer*
Richard Strauss	German	1864–1949	*Der Rosenkavalier*
Sergei Rachmaninov	Russian	1873–1943	*Piano works*
Gustav Holst	English	1874–1934	*The Planets*
Maurice Ravel	French	1875–1937	*Boléro*
Benjamin Britten	English	1913–1976	*Billy Budd*
Philip Glass	American	b.1937	*Einstein on the Beach*

FAMOUS OPERA HOUSES

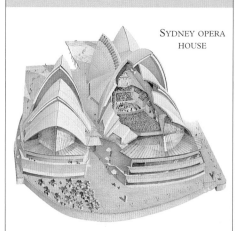

SYDNEY OPERA HOUSE

SYDNEY OPERA HOUSE, AUSTRALIA
Officially opened by Queen Elizabeth in 1973, Sydney's opera house is on the harbor and has distinctive sail-like roofs.

ROYAL OPERA HOUSE, LONDON, UK
The present building was designed by E. M. Barry in 1858.

LA SCALA, MILAN, ITALY Home of Teatro alla Scala opera company and a major feature of the city.

METROPOLITAN OPERA, NEW YORK
The world's largest opera house, "The Met" seats 4,065 people and is the focal point of Lincoln Center's Plaza.

BAYREUTH FESTIVAL THEATER, GERMANY This opera house was built for performances of Wagner's operas.

VIENNA STATE OPERA, AUSTRIA Opened in 1869, this was bombed in 1945. The new auditorium was opened in 1955.

GREAT OPERA SINGERS

NAME	DATES	COUNTRY	VOICE
Jenny Lind	1820–1887	Swedish	Soprano
Dame Nellie Melba	1861–1931	Australia	Soprano
Kathleen Ferrier	1912–1953	UK	Contralto
Tito Gobbi	1915–1984	Italy	Baritone
Maria Callas	1923–1977	Greece	Soprano
Luciano Pavarotti	b.1935	Italy	Tenor
Placido Domingo	b.1941	Spain	Tenor
Kiri Te Kanawa	b.1944	New Zealand	Soprano
Frederica von Stade	b.1945	US	Mezzo-soprano
José Carreras	b.1946	Spain	Tenor

VOICE RANGES

SOPRANO Highest female voice.

MEZZO-SOPRANO Between soprano and contralto.

CONTRALTO Lowest female voice.

ALTO Highest male voice, traditionally sung by choirboys.

TENOR High male voice – countertenor is very high.

BARITONE Male voice, higher than bass, but lower than tenor.

BASS Lowest male voice.

OPERA FACTS

LONGEST OPERA *Die Meistersinger von Nurnberg* lasts 5 hours.

SHORTEST OPERA *The Sands of Time*, by Rees and Reynolds, lasts just 4 minutes.

OPERA TEXT The text of an opera is called the libretto.

DID YOU KNOW?
Many believe that an opera singer's voice improves with increased body weight, but there is no evidence of this.

POPULAR MUSIC ARTISTS

TOP SINGLES OF ALL TIME WORLDWIDE

Global sales are hard to calculate, since for many decades, a large part of the world carried out very little statistical research on record sales. "Worldwide" is thus usually taken to mean the known minimum sales in the West.

ARTIST/TITLE	SALES EXCEED
Elton John, *Candle in the Wind* (1997)	35,000,000
Bing Crosby, *White Christmas*	30,000,000
Bill Haley and The Comets, *Rock Around the Clock*	17,000,000
The Beatles, *I Want to Hold Your Hand*	12,000,000
Elvis Presley, *It's Now or Never*	10,000,000

TOP JOHN LENNON & PAUL McCARTNEY HITS

John Lennon and Paul McCartney were two members of the famous and influential group, The Beatles. Their songs dominated the sixties, and still influence many musicians today.

TITLE	CHARTING ARTIST(S)
She Loves You	The Beatles
I Want to Hold Your Hand	The Beatles
Can't Buy Me Love	The Beatles, Ella Fitzgerald
I Feel Fine	The Beatles
We Can Work It Out	The Beatles, Stevie Wonder
Help!	Bananarama & La La Nee Nee Noo Noo, The Beatles, Tina Turner
Day Tripper	The Beatles, Otis Redding
Hey Jude	The Beatles, Wilson Pickett
Let It Be	The Beatles, Ferry Aid
A Hard Day's Night	The Beatles, Peter Sellers

DID YOU KNOW? Items such as the barber's shop in the song *Penny Lane* have been put up for sale as Beatles' memorabilia!

TOP ALBUMS OF ALL TIME

Total worldwide sales of albums have traditionally been hard to gauge, but even with the huge expansion of the album market during the 1980s, and multiple million sales of many major releases, this Top 11 is still elite territory.

ARTIST/ALBUM	ESTIMATED SALES
Michael Jackson, *Thriller*	40,000,000
Pink Floyd, *Dark Side of the Moon*	28,000,000
Meat Loaf, *Bat out of Hell*	27,000,000
Soundtrack, *The Bodyguard*	26,000,000
Soundtrack, *Saturday Night Fever*	25,000,000
The Beatles, *Sgt. Pepper's Lonely Hearts Club Band*	24,000,000
Eagles, *Their Greatest Hits 1971–1975*	24,000,000
Mariah Carey, *Music Box*	23,000,000
Carole King, *Tapestry*	22,000,000
Simon and Garfunkel, *Bridge over Troubled Water*	22,000,000
Soundtrack, *Grease*	22,000,000

TOP JUKEBOX SINGLES

This list was compiled by the Amusement & Music Operators Association, whose members service and operate more than 250,000 jukeboxes in the US. It is based on jukebox singles from 1950 to the present.

ARTIST/GROUP	SINGLE
Patsy Cline	*Crazy* (1962)
Bob Seger	*Old Time Rock 'n' Roll* (1979)
Elvis Presley	*Hound Dog/Don't Be Cruel* (1956)
Bobby Darin	*Mack the Knife* (1959)
Steppenwolf	*Born to Be Wild* (1968)
Frank Sinatra	*New York, New York* (1980)
Bill Haley and The Comets	*Rock Around the Clock* (1955)
Marvin Gaye	*I heard It Through the Grapevine* (1968)
Otis Redding	*(Sittin' on) the Dock of the Bay* (1968)

DID YOU KNOW? Conductor Sir Georg Solti has won the most Grammy Awards ever – a total of 31.

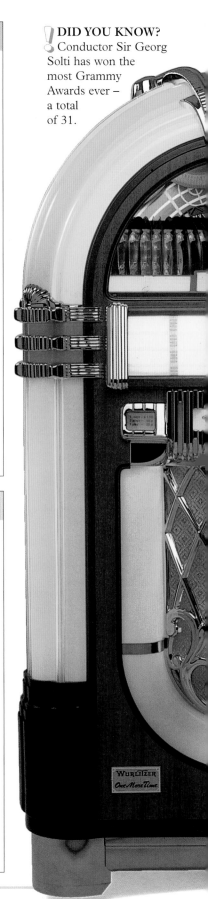

DID YOU KNOW?

An Edison phonograph [ju]kebox, invented by Louis [Gl]ass, was set up in 1889 [in] San Francisco. The first [ju]kebox based on disc [re]cordings was made in Chicago in 1906.

MOST BRIT AWARDS

The Brit Awards, which started in 1982, are sponsored by Britannia Music, Europe's largest music club. They are presented to UK and international pop musicians in various categories.

ARTIST	AWARDS
Annie Lennox	7
Phil Collins	6
The artist formerly known as Prince	6
Michael Jackson	5
George Michael	5
Blur	4
Oasis	4
Take That	4
U2	4

MOST GRAMMY AWARDS

The Grammy Awards have been presented since 1959 by the National Academy of Recording Arts and Sciences. These are the leading nonclassical winners.

ARTIST	AWARDS
Quincy Jones	26
Henry Mancini	20
Stevie Wonder	19
Paul Simon	16
John Williams	16
Aretha Franklin	15
Chet Atkins	14
David Foster	14
Ella Fitzgerald	13
Michael Jackson	13

DID YOU KNOW?

Buddy Holly's eyeglasses were sold in 1990 for $45,100 (£30,000).

MOST EXPENSIVE POP MEMORABILIA

Pioneered particularly by Sotheby's in London, pop memorabilia has become big business. In some instances, the same items have been re-auctioned by a sequence of celebrity owners to raise money for charities.

ITEM/SALE	PRICE
John Lennon's 1965 Rolls-Royce Phantom V touring limousine, Sotheby's, New York, June 29, 1985	£1,768,462
Acoustic guitar owned by David Bowie, Paul McCartney, and George Michael, Christie's, London, May 18, 1994	£220,000
Jimi Hendrix's Fender Stratocaster electric guitar, Sotheby's, London, April 25, 1990	£198,000
Paul McCartney's handwritten lyrics for *Getting Better*, 1967, Sotheby's, London, September 14, 1995	£161,000

FIRST MEMBERS OF THE ROCK AND ROLL HALL OF FAME

These seminal artists were all inducted at the first ceremony which took place on January 23, 1986, at the Waldorf-Astoria Hotel, New York. The Rock and Roll Hall of Fame and Museum is a futuristic building in Cleveland, Ohio, which opened in 1995 at a cost of $90 million (£56 million):

Chuck Berry (b.1926) • James Brown (b.1934) • Ray Charles (b.1930) • Sam Cooke (1935–1964) • Fats Domino (b.1928) Everly Brothers (Don, b.1937; Phil, b.1939) • Buddy Holly (1936–1959) • Jerry Lee Lewis (b.1935) • Elvis Presley (1935–1977) • Little Richard (b.1935)

POPULAR MUSIC STYLES/TRENDS

BLUES A slow type of US folk music that developed from the spiritual music and work songs of the 19th-century slaves.

ROCK 'N' ROLL The first of the modern popular music styles, it started in the mid-1950s as a fast blues that could be danced to.

RHYTHM AND BLUES (R & B) A style that merged traditional blues and popular music.

REGGAE West Indian rock jazz, with a simple two-beat rhythm.

HEAVY METAL A highly amplified type of rock music that appeared in the 1970s.

PUNK ROCK A style that emerged in the 1970s from groups that rebelled against authority, as their music and wild appearance showed.

DISCO Recorded music designed to be danced to. Various dance music styles have also developed in recent years, including garage and electronic styles such as techno and house music.

DANCE

DID YOU KNOW? Italian ballerina Marie Taglioni (1804–1884) became the first to go *en pointe* on points in 1832.

BALLET TERMS

BARRE The bar used by dancers to help balance when they are practicing.

CHOREOGRAPHY The composition, movement, and steps in a ballet.

CORPS DE BALLET Chorus of dancers (not those dancing solo).

PAS DE DEUX A dance for two (usually the principal male and female dancers in the company).

PAS SEULE A solo dance.

PRIMA BALLERINA The leading ballerina in a company.

BALLET POSITIONS

ARABESQUE Position in which the dancer stands on one leg, with extended arms and body bent forward, with the other leg stretched back.

ENTRECHAT Rapid crossing and uncrossing of the feet during a jump.

GLISSADE Gliding move.

JETÉ A jump from one foot to the other.

PIROUETTE A complete turn on one leg.

PLIÉ A knee-bending movement.

POINTES Dancing on the tips of the toes.

MILESTONES OF DANCE

c.15,000 BC Stone Age rock paintings show dance formations.

3000–1000 BC Egyptians use dance in the worship of gods and goddesses.

1300s Ballroom dances are held in royal palaces.

1400s Ballo, an Italian story-based dance, is the earliest form of ballet.

1681 Women are allowed to dance in ballets. By the 1840s, ballerinas are the most important of ballet dancers.

1870s The French high-kicking dance, the cancan, becomes popular.

c.1900 Isadora Duncan (1878–1927), US, is the first modern dancer.

1920s Tap, Charleston, jazz, and many other dance forms of African-American influence become increasingly popular.

1930s Dancing pair Fred Astaire (1899–1987) and Ginger Rogers (1911–1995) appear in musical films.

1950s Rock 'n' Roll established.

1970s Disco dancing evolves.

1980s Robotic break dancing is born.

DEBUTS OF POPULAR BALLETS

BALLET	FIRST DANCED
La Sylphide	1832
Giselle	1841
Coppélia	1870
Sleeping Beauty	1890
The Nutcracker	1892
Swan Lake	1895
The Rite of Spring	1913
Manon	1974
Fait Accompli	1984
Still Life at the Penguin Cafe	1988

DANCERS

ISADORA DUNCAN (1878–1927) The American contemporary dancer developed free forms of dance

MARIE RAMBERT (1888–1982) A Polish teacher and dancer, Rambert founded the Ballet Rambert (now the Rambert Dance Company).

DAME MARGOT FONTEYN (1918–1991) Fonteyn and her celebrated dancing partner Rudolf Nureyev (1938–1993), become one of the most famous dancing pairs ballet has ever seen.

GENE KELLY (1912–1996) This American dancer used his athletic dance style in film musicals, including *Singin' in the Rain* (1952).

ANNA PAVLOVA (1885–1931) The famous Russian ballerina formed her own ballet company.

WAYNE SLEEP (b.1948) The British dancer set a record for achieving 12 *entrechats* in a single jump!

ARTHUR MITCHELL (b.1934) Founded the first black classical ballet company, the Dance Theater of Harlem, New York.

POPULAR DANCE FILMS

All That Jazz (1979) • *Fame* (1980) • *Flashdance* (1983) *Lambada* (1990) • *Oklahoma!* (1955) • *The Red Shoes* (1948) *Saturday Night Fever* (1977) *Seven Brides for Seven Brothers* (1954) • *Singin' in the Rain* (1952) • *Staying Alive* (1983) *Strictly Ballroom* (1992) • *Tales of Beatrix Potter* (1971)

UNUSUAL DANCES

PYRRHIC DANCE A dance performed in ancient Greece, by soldiers wearing full armor.

TARANTELLA A wild dance originating in Naples, Italy. Its gyrations were said to resemble those of a person who had been bitten by a tarantula spider.

FURRY DANCE This dance, held annually in Helston in Cornwall, UK, is believed to have its origin in ancient times. It involves large groups of people, with men in top hats, leading their partners in and out of the town's houses.

DANCE MARATHONS Starting in 1923, endurance dances were held in the US, and gained in popularity during the Depression, when people tried to win prize money by dancing until they dropped, exhausted. The craze was eventually made illegal in many states.

DID YOU KNOW? Classical Asian dance is slow with complex hand movements.

DANCE PROPS

WEAPONS The use of weapons in dance originates from early religious ceremonies, such as war and rain dances.

SNAKES The Hopi people of North America use snakes in rain dances.

INSTRUMENTS Instruments such as castanets, are often used to help accentuate rhythm.

DANCE RECORDS

LONGEST CONGA LINE The Miami Super Conga, held on March 13, 1988, consisted of 119,986 people.

LOWEST LIMBO Dennis Walston (known as "King Limbo") of the US limboed under a bar 6 in (15.25 cm) high on March 2, 1991.

FASTEST TAP DANCER Stephen Gare, UK, achieved 32 taps per second in March 1990.

MOST CURTAIN CALLS FOR A BALLET PERFORMANCE Margot Fonteyn and Rudolf Nureyev received 89 for their performance in *Swan Lake* in Vienna, Austria, in October 1964.

FASTEST FLAMENCO Solero de Jerez tapped his heels at a record speed of 16 taps per second in Brisbane, Australia, in September 1967.

MOST EXPENSIVE COSTUME Designed by Pablo Picasso in 1917, the costume of the conjurer in *Parade* fetched $42,000 (£28,000) in 1984.

WORLD DANCE STYLES

AFRICAN DANCE In Africa, important events such as births and deaths are observed by dancing. Usually, African dance is accompanied by rhythmic drumbeats.

ASIAN DANCE Many Asian dances make use of stylized hand movements. Thai dancers, for example, use slow, controlled movements, with graceful arm and hand gestures.

EUROPEAN FOLK DANCING Folk dances are often performed in traditional costumes, and many involve people forming simple patterns such as lines or circles. Irish jigs are usually performed by pairs or individuals.

FLAMENCO This dance is a mixture of both Spanish and Arab cultures. Men use complicated footwork, while women weave patterns with their arms. The dancers are accompanied by fast, dramatic guitar music.

SOUTH AMERICAN The dances of Central and South America reflect the cultures of the native peoples, the European colonists, and their African slaves.

BALLROOM Developed in the courts of Europe, ballroom dances, such as the waltz, were adapted from folk dances. They were danced on flat, polished floors, which allowed for elegant gliding movements.

TAP DANCE In 19th-century America, slaves combined African rhythms with the jigs of English and Irish settlers.

DANCE MARATHONS

LONGEST DANCE Ritof and Edith Boudreaux danced the marathon of their lives in the US from August 29, 1930, to April 1, 1931. Their final total of 5,148 hours 28.5 minutes won them a prize of $2,000.

DISCO MARATHON Peter Stewart disco danced for a record-breaking 408 hours in Birmingham, UK, from August 6 to 21, 1983.

MARATHON TWIST Super dancer Ra Denny twisted the night away for 100 hours at Christchurch, New Zealand, in March 1962.

BELLY DANCING MARATHON Supple dancer Eileen Foucher belly danced for a total of 106 hours at Romford, Essex, UK, from July 30 to August 10, 1984.

MARATHON CHARLESTON John Giola did the Charleston dance for 22.5 hours at the Roseland Ballroom, New York, in 1926.

DID YOU KNOW? Judges at Irish jigging contests sit under the stage to assess the dancer's steps in detail.

THEATER

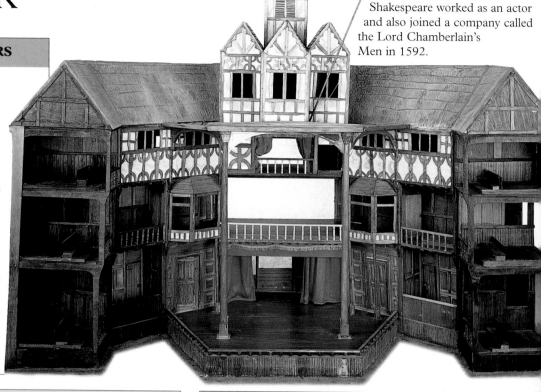

DID YOU KNOW? The English playwright William Shakespeare worked as an actor and also joined a company called the Lord Chamberlain's Men in 1592.

FAMOUS THEATERS

EPIDAURUS, GREECE Built around 400 BC, this open-air theater can seat 14,000 spectators. Fifty-five tiers of stone seats are arranged in a semi-circle around the orchestra and the stage.

GLOBE, LONDON This famous theater was first built in 1599. Many of Shakespeare's plays were performed on its stage. Spectators stood on the open-air courtyard in front of the stage or sat in covered galleries.

TEATRO OLIMPICO, VICENZA, ITALY Completed in 1583, it is the world's oldest indoor theater. It was designed in the Roman style by Palladio.

SHAKESPEARE'S MOST DEMANDING ROLES

ROLE	PLAY	NUMBER OF LINES
Hamlet	*Hamlet*	1,422

DID YOU KNOW? Hamlet's role comprises 11,610 words – over 36 percent of the total number of lines spoken in the play.

Falstaff	*Henry IV*, Parts I and II	1,178

DID YOU KNOW? Falstaff also appears in *The Merry Wives of Windsor* where he has 436 lines. His total of 1,614 lines would thus make him the most talkative of all Shakespeare's characters.

Richard III	*Richard III*	1,124
Iago	*Othello*	1,097
Henry V	*Henry V*	1,025

LONGEST-RUNNING PLAYS

SHOW	VENUE	DATES	PERFORMANCES
The Golden Horseshoe Revue	Disneyland, California	1955–1986	47,250
The Mousetrap	London	1952–	18,872
La Cantatrice Chauve	Paris	1957–	12,772
The Drunkard	Los Angeles	1933–1959	9,477
No Sex, Please – We're British	London	1971–1987	6,761

AMAZING FACT! Samuel Beckett's play *Breath* is the shortest recorded play ever written, consisting of 35 seconds of human cries and breaths.

SHAKESPEARE'S LONGEST PLAYS

Acclaimed English playwright William Shakespeare (1564–1616) wrote 37 plays and 154 14-line poems called sonnets.

PLAY	LINES
Hamlet	3,901
Richard III	3,886
Coriolanus	3,820
Cymbeline	3,813
Othello	3,672

THEATER LORE

GREEN FOR CALM Before going on stage, actors wait in a green room, since this color is believed to calm nerves.

GOOD LUCK The phrase "break a leg" is often used instead of "good luck."

UNLUCKY NAME Some actors consider it unlucky to call *Macbeth* by its title, so they call it "the Scottish play" or use another name.

ONE-NIGHT STANDS

PLAY WITHOUT AN A The one and only performance of J. R. Ronden's play took place at the Paris Théâtre des Variétés on December 18, 1816. The total absence of words containing the lette "a" was trying for the actors and the audience, who riotec and did not allow it to finish

LADY OF LYONS In 1888, at London's Shaftesbury Theatre this play failed to make its own first night whe the safety curtain jammed.

THE INTIMATE REVUE A disaster from start to finish, this play opened and closed in London, on March 11, 1930. Scenery changes took so long that seven scenes were left out to allow the audience to go home.

MUSICAL EXTRAVAGANZA In 1982, *i*, combining opera, ballet, and circus, by Arturo Brachetti, was closed before it opened – the dress rehears ran over by two hours!

FAMOUS PUPPETS

THE MUPPETS Colorful puppets who rose to fame through children's television programs and films.

PUNCH AND JUDY Punch quarrels with his wife, Judy, in a popular street show.

PINOCCHIO This storybook wooden puppet has a nose that grows longer every time he tells a

PUPPET THEATER

ANIMATRONICS Realistic animal puppets are moved by electric motors mounted within them. Operators use remote controls to activate prerecorded movements.

JAPANESE BUNRAKU Four 12-in (30.5-cm) tall puppets are carried onstage by operators dressed in black. A narrator chants the story, while a samisen player provides music.

INDONESIAN SHADOW PUPPETRY Intricately cut leather puppets appear as black shadows on a screen. Performances are accompanied by an orchestra of gongs and cymbals called a gamelan.

VIETNAMESE WATER PUPPETRY Very large puppets perform on a covered stage set up on a floating raft. The audience watches the show from the water's edge.

KEY PLAYWRIGHTS

NAME	NATIONALITY	DATES	FAMOUS PLAY
William Shakespeare	English	1564–1616	Hamlet
Pierre Corneille	French	1607–1684	Le Cid
Molière	French	1622–1673	Tartuffe
Jean Racine	French	1639–1699	Phèdre
Johann Goethe	German	1749–1832	Faust
Richard Sheridan	Irish	1751–1816	The Rivals
Henrik Ibsen	Norwegian	1828–1906	A Doll's House
George Bernard Shaw	Irish	1856–1950	Pygmalion
Anton Chekov	Russian	1860–1904	Uncle Vanya
Luigi Pirandello	Italian	1867–1936	Six Characters in Search of an Author
Susan Glaspell	American	1882–1948	Alison's House
Eugene O'Neill	American	1888–1953	Strange Interlude
Bertolt Brecht	German	1898–1956	The Threepenny Opera
Samuel Beckett	Irish	1906–1989	Waiting for Godot
Tennessee Williams	American	1911–1983	The Glass Menagerie
Eugène Ionesco	French	1912–1994	The Bald Prima Donna
Arthur Miller	American	b.1915	Death of a Salesman
John Osborne	English	1929–1994	Look Back in Anger
Harold Pinter	English	b.1930	The Caretaker

LARGEST INDOOR THEATERS

THEATER	COUNTRY	DATE OPENED	NO OF SEATS
National People's Congress Building Theatre	Beijing, China	1959	10,000
Perth Entertainment Centre	Australia	1976	8,003
Chaplin (originally Blanquetta)	Havana, Cuba	1949	6,500
Radio City Music Hall	New York, NY	1932	6,200+

LONGEST-RUNNING MUSICALS

SHOW, VENUE	DATE	PERFORMANCES
The Fantasticks, New York	1960–	15,653
Cats, London	1981–	7,242
Cats, New York	1982–	6,463
A Chorus Line, New York	1975–1990	6,137
Starlight Express, London	1984–	5,846
Les Misérables, London	1985–	5,109

TYPES OF THEATER

MIME Emotions or tales are expressed through body and face movements. Medieval court jesters and wandering minstrels used mime to entertain.

CABARET Composed of a mix of songs, dances, and theatrical sketches. The earliest shows were given in Paris, in front of dining audiences.

PANTOMIME Amusing drama that combines music, dancing, and acrobatics. Harlequin the clown is a traditional character.

MYSTERY PLAYS These link biblical scenes with current events. A group of plays is called a cycle and is traditionally performed in summer.

COMMEDIA DELL'ARTE Stock characters are played by leather-masked actors. Basic plots are improvised with acrobatics and farcical routines.

GREEK TRAGEDY Three principal characters and a chorus were part of each drama. Lead actors wore masks that indicated the character's emotion.

NOH AND KABUKI Traditional Japanese theater, which features a mixture of acting, miming, and dancing. Noh actors wear masks and ornate costumes. Kabuki actors have dramatically painted faces and perform on a revolving stage.

MUSICALS Plots are told through a mixture of music, lyrics, and dance.

FILMS

MOST EXPENSIVE FILMS EVER MADE

FILM	COUNTRY	YEAR	ESTIMATED COST ($)
Titanic	US	1997	200,000,000
Waterworld	US	1995	175,000,000
Armageddon	US	1998	140,000,000
Dante's Peak	US	1997	116,000,000
Batman and Robin	US	1997	110,000,000
Tomorrow Never Dies	US	1997	110,000,000
True Lies	US	1994	110,000,000
Speed 2: Cruise Control	US	1997	110,000,000
Inchon	US, Korea	1981	102,000,000

LONGEST FILMS EVER SCREENED

The list includes commercially screened films, but not "stunt" films created solely to break endurance records. *The Longest and Most Meaningless Movie in the World* was cut to a more manageable 1 hr 30 min, but remained just as meaningless.

TITLE	COUNTRY	YEAR	DURATION HR:MIN
The Longest and Most Meaningless Movie in the World	UK	1970	48:00
The Burning of the Red Lotus Temple	China	1928–1931	27:00
****	US	1967	25:00
Heimat	Germany	1984	15:40
Berlin Alexanderplatz	Germany/ Italy	1980	15:21

TOP MOVIE-GOING COUNTRIES

COUNTRY	ANNUAL VISITS PER PERSON
Lebanon	35.3
China	12.3
Georgia	5.6
India	5.0
Iceland	4.5
Australia	3.9
New Zealand	3.9
US	3.9
Monaco	3.7

COUNTRIES WITH THE MOST CINEMAS

COUNTRY	NUMBER OF CINEMAS
US	23,66
Ukraine	14,96
India	8,97
China	4,63
France	4,36
Italy	3,81
Germany	3,81
Belorussia	3,78
Uzbekistan	2,36

FILM EQUIPMENT

PROPS All the items that are needed to make the costumes and setting authentic.

BOOM A long pole on which a microphone is mounted.

DOLLY A wheeled stand for the camera and tripod, to help smooth movement.

GEL A colored piece of film that can filter light to create a different atmosphere.

SPECIAL FX "Special effects" – everything from creating the weather to exploding buildings!

MOST PROLIFIC FILM PRODUCERS

COUNTRY	ANNUAL PRODUCTION
India	851
US	569
Japan	252
Russia	192
France	143
China	137
Italy	107
South Korea	80
Turkey	71
UK	65

HIGHEST-GROSSING FILMS OF ALL TIME

FILM	YEAR OF RELEASE	WORLD GROSS INCOME $
Titanic	1997	1,749,900,000
Jurassic Park	1993	920,100,000
Independence Day	1996	811,200,000
Star Wars	1977	783,700,000
The Lion King	1994	766,900,000
E.T.: The Extra-Terrestrial	1982	704,800,000
Forrest Gump	1994	679,700,000
The Lost World: Jurassic Park	1997	614,100,000
Men in Black	1997	586,100,000
Return of the Jedi	1983	572,800,000
The Empire Strikes Back	1980	533,900,000

MOST EXPENSIVE ITEMS OF FILM MEMORABILIA

This list excludes color cels from animated films, which attain colossal prices: one cel from *Snow White* (1937) sold for $209,000. Cels are individual painted scenes shot in sequence to make up cartoon films.

ITEM AND SALE	PRICE $
Clark Gable's Oscar® for *It Happened One Night* Christie's, Los Angeles, December 15, 1996	607,500
Vivien Leigh's Oscar® for *Gone with the Wind* Sotheby's, New York, December 15, 1993	562,500
Poster for *The Mummy*, 1932 Sotheby's, New York, March 1, 1997	453,500
James Bond's Aston Martin DB5 from *Goldfinger* Sotheby's, New York, June 28, 1986	275,000
Clark Gable's personal script for *Gone with the Wind* Christie's, Los Angeles, December 15, 1996	244,500
"Rosebud" sled from *Citizen Kane* Christie's, Los Angeles, December 15, 1996	233,500

FILMS TO WIN THE MOST OSCARS®

FILM	YEAR	NOMINATIONS	AWARDS
Ben-Hur	1959	12	11
Titanic	1997	14	11
West Side Story	1961	11	10
Gigi	1958	9	9
The Last Emperor	1987	9	9
The English Patient	1996	12	9
Gone with the Wind	1939	13	8
From Here to Eternity	1953	13	8
On the Waterfront	1954	12	8
My Fair Lady	1964	12	8

TOP HOLLYWOOD STUDIOS

COLUMBIA Along with Tri-Star, Columbia is owned by Japanese company Sony. Among its blockbusters is *Men in Black* (1997).

MGM Among other films, Metro Goldwyn Mayer made the *Tom and Jerry* cartoons. It merged with United Artists in 1981.

PARAMOUNT Based on a studio founded in 1912, Paramount has earned huge amounts from the three Indiana Jones films, and in 1997 made *Titanic*, the highest-earning film to date.

TWENTIETH CENTURY FOX Founded in 1912, it is notable for smash hits such as *Independence Day* (1996).

UNIVERSAL Once the world's largest studio, Universal is most famous for *Jurassic Park* (1993) and *E.T.* (1982).

WARNER BROS Warner Brothers made the first sound film, *The Jazz Singer* in 1927. *Batman* (1989) is one of its highest-earning films ever.

FILM MILESTONES

1895 The film era begins when the Lumière brothers present a program of films to a paying audience in the basement of a Paris café.

1913 German filmmakers film stories of intrigue and mysterious death.

1915 *The Birth of a Nation*, directed by D. W. Griffith, is released. It is the first "epic" film and is famous for its spectacular battle scenes.

1920s The first film studios in India spring up in Bombay, later known as "Bollywood."

1927 *The Jazz Singer* is the first film to record spoken dialogue. The "talkies" revolutionize the industry and silent films soon die out.

1929 The Oscar® awards are presented for the first time. Today, the ceremony is a TV spectacular.

1932 The Technicolor process is perfected. Color films begin to replace black-and-white films.

1940s Song-and-dance musicals become popular.

1953 Twentieth Century Fox's CinemaScope introduces wide-screen cinema.

1977 *Star Wars* ushers in the era of the modern blockbuster.

1996 *Toy Story* is the first full-length computer-generated film.

DID YOU KNOW?
The Oscar® is so-called because the librarian at the Academy said that the statue reminded her of her Uncle Oscar. The name stuck!

ACADEMY FIRST AWARD
TO
CECIL BEATON
FOR COLOR COSTUME DESIGN OF
"MY FAIR LADY"

FILM STARS

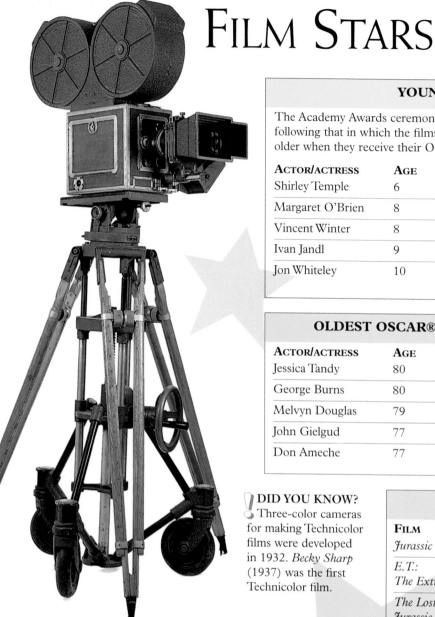

YOUNGEST OSCAR® WINNERS

The Academy Awards ceremony usually takes place at the end of March in the year following that in which the films were released, so the winners are generally at least a year older when they receive their Oscar® than when they acted in their award-winning films.

ACTOR/ACTRESS	AGE	AWARD	FILM	YEAR
Shirley Temple	6	Special Award	For all her films	1934
Margaret O'Brien	8	Special Award	*Meet Me in St. Louis*	1944
Vincent Winter	8	Special Award	*The Little Kidnappers*	1954
Ivan Jandl	9	Special Award	*The Search*	1948
Jon Whiteley	10	Special Award	*The Little Kidnappers*	1954

OLDEST OSCAR®-WINNING ACTORS AND ACTRESSES

ACTOR/ACTRESS	AGE	AWARD	FILM	YEAR
Jessica Tandy	80	Best Actress	*Driving Miss Daisy*	1989
George Burns	80	Best Supporting Actor	*The Sunshine Boys*	1975
Melvyn Douglas	79	Best Supporting Actor	*Being There*	1979
John Gielgud	77	Best Supporting Actor	*Arthur*	1981
Don Ameche	77	Best Supporting Actor	*Cocoon*	1985

DID YOU KNOW?
Three-color cameras for making Technicolor films were developed in 1932. *Becky Sharp* (1937) was the first Technicolor film.

TOP FILMS WITH CHILD STARS

FILM	DATE	CHILD STAR(S)
Jurassic Park	1993	Joseph Mazello, Ariana Richards
E.T.: The Extra-Terrestrial	1982	Drew Barrymore, Robert McNaughton, K. C. Martel
The Lost World: Jurassic Park	1997	Joseph Mazello, Ariana Richards
Home Alone	1990	Macaulay Culkin
Mrs. Doubtfire	1993	Lisa Jakub, Matthew Lawrence, Mara Wilson
Indiana Jones and the Temple of Doom	1984	Jonathan Ke Quan

CLASSIC HOLLYWOOD FILM STARS (1920–1950)

GRETA GARBO One of Hollywood's most successful female stars, Swedish Greta Garbo captured the hearts of many men.

CARY GRANT British-born Cary Grant usually played the hero in light comedies, often with Katharine Hepburn.

KATHARINE HEPBURN The winner of four Oscars®, Katharine Hepburn often played strong female roles.

INGRID BERGMAN Winning an Oscar® in 1944 for her part in *Gaslight*, Swedish Ingrid Bergman was a leading lady.

HUMPHREY BOGART A star in the 1940s, Humphrey Bogart starred in many film noirs. His most famous film is *Casablanca*.

MARILYN MONROE A notorious Hollywood star, Monroe found fame in 1953. Her films include *Gentlemen Prefer Blondes*.

JAMES DEAN Dean became famous for his roles as a rebellious teenager, in films such as *Rebel Without a Cause*.

FILMS WITH CASTS OF THOUSANDS (OF EXTRAS)

FILM	COUNTRY	YEAR	EXTRAS
Gandhi	UK	1982	300,000
Kolberg	Germany	1945	187,000
Monster Wang-magwi	South Korea	1967	157,000
War and Peace	USSR	1967	120,000
Ilya Muromets	USSR	1956	106,000

ACTORS WHO HAVE PLAYED...

ROBIN HOOD A forest-dweller, who, with his band of Merry Men, stole from the rich and gave to the poor.
Douglas Fairbanks (1922) • Errol Flynn (1938) • Russell Hicks 1948) • Jon Hall (1948) • Robert Clarke (1951) • Richard Todd 1952) • Don Taylor (1954) • Richard Greene (1960) • Barrie Ingram (1967) • Sean Connery (1976) • John Cleese (1981) Kevin Costner (1991) • Patrick Bergin (1991) • Cary Elwes (1993)

SUPERMAN A superhero with special powers.
Kirk Alyn (1948, 1950) • George Reeves (1951, 1953–1957) Christopher Reeve (1978, 1980, 1983, 1987) • Dean Cain (1993–)

TARZAN A man reared by apes.
Elmo Lincoln (1918–1921) • Johnny Weismuller (1932–1958) Buster Crabbe (1933) • Herman Brix (changed name to Bruce Bennett) (1935) • Lex Barker (1949–1952) • Gordon Scott 1955–1960) • Denny Miller (1959) • Jock Mahoney 1962–1963) • Mike Henry (1966–1968) • Ron Ely (1970) Miles O'Keeffe (1981) • Christopher Lambert (1984)

DRACULA A vampire from Transylvania.
Bela Lugosi (1931–1948) • Lon Chaney, Jr (1943) • John Carradine (1944–1979) • Christopher Lee (1958–1976) • David Niven (1975) • George Hamilton (1979) • Frank Langella (1979) Gary Oldman (1992) • Leslie Nielsen (1995)

JESUS The son of God, according to Christian faith.
Jeffrey Hunter (1961) • Luis Alvarez (1965) • Max Von Sydow 1965) • Victor Garber (1973) • Robert Powell (1977) • Kenneth Colley (1979) • Brian Deacon (1979) • John Hurt (1981) Willem Dafoe (1988)

JAMES BOND A British secret agent.
David Niven (1967) • Sean Connery (1962–1983) • George Lazenby (1969) • Roger Moore (1973–1983) • Timothy Dalton (1987–1990) • Pierce Brosnan (1995–1997)

DID YOU KNOW? Pierce Brosnan was the favorite to replace Roger Moore in the James Bond series, but he was unavailable due to other acting obligations, so the role went to Timothy Dalton.

MODERN COMEDY STARS

STAR	FAMOUS FILM
Dan Ackroyd	*Ghostbusters* (1984)
Woody Allen	*Manhattan* (1979)
Jim Carrey	*The Mask* (1994)
Danny DeVito	*Get Shorty* (1995)
Whoopi Goldberg	*Sister Act* (1992)
Goldie Hawn	*Private Benjamin* (1980)
Steve Martin	*Parenthood* (1989)
Eddie Murphy	*Beverly Hills Cop* (1984)
Robin Williams	*Mrs. Doubtfire* (1993)

DID YOU KNOW? Stan Laurel, from the UK, and Oliver Hardy, from the US, teamed up in 1926 and were to become one of the most famous comedy duos of all time.

CARTOON CHARACTERS' FIRST SCREEN APPEARANCES

CHARACTER	FILM	YEAR
Felix the Cat	*Feline Follies*	1919
Mickey Mouse	*Steamboat Willie*	1928
Pluto	*The Chain Gang*	1930
Goofy	*Mickey's Review*	1932
Popeye	*Popeye the Sailor Man*	1933
Donald Duck	*The Wise Little Hen*	1934
Porky Pig	*I Haven't Got a Hat*	1935
Bugs Bunny	*Porky's Hare Hunt*	1938
Daffy Duck	*Porky's Hare Hunt*	1938
Tom and Jerry	*Puss Gets the Boot*	1939
Woody Woodpecker	*Knock Knock*	1940
Tweety Pie	*Birdie and the Beast*	1944
Sylvester the Cat	*Kitty Kornered*	1945
Road Runner	*Fast and Furry-ous*	1948
Speedy Gonzales	*Speedy Gonzales*	1955
Teenage Mutant Ninja Turtles	*Teenage Mutant Ninja Turtles*	1990

TOP FILMS

TOP COP FILMS

Although films in which one of the central characters is a police officer have never been the most successful films of all time, many have done well at the box office.

FILM	YEAR	ACTORS
Die Hard III	1995	Bruce Willis
The Fugitive	1993	Harrison Ford
Se7en	1995	Brad Pitt
Lethal Weapon 3	1993	Mel Gibson
Beverly Hills Cop	1984	Eddie Murphy
Beverly Hills Cop II	1987	Eddie Murphy
Speed	1994	Keanu Reeves
Lethal Weapon 2	1987	Mel Gibson

TOP SCIENCE-FICTION FILMS

A science-fiction film is one that draws on scientific knowledge and speculation for its theme or setting.

Jurassic Park (1993)
Independence Day (1996)
Star Wars (1977) • *E.T.: The Extra-Terrestrial* (1982)
The Lost World: Jurassic Park (1997) • *Men in Black* (1997)
The Empire Strikes Back (1980)
Terminator 2: Judgment Day (1991) • *Return of the Jedi* (1983) • *Batman* (1989)

TOP COMEDY FILMS

All of the films listed here have earned a total of more than $200,000,000 each worldwide.

Forrest Gump (1994) • *Home Alone* (1990) • *Ghost* (1990)
Pretty Woman (1990)
Mrs. Doubtfire (1993)
Flintstones (1995) • *The Mask* (1994) • *Liar Liar* (1997)
Look Who's Talking (1989)
Coming to America (1988)
My Best Friend's Wedding (1997) • *Home Alone 2: Lost in New York* (1992)

TOP MUSICAL FILMS

Traditional musicals (films in which the cast sing) and films in which a musical soundtrack is a major component of the film are included here.

FILM	YEAR	FAMOUS SONG
Grease	1978	*The One that I Want*
Saturday Night Fever	1977	*Stayin' Alive*
The Sound of Music	1965	*My Favorite Things*
Footloose	1984	*Let's Hear It for the Boy*
American Graffiti	1973	*That'll Be the Day*
Mary Poppins	1964	*Supercalifragilistic…*
Flashdance	1983	*What a Feeling!*

DID YOU KNOW? The popular Disney films *Aladdin*, *The Lion King*, and *Pocahontas* have all won an Oscar® for "Best Original Song."

DID YOU KNOW? The first full-length Disney film was *Snow White and the Seven Dwarfs*, made in 1937.

WHAT DOES "TOP" MEAN?

The lists here are about "top" films. This refers to the highest-earning films worldwide.

ANIMATED FILMS

Animated films stand out among the leading money-makers of each decade, some earning more than $250,000,000 apiece.

1930s *Snow White and the Seven Dwarfs* (1937) was the second highest earning film of the 1930s (after *Gone with the Wind*).

1940s *Bambi* (1942) and *Fantasia* (1940), and through additional earnings from its re-release, *Pinocchio* (1940), were the most successful films of the 1940s.

1950s *Lady and the Tramp* (1955) was the second most successful film of the 1950s (after *The Ten Commandments*).

1960s *101 Dalmatians* (1960) is the second most successful film of this decade (after *The Sound of Music*). It is followed by *Jungle Book* (1967).

1970s *The Aristocats* (1970) and *The Rescuers* (1977) were popular hits.

1980s *Who Framed Roger Rabbit*, a part animated, part live-action film (1988), was the most successful animated film of the 1980s, and is the fifth most successful animated film of all time.

1990s Eight of the top ten animated films were made in the 1990s: *The Lion King* (1994), *Aladdin* (1992), *Toy Story* (1995), *Beauty and the Beast* (1991), *Pocahontas* (1995), *The Hunchback of Notre Dame* (1996) *Casper* (part live-action – 1995), and *Hercules* (1997).

TOP CHILDREN'S FILMS

This list is of live-action films aimed at a young audience – though no doubt they are appreciated by parents!

FILM	YEAR OF RELEASE
Hook	1991
Space Jam	1996
Honey, I Shrunk the Kids	1989
Ace Ventura: When Nature Calls	1995
Teenage Mutant Ninja Turtles	1990
George of the Jungle	1997
The Karate Kid Part II	1986
Mary Poppins	1964
The Karate Kid	1984

DID YOU KNOW? Some of the most successful films of all time, such as *E.T.*, *Star Wars*, *Ghostbusters*, and *Home Alone* would top this list if it were based on "family audience" films.

TOP DISASTER FILMS

FILM	YEAR	DISASTER SUBJECT
Titanic	1997	Sinking of ocean liner
Twister	1996	Tornadoes
Die Hard III	1995	Terrorists
Apollo 13	1995	Aborted space mission
Outbreak	1995	Killer viruses

TOP HORROR FILMS

Horror films entertain or fascinate audiences by shocking or frightening, using an emphasis on bloodshed or supernatural forces.

FILM	DATE	SCARY CHARACTER
Jaws	1975	Shark
Interview With the Vampire	1994	Vampires
Jaws II	1978	Shark
Bram Stoker's Dracula	1992	Vampire
The Exorcist	1973	Evil spirit
Mary Shelley's Frankenstein	1994	Monster

TOP DINOSAUR FILMS

Jurassic Park (1993) • *The Lost World: Jurassic Park* (1997) • *Fantasia* (animated) (1940) • *The Land Before Time* (animated) (1988) • *Baby… Secret of the Lost Legend* (1985) • *One of Our Dinosaurs Is Missing* (1975) • *Journey to the Center of the Earth* (1959)

MOST-FILMED STORIES OF ALL TIME

Alice in Wonderland (Lewis Carroll) • *A Christmas Carol* (Charles Dickens) • *Cinderella* (fairy tale) • *Dr. Jekyll and Mister Hyde* (Robert Louis Stevenson) • *Dracula* (Bram Stoker) • *Frankenstein* (Mary Shelley) • *Hamlet* (William Shakespeare) • *Julius Caesar* (William Shakespeare) • *Macbeth* (William Shakespeare) • *Oliver Twist* (Charles Dickens) • *Robinson Crusoe* (Daniel Defoe) • *Romeo and Juliet* (William Shakespeare)

TOP WESTERNS

A western is a film that is set in the American West in the 19th century.

Dances with Wolves (1990) • *Maverick* (1994) • *Unforgiven* (1992) • *Butch Cassidy and the Sundance Kid* (1969) • *Jeremiah Johnson* (1972) • *How the West Was Won* (1962) • *Young Guns* (1988) • *Young Guns II* (1990) • *Pale Rider* (1985) • *Bronco Billy* (1980) • *Little Big Man* (1970)

TOP FILMS STARRING ANIMALS

This is a list of top live-action films where an animal is acknowledged as the central, rather than a secondary character.

FILM	YEAR	ANIMAL
Jaws	1975	Man-eating shark
101 Dalmatians	1996	Dalmatian puppies
Jaws II	1978	Man-eating shark
Free Willy	1993	Orca whale
Turner & Hooch	1989	A bloodhound

TOP FILM SEQUELS OF ALL TIME

ORIGINAL FILM	SEQUELS	CATEGORY
Star Wars	The Empire Strikes Back, Return of the Jedi (1977–1983)	Sci-fi
Jurassic Park	The Lost World: Jurassic Park (1993–1997)	Sci-fi
Batman	Batman Returns, Batman Forever, Batman & Robin (1989–1997)	Sci-fi
Raiders of the Lost Ark	Indiana Jones and the Temple of Doom, Indiana Jones and the Last Crusade (1981–1989)	Action

DID YOU KNOW? The original Hollywood sign read "Hollywoodland" and was lit up by 4,000 lights. A 400-ft (120-m) high replacement was erected in 1978, Hollywood's 75th anniversary.

RADIO and TELEVISION

FIRST TO HAVE TELEVISION

This lists the first to receive a high-definition regular public broadcasting service.

COUNTRY	YEAR
UK	1936
US	1939
USSR	1939
France	1948
Brazil	1950
Cuba	1950
Mexico	1950
Argentina	1951
Denmark	1951

RADIO RECORDS

FIRST BROADCAST The world's first radio broadcast took place on December 24, 1906. Canadian-born physicist Professor Reginald Augrey Fessenden played music and read from the Bible from Brant Rock in the US to ships in the Atlantic Ocean.

LARGEST AUDIENCE The BBC World Service, which is broadcast in 41 languages, is estimated to have more than 140 million regular listeners around the world.

MOST RADIO STATIONS The US has more than 12,000 authorized radio stations – more than any other country in the world.

LONGEST-RUNNING RADIO PROGRAM *Rambling with Gambling* aired six days a week on WOR radio in New York City. It was first broadcast in March 1925 and is still running.

LONGEST-RUNNING MUSIC PROGRAM BBC Radio's *Desert Island Discs* began in January 1942. In the program, guests are asked to select the records they would take with them if stranded on a desert island.

LONGEST-RUNNING SOLO PROGRAM Alistair Cooke has been presenting BBC's *Letter from America* since March 1946.

LONGEST-RUNNING SOAP *Guiding Light* is the longest-running drama in broadcasting history. Still on TV, it began on radio in 1937 and on television in 1952.

TOP RADIO-OWNERS

COUNTRY	RADIOS PER 1,000 POPULATION
US	2,093
UK	1,433
Australia	1,304
Canada	1,053
Denmark	1,034
South Korea	1,024
Monaco	1,019
Finland	1,008
New Zealand	997
Germany	944
Netherlands	937
Japan	916
France	895
Lebanon	891
Sweden	882
Ukraine	856
Switzerland	851
Italy	822

DID YOU KNOW? The top eight countries on this list have at least one radio per person.

DID YOU KNOW? The US soap *Guiding Light* is the world's longest-running serial. Still on TV after almost 50 years, it introduced daytime's first significant black character, a nurse. Its characters were so well known that in 1983, several appeared in a TV movie.

TV MILESTONES

THE FIRST DAILY BROADCAST The BBC, based in London, UK, made the first daily broadcast on November 10, 1936.

THE FIRST TV COMMERCIAL A 20-second commercial for a Bulova clock, which cost $9 to air, was broadcast by WNBT, New York, during a game between the Brooklyn Dodgers and the Philadelphia Phillies, on July 1, 1941.

THE FIRST SOAP OPERA ON TV The first regular daytime serial, DuMont TV network's *A Woman to Remember*, began its run on February 21, 1947.

THE FIRST BROADCAST OF A CURRENT AFFAIRS TV SHOW NBC's *Meet the Press* was first broadcast on November 6, 1947.

THE FIRST COMMERCIAL COLOR BROADCAST Hallmark's presentation of Gian Carlo Menotti's opera *Amahl and the Night Visitors*, aired on December 24, 1951, was the first color broadcast.

THE FIRST NETWORKED COAST-TO-COAST COLOR TV SHOW *The Tournament of Roses* parade in Pasadena, California, hosted by Don Ameche, was seen in color in 21 cities across America on January 1, 1954.

TV RECORDS

WORLD'S LONGEST-RUNNING SHOW NBC's *Meet the Press* was first transmitted on November 6, 1947, and it was shown weekly from September 12, 1948.

LONGEST CONTINUOUS BROADCAST GTV in Australia was on the air between July 19 and 26, 1969, for a record 163 hours 18 minutes, while transmitting *Apollo XI's* Moon mission during which two men walked on the Moon for the first time in history.

LONGEST-SERVING HOST The BBC's monthly *Sky at Night,* an astronomy show, has been presented by Patrick Moore without a break since April 24, 1957. It celebrated its 500th broadcast in April 1995.

DID YOU KNOW? The number of homes with TV sets is now more than 500 million worldwide.

DID YOU KNOW? The children's TV show *Sesame Street* is seen in 80 countries.

TV FIRSTS

FIRST PRESIDENT TO APPEAR ON TV The former American President Franklin D. Roosevelt was seen by US television viewers opening the World's Fair, New York, on April 30, 1939.

FIRST CORONATION The coronation of the British Queen, Elizabeth II, in 1953 was broadcast live in the UK, and also in Germany, the Netherlands, and France.

FIRST TELEVISED ATOMIC BOMB EXPLOSION An "Operation Ranger" detonation at Frenchman Flats, Nevada, on February 1, 1951, was televised by KTLA, Los Angeles.

FIRST TV INTERVIEW Irish actress Peggy O'Neil appeared on television at the Ideal Home Exhibition, UK, on April 29, 1930.

TOP TV OWNERS

COUNTRY	TVs PER 1,000 POPULATION
US	805
Monaco	750
Malta	749
Canada	714
El Salvador	689
Japan	684
Oman	657
France	589
Denmark	574
Germany	564
Finland	519
New Zealand	514
Austria	497
Netherlands	497
Australia	495
Czech Republic	482
Sweden	478
Latvia	477
Slovakia	476
Georgia	468

TOP AMERICAN TV AUDIENCES OF ALL TIME

PROGRAM	DATE	HOUSEHOLDS VIEWING: TOTAL	PERCENT
*M*A*S*H* (Finale)	Feb. 28, 1983	50,150,000	60.2
Dallas (Who Shot J.R.?)	Nov. 21, 1980	41,470,000	53.3
Roots (Part 8)	Jan. 30, 1977	36,380,000	51.1
Super Bowl XVI: 49ers v. Bengals	Jan. 24, 1982	40,020,000	49.1

As more households acquire TV sets, the most recent TV shows are naturally watched by larger audiences. Listing the top audiences by *percentage* of households viewing rather than by *total number* gives us a more accurate historical picture of TV audiences.

MOST VCRs

COUNTRY	% OF HOMES	NUMBER OF VCRs
US	89.6	86,825,000
China	13.3	40,000,000
Japan	80.4	34,309,000
Germany	71.8	26,328,000
UK	81.7	18,848,000
Brazil	37.2	15,488,000
France	70.4	15,483,000
Italy	60.2	13,161,000
Russia	20.6	10,315,000
Mexico	56.7	8,540,000
Canada	70.5	8,180,000
Spain	60.1	7,293,000

VIDEO QUESTIONS AND ANSWERS

WHO NAMED VIDEO? The terms "video recording" and "videotape" were first used in the early 1950s by TV professionals.

WHERE DOES VCR COME FROM? VCR (video cassette recorder) was used in the UK and US in 1971.

WHEN WAS VIDEO AVAILABLE? The first domestic video recorders were sold in 1974, but were very expensive.

WHEN WAS VHS LAUNCHED? The VHS (Video Home System) was launched in 1976 in the US and 1978 in Europe.

HOW MANY PEOPLE OWN VCRS? The number of homes with video recorders has increased 50-fold since 1980.

WHICH IS THE BEST-SELLING VIDEOTAPE? Disney's *Lion King* sold 20 million copies in the first six months of release.

DID YOU KNOW? The video camera was invented in 1981. Its built-in recorder saves images onto a cassette. Today, some video cameras are small enough to fit into the palm of your hand!

WORLD SPORTS

SPORTS MISCELLANY

COMMON SPORTS INJURIES

Even the fittest athletes can injure themselves during strenuous training. The most common sports injuries are:

Bruising • Sprained ankle • Sprained knee • Lower back strain • Hamstring tear • Jumper's knee • Achilles tendinitis • Shin splints • Tennis elbow

SPORTS INVOLVING ANIMALS OTHER THAN HORSES!

Not only horses are used for racing!

PIGEON RACING Homing pigeons are transported to a designated place and released to fly home. Several pigeons compete at a time, and the first to reach home is the winner.

DOG-SLED RACING This sport is popular in Alaska. Each sled is pulled by a team of dogs and is controlled by a driver called a musher. The most famous annual sled dog race is the 1,299-mile (2,090-km) Iditarod, from Anchorage to Nome.

GREYHOUND RACING Specially bred greyhound dogs chase an electric hare around a track over distances between 689 ft (210 m) and 3,609 ft (1,100 m). Races may involve six or eight dogs.

ATHLETIC HEARTS

The more demanding a sport, the bigger the heart of the athlete. Here are the categories of athlete with the biggest hearts:

Tour de France cyclists • Marathon runners • Rowers • Boxers • Sprint cyclists Middle-distance runners • Weight lifters

POPULAR SPORTS SUPERSTITIONS

GENERAL The number 13 is widely considered to be unlucky and no player wants to wear the number 13.

TENNIS It is bad luck to hold more than two balls at a time when serving.
• When switching sides, it is lucky to walk around the outside of the court.

BASEBALL It is lucky to spit into your hand before you pick up the bat.
• Never lend your bat to another player – it's considered unlucky.
• It is bad luck if a dog walks across the diamond before the first pitch.

FISHING Fish may not bite if a barefoot woman passes you on the way to the dock.
• Throw back your first catch for good luck.
• It's bad luck to change rods while fishing.
• Spitting on your bait before you cast your rod is said to make fish bite.

BOWLING If you are in the middle of a phase of winning, keep wearing the same clothes each time you play.

GOLF Start only with odd-numbered clubs.
• Carry coins in your pockets for good luck.
• Balls with a number higher than four are thought to be bad luck.

ICE HOCKEY It is bad luck for hockey sticks to lie crossed.
• Players believe that they will win if they tap the goalie on his shin pads before a game.

THE WORLD'S HIGHEST-EARNING ATHLETES

NAME	SPORT	SALARY	ENDORSEMENTS	TOTAL
Michael Jordan	Basketball	31,300,000	47,000,000	78,300,000
Evander Holyfield	Boxing	53,000,000	1,300,000	54,300,000
Oscar De La Hoya	Boxing	37,000,000	1,000,000	38,000,000
Michael Schumacher	Car racing	25,000,000	10,000,000	35,000,000
Mike Tyson	Boxing	27,000,000	—	27,000,000
Tiger Woods	Golf	2,100,000	24,000,000	26,100,000
Shaquille O'Neal	Basketball	12,900,000	12,500,000	25,400,000
Dale Earnhardt	Stock car racing	3,600,000	15,500,000	19,100,000
Joe Sakic	Ice-hockey	17,800,000	100,000	17,900,000
Grant Hill	Basketball	5,000,000	12,000,000	17,000,000

This list gives the total annual income in US dollars of each athlete during 1997. The total is, in each case, broken down into salary and endorsements, which is the money earned from sponsorship and royalties. All the athletes listed are American, with the sole exception of Michael Schumacher, who was born in Germany.

TIMELINE OF SPORTS

c.3000–1500 BC Bull sports played in ancient Crete, Greece.

c.1500 BC Wrestling, fighting, and running events in Egypt.

c.776 BC First Olympic Games held at Olympia in Greece.

c.200 BC Roman crowds watch gladiators fight to the death.

c.20 BC Sumo wrestling develops in Japan from Chinese wrestling.

c.AD 400 Aztecs of Central America play *tlachtli*, a ball game.

c.1100 Jousting is popular with English and French knights.

1200s Clergy and royalty of France play "real tennis"; skating is popular on frozen canals in Holland; bowls played in England.

1400s *Calcio* (kick), a form of early soccer, is played in Florence, Italy. Each side has 27 players.

1636 The game of lacrosse develops from baggataway, which is still played by the Huron people in present-day Ontario, Canada.

1777 British explorer Captain James Cook (1729–1779) observes people surfing off the Pacific islands of Tahiti and Oahu.

1811 First outdoor gymnasium opened by German teacher Friedrich Jahn (1778–1852), inventor of the rings and parallel bars.

1823 Rugby is born when William Webb Ellis, a pupil at Rugby School, England, picks up and runs with the ball in a soccer match.

c.1829 Baseball is first played in the US.

1839 First Grand National steeplechase is held at Aintree, England.

1843 First cross-country ski race held in Tromso, Norway.

1846 Soccer rules drawn up at Cambridge University, England.

1847 Ten-pin bowling is born in Connecticut.

1861 First hockey club formed in London.

1865 Gloved boxing develops from bare-knuckle fighting.

1866 First show-jumping event is held in Paris.

1874 Football develops from soccer and rugby.

1876 Modern badminton rules are drawn up in Poona, India.

1877 First cricket Test Match held in Melbourne, Australia; first Wimbledon lawn tennis championships held in England.

1882 Judo developed by Jigoro Kano (1860–1938) in Japan.

1891 Basketball invented in Massachusetts.

1895 Volleyball devised by William G. Morgan in Massachusetts. First auto race held, Paris–Bordeaux–Paris.

1896 First modern Olympic Games held in Athens.

1903 First Tour de France multistage bicycle race.

1924 First Winter Olympics staged at Chamonix, France.

1930 Soccer's first World Cup is held in Uruguay.

1960 First Paralympics is held for disabled people in Rome, Italy.

1980–1990s Regular mass marathons staged worldwide.

FEMALE ATHLETES OF THE 20TH CENTURY

FANNY BLANKERS-KOEN Known as "The Flying Dutchwoman," this athlete won the 80-m hurdles, 100 m, 200 m, and the sprint relay at the 1948 Olympics in London.

ZOLA BUDD In 1985, South African runner Zola Budd set a new world record of 14 min 48.07 sec for the 5,000-m race.

NADIA COMANECI This Romanian gymnast was the first ever to score a perfect 10 at the 1976 Olympics.

CHARLOTTE COOPER In 1900, this UK tennis player became first woman Olympic champion.

DAWN FRASER This Australian swimmer won gold for the 100-m freestyle in three successive Olympic Games – 1956, 1960, and 1964.

MARTINA NAVRATILOVA This Czech-born tennis player won her ninth Wimbledon singles title in 1990.

MALE ATHLETES OF THE 20TH CENTURY

ROGER BANNISTER In 1954, this UK runner was the first to run a mile in under four minutes. His time was 3 min 59.4 sec.

PRINCE BORGHESE In 1907, after 62 days, this Italian racer won the 8,045-mile (12,872-km) Peking to Paris auto race.

DONALD BRADMAN This Australian cricketer set a Test Match record on July 12, 1930, with a score of 334 runs in Leeds, UK.

JOE LOUIS This heavyweight boxer was world champion from 1937 to 1949. He defended his title 25 times.

DIEGO MARADONA Barcelona paid a record $7.5 million for Argentine soccer-player Maradona in 1982.

JOE MONTANA This US football player led his team, the San Francisco 49ers, to victory in four Super Bowls in the 1980s.

BABE RUTH This US baseball player of the Boston Red Sox was sold to the New York Yankees for $125,000 in 1920.

MAXIMUM OFFICIAL BALL WEIGHTS

BALL	WEIGHT	
	OZ	G
Table tennis ball	0.09	2.53
Squash ball	0.87	24.60
Golf ball	1.61	45.93
Tennis ball	2.06	58.50
Cricket ball	5.74	163.01
Ice-hockey puck	5.98	170.00
Billiard ball	5.99	170.10
Volleyball	9.86	280.00
Rugby ball	15.47	439.42
Bowling ball	255.55	7,260.00

BALL GAMES

VOLLEYBALL FACTFILE

WHAT IS THE GAME? Players hit a ball over a high net using any part of their upper body. Play is usually on a hard court but can take place on the beach.

NUMBER OF PLAYERS Teams usually have six players each, unlike beach volleyball, where teams of two compete. Six substitutions per set are allowed.

POSITIONS Three players play from the front attack line. The remaining three cover the rear, with the right player acting as server. Positions are rotated at each change of service.

RULES The ball may not be caught. • A team has up to three hits to return the ball. • Service changes when a serve goes out or fails to clear the net.

BEACH VOLLEYBALL

WHAT IS THE GAME? As in volleyball, players use their upper bodies to hit a ball over a net, but the game is played on the beach with only two players per team.

THE STEREOTYPE The sport has been falsely characterized as a partyer's pastime – all sun, surf and sand, blonds and bikinis.

THE TRUTH Beach volleyball players exhibit great strength, endurance, and discipline. Two-player teams run through deep sand, covering the same amount of court space as six-person teams – sometimes in 100°F (38°C) heat. They must master every single skill, especially ball control, serves, and passes.

MILESTONE Beach volleyball made its Olympic debut at the 1996 Summer Games. The US men triumphed, capturing gold and silver. The US women fared poorly, losing gold and silver to Brazil, bronze to Australia.

TOP OLYMPIC VOLLEYBALL MEDALISTS

COUNTRY	GOLD	SILVER	BRONZE	TOTAL
USSR	7	4	1	12
Japan	3	3	2	8
US	2	1	2	5
Cuba	2	–	1	3
Brazil/China	1	1	1	3
Poland	1	–	2	3
Italy	–	2	1	3
Netherlands	1	1	–	2
East Germany	–	2	–	2
Bulgaria/Czechoslovakia		1	1	2

TOP OLYMPIC HANDBALL MEDALISTS

Team handball was introduced at the 1936 Berlin Olympics as an 11-a-side outdoor game, played only by men. It was dropped from the Games until 1972, when it was reintroduced as a seven-a-side indoor game at the Olympics. It was first played at competition by women in 1976.

COUNTRY	GOLD	SILVER	BRONZE	TOTAL
USSR	5	1	2	8
Yugoslavia	3	1	1	5
South Korea	2	3	–	5
Romania	–	1	3	4
East Germany	1	1	1	3
Sweden	–	2	–	2
Hungary	–	–	2	2

BOWLING GAMES

BOWLING An indoor sport where players roll a ball down an alley aiming to knock down ten pins. It was first played in the US circa 1850 as an alternative to the German game of nine-pins. World championships are held by the Fédération Internationale des Quilleurs (FIQ).

BOWLS In bowls, individuals roll bowls called woods along a flat green, aiming at a target ball called a jack. The rules of outdoor bowls were set out in 1848 by Scotsman William Mitchell. World Championships for outdoor and indoor bowls are held every four years.

BOULES Similar to bowls, the French game of boules is usually played on sandy ground. The metal bowls are lobbed at the target ball instead of rolled along the ground as they are in bowls.

BASKETBALL FACTS The basketball court measures 85 ft (26 m) long and 46 ft (14 m) wide. • The rim of the basketball net is positioned 10 ft (3.05 m) high. • The ball weighs 21 oz (600 g) and has a circumference of 30 in (75 cm).

HANDBALL FACTFILE

WHAT IS THE GAME? One of the world's fastest team games, this Olympic sport is played between two teams on an indoor court. Goals are scored by shooting with the hands.

AIM OF THE GAME To score as many goals as possible by shooting into a 10-ft (3-m) wide goal. Players pass or bounce the ball using their hands, arms, head, or upper body.

NUMBER OF PLAYERS Up to seven may be in play at any time but at least five must be on the court when the game begins.

POSITIONS All field players play both attack and defense. Each team has a goalkeeper.

RULES No part of the leg below the knee may be used in play. The ball must not be held for longer than three seconds. Only the goalkeeper is allowed in the goal area.

TOP BASKETBALL TEAMS

MOST GAMES PLAYED Robert Parish has played 1,611 games in the National Basketball Association (NBA). This includes games played for the American Basketball Association (ABA), which folded in 1976. Parish gained this title on April 6, 1996, at the Gateway Arena, Cleveland, playing his 1,561st game.

MOST NBA TITLES The Boston Celtics have won no fewer than 16 NBA titles.

TOP POINTS IN THE WNBA In a game between the Utah Starzz and the Los Angeles Sparks, in the Women's National Basketball Association (WNBA), the score was 102–89 to the Starzz!

BASKETBALL MILESTONES

1891 Basketball is invented by Dr. James Naismith in Springfield, Massachusetts.

1895 Five-a-side is agreed as the standard size of the basketball team.

1898 The playing of professional basketball starts in the US.

1932 Basketball's world governing body, Fédération Internationale de Basketball (FIBA), is formed.

1936 Basketball becomes an Olympic sport at the Berlin Olympics; won by the US.

1939 NCAA Championships are held for the first time; won by Oregon.

1949 National Basketball Association (NBA) is formed when the National Basketball League and Basketball Association of America merge.

1950 World Championship held for the first time in Buenos Aires; won by Argentina. Staged every four years.

1953 World Championships for women basketball players are first held.

1956 NBA "Most Valuable Player" is first awarded to Bob Petit, St. Louis, Missouri.

1982 NCAA Women's Championship are first held; won by Louisiana Tech.

1989 178 national federations have become members of FIBA.

DID YOU KNOW? A game very similar to basketball was played in Mexico in the tenth century BC, by the Olmec people.

DID YOU KNOW? Many basketball players are superstitious, and believe that the last person to shoot a basket during the warm-up will have good luck during the game!

TOP POINTS-SCORERS IN AN NBA CAREER

PLAYER	TOTAL POINTS
Kareem Abdul-Jabbar	38,387
Wilt Chamberlain	31,419
Michael Jordan	29,277
Karl Malone	27,782
Moses Malone	27,409
Elvin Hayes	27,313
Oscar Robertson	26,710
Dominique Wilkins	26,534
John Havlicek	26,395
Alex English	25,613

BASKETBALL FACTFILE

WHAT IS THE GAME? Popular in nearly 200 countries worldwide, players of this fast game bounce a large ball or throw it to each other as they move around a hard court.

AIM OF THE GAME To score points by putting the ball into a basket placed at the opposing team's end of the court. The high position of each basket favors taller players.

NUMBER OF PLAYERS Each team has five players and can substitute freely. Players may both attack and defend.

POSITIONS Forwards play near the sides and guards in the middle of the court. Centers usually are the tallest players and stay near the basket.

TIME A professional game lasts for four quarters of 12 minutes each. Teams can call a one minute "time out" to discuss tactics.

RULES Moving players may take one stride holding the ball, but can move freely while bouncing it. If an opponent is pushed, a personal foul is committed. Attacking players may stay in the free throw area for three seconds only.

BASKETBALL WORLD CHAMPIONS

YEAR	MEN	YEAR	WOMEN
1978	Yugoslavia	1979	US
1982	USSR	1983	USSR
1986	US	1986	US
1990	Yugoslavia	1990	US
1994	US	1994	Brazil

SOCCER

MAJOR SOCCER EVENTS

INTERNATIONAL World Cup (1930) Olympics (1908): both every four years World Club Championship (1960): annual

EUROPE European Championship (1960): every four years • European (Champions League) Cup (1956): annual • European Cup Winners' Cup (1961): annual • UEFA (Union des Associations Européennes de Football) Cup (1955): annual

US US Open Cup (1914) • MLS (Major League Soccer) Cup (1996) • Nike US Men's Cup (1993) • Nike US Women's Cup (1993) • NCAA Men's Soccer Championship (1959) • NCAA Women's Soccer Championship (1982): all annual

ENGLAND FA (Football Association) Cup (1872) • Coca Cola (League) Cup (1961) • Auto Windscreens Shield • FA Vase (1975) • FA Trophy (1969) • Charity Shield (1898) • Women's FA Cup (1993) Women's League Cup (1993): all annual

SOUTH AMERICA Copa America (1910): every two years • Copa Libertadores (1960): annual

DID YOU KNOW? The first soccer boots were steel or chrome toe-capped. They were protective, but heavy!

SOCCER MILESTONES

1848 Cambridge students draft a set of soccer rules.

1852 First English interschool soccer match takes place at Harrow School.

1863 England's Football Association (FA) founded.

1863 Official FA rules published.

1865 In Argentina, British residents found Buenos Aires Football Club.

1874 Shinguards introduced.

1878 Referee's whistle is first used.

1888 English Football League formed.

1889 The term "Soccer" (abbreviation for "Association") is first used.

1890 Goal nets are invented.

1891 Penalty kick is introduced.

1904 Fédération Internationale de Football Association (FIFA) is set up.

1930 First World Cup.

1965 Substitutes first allowed.

1967 In US, North American Soccer League founded (folds in 1985).

1975 Soccer sensation Pelé joins the New York Cosmos, becoming the highest paid athlete in the world.

1977 Pelé's presence makes soccer the fastest-growing sport in the US.

1996 US Major League Soccer created.

1998 Brazil's Denilson Oliveirá moves to Spain's Real Betis for a record transfer fee of $35 million.

AMAZING FACT! According to rumor, a bus full of Celtic supporters traveled from Glasgow in Scotland to Nuremberg in Germany to watch their team play, only to discover they had gone to the wrong venue!

SOCCER HALL OF FAME

FIFA launched its first Hall of Champions on January 12, 1998. These players were the first ten retired players inducted into the Hall "for sporting success that contributed to the positive image of the game."

Franz Beckenbauer (Germany) • Bobby Charlton (England) • Johan Cruyff (Holland) • Alfredo di Stefano (Argentina) • Eusebio (Portugal) Stanley Matthews (England) • Pelé (Brazil) • Michel Platini (France) Ferenc Puskas (Hungary) • Lev Yashin (USSR)

WOMEN'S SOCCER

Women's soccer is on the rise in the US. In 1991, at the first women's World Cup Final in Guangzhou, China, the US women became international champions, defeating Norway 2–1. They lost the 1995 World Cup to Norway, but captured gold at the 1996 Olympics, beating China 2–1. They also won the first ever female competition at the 1998 Goodwill Games.

SOCCER FACTFILE

AIM OF THE GAME The aim is to score goals by hitting the ball into the opponents' goal. Shots are usually attempted with the feet or head.

NUMBER OF PLAYERS Each team is made up of 11 players, but play continues with fewer if one is penalized.

POSITIONS Attacking players, called forwards, are the main goal-scorers. Defenders make it difficult for opponents to shoot. Midfielders act as links between attack and defense. Each team has one goalkeeper who tries to prevent balls from entering the goal.

RULES No player, except the goalkeeper, may handle the ball with the arms or hands. Fouls are committed if players trip, obstruct, or hold opponents. Yellow and red cards indicate a player is cautioned or dismissed.

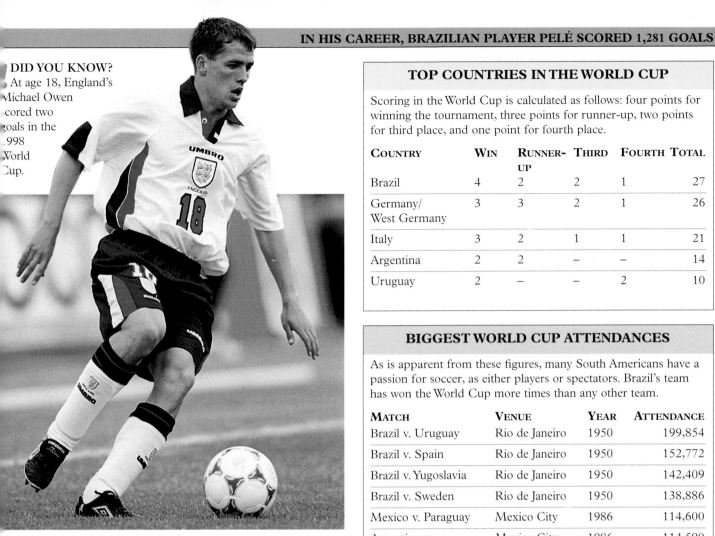

DID YOU KNOW? At age 18, England's Michael Owen scored two goals in the 1998 World Cup.

TOP COUNTRIES IN THE WORLD CUP

Scoring in the World Cup is calculated as follows: four points for winning the tournament, three points for runner-up, two points for third place, and one point for fourth place.

COUNTRY	WIN	RUNNER-UP	THIRD	FOURTH	TOTAL
Brazil	4	2	2	1	27
Germany/West Germany	3	3	2	1	26
Italy	3	2	1	1	21
Argentina	2	2	–	–	14
Uruguay	2	–	–	2	10

BIGGEST WORLD CUP ATTENDANCES

As is apparent from these figures, many South Americans have a passion for soccer, as either players or spectators. Brazil's team has won the World Cup more times than any other team.

MATCH	VENUE	YEAR	ATTENDANCE
Brazil v. Uruguay	Rio de Janeiro	1950	199,854
Brazil v. Spain	Rio de Janeiro	1950	152,772
Brazil v. Yugoslavia	Rio de Janeiro	1950	142,409
Brazil v. Sweden	Rio de Janeiro	1950	138,886
Mexico v. Paraguay	Mexico City	1986	114,600
Argentina v. West Germany	Mexico City	1986	114,590
Mexico v. Bulgaria	Mexico City	1986	114,580
Argentina v. England	Mexico City	1986	114,580

AMAZING FACT! In the 1994 World Cup, Oleg Salenko, playing for Russia, scored a record five goals for his team in one game, against Cameroon!

WORLD CUP WINNERS

YEAR	WINNERS	BEAT	SCORE
1930	Uruguay	Argentina	4:2
1934	Italy	Czechoslovakia	2:1
1938	Italy	Hungary	4:2
1950	Uruguay	Brazil	2:1
1954	West Germany	Hungary	3:2
1958	Brazil	Sweden	5:2
1962	Brazil	Czechoslovakia	3:1
1966	England	West Germany	4:2
1970	Brazil	Italy	4:1
1974	West Germany	Holland	2:1
1978	Argentina	Holland	3:1
1982	Italy	West Germany	3:1
1986	Argentina	West Germany	3:2
1990	West Germany	Argentina	1:0
1994	Brazil	Italy	3:2
1998	France	Brazil	3:0

DID YOU KNOW? The lowest-scoring World Cup competition ever was Italia 1990, which produced 115 goals from 52 matches – an average of just 2.21 per game.

TOP US FEMALE PLAYERS

PLAYER	POSITION	APPEARANCES	GOALS
Mia Hamm (1987–)	Forward	156	101
Michele Akers (1985–)	Midfielder	126	98
Kristine Lilly (1987–)	Midfielder	162	61
Tiffeny Milbrett (1991–)	Forward	101	46
Julie Foudy (1988–)	Midfielder	137	24
Carla Overbeck (1988–)	Defender	127	7
Briana Scurry (1994–)	Goalkeeper	77	–

FOOTBALL <u>and</u> RUGBY

SUPER BOWL WINNERS AND LOSERS

The Super Bowl is the annual championship football game between the best team of the National Football Conference (NFC) and that of the American Football Conference (AFC). Together, the NFC and AFC form the National Football League (NFL). The Super Bowl is the climax of the football season.

YEAR	WINNERS	LOSERS	SCORE	VENUE
1990	San Francisco 49ers	Denver Broncos	55–10	Superdome, New Orleans
1991	New York Giants	Buffalo Bills	20–19	Tampa Stadium
1992	Washington Redskins	Buffalo Bills	37–24	Metrodome, Minneapolis
1993	Dallas Cowboys	Buffalo Bills	52–17	Rose Bowl, Pasadena
1994	Dallas Cowboys	Buffalo Bills	30–13	Georgia Dome, Atlanta
1995	San Francisco 49ers	San Diego Chargers	49–26	Joe Robbie Stadium, Miami
1996	Dallas Cowboys	Pittsburgh Steelers	27–17	Sun Devil Stadium, Tampa
1997	Green Bay Packers	New England Patriots	35–21	Superdome, New Orleans
1998	Denver Broncos	Green Bay Packers	31–24	Qualcomm Stadium, San Diego

DID YOU KNOW? Each football team has up to 40 players, but only 11 may play at one time.

LARGEST NFL STADIUMS

The first professional American football game was played in Pennsylvania, in 1895. Today, the sport is immensely popular, as the seating capacities of the stadiums below illustrate.

STADIUM	HOME TEAM	CAPACITY
Pontiac Silverdome	Detroit Lions	80,368
Rich Stadium	Buffalo Bills	80,091
Arrowhead Stadium	Kansas City Chiefs	79,101
Jack Cooke Stadium	Washington Redskins	78,600
Giants Stadium	New York Giants	78,148
Mile High Stadium	Denver Broncos	76,078

SUCCESSFUL FOOTBALL TEAMS

The winner of a Super Bowl is awarded two points; the runner-up receives one. Wins take precedence over runners-up in determining ranking.

TEAM	WINS	RUNNERS-UP	POINTS
Dallas Cowboys	5	3	13
San Francisco 49ers	5	0	10
Pittsburgh Steelers	4	1	10
Washington Redskins	3	2	8
Green Bay Packers	3	1	7
Oakland/ Los Angeles Raiders	3	1	7
Miami Dolphins	2	3	7
Denver Broncos	1	4	6

FOOTBALL FACTFILE

AIM OF THE GAME Two teams of 11 players score points by carrying the ball over the opponents' goal line or kicking it between their goal posts.

POSITIONS Quarterback Punter • Kicker • Running back Defensive back • Center Lineback • Defensive linesman Offensive guard • Tackle Wide receiver • Tight end

TIME Playing time consists of four 15-minute quarters. Each team is allowed three "time-outs," of 90 or 270 seconds duration, per half. Halftime lasts 15 minutes.

RULES The attacking team has four attempts ("downs") to advance the ball 10 yd (9.1 m). If they fail, their opponents get the ball. Each down must start with a snap – a backward pass through the legs of a player.

SCORING A touchdown is scored by crossing the goal line with the ball, or gaining possession within the end zone. A field goal is scored by kicking the ball through the goal posts.

MOST CAREER POINTS

In football, a touchdown scores six points and a field goal scores three. Individual points are made up of a combination of these.

PLAYER	POINTS
George Blanda	2,002
Nick Lowery	1,711
Jan Stenerud	1,699
Gary Anderson	1,681
Morten Andersen	1,641

MOST CAREER TOUCHDOWNS

In football, players earn six points for their team by scoring a touchdown. This is when a player is in possession of the ball on, above, or behind the opponents goal line.

PLAYER	TOUCHDOWNS
Jerry Rice	166
Marcus Allen	145
Jim Brown	126
Walter Payton	125
Emmitt Smith	119

TOP POINTS-SCORERS IN MAJOR RUGBY INTERNATIONALS

PLAYER	COUNTRY	YEARS	POINTS
Michael Lynagh	Australia	1984–1995	911
Gavin Hastings	Scotland	1986–1995	667
Grant Fox	New Zealand	1985–1993	645
D. Dominguez	Italy	1991–1998	609
Neil Jenkins	Wales	1991–1998	594
S. Bettarello	Italy	1979–1988	483
Rob Andrew	England	1985–1997	396
T. Lacroix	France	1989–1997	367
A. P. Mehrtens	New Zealand	1995–1997	364

RUGBY UNION AND LEAGUE FACTFILE

WHAT IS THE GAME? This highly physical sport is divided into two forms – Union and League. Rules and scoring differ between the two types, but the aim in both is to score points by placing a ball on or over the opponents' touchline (goal line), or by kicking it over the crossbar of their goal.

NUMBER OF PLAYERS Union rugby is played between two teams of 15 players; League features two teams of 13.

POSITIONS Prop forward • Hooker • Lock forward Flank forward • Number 8 forward • Scrum half back • Fly half Left wing • Left center • Right center • Right wing • Full back

RULES The ball may not be passed forward to a teammate. The player scoring a try must be touching the ball when it meets the ground. Games start with a place kick from the center point.

SCORING In Union, a try (five points) is scored by grounding the ball on or over the touchline. Kicking the ball over the crossbar scores differently if it follows a try (two points), occurs during play (three points), or is a penalty (three points). In League, a try scores three points, and a conversion or a penalty goal both score two.

AUSTRALIAN FOOTBALL FACTS

WHAT IS THE GAME? Contested on an oval field, this sport originated in the Australian state of Victoria. The aim is to score points by kicking a ball between posts placed at either end of the field. The 18 players per team kick, "mark," or "handball" the ball.

POSITIONS Full back • Back pocket • Halfback flank • Center half back • Follower • Rover Wing • Center • Half forward flank • Center half forward Forward pocket • Full forward

RULES One player may "shepherd" another using the hip and shoulder if he or she is within 16 ft (5 m) of the ball. A running player must touch the ball on the ground every 33 ft (10 m).

SCORING Kicking the ball cleanly between the two central posts scores a goal worth six points. A "behind" – worth one point – is scored if the ball passes between the behind post and the goal post.

RUGBY UNION WORLD CUP WINNERS

YEAR	VENUE	WINNING TEAM
1987	Australia and New Zealand	New Zealand
1991	British Isles and France	Australia
1995	South Africa	South Africa

MOST-CAPPED RUGBY UNION PLAYERS

When a player is selected for a representative team, in this case, for a national squad, he is "capped."

PLAYER	COUNTRY	YEARS	CAPS
Philippe Sella	France	1982–1995	111
David Campesi	Australia	1982–1996	101
Serge Blanco	France	1980–1991	93
S.B.T. Fitzpatrick	New Zealand	1986–1997	92
Rory Underwood	England	1984–1996	85
Will Carling	England	1988–1997	72
Ieuan Evans	Wales	1987–1998	72
Rob Andrew	England	1985–1997	71
I. D. Jones	New Zealand	1990–1997	70
Mike Gibson	Ireland	1964–1979	69

DID YOU KNOW? In 1932, a rugby ball was kicked a distance of 270 ft (82 m).

STICK GAMES

TEAM STICK AND BALL GAMES AND EVENTS

GAME	MAIN COMPETITIONS	ESTABLISHED
Bandy	World Championships	1957
Croquet	The Croquet Championship	1867
	President's Cup	1934
	World Championships	1989
Hockey (field)	FIH World Cup:	
	Men's Cup	1971
	Women's Cup	1974
Hurling	All Ireland Championship	1887
Lacrosse	World Championship	1967
Roller hockey	World Championships	1936
Shinty	Camanachd Association Challenge Cup	1896
Softball	World Championship:	
	Women's Championship	1965
	Men's Championship	1966
	US National Fast Pitch Championship	1950
	Slow Pitch Championship:	
	Men's Championship	1953
	Women's Championship	1962

TOP OLYMPIC HOCKEY MEDALISTS

In this list, Great Britain includes England, Ireland, Scotland, and Wales, which competed separately in the 1908 Olympics. Germany competed as a combined team in 1956; West Germany competed separately from East Germany in 1972 and 1984.

COUNTRY	GOLD	SILVER	BRONZE	TOTAL
India	8	1	2	11
Great Britain	3	2	5	10
Netherlands	2	2	5	9
Pakistan	3	3	2	8
Australia	2	3	2	7
Germany	2	2	2	6
Spain	1	2	1	4
South Korea	–	2	–	2
US	–	–	2	2
USSR	–	–	2	2

DID YOU KNOW? Field hockey first appeared as an event in the 1908 London Olympics. More than 70 years later, women's hockey qualified as an Olympic event, making its debut at the 1980 Olympic Games held in Moscow.

DID YOU KNOW? Early Greek wall carvings from about 500 BC show hockey-like games, while curved-stick games appear on Egyptian tomb paintings from about 2050 BC.

FIELD HOCKEY FACTFILE

AIM OF THE GAME To shoot a cork ball into an opponents' goal using a hooked stick.

NUMBER OF PLAYERS Each team has 11 players, including a captain and a goalkeeper. Up to three players may be substituted during the game.

POSITIONS Field players serve as attack and defense. Goalkeepers stand guard in front of each goal. They wear protective clothing – including helmets and leg guards – to shield them from injury by the ball, which can move at great speeds.

TIME There are two halves of 35 minutes each. Teams change ends at half-time, when there is an interval lasting 10 minutes. Time lost during play is added to the end of the second half of the game.

RULES Players may hit the ball with the flat side of the stick only. A player must not raise the stick above the shoulder. Goal shots must only be attempted from within the shooting circle.

SCORING A goal is scored when the ball completely crosses the goal line between the goal posts and under the crossbar. The team with the greater number of goals at the end of the game wins the match.

DID YOU KNOW? There are several different weights of hockey stick available.

WORLD CUP FIELD HOCKEY

The men's World Cup field hockey event has been contested since 1971, and the women's since 1974. These are the winners of the men's competition since the event began.

TEAM	NO. OF WINS
Pakistan	
Netherlands	
India	
Australia	

DID YOU KNOW? Although its origins are ancient, the earliest mention of field hockey dates back to 1527, when a Scottish law described the game as "the horlinge (hurling) of litill balle with stickes or staves" – and banned it!

CHAMPION LACROSSE TEAMS

The lacrosse World Championships for men are now contested every four years. These are the results since the Championships began in 1967.

COUNTRY	NO. OF WINS
US	7
Canada	1

The Women's World Cup was formerly the World Championship. These are the results since the World Cup started in 1982.

COUNTRY	NO. OF WINS
US	4
Australia	1

WINNERS OF TOP GOLF TOURNAMENTS

JACK NICKLAUS (b.1940) US golfer Nicklaus has won 70 PGA Tours and 14 internationals. He is the winner of the most Majors, and was named "Player of the Century" in 1988.

GREG NORMAN (b.1955) Australian player Norman has won 18 PGA Tours, 57 internationals, and is the all-time highest-earning golfer.

TIGER WOODS (b.1975) High-ranking American golfer Woods has played golf professionally since 1996. He has seven PGA Tour wins, two internationals, and was voted the 1997 Player of the Year.

SEVE (SEVERIANO) BALLESTEROS (b.1957) Top Spanish golfer Ballesteros has won the PGA Tour on six occasions, and was captain of the winning European Ryder Cup team in 1997.

NICK FALDO (b.1957) British golfer Faldo has six PGA Tour wins, 33 internationals, including three British Opens, and was the first non-American to be named Player of the Year in 1990.

GOLF FACTFILE

AIM OF THE GAME
To knock a small, dimpled ball into holes that are set far apart. The game is played on a landscaped area of grass that features obstacles, such as streams, sand bunkers, bushes, and uneven ground.

EQUIPMENT There are three types of club: woods, irons, and putters. Woods send the ball the farthest and are used for the first shot; irons are used along the course; and putters are used at the hole.

NUMBER OF PLAYERS
Individuals or teams of up to four usually compete. In the biennial Ryder Cup competition, European and American teams of 12 men play individually and in pairs.

RULES The ball must be played from the position it lies in on the course. The ball must be struck with the club's head, not pushed. A player may use a maximum of 14 clubs.

SCORING The score is calculated from the number of strokes above or below par that it takes to play a hole.

LACROSSE FACTFILE

AIM OF THE GAME To send a ball into a goal placed at the opponents' end of the field, using a stick with a netted head to throw, catch, and carry it.

NUMBER OF PLAYERS
Women's teams have a maximum of 16 players, including four substitutes. Men's teams have ten players and are permitted up to 13 substitutes in international competition.

POSITIONS Men's teams consist of three defenders, three midfielders, three attackmen, and a goalkeeper. Each team must keep four players in its own half and three in its opponents' half at all times.

TIME Men's matches last four 25-minute quarters; each team is allowed two 90-second time-outs per half. Women's matches consist of two 25-minute halves; during the first 23 minutes, the clock is stopped after every goal.

RULES Women may not kick the ball or engage in physical contact. Men are permitted shoulder-to-shoulder contact and bodychecking. No attacking player may enter the goal crease. A goal is scored when the ball passes completely over the goal line.

GOLF WORDS AND THEIR MEANINGS

PAR The standard score for a hole or round (18 holes) on a course, based on what a top player would be expected to shoot, and allowing for two putts.

BIRDIE A score of one stroke under par for a hole.

BOGEY A score of one stroke over par for a hole.

EAGLE A score of two strokes under par for a hole.

HOLE A complete section, from tee to putting green; the round hole into which the ball is played.

TEE The ground that marks the start of a hole; a peg on which the ball is put for the first stroke of a hole.

ALBATROSS Holing out in three under par on a hole.

BUNKER A sandpit on a course, known in the US as a trap.

FAIRWAY A course between the tee and the green.

GREEN The cut grass area around the hole used for putting.

GOLF TOURNAMENTS

TOURNAMENT	FIRST HELD
British Open	1860
US Open	1895
US PGA	1916
US Masters	1934
Ryder Cup (male team event)	1927
Curtis Cup (female team event)	1932

DID YOU KNOW? During a golf match in America held in the early 1900s, one of the entrants drove her ball into a river at the 16th hole. She finally completed the hole in 166 shots after going out in a boat to retrieve the ball!

181

RACKET SPORTS

TENNIS MILESTONES

c.1050 French monks play *jeu de paume* – hitting the ball with the palm of the hand.

c.1500 Long-handled racket introduced – the start of "real tennis," which is still played today as a separate sport.

1793 "Field tennis" mentioned in British *Sporting Magazine*.

1873 Lawn tennis, called *sphairistike* (Greek for "ball game"), invented.

1874 First tennis rules published.

1875 All-England Croquet Club, Wimbledon, builds first tennis courts.

1877 First Wimbledon Championships held (men only). Standard size of singles court and height of net agreed.

1881 US Championship inaugurated.

1896 Tennis included in first Olympics (dropped 1934).

1900 Davis Cup first contested.

1923 Wightman Cup (female UK and US competition) first contested.

1925 French Championships started.

1925 Australian Championships begin.

1926 First professional tennis players.

1938 Don Budge (US) first to achieve Grand Slam.

1968 Start of open era (amateurs and professionals in same events).

1988 Tennis reintroduced at Olympics.

WOMEN WITH THE MOST WIMBLEDON TITLES

PLAYER	COUNTRY	YEARS	SINGLES	DOUBLES	MIXED	TOTAL
Billie Jean King	US	1961–1979	6	10	4	20
Elizabeth Ryan	US	1914–1934	0	12	7	19
Martina Navratilova	Czechoslovakia/ US	1976–1995	9	7	3	19
Suzanne Lenglen	France	1919–1925	6	6	3	15
Louise Brough	US	1946–1955	4	5	4	13
Helen Wills-Moody	US	1927–1938	8	3	1	12

MEN WITH THE MOST WIMBLEDON TITLES

PLAYER	COUNTRY	YEARS	SINGLES	DOUBLES	MIXED	TOTAL
William Renshaw	UK	1880–1889	7	7	0	14
Lawrence Doherty	UK	1897–1905	5	8	0	13
Reginald Doherty	UK	1897–1905	4	8	0	12
John Newcombe	Australia	1965–1974	3	6	0	9
Ernest Renshaw	UK	1880–1889	1	7	0	8
Tony Wilding	New Zealand	1907–1914	4	4	0	8
Wilfred Baddeley	UK	1891–1896	3	4	0	7

TENNIS FACTFILE

WHAT IS THE GAME? A racket game played on a marked clay, grass, or synthetic court.

AIM OF THE GAME To hit the ball over the net so it lands in the correct area of the court and cannot be returned by the opponent.

NUMBER OF PLAYERS Individuals play singles competitions, while pairs play in doubles matches. In mixed doubles, each pair consists of a man and a woman.

EQUIPMENT Rackets are made of lightweight artificial materials, such as graphite. Balls are made of rubber and covered with a woolly material that makes them less slippery.

RULES The ball being served must clear the net and bounce once in the opponent's service court before being returned by the opponent.

SCORING Each rally won is worth a point; a score of four points wins the game. A player must win at least six games, and have a two-game lead, to win the set. A match lasts the best of five sets for men and the best of three for women.

DID YOU KNOW? Wimbledon, the world's oldest tennis championship, takes place every June. It has become traditional for spectators to eat strawberries and cream during their visit.

FASTEST TENNIS SERVES

NAME	COUNTRY	YEAR	MPH	KM/H
Mark Philippoussis	Australia	1997	142	229
Steve Denton	US	1984	138	222
Brenda Schulz-McCarthy	Netherlands	1996	123	196
Jana Novotna	Czech Republic	1993	115	185

HISTORY OF INTERNATIONAL RACKET SPORTS

JAI ALAI In this fast-moving game, of which several forms exist round the world, players hit the ball with a wicker basket, called a *cesta*, attached to a glove.

RACKETS Originally a medieval ball and racket game for two or four players, rackets was popular in 18th-century England.

RACQUETBALL There are two versions of this squashlike game: in the US it is called racquetball, and in Britain, it is called racketball. The original game was invented in 1949 by Joe Sobek of the US, when he sawed half the handle off a tennis racket!

REAL TENNIS A forerunner of the modern tennis, real tennis is played only in France, the UK, the US, and Australia. The World Championship began in c.1740 and is the oldest of any sport.

SQUASH First played in 1817 at Harrow School, UK, squash was used as a means of practicing rackets with a softer, "squashy" ball.

TABLE TENNIS First played in the UK in the 1880s, table tennis is commonly called Ping-Pong. It is now played worldwide.

WINNERS OF MEN'S GRAND SLAM TENNIS SINGLES TITLES

PLAYER	COUNTRY	A	F	W	US	TOTAL
Roy Emerson	Australia	6	2	2	2	12
Bjorn Borg	Sweden	0	6	5	0	11
Rod Laver	Australia	3	2	4	2	11
Pete Sampras	US	2	0	4	4	10
Jimmy Connors	US	1	0	2	5	8
Ivan Lendl	Czechoslovakia	2	3	0	3	8

A – Australian Open; F – French Open; W – Wimbledon; US – US Open

GRAND SLAM? The world's four major tournaments are known as "grand slam" tournaments. For a player to achieve the grand slam itself, he or she must win all four major titles within a season.

WINNERS OF WOMEN'S GRAND SLAM TENNIS SINGLES TITLES

PLAYER	COUNTRY	A	F	W	US	TOTAL
Margaret Court	Australia	11	5	3	5	24
Steffi Graf	Germany	4	5	7	5	21
Helen Wills-Moody	US	0	4	8	7	19
Chris Evert-Lloyd	US	2	7	3	6	18
Martina Navratilova	Czechoslovakia/US	3	2	9	4	18
Billie Jean King	US	1	1	6	4	12
Maureen Connolly	US	1	2	3	3	9
Monica Seles	Yugoslavia/US	4	3	0	2	9

DID YOU KNOW? Martina Navratilova holds the most Wimbledon singles titles – nine, which she won between 1978 and 1990.

TOP BALL SPEEDS

Jai alai 188 mph (302 km/h) • Squash 144 mph (232 km/h) Tennis 142 mph (229 km/h) • Badminton 124 mph (200 km/h) • Table tennis 106 mph (170 km/h)

SQUASH FACTFILE

WHAT IS THE GAME? A fast racket game for two (occasionally four) people, played using all four walls of an enclosed court.

EQUIPMENT A small, round-headed racket; hollow rubber ball, color-coded to indicate its speed.

RULES The server must first hit the ball onto the front wall above the cut line, but below the out-of-court line. The ball must be returned before it bounces twice.

SCORING A match consists of the best of five games. The winner of a game is the first player to reach nine points.

TABLE TENNIS FACTFILE

WHAT IS THE GAME? An indoor game for two or four players, who use small wooden paddles faced with pimpled rubber to hit a lightweight plastic ball over a low net across a table.

RULES The ball must always bounce before being returned over the net. When serving, the ball is thrown vertically from the flat hand to avoid spin.

SCORING The first side to score 21 points wins the game, but if the score reaches 20-all, the game continues until one side has a two-point lead. A match is decided by the best of three or five games.

BADMINTON FACTFILE

WHAT IS THE GAME? Players use a long-handled racket to hit a feathered birdie over a high net. Games take place indoors on a court that provides a nonslip surface for play.

AIM OF THE GAME To hit the birdie over a high net so it lands in the opponent's area of the court. Players serve underhand, but may return with an overhead swing.

NUMBER OF PLAYERS Singles matches take place between individuals. Pairs of players compete in doubles competitions. The rules of service are different for singles and doubles play.

EQUIPMENT The racket is made of lightweight metal or carbon graphite, and is strung with gut. The birdie has a cork base, which contains a ball-bearing to add weight and is circled by 16 feathers.

TIME A match lasts the best of three games. An interval of five minutes between the second and third games of a set is permitted in international competitions.

RULES A player must return the birdie before it touches the ground. When serving, the player must hit the birdie below waist level. A player may not strike the birdie with two successive shots.

SCORING Doubles and men's matches have 15 points; women's have 11. Only the server can score points. Service is passed to the other side when the server commits a fault.

CRICKET and BASEBALL

CRICKET FACTFILE

WHAT IS THE GAME? A bat-and-ball game played by two teams of 11 on a pitch with a large outfield.

AIM OF THE GAME In each "innings" the batting side defends the "wicket" and scores runs by hitting the ball bowled by a bowler. The fielding side gets the batting side out by dismissing the batsmen.

NUMBER OF PLAYERS There are two teams of 11 players. The fielding side has all 11 players on the field. The batting side has only two batsmen on the field at the same time.

POSITIONS The two batsmen each stand in front of their wickets. The fielders take up different positions on the field.

TIME Test matches are two-innings games played over five days. Limited-overs cricket is a one-day, one-innings game.

TEST COUNTRIES

Test Matches are internationals between major cricket-playing countries. These currently include the following:

Australia	England
India	New Zealand
Pakistan	South Africa
Sri Lanka	West Indies
Zimbabwe	

MOST TEST CENTURIES

When a cricketer scores 100 runs it is called a century. A century scored in a Test Match is called a Test century.

PLAYER (COUNTRY)	CENTURIES
Sunil Gavaskar (India)	34
Don Bradman (Australia)	29
Allan Border (Australia)	27
Gary Sobers (West Indies)	26
Greg Chappell (Australia)	24
Viv Richards (West Indies)	24
Javed Miandad (Pakistan)	23

HIGHEST INNINGS TOTALS IN TEST CRICKET

MATCH	VENUE	YEAR	SCORE
Sri Lanka v. India	Colombo, Sri Lanka	1997–1998	952–6d
England v. Australia	London, UK	1938	903–7d
England v. West Indies	Kingston, Jamaica	1929–1930	849d
West Indies v. Pakistan	Kingston, Jamaica	1957–1958	790–3d

d = innings declared closed by the batting side's captain

CRICKET MILESTONES

1646 First recorded cricket match at Coxheath, Kent, England. At this time, wickets were up to 6 ft (1.8 m) wide.

1676 First overseas cricket game recorded in Aleppo, Syria.

1709 First match between two English counties (Kent v. Surrey) at which there is also evidence of betting on the sport.

1729 Oldest surviving cricket bat made – now on display in the pavilion at The Oval, London, UK.

1744 Standard 22-yard (20.12-m) pitch introduced; first laws of cricket published.

1775 First six-seamed ball made of crimson leather around an interior of cork; third stump introduced.

1786 First use of two bails for each wicket. Early wickets carried only one – sometimes several feet long!

1853 Modern bat, with a willow blade and cane handle, invented

1877 First Test Match (Australia v. England).

1887 First women's cricket club.

1890 First professional women cricketers.

1934 First women's Test Match (England v. Australia).

1972 Benson & Hedges Cup (one-day match) started.

1973 First women's World Cup.

1975 First World Cup – a one-day international tournament.

MAIN WAYS OF BEING OUT IN CRICKET

BOWLED The ball breaks the batsman's wicket.

CAUGHT A fielder catches the ball after it has hit the batsman's bat or gloves.

HIT WICKET The batsman breaks his wicket while playing a shot.

LEG BEFORE WICKET (LBW) The batsman obstructs a delivery that would have otherwise touched the wicket, without previously playing the ball with his bat.

RUN OUT The wicket is broken by the fielding team before the batsman reaches the popping crease (a line that marks the limit of a batsman's approach when hitting the ball).

STUMPED The wicketkeeper breaks the batsman's wicket while the batsman is outside his ground when receiving a ball.

HANDLING THE BALL The batsman touches the ball in play.

TIMED OUT The batsman takes too long to reach the crease.

CRICKET SCORES LIST

RUNS	HOW RUNS ARE GAINED
1	The two batsmen pass each other to reach opposite wicket
1	No ball: bowler steps outside batting creases or throws, rather than bowls the ball
1	Wide: a delivery is too high or wide of the stumps for the batsman to play the ball
4	Ball reaches boundary after touching ground
6	Ball reaches boundary without touching ground

GREAT BASEBALL PLAYERS

CY (TYRUS RAYMOND) COBB (1886–1961) He played for Detroit between 1905 and 1926, and was regarded as the greatest offensive player of all time. His records for "career batting average" and "most runs in a career" stand to this day.

LOU GEHRIG (1903–1941) This New York Yankees player hit 49 home runs in 1936, and was the only player to hit 14 home runs against one opponent in a season.

WILLIE MAYS (b.1931) Mays was a Giants center fielder, who scored 660 home runs. He was the youngest player to achieve 50 home runs in a season, which he did in 1955, at the age of just 24.

PETE ROSE (b.1941) Nicknamed "Charlie Hustle," Rose played for Cincinnati and scored a record 4,256 hits in his career.

"BABE" (GEORGE HENRY) RUTH (1895–1948) Yankees outfielder who, at his retirement, was holder of more than 50 records. He is regarded as baseball's greatest player.

"HONUS" (JOHN PETER) WAGNER (1874–1955) Baseball's most popular player prior to Ruth, and was considered the game's greatest shortstop.

"CY" (DENTON TRUE) YOUNG (1867–1955) Pitcher record-holder after whom the coveted pitching award is named. He played 22 seasons between 1890 and 1911.

BASEBALL FIELDING POSITIONS

The nine fielding positions are:

Pitcher • Catcher • First baseman • Second baseman • Third baseman • Shortstop • Left fielder • Center fielder • Right fielder

FIRST PITCHERS TO THROW PERFECT GAMES

In all, only 14 pitchers have ever thrown perfect games, which means that they allow the opposition no hits, no runs, and do not allow a player to reach first base.

PLAYER	MATCH	DATE
Lee Richmond	Worcester v. Cleveland	June 12, 1880
Monte Ward	Providence v. Buffalo	June 17, 1880
Cy Young	Boston v. Philadelphia	May 5, 1904
Addie Joss	Cleveland v. Chicago	October 2, 1908
Charlie Robertson	Chicago v. Detroit	April 30, 1922

MOST HOME RUNS IN A SINGLE SEASON

A home run is when the batter hits the ball so far that he or she manages to run around all four bases in one at-bat.

PLAYER	TEAM	SEASON	HOME RUNS
Mark McGwire	St. Louis	1998	70
Sammy Sosa	Chicago	1998	66
Roger Maris	New York	1961	61
Babe Ruth	New York	1927/1921	60/59
Jimmy Foxx	Oakland	1932	58

WORLD SERIES STARS

The World Series is a post-season event played between American League and National League teams on a best-of-seven basis to determine the major league baseball champions.

TEAM	WINS
New York Yankees	23
St. Louis Cardinals	9
Philadelphia/Kansas City/ Oakland Athletics	9
Brooklyn/Los Angeles Dodgers	6
New York/San Francisco Giants	5
Boston Red Sox	5
Cincinnati Reds	5
Pittsburgh Pirates	5
Detroit Tigers	4

Teams separated by / show changes of franchise and are regarded as the same team for record purposes.

BASEBALL FACTFILE

WHAT IS THE GAME? Baseball is a bat-and-ball game played by two teams of nine players. Each team takes turns to bat and field. It is the official national pastime of the US.

AIM OF THE GAME The batting side scores runs by hitting the ball and running around four bases, touching or "tagging" each base in turn.

RULES The pitcher throws the ball at a height between the batter's armpits and knees – the "strike zone." The batter is out if he misses three strikes in a row, the ball is caught, or he is "tagged."

TIME There are nine periods called "innings." An inning ends when three members of the batting team are out.

ATHLETICS and GYMNASTICS

OLYMPIC TRACK AND FIELD EVENTS

DECATHLON Ten events (men): 100 m, long jump, shot put, high jump, 400 m, 110-m hurdles, discus, pole vault, javelin, 1,500 m.

DISCUS Thrown from a circle, it must land within a 40° arc.

HAMMER THROW Like the discus, the hammer is thrown from a circle and must fall within a 40° arc.

HEPTATHLON Seven events (women): 100-m hurdles, high jump, shotput, 200 m, long jump, javelin, 800 m.

HIGH JUMP Competitors have three jumps to clear the bar. As the bar is raised, jumpers are eliminated until the winner is left.

HURDLING Races have ten hurdles and are run over 110 m (100 for women) and 400 m.

JAVELIN The javelin is thrown from behind a curved line at the end of a run-up track and must land within a 29° arc.

LONG JUMP Athletes take a fast run-up to launch themselves.

MARATHON These long-distance runs over 26 miles 385 yd (42,195 m) are run on roads but start and end in the stadium.

POLE VAULT Athletes jump over a bar with the aid of a long pole.

RELAY RACING The major events are the 4 x 100 m and 4 x 400 m. Each athlete runs with the baton and passes it to the next runner.

RUNNING Races are run over distances of 100 m, 200 m, 400 m, 800 m, 1,500 m, 5,000 m, and 10,000 m.

SHOT PUT Athlete throws, or "puts," a heavy ball.

TRIPLE JUMP This consists of a hop, step, and jump starting with a run-up to the take off board and finishing in the sand pit.

WALK The men's walking race is held over a distance of 20 km and 50 km, and the women's is over 10 km.

DID YOU KNOW? Rhythmic gymnastics is performed by women only, using hand apparatus

ATHLETICS AND GYMNASTICS RECORDS

FOUR-MINUTE MILE Roger Bannister, UK, broke through this barrier with 3 min 59.4 secs on May 16, 1954. The current world record of 3 min 44.39 secs has been held by Noreddine Morceli (Algeria) since September 5, 1993.

GYMNASTICS Larisa Latynina (USSR) won an unbeaten record of nine gold (six individual, three team), five silver, and four bronze medals in the Olympics in the 1956, 1960, and 1964 Games.

DISCUS The women's record of 252 ft (76.80 m), by Gabriele Reinsch, is greater than the men's 243 ft (74.08 m) held by Jürgen Schult, both of East Germany. The men's discus is twice as heavy!

HIGH JUMP In 1993, Javier Sotomayor of Cuba broke his own record with a jump of 8 ft (2.45 m).

JAVELIN Jan Zelezny (Czech Republic) set the record of 323 ft 1 in (98.48 m) on May 25, 1996.

LONG JUMP Mike Powell (US) set the world record of 29 ft 4 in (8.95 m) on August 30, 1991.

SHOT PUT The world men's record of 75 ft 10 in (23.12 m) was set by Randy Barnes of the US on May 20, 1990.

LONGEST LONG JUMPS

ATHLETE	COUNTRY	YEAR	DISTANCE		
			M	FT	IN
Mike Powell	US	1991	8.95	29	4.3
Bob Beamon	US	1968	8.9	29	2.4
Carl Lewis	US	1991	8.87	29	1.2
Robert Emmiyan	USSR	1987	8.86	29	0.7

HIGHEST HIGH JUMPS

ATHLETE	COUNTRY	YEAR	HEIGHT		
			M	FT	IN
Javier Sotomayor	Cuba	1993	2.45	8	0
Patrik Sjöberg	Sweden	1987	2.42	7	11.2
Igor Paklin	USSR	1985	2.41	7	10.8
Rudolf Povarnitsyn	USSR	1985	2.40	7	10.4

LONGEST-STANDING OUTDOOR EVENT RECORDS

EVENT	HOLDER	TIME/DISTANCE	DATE SET
x 1500 m relay	West Germany	14:38.7	August 17, 1977
x 200 m relay	East Germany	1:28.15	August 9, 1980
5,000 m	Toshihiko Seko (Japan)	1:13:55.8	March 22, 1981
0,000 m	Toshihiko Seko (Japan)	1:29:18.7	March 22, 1981
hour*	Silvana Cruciata (Italy)	18,084 m	May 4, 1981
000 m	Sebastian Coe (UK)	2:12.18	July 11, 1981
x 800 m relay	UK	7:03.89	August 30, 1982
00 m*	Jarmila Kratochvilová (Czechoslovakia)	1:53.28	July 26, 1983
x 800 m relay*	USSR	7:50.17	August 5, 1984

Denotes women's races

DID YOU KNOW? UK athlete Sebastian Coe's 800-m world record of 1:41.73, set on June 10, 1981, was matched exactly by Wilson Kipketer of Denmark on July 7, 1997. This was the first time since records have been kept to one-hundredths of a second that a world outdoor record had been exactly equaled. However, Kipketer finally succeeded in breaking the world record on August 24, 1997.

FASTEST TIMES FOR THREE WORLD MARATHONS

COMPETITOR	COUNTRY	EVENT	YEAR	HR:MIN:SEC
Boston Marathon	Kenya	Cosmas Ndeti	1994	2:07:15
Boston Marathon	Germany	Uta Pippig*	1994	2:21:45
London Marathon	Spain	Abel Anton	1998	2:07:56
London Marathon	Norway	Ingrid Kristiansen*	1985	2:21:06
New York Marathon	Tanzania	Juma Ikangaa	1989	2:08:01
New York Marathon	Australia	Lisa Ondieki*	1992	2:24:40

Denotes best women's times

DID YOU KNOW? The marathon originated in ancient Greece in 490 BC when a messenger called Pheidippides ran 24 miles (39 km) to report the Athenian victory over the Persians at the Battle of Marathon. Today, marathons are standardized at 26 miles 385 yards (42,195 m). Many of the world's major cities have hosted marathon events for members of the public who are sponsored for money which goes to different charity organizations.

DID YOU KNOW? There are two Olympic gymnastic events: rhythmic gymnastics for women only, and artistic gymnastics, which includes rings, parallel bars, horse vault, asymmetric bars, and floor routines.

FASTEST MEN OVER 100 METERS

ATHLETE	COUNTRY	YEAR	SEC
Donovan Bailey	Canada	1996	9.84
Leroy Burrell	US	1994	9.85
Carl Lewis	US	1991	9.86
Frank Fredericks	Namibia	1996	9.86
Linford Christie	UK	1993	9.87
Ato Boldon	Trinidad	1997	9.89

DID YOU KNOW? In 1984, Carl Lewis (b.1961) won Olympic golds in the 100 m, 200 m, 4 x 100 m relay, and the long jump. He won five more golds in later Olympics, and retained his long-jump title three times (1988–1996), becoming only the second athlete in history to win four golds in one event.

FASTEST WOMEN OVER 100 METERS

ATHLETE	COUNTRY	YEAR	SEC
Florence Griffith Joyner	US	1988	10.49
Merlene Ottey	Jamaica	1996	10.74
Evelyn Ashford	US	1984	10.76
Irina Privalova	Russia	1994	10.77
Dawn Sowell	US	1989	10.78
Marlies Göhr	East Germany	1983	10.81
Gail Devers	US	1992	10.82
Gwen Torrence	US	1994	10.82
Marita Koch	East Germany	1983	10.83
Juliet Cuthbert	Jamaica	1992	10.83

TOP PENTATHLON COUNTRIES

Both men and women compete in the Modern Pentathlon, though only men compete in the Olympics. It covers five events: fencing, swimming, pistol shooting, cross-country running, and riding.

COUNTRY	GOLD	SILVER	BRONZE	TOTAL
Sweden	9	8	5	22
Hungary	8	6	4	18
USSR/Russia	5	7	6	18
US	0	5	3	8
Italy	2	2	3	7

HIGHEST POLE VAULTS

ATHLETE	COUNTRY	YEAR	HEIGHT M	FT	IN
Sergey Bubka	Ukraine	1994	6.14	20	1.6
Okkert Brits	S. Africa	1995	6.03	19	9.4
Igor Trandenkov	Russia	1996	6.01	19	8.6
Rodion Gataullin	USSR	1989	6.00	19	8.1

DID YOU KNOW? The men's javelin weighs 28.22 oz (800 g) and the women's javelin 27.74 oz (600 g).

THE OLYMPIC GAMES

OLYMPIC GAMES SUMMER VENUES

The modern Olympic Games, which began in 1896, were the brainchild of French scholar Pierre de Coubertin, who had been inspired by stories of the ancient Greek games. Every four years, athletes from all over the world meet to compete in the Summer Olympic Games. The only pauses since 1896 came in 1916, 1940, and 1944 when the games were canceled as a result of war. Today, over 10,000 competitors take part in more than 20 sports.

Year	Location
1896	Athens, Greece
1900	Paris, France
1904	St. Louis, MO
1906	Athens, Greece
1908	London, UK
1912	Stockholm, Sweden
1920	Antwerp, Belgium
1924	Paris, France
1928	Amsterdam, Netherlands
1932	Los Angeles, CA
1936	Berlin, Germany
1948	London, UK
1952	Helsinki, Finland
1956	Melbourne, Australia*
1960	Rome, Italy
1964	Tokyo, Japan
1968	Mexico City, Mexico
1972	Munich, Germany
1976	Montreal, Canada
1980	Moscow, USSR
1984	Los Angeles, CA
1988	Seoul, South Korea
1992	Barcelona, Spain
1996	Atlanta, GA
2000	Sydney, Australia
2004	Athens, Greece

Equestrian events held in Stockholm, Sweden

LONGEST-STANDING CURRENT OLYMPIC TRACK AND FIELD RECORDS

Event	Distance/ Time/Score	Competitor	Country	Date
Men's long jump	29 ft 2.4 in (8.90 m)	Bob Beamon	US	October 18, 196
Men's javelin	310 ft 4 in (94.58 m)	Miklos Nemeth	Hungary	July 25, 197
Women's shot	73 ft 6 in (22.41 m)	Ilona Slupianek	GDR	July 24, 198
Women's 800 m	1 min 53.43 sec	Nadezhda Olizarenko	USSR	July 27, 198
Women's 4 x 100 m	41.60 sec	Team names	GDR	August 1, 198
Men's 1500 m	3 min 32.53 sec	Sebastian Coe	GB	August 1, 198
Women's marathon	2 hr 24 min 52 sec	Joan Benoit	US	August 5, 198
Men's 800 m	1 min 43 sec	Joaquim Cruz	Brazil	August 6, 198
Decathlon	8,847 points	Daley Thompson	GB	August 9, 198
Men's 5000 m	13 min 05.59 sec	Said Aouita	Morocco	August 11, 198

At the 1968 Olympics in Mexico, Bob Beamon added a staggering 21.75 in (55.25 cm) to the old long jump record, and won the competition by a lead of 28.5 in (72.39 cm). His jump of 29 ft 2.4 in (8.90 m) was the first beyond both 28 and 29 feet (8.53 and 8.84 m). The first 28-ft (8.53-m) jump in the Olympics was not until 1980, 12 years later.

FAMOUS OLYMPIC COMPETITORS

General Patton George Patton (1885–1945), US World War II general, took part in the Modern Pentathlon at the 1912 Stockholm Games, coming fifth in the event. He might have won, but for the fact that shooting was his weakest sport!

Dr. Spock A member of the winning US rowing eights team at the 1924 Paris Olympics was Benjamin Spock (1903–1998), who later became famous as the author of *The Common Sense Book of Baby and Child Care* (1946), one of the best-selling books of all time.

Tarzan Johnny Weismuller (1904–1984), winner of swimming gold medals at the 1924 Paris Olympics and 1928 Amsterdam Olympics, went on to appear as Tarzan in numerous films.

LAST APPEARANCES OF OLYMPIC SPORTS

Each Olympic Games includes different, new sports. However, as new ones arrive, other sports are discontinued.

Sport	Last appearance
Cricket	Paris, 190
Croquet	Paris, 190
Golf	St Louis, 190
Lacrosse	London, 190
Motor boating	London, 190
Tug-of-war	Antwerp, 192
Rugby	Paris, 192
Polo	Berlin, 193

OLYMPIC DECATHLON EVENTS

The decathlon event, in which only men compete, has been included in every Olympic Games since 1904. Ten different events make up the decathlon:

100 m • Long jump • Shot put • High jump • 400 m • 110-m hurdles • Discus • Pole vault • Javelin • 1500 m

AMAZING FACT! A number of decathletes have gone on to become film actors. Floyd Simmons, who was a bronze medalist in Helsinki in 1952, appeared in *South Pacific* (1958), and Bruce Jenner, a gold medalist in Montreal in 1976, found fame through his role in *Can't Stop the Music* (1980).

TOP INDIVIDUAL MEDAL WINNERS IN A SUMMER OLYMPICS CAREER

MEDALLIST	COUNTRY	SPORT	YEARS	GOLD	SILVER	BRONZE	TOTAL
Larissa Latynina	USSR	Gymnastics	1956–1964	9	5	4	18
Nikolay Andrianov	USSR	Gymnastics	1972–1980	7	5	3	15
Edoardo Mangiarotti	Italy	Fencing	1936–1960	6	5	2	13
Takashi Ono	Japan	Gymnastics	1952–1964	5	4	4	13
Boris Shakhlin	USSR	Gymnastics	1956–1964	7	4	2	13
Sawao Kato	Japan	Gymnastics	1968–1976	8	3	1	12
Paavo Nurmi	Finland	Athletics	1920–1928	9	3	0	12
Viktor Chukarin	USSR	Gymnastics	1952–1956	7	3	1	11
Vera Cáslavská	Czechoslovakia	Gymnastics	1964–1968	7	4	0	11
Carl Osborn	US	Shooting	1912–1924	5	4	2	11
Mark Spitz	US	Swimming	1968–1972	9	1	1	11

AMAZING FACT! The only event at which outstanding gymnast Larissa Latynina did not win a medal between 1956 and 1964 was the beam, in 1956. She came in fourth!

DID YOU KNOW? The Olympic symbol is made up of five interlocking rings, standing for the continents of Europe, Asia, Africa, Australasia, and America.

MOST SUMMER OLYMPICS MEDALS

COUNTRY	GOLD	SILVER	BRONZE	TOTAL
US	815.5	622	534	1,971.5
USSR	395	319	295	1,009.0
UK	165	215.5	213	593.5
France	161	172	187.5	520.5
Germany	147.5	173	178	498.5

AMAZING FACT! "Half medals" result when nationality is uncertain and they are shared between two countries.

MOST SUMMER OLYMPICS COMPETITORS

CITY	YEAR	COUNTRIES	COMPETITORS
Atlanta	1996	197	10,310
Barcelona	1992	172	9,364
Seoul	1988	159	9,101
Munich	1972	122	7,156
Los Angeles	1984	141	7,058
Montreal	1976	92	6,085
Mexico City	1968	112	5,530

ONE-TIME OLYMPIC EVENTS

As well as sports such as cricket, croquet, golf, lacrosse, polo, and rugby, which remain popular in many countries but are no longer included in the Olympics, there are a number of "oddity" sports that have appeared once or twice, but never again:

100 M SWIMMING FOR SAILORS Only members of the Greek navy could enter this event, included in the 1896 Athens Olympics.

JUMPING ON HORSEBACK Both long jump and high jump on horseback were included in the Paris Olympics in 1900.

UNDERWATER SWIMMING In this event, which appeared only once, in the 1900 Paris Olympics, contestants received extra points for the length of time they managed to stay submerged.

WATER OBSTACLE RACE In this unusual race, held at the Paris Games, 1900, swimmers had to swim under and climb over boats.

DUELING Dueling pistol shooting was included in the Athens Games, 1906.

ARCHERY At Antwerp, 1920, archers used live birds as targets.

PARALYMPICS FACTS

WHAT ARE THE PARALYMPICS? The Paralympic Games are the Olympics for athletes with disabilities. They are held every four years, after the Olympic Games, and always at the same venue.

WHEN DID THEY START? The first Paralympics were held in Rome in 1960, with about 400 athletes from 23 countries. Until 1972, they were restricted to athletes with spinal injuries, but now include those with other disabilities. Winter Paralympics have been held since 1976.

NUMBER OF ATHLETES At the 1996 Atlanta Paralympics, 4,000 athletes from 118 countries competed.

CHAMPION GOLD MEDALLIST Louise Sauvage (Australia) won four gold medals at the 1996 Atlanta Games. She also won the Boston Wheelchair Marathon in both 1997 and 1998.

YOUNGEST COMPETITOR LeAnn Shannon (US) is the youngest person ever to compete in the Paralympic Games. Aged 13 at the time of the 1996 Atlanta Games, she won three gold medals and one silver, and holds the world record in the 400, 800, and 1,500 m wheelchair events.

WINTER SPORTS

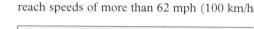

TOP ALPINE SKIING WORLD CUP TITLES

The Alpine Skiing World Cup, comprising a series of slalom and downhill events, has been staged annually since 1967. Points are awarded for race performances worldwide during the winter.

NAME	COUNTRY	YEARS	TITLES
Annemarie Moser-Proll	Austria	1971–1979	6
Marc Girardelli	Luxembourg	1985–1993	5
Gustavo Thoeni	Italy	1971–1975	4
Pirmin Zurbriggen	Switzerland	1984–1990	4
Ingemar Stenmark	Sweden	1976–1978	3
Phil Mahre	US	1981–1983	3

DID YOU KNOW? Downhill races are the fastest races in which skiers follow a set rou[t] down the mountain. Competitors regularly reach speeds of more than 62 mph (100 km/h[)]

SPORTS INCLUDED IN THE WINTER OLYMPICS

BIATHLON Introduced into the Olympics in 1960, this combined event involves cross-country skiing and shooting at targets.

BOBSLEDDING The sport dates from 1888 and has been part of the Olympics since 1924. Sleds are four- and two-man.

CURLING A bowls-like game played with big stones on ice, curling dates back to the 1600s or earlier. It entered the Olympics in 1998.

ICE HOCKEY A fast and furious game, in the Olympics since 1920.

FIGURE SKATING First included in the 1908 Olympics.

LUGE The modern luge, which is a small one- or two-person sled on which contestants lie back, was included in the 1964 Olympics.

SKIING Alpine skiing, introduced in the 1948 Olympics, includes downhill, slalom, and freestyle. Nordic skiing includes cross-country and ski-jumping.

SKI JUMPING Introduced into the Olympics in 1924, jumps have become progressively longer; the men's world men's record now stands at 669 ft (204 m).

SNOWBOARDING The development of high-tech boards has made snowboarding one of the most popular snow sports. It was first included in the 1998 Winter Olympics.

SPEED SKATING An Olympic sport since 1924. Speed skaters are the fastest self-propelled humans on a level surface. Short track speed skating was introduced in 1992.

VENUES FOR THE WINTER OLYMPIC GAMES

Until 1992, the Winter Games were held in the same year as the Summer Games. They ar[e] now held two years after the Summer Games[.]

YEAR	LOCATION	COUNTRY
1924	Chamonix	France
1928	St. Moritz	Switzerland
1932	Lake Placid	US
1936	Garmisch-Partenkirchen	Germany
1948	St. Moritz	Switzerland
1952	Oslo	Norway
1956	Cortina d'Ampezzo	Italy
1960	Squaw Valley	US
1964	Innsbruck	Austria
1968	Grenoble	France
1972	Sapporo	Japan
1976	Innsbruck	Austria
1980	Lake Placid	US
1984	Sarajevo	Yugoslavia
1988	Calgary	Canada
1992	Albertville	France
1994	Lillehammer	Norway
1998	Nagano	Japan
2002	Salt Lake City	US

DID YOU KNOW? The Winter Olympics that were planned to take place in Japan, Switzerland, and Germany in 1940 and at Cortina d'Ampezzo, Italy, in 1944 had to be canceled due to World War II.

COUNTRIES WITH THE MOST WINTER OLYMPICS MEDALS 1924–1998

COUNTRY	GOLD	SILVER	BRONZE	TOTAL
Norway	83	89	67	239
Russia (former USSR)	78	57	59	194
US	60	59	42	161
Austria	39	53	54	146

ICE HOCKEY FACTFILE

WHAT IS THE GAME? Ice hockey is a fast, six-a-side game played on an iced surface surrounded by wooden boards, with a goal net at each end. It originated as the winter version of hockey.

AIM OF THE GAME The object of the game is to hit a frozen rubber disk, called a puck, into the opposing team's net with an ice hockey stick. The team scoring most goals wins.

NUMBER OF PLAYERS Ice hockey is played six-a-side with up to 14 substitutes. Substitutions are allowed at any time during the game. Teams are sometimes forced to continue short-handed when penalized players are serving time in the penalty box.

POSITIONS The rink is divided into the defending, neutral, and attacking zones. Players may move with the puck and pass it to one another but may not pass it more than two zones across the rink markings.

TIME Each game consists of three periods of 20 minutes, divided by breaks of 15 minutes, when the ice is resurfaced.

RULES The game begins when the referee drops the puck between the sticks of two players from opposing teams, who "face off." After a foul, the game is restarted by a "face off" in the nearest circle.

SCORING A goal is scored when the puck crosses the goal line between the posts and under the crossbar of the goal.

TOP POINTS-SCORERS IN A NATIONAL HOCKEY LEAGUE CAREER

Founded in 1917, the major professional competition in North America is the National Hockey League. Players win points by scoring goals and by helping to score goals (assists).

PLAYER	SEASONS	GOALS	ASSISTS	TOTAL POINTS
Wayne Gretzky (still playing)	19	885	1,910	2,795
Gordie Howe	26	801	1,049	1,850
Marcel Dionne	18	731	1,040	1,771
Mark Messier (still playing)	19	597	1,015	1,612
Phil Esposito	18	717	873	1,590

FASTEST SPEED SKATERS

EVENT	MEN	COUNTRY	MIN:SEC	WOMEN	COUNTRY	MIN:SEC
500 m	H. Shimazu	Japan	0:34.82	C. Le May	Canada	0:37.55
1000 m	J. Wotherspoon	Canada	1:10.16	C. Witty	Canada	1:14.96
1500 m	A. Sondral	Norway	1:46.43	M. Timmer	Netherlands	1:57.58
3000 m	B. Veldkamp	Belgium	3:48.91	G. Niemann	Germany	4:01.67
5000 m	G. Romme	Netherlands	6:21.49	G. Niemann	Germany	6:58.63
10000 m	G. Romme	Netherlands	13:15.33	No women's event		

TOP OLYMPIC BOBSLED MEDALISTS

COUNTRY	GOLD	SILVER	BRONZE	TOTAL
Switzerland	9	9	8	26
Germany/ West Germany	5	5	7	17
US	5	4	5	14
East Germany	5	6	2	13
Italy	4	4	3	11
UK	1	1	2	4

DID YOU KNOW? Ice hockey is the fastest team game in the world. The puck, which is usually black and made of toughened rubber, is hit at speeds of up to 118 mph (190 km/h).

TEAMS WITH MOST STANLEY CUP WINS

The Stanley Cup is North America's most prestigious ice hockey trophy. It is named after Sir Frederick Arthur Stanley, who was Governor General of Canada from 1888 to 1893 and who presented the first Cup.

TEAM	WINS
Montreal Canadiens	23
Toronto Maple Leafs	13
Detroit Red Wings	8
Boston Bruins	5
Edmonton Oilers	5
New York Islanders	4
New York Rangers	4
Chicago Black Hawks	3
Philadelphia Flyers	2
Pittsburgh Penguins	2

DID YOU KNOW? Cross-country races have no steep slopes but are a test of stamina, covering up to 155 miles (50 km). Nordic skis are lighter and narrower than Alpine skis.

FIGURE SKATING FACTS

OLYMPIC COUNTRIES The US and Russia (formerly USSR) have each won 40 Olympic medals, but Russia has 20 golds compared with the US's 12.

MOST OLYMPIC GOLDS Gillis Grafstöm (Sweden), Sonja Henie (Norway), and Irina Konstantinovna (USSR) each won three gold medals in consecutive Olympic Games.

MEN'S WORLD TITLES Ulrich Salchow (Sweden) won ten skating titles between 1901 and 1905 and 1907 and 1911.

WOMEN'S WORLD TITLES Sonja Henie (Norway) won ten titles between 1927 and 1936. She later became a Hollywood film star.

MOST POINTS Jayne Torvill and Christopher Dean (UK) were awarded maximum points in the 1984 Olympic ice dance event.

191

WATER SPORTS

WATER SPORTS

BOARDSAILING A sailboard is steered by moving the position of the sail. The three main types of competition are wave performance, course racing, and slalom.

CANOEING AND KAYAKING There are two types of competition canoe. A kayak has a closed top and the canoeist sits inside, with legs outstretched. The paddle has a blade at each end. A Canadian canoe is usually open and the canoeist sits or kneels. The paddle has only one blade. Canoe races may be sprints, long distance, or white water; the last includes slalom racing.

DIVING There are two divisions of diving: highboard and springboard. Snorkeling, scuba diving, and skin diving are all underwater leisure sports.

POWERBOAT RACING The two main types of powerboat racing are inshore and offshore. There are several classes, depending on size and type of engine.

ROWING This is a racing sport for lightweight, narrow boats of up to eight rowers, often with a coxswain to steer. In sculling, each rower uses two oars instead of one. All boats have the same basic design made of reinforced plastic or wood, but length varies. Rowers sit on sliding seats for extra power.

SURFING Most competition boards are tri-fins, with three fins on the tail. Surfers paddle out to sea on lightweight boards and "ride" the waves back to shore. Judges assess style and timing.

SWIMMING This includes individual and team racing events, as well as synchronized swimming in which swimmers perform movements to music.

WATER POLO This game is played seven-a-side in water. Only the goalkeeper can stand to play the ball, touch it with both hands, or punch it.

WATERSKIING Water-skiers, towed behind a motorboat, compete in slalom, trick, and jumping events.

YACHTING Apart from the Olympics, major competitions are the biennial Admiral's Cup in the UK and the Americas Cup.

WATER SPORT COMPARISONS

SPORT	TOP SPEED	
	KM/H	MPH
Canoeing	20	12
Rowing	21	13
Sailing	69	43
Windsurfing	82	51
Powerboat racing	166	103
Waterskiing	230	143

SPEED DATA! The top rowing speed of 13 mph (21 km/h) is the average Olympic record speed for an eight over 1.24 m (2 km). The fastest Olympic powerboat speed is 103 mph (166 km/h), but much faster records have been set by boats that have been specially designed to break the record. The top canoeing speed is the average Olympic record speed for a K4 over 0.62 mile (1 km).

TOP OLYMPIC ROWING MEDALISTS

COUNTRY	GOLD	SILVER	BRONZE	TOTAL
US	30	23	16	69
East Germany	33	7	8	48
Germany/West Germany	19	13	13	45
Russia/USSR	12	20	12	44
UK	17	15	7	39
Italy	13	10	8	31
France	4	14	12	30
Canada	4	12	9	25
Romania	10	6	6	22

TOP OLYMPIC CANOEING MEDALISTS

COUNTRY	GOLD	SILVER	BRONZE	TOTAL
Hungary	10	23	20	53
Russia/USSR	30	13	10	53
Germany/West Germany	19	18	14	51
East Germany	15	7	10	32
Romania	9	10	12	31
Sweden	14	4	10	48

DID YOU KNOW? Canoeing was not recognized as an official Olympic sport until 1936 at the games in Berlin, Germany, although it first appeared as a demonstration sport at the 1924 Olympics in Paris, France.

ROWING FACTFILE

WHAT IS THE SPORT? Boats are raced through water by individuals or crews using bladed sticks called oars. Rowers use a single oar each; scullers have two oars each.

AIM OF THE SPORT The aim is to be the first boat to finish, or, in the case of processional events, the quickest.

TEAM SIZES Boats seat two, four, or eight, sometimes a coxswain. Scullers race as singles, doubles, or quadruples.

POSITIONS Rowers sit one behind the other. The coxswain, who steers and directs the boat, sits at the stern (back).

RACES Championship races, or regattas, take place in lanes over 1.24 miles (2 km). In processional races crews start at intervals and race against the clock.

DID YOU KNOW? Canoes and kayaks originated among the Native Americans and Inuit of eastern North America.

SWIMMING AND DIVING FACTFILE

ABOUT SWIMMING Swimmers race in pools over a preset distance in one of four recognized strokes. The aim is to be the first to finish the race.

NUMBER OF COMPETITORS Swimming is both an individual and a team sport.

TIMING Swimmers are timed to one-thousandth of a second by touching sensitive electronic pads at the end of the race.

SWIMMING RULES Swimmers must not start before the gun or, in relays, until the previous swimmer has touched the pad. Rules govern each stroke (except for freestyle), including turns made.

ABOUT DIVING Divers perform a set number of dives in springboard and highboard events. There are six main diving styles. The aim is to score the highest number of points.

COMPETITORS Diving is an individual sport, but teams compete in international events.

SCORING A panel of judges awards points according to the style and degree of difficulty of the dive being performed.

DID YOU KNOW! Developed and promoted in the 19th century, the front crawl is sometimes called the "American crawl." It is the fastest competition stroke.

OLYMPIC YACHT CLASSES

CLASS	LENGTH		
	M	FT	IN
Soling	8.20	26	9
Star	6.92	22	8
Tornado	6.09	20	0
470	4.70	15	5
Finn	4.54	14	9
Laser	4.23	13	9
Mistral	3.72	12	2
Europe	3.35	11	0

TOP OLYMPIC SWIMMING MEDALISTS

This prize table includes medals for the diving and water polo events that form part of the Olympic swimming program.

COUNTRY	GOLD	SILVER	BRONZE	TOTAL
US	231	176	136	543
Australia	41	37	47	125
Germany/West Germany	22	44	49	115
Russia/USSR	29	34	40	103
East Germany	39	34	25	98
UK	18	23	30	71
Hungary	29	23	19	71
Sweden	13	20	21	54

YACHTING RACES

INSHORE RACING takes place off the coast on predetermined courses marked by buoys.

OFFSHORE RACING takes place across the ocean. There are different classes of yachts based on size.

ONE-DESIGN EVENTS are for boats of the same class.

HANDICAP EVENTS are for boats of different designs.

TOP OLYMPIC YACHTING MEDALISTS

COUNTRY	GOLD	SILVER	BRONZE	TOTAL
US	16	18	15	49
Great Britain	15	10	9	34
Sweden	9	12	9	30
Norway	15	11	3	29
France	10	6	9	25
Denmark	10	8	4	22

DID YOU KNOW? Paul Elvström of Denmark became the first person to win gold medals at four consecutive games (1948, 1952, 1956, and 1960), and went on to compete in an additional four Games.

SWIMMING STROKES

BREASTSTROKE In breaststroke, used recreationally and for competitions, the arms and legs remain under water, and leg movement is froglike. The sidestroke, with a scissor leg action, developed from breaststroke.

FRONT CRAWL Fast up-and-down leg motion and alternate arm movements typify front crawl.

BACKSTROKE Swimmers lie on their back, move their arms "windmill" style, and kick with their legs.

BUTTERFLY In butterfly, the arms enter the water simultaneously and the legs perform a "dolphin kick." It first appeared in the 1930s.

TAKE A DIVE

Competitive springboard and highboard diving began in the 1890s and have been featured in the Olympic Games since 1904 for men and 1912 for women. The main dives are:

FORWARD Performed from a run-up or a standing position, the feet are kept together with the body as straight as possible.

BACKWARD With straight body and head up, arms are swung upward just before diving.

REVERSE The diver starts facing forward and rotates midair.

ARMSTAND The diver does a hand-stand on the platform and dives off.

INWARD The diver faces the board and rotates forward while diving.

SAFETY TIP! Always check the depth of the water before you dive – serious injuries may result from diving into shallow water.

EQUESTRIAN SPORTS

MAJOR HORSE RACES

RACE	TYPE	COURSE	DISTANCE	FIRST RUN
St. Leger	Flat	Doncaster, UK	1 mile 6 furlongs 132 yd	1776
Oaks	Flat	Epsom, UK	1 mile 4 furlongs	1779
Derby	Flat	Epsom, UK	1 mile 4 furlongs	1780
Ascot Gold Cup	Flat	Ascot, UK	2 miles 4 furlongs	1807
2,000 Guineas	Flat	Newmarket, UK	1 mile	1809
1,000 Guineas	Flat	Newmarket, UK	1 mile	1814
Grand National	Steeplechase	Aintree, UK	4 miles 4 furlongs	1837
Melbourne Cup	Flat	Melbourne, Australia	3,200 m	1861
Irish Sweeps Derby	Flat	The Curragh, Ireland	1 mile 4 furlongs	1866
Kentucky Derby	Flat	Churchill Downs, KY	1 mile 2 furlongs	1875
Prix de l'Arc de Triomphe	Flat	Longchamp, France	2,400 m	1920

DID YOU KNOW? There are two types of horse race: flat or with jumps. Flat races are for horses aged two or more years and cover between 5 furlongs (1 km) and 2 miles (3 km). Races with low hurdles are for three-year-old horses upward; steeplechases have ditches, water jumps, and large fences, and are for horses aged four or more years. A furlong is equal to 220 yd (201 m).

DID YOU KNOW? Cushioned saddles were invented in China in c.AD 25–22

POLO FACTS

ORIGIN Polo originated from Persia (now Iran) in about 600 BC. British soldiers in India discovered the game in the mid-19th century.

FIRST UK AND US MATCHES Polo was first played in the UK in the 1870s. It was promoted in the US by James Gordon Bennett.

THE GAME Four mounted players on each team. Play is divided into periods called "chukkas." The 900-ft (274.32-m) field is the largest of any sport.

EQUESTRIAN EVENTS FACTFILE

WHAT IS THE SPORT? Races and trials that test the abilities of a horse and its rider.

SHOW JUMPING Horse and rider must negotiate jumps, and are penalized for errors. Those with fewest faults win.

EVENTING Tests of show jumping, speed and endurance, and dressage.

DRESSAGE Horse and rider carry out a variety of paces, figures, and movements. Marks are given for quality.

RACING Flat or fenced courses that test speed and agility.

TOP OLYMPIC EQUESTRIAN MEDALISTS

These figures include the medal totals for both individual and team disciplines: Show Jumping, Three-Day Event, and Dressage.

COUNTRY	GOLD	SILVER	BRONZE	TOTAL
West Germany/ Germany	31	17	20	68
Sweden	17	8	14	39
US	8	17	13	38
France	11	12	11	34
Italy	7	9	7	23
Great Britain	5	7	9	21

DID YOU KNOW? US jockey Willie Shoemaker won a record 8,833 out of 40,350 races during his career (1949–1990).

DID YOU KNOW? The fastest-ever racehorse is Big Racket, who ran at 43.26 mph (69.62 km/h) in Mexico City, 1945.

COMBAT SPORTS

BOXING WEIGHT DIVISIONS

Divisions according to the bodyweight of a boxer were introduced into the sport during the mid-19th century. Today there are 17 weight divisions, as listed below:

WEIGHT DIVISION	LIMIT	
	LB	KG
Heavyweight	190+	86+
Cruiserweight	190	86
Light heavyweight	175	79
Super middleweight	168	76
Middleweight	160	73
Junior middleweight, Super welterweight	154	70
Welterweight	147	67
Junior welterweight, Super lightweight	140	65
Lightweight	135	61
Junior lightweight, Super featherweight	130	59
Featherweight	126	57
Junior featherweight, Super bantamweight	122	55
Bantamweight	118	54
Junior bantamweight, Super flyweight	115	52
Flyweight	112	51
Junior flyweight, Light flyweight	108	49
Straw weight, Mini flyweight	105	48

DID YOU KNOW?

The earliest record of gloves for boxing is in a painting from c.1520 BC, but boxing did not become a legal sport until 1901.

8 OZ /227 GR

BOXING FACTFILE

WHAT IS THE SPORT? Boxing is a combat sport in which two contestants, wearing padded leather gloves, aim to punch each other on the head or upper body while avoiding each other's blows. The contest takes place in a raised, square "ring" bounded by ropes.

DURATION OF CONTEST Amateur boxing is staged over three three-minute rounds. Professional fights last up to 12 rounds (15 in title fights).

SCORING Fights are won by a knockout, by the referee calling time, or on points.

COMBAT AND STRENGTH SPORTS

AIKIDO Martial art similar to judo.

BOXING A carefully controlled, but dangerous combat sport.

FENCING Evolved from sword-fighting, and held since the first Olympics.

JUJITSU Based on a range of throws, kicks, and punches. World Championships were first staged in 1984.

JUDO Dating from the 1880s, judo has been in the Olympics since 1964. World Championships were first held in 1956.

KARATE A Japanese martial art. World Championships were first held in 1970.

KENDO Japanese sword art. World Championships have been held since 1970.

WEIGHTLIFTING Has always been in the Olympics. Like boxing, it is competed for in a range of weight classes.

WRESTLING One of the oldest of all combat sports, a feature of both the ancient and modern Olympics. The first World Championship was staged in 1921.

FASTEST KNOCKOUTS IN WORLD TITLE FIGHTS

BOXERS (WINNERS FIRST)	WEIGHT	DATE	DURATION IN SECONDS
Gerald McClellan v. Jay Bell	Middleweight	August 7, 1993	20
James Warring v. James Pritchard	Cruiserweight	September 6, 1991	24
Lloyd Honeyghan v. Gene Hatcher	Welterweight	August 30, 1987	45

FENCING FACTFILE

WHAT IS THE SPORT? The sport of fencing takes place between opponents on a narrow "piste." They use three sword types – the foil, épée, and saber – all designed with safety in mind.

AIM OF THE SPORT Competitors try to touch target areas on their opponent with their sword. The winner is the one who scores the greatest number of "hits."

NUMBER OF COMPETITORS Two.

POSITIONS Attack, parry, and riposte.

MARTIAL ARTS FACTFILE

WHAT ARE THEY? Martial arts originate in the East and are used in self-defense.

JUDO Aim is to display superior holding and throwing technique to the opponent.

KARATE Relies on high-energy punches, strikes, and kicks aimed at the opponent.

AIKIDO Uses flowing, defensive techniques to throw opponent off balance.

JUJITSU Forerunner of judo and aikido.

KENDO "Sword"-fight with bamboo sticks.

TOP OLYMPIC JUDO MEDALISTS

Judo made its debut at the 1964 Tokyo Olympics, but for men only. Women's judo was not introduced until 1992.

COUNTRY	GOLD	SILVER	BRONZE	TOTAL
Japan	19	10	11	40
France	8	3	15	26
South Korea	6	9	9	24
USSR	5	5	13	23
Cuba	3	5	9	17

WHEELED SPORTS

SPORTS ON WHEELS

BICYCLE RACING Olympic biking events include road racing, off-road racing, and track racing. Bicycles are lightweight and streamlined to maximize speed. Cycling has been an Olympic sport since 1896.

DRAG RACING Dragster cars are very light, with powerful engines, and much larger tires on the back than the front. Races are won on speed. Drag racing is most popular in the US.

KARTING Small, open karts race on indoor and outdoor circuits.

MOTORCYCLE RACING The first motorcycle race was held in 1897. World Championships started in 1949 and consist of a range of grand prix races for bikes of different engine sizes. The Isle of Man TT races, first held in 1907, are a main event.

MOTOCROSS The cross-country branch of motorcycle racing, where riders must negotiate steep climbs and drops, difficult bends, and muddy water.

INDYCAR RACING Streamlined, super-fast cars race on oval circuits in the US.

MOUNTAIN BIKING This became an Olympic event in 1996. It includes trials and cross-country racing.

RALLY DRIVING Enhanced sedans race over public roads, often for thousands of miles in stages. The aim is to achieve the fastest time.

SPEEDWAY Motorcycle racing on dusty tracks. Four riders race for four laps. The annual World Championships were first held in 1936 in London.

ROLLER SKATING Invented in 1760, roller skating is a popular leisure activity as well as a competitive sport. Competitions include speed, figure, and dance.

BICYCLING FACTFILE

WHAT IS THE SPORT? In cycle sports, cyclists ride specially designed bicycles in races held on tracks, roads, and cross-country circuits. Races range from sprints to multi-stage events that last several weeks and cover hundreds of miles (kilometers).

OFF-ROAD RACING The original form of cross-country cycling is cyclocross, where riders carry their bikes over obstacles and may have to run up hills. Mountain biking is now the most popular off-road bicycle sport.

ROAD RACING Road races take place on courses set along ordinary roads. Races are either single-stage races or multi-stage events in which aggregate, or total, time decides the finishing positions.

TRACK RACING Track races take place on wooden indoor tracks, with banked sides, or flat asphalt outdoor tracks. Races include sprints, where riders make a dash for the line on the last lap, and pursuits, where the winner is the fastest rider.

TOP TOUR DE FRANCE WINNERS

The Tour de France is the world's top multi-stage road race, held over three weeks every summer.

RIDER (COUNTRY)	WINS
Jacques Anquetil (France)	5
Eddy Merckx (Belgium)	5
Bernard Hinault (France)	5
Miguel Indurain (Spain)	5
Philippe Thys (Belgium)	3
Louison Bobet (France)	3
Greg LeMond (US)	3
Lucien Petit-Breton (France)	2
Firmin Lambot (Belgium)	2
Ottavio Bottecchia (Italy)	2
Nicholas Frantz (Luxembourg)	2
André Leducq (France)	2
Antonin Magne (France)	2
Gino Bartali (Italy)	2
Sylvere Maës (Belgium)	2
Fausto Coppi (Italy)	2
Bernard Thevenet (France)	2
Laurent Fignon (France)	2

DID YOU KNOW? You can tell the leaders in the Tour de France from their tops: yellow is the race leader, red polka dots is the rider with most points from climbs, and green is the rider with most points from sprints.

TOP OLYMPIC BICYCLING MEDALISTS

There are five Olympic bicycling events: sprint, pursuit, points race, time trial (men only), and team pursuit (men only). Women's events only began in 1984.

COUNTRY	GOLD	SILVER	BRONZE	TOTAL
France	32	18	21	71
Italy	30	15	6	51
Great Britain	8	21	16	45
Germany	7	12	14	33
Holland	10	12	5	27
USSR/Russia	12	5	9	26

MOTORCYCLING FACTFILE

WHAT IS THE SPORT? In motorcycling, riders race around circuits on powerful motorcycles. There are competitions for different types of bike. Motocross, or scrambling, is held over a cross-country course.

RACING BIKES Racing motorcycles are powerful machines designed for speed. Classes range from 125cc upward, with a special class for sidecars.

GRAND PRIX RACING The world's leading drivers and manufacturers compete in 12 or more grands prix each season for world championships in several classes: 500cc, 250cc, 125cc, and sidecar. Points are awarded for the first 15 home in each grand prix – 25 points for first, 20 for second, down to one point for 15th.

MOTOCROSS In big motocross events as many as 40 riders race over several laps of a winding, muddy, hilly course. Motocross bikes are light but strong.

RACING SIDECARS Sidecars are attached to the motorcycle to make one unit. The driver and passenger work together as a team, the latter leaning over behind the driver to balance the bike when cornering.

RALLY AND INDYCAR RECORDS

MOST FAMOUS INDYCAR CIRCUIT The Indianapolis track, home to Indycar racing, is 2.5 miles (4 km) long.

TOP DRIVING FAMILY Al Unser from the US has won the Indy 500 four times; his brother Bobby three times, and son Al, Jr., twice.

LONGEST RALLY In 1977, the London to Sydney Rally race covered a distance of 19,329 miles (31,107 km).

LONGEST ANNUAL RALLY The Safari Rally, held annually in Kenya, Africa.

DID YOU KNOW? The fastest ever Indycar speed is 239 mph (385 km/h)!

MOTOR RACING FACTFILE

FORMULA ONE Streamlined, Formula One cars compete in 16 worldwide races.

INDYCAR RACING Mostly US-based, on oval circuits.

DRAG RACING Dragsters race along a 440-yd (400-m) "drag strip." The fastest can reach 300 mph (485 km/h). Parachutes slow them down.

KARTING Karts are like miniature racing cars. The simplest have 60cc or 100cc engines and no gear box.

RALLY DRIVING "Souped-up" sedans compete on regular roads, country roads, and tracks. Drivers lose points for exceeding set times.

FORMULA ONE GRAND PRIX CIRCUITS

In Formula One, teams of car manufacturers and drivers compete for the World Championship title, in a series of worldwide races.

COUNTRY	LOCATION	LAPS NO.	MILES	KM
Argentina	Buenos Aires	72	2.646	4.259
Australia	Melbourne	58	3.295	5.303
Austria	Al-Ring	71	2.684	4.319
Belgium	Spa-Francorchamps	44	4.330	6.968
Brazil	Interlagos	72	2.667	4.292
Canada	Gilles Villeneuve	69	2.747	4.421
France	Magny-Cours	71	2.641	4.250
Germany	Hockenheim	45	4.240	6.823
Hungary	Hungaroring	77	2.468	3.972
Italy	Monza	53	3.585	5.770
Japan	Suzuka	53	3.643	5,864
Luxembourg	Nürburgring	67	2.831	4.556
Monaco	Monaco	78	2.092	3.367
San Marino	Enzo e Dino Ferrari	62	3.063	4.930
Spain	Catalunya	65	2.938	4.728

DRIVERS WITH THE MOST GRAND PRIX WINS

DRIVER	NATIONALITY	YEARS	WINS
Alain Prost	France	1981–1993	51
Ayrton Senna	Brazil	1985–1993	41
Nigel Mansell	UK	1985–1994	31
Jackie Stewart	UK	1965–1973	27
Jim Clark	UK	1962–1968	25
Niki Lauda	Austria	1974–1985	25
Michael Schumacher	Germany	1992–1997	25
Juan Manuel Fangio	Argentina	1950–1957	24
Nelson Piquet	Brazil	1980–1991	23

Up to and including 1997 season

DID YOU KNOW? Ferrari has taken part in the World Championships since 1950 and boasts 113 wins to date – more wins than any other Formula One team!

YOUNGEST FORMULA ONE WORLD CHAMPIONS

DRIVER	NATIONALITY	YEAR	AGE YEARS	MONTHS
Emerson Fittipaldi	Brazil	1972	25	9
Michael Schumacher	Germany	1994	25	10
Jacques Villeneuve	Canada	1997	26	5
Niki Lauda	Austria	1975	26	7
Jim Clark	UK	1963	27	7
Jochen Rindt	Austria	1970	28	6

If a driver has won the World Championship more than once, only his youngest age is considered in this list.

ULTIMATE LISTS

EVENTS of the 20TH CENTURY

1900s

1900 Umberto I, king of Italy, is shot by an anarchist in Milan.

1903 US brothers Orville and Wilbur Wright make first powered flight.

1902 Boer War ends in South Africa.

1904 Double-sided records produced for the first time in the US.

1904 Japanese torpedo the Russian fleet following tension over control of China.

1905 Russian troops fire on workers' demonstration in "Bloody Sunday" attack.

1906 Women over age 24 get the vote in Finland.

1906 San Francisco is razed to the ground by a violent earthquake.

1907 New Zealand becomes independent from British rule.

1907 Over a million emigrate to the US.

1908 Two-year-old Pu Yi becomes Emperor of China.

1910s

1910 In Portugal, republican revolutionaries overthrow King Manuel II.

1912 The ocean liner *Titanic* sinks after hitting an iceberg in the North Atlantic.

1913 Grand Central Terminal, New York's new railroad station, opens.

1914 France, Russia, and Britain declare war on Germany and Austria-Hungary at the start of World War I.

1914 Western Front truce halts the war for Christmas Day.

1916 Irish nationalists stage the Easter Uprising in Dublin.

1917 Russian Tsar Nicholas II abdicates.

1917 US troops enter World War I.

1917 Lenin seizes power in Russia.

1918 The Russian royal family is executed by revolutionaries in the Urals.

1918 Arab forces capture Damascus.

1918 World War I ends.

1920s

1920 Prohibition (ban) of the making and selling of alcohol begins in the US.

1920 29 countries attend the first meeting of the League of Nations.

1920 US women win right to vote.

1921 Chinese Communist party founded

1921 Famine devastates Russia.

1922 Tutankhamun's tomb is discovered in Valley of the Kings, Egypt.

1922 Indian nationalist Mohandas Gandhi is imprisoned by the British.

1923 German currency collapses.

1927 US pilot Charles Lindbergh is the first to fly solo across the Atlantic.

1927 Chinese Communist coup crushed.

1929 St. Valentine's Day massacre in Chicago, US.

1929 Wall Street crash in the US leads to world financial crisis.

1930s

1930 Stalin declares all farmland in USSR "collectively owned."

1931 German Danatbank goes bankrupt.

1931 Spain declares itself a republic.

1931 In the US, the General Electric Building is finished.

1933 Hitler becomes German Chancellor.

1934 US gangsters Bonnie and Clyde are gunned down.

1935 Hitler's Nuremberg decrees deprive German Jews of citizenship.

1935 Italy, under Mussolini, invades the North African kingdom of Abyssinia.

1935 In China, the Communists' long march, led by Mao Zedong, ends.

1936 In the UK, 200 men go on the Jarrow Crusade to protest unemployment.

1936 Civil war breaks out in Spain.

1936 German troops enter the French-controlled cities of the Rhineland.

1939 After the invasion of Poland, Britain and France declare war on Germany, marking the start of World War II.

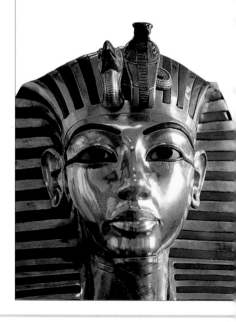

1940s

1940 Charles de Gaulle sets up Free French National committee.

1941 Japanese attack US Pacific Fleet Base at Pearl Harbor.

1943 Soviet women fly bomber aircraft.

1943 Italian dictator Mussolini resigns.

1944 Launch of the German V-1, "flying bomb," the first cruise missile.

1944 Allied troops land in northern France and go on to liberate Paris.

1945 Hitler commits suicide in Berlin.

1945 Germany surrenders and Europe celebrates VE day.

1945 Japan surrenders after US drops atom bombs at Hiroshima and Nagasaki.

1946 The United Nations is established.

1948 Mahatma Gandhi is assassinated.

1948 Jewish leaders declare the new Jewish state of Israel.

1949 NATO (North Atlantic Treaty Organization) is formed.

1950s

1950 North Korea invades South Korea in an attempt to unify the peninsula.

1952 Crown Prince Hussein becomes King of Jordan.

1953 New Zealander Edmund Hillary and Sherpa Tenzing Norgay climb Everest.

1956 Egyptian president Nasser seizes control of the Suez Canal.

1956 Prodemocracy protesters rebel against Soviet forces in Hungary.

1957 USSR launches *Sputnik 1*, the first artificial satellite in space.

1957 Six countries – France, West Germany, Italy, Belgium, Holland, and Luxembourg – form the European Common Market.

1957 François Duvalier is elected president of Haiti.

1958 Iraq's Faisal II is assassinated.

1958 General Charles de Gaulle is elected President of France.

1959 Fidel Castro takes control of Cuba.

1960s

1960 In South Africa, 69 blacks are killed as they demonstrate for their rights.

1960 Sirimarvo Bandaraniake of Ceylon is the first woman Prime Minister.

1961 East Germans build wall to separate east and west Berlin.

1965 The US sends troops to Vietnam.

1968 US black civil rights leader Martin Luther King, Jr., is assassinated.

1969 US *Apollo 11* lands on the Moon.

DID YOU KNOW?
US President John F. Kennedy was assassinated in Dallas in 1963.

1970s

1970 King Hussein of Jordan and Yassir Arafat of the PLO sign a truce to end war.

1973 The Vietnam ceasefire is signed in Paris, but the war does not end.

1973 President Allende of Chile is assassinated.

1974 US President Nixon resigns.

1975 The Vietnam war ends.

1975 Civil war breaks out in Angola.

1976 White police fire on black children in Soweto, South Africa.

1976 China's Chairman Mao Zedong dies.

1977 Thousands flee Vietnam in boats to escape Communist regime.

1979 Nuclear accident at Three Mile Island, US.

1990s

1991 Coup in the USSR topples Premier Gorbachev.

1993 Terrorists explode bomb under World Trade Center in New York.

1993 Israeli Prime Minister Yitzhak Rabin and PLO leader Yassir Arafat sign peace accord in the US.

1994 New South African flag is raised, marking the end of white rule.

1994 Serb troops bomb Sarajevo in Bosnia, killing 68 people.

1994 Conflict between Tutsi rebels and the Hutu government in Rwanda erupts.

1995 Israel's prime minister Yitzhak Rabin is assassinated.

1995 Talks are held to bring peace to war-torn Bosnia.

1997 Diana, Princess of Wales dies in a car crash in Paris, France.

1980s

1980 The Iran-Iraq war escalates.

1981 Nobel Peace Prize winner President Sadat of Egypt is assassinated.

1984 Famine in Ethiopia.

1984 Scientists warn of global warming.

1984 Discovery of virus that causes AIDS.

1985 Live Aid concert is watched by 1.5 million people, raising $60 million (£40 million) for African famine relief.

1986 Space Shuttle *Challenger* explodes 73 seconds after liftoff.

1986 The Ukraine suffers the effects of a major nuclear accident at the Chernobyl power plant.

1987 US President Reagan and Soviet Premier Gorbachev sign treaty to cut nuclear arsenal.

1988 Bangladesh is hit by terrible floods.

1988 More than 100,000 people die when Armenia in the USSR is hit by an earthquake.

1989 The wall dividing East and West Berlin, in East Germany, is torn down.

DEAD ENDS

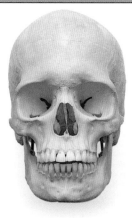

DID YOU KNOW? Halley's Comet appeared in 1835, the year American writer Mark Twain was born. He believed that he would die when it next appeared. The comet appeared again on April 20, 1910, and the following day, Twain died.

WEIRD DEATHS OF FAMOUS PEOPLE

AESCHYLUS A dramatist known as the "Father of Greek Tragedy," Aeschylus died in 456 BC. It is said that a prediction that he would be killed by a blow from heaven came true, when an eagle dropped the tortoise it was carrying on his head.

FRANCIS BACON This Elizabethan philosopher died on April 9, 1626, after he caught a chill while experimenting with deep-freezing a chicken by stuffing it with snow.

HILAIRE BELLOC This French-born English writer and Liberal MP died on July 16, 1953, after a burning coal fell out of his fire and set him ablaze.

HARRY HOUDINI The Hungarian-born American escapologist, whose real name was Erich Weiss, died on October 31, 1926, after being punched in the stomach.

THOMAS MAY This English poet was strangled to death by the cloth he used to support his double chin, on November 13, 1650.

FAMOUS PEOPLE WHO DIED YOUNG

NAME	AGE AT DEATH
Anne Frank, German diarist, in concentration camp, 1945	15
Lady Jane Grey, Queen of England, executed, 1554	16
Ritchie Valens, American rock singer, plane crash, 1959	17
Joan of Arc, French heroine, burned at the stake, 1431	19
Buddy Holly, American rock singer, plane crash, 1959	22

FAMOUS PEOPLE WHOSE BODIES WERE MOVED

CHARLIE CHAPLIN The British-born film actor died in 1977 and was buried in Switzerland. His body was stolen and held for ransom, but the thieves were apprehended, and the body reburied in a concrete vault.

ELVIS PRESLEY Presley died of heart failure in 1977, and was buried at Memphis Forest Hill cemetery. He was reburied at Graceland, his home, after threats of body-snatching.

SITTING BULL Sitting Bull was a Native American chief who died in 1890, and whose remains were stolen in 1952. They were reburied under concrete in Sitting Bull Park, South Dakota.

FAMOUS PEOPLE WHO COMMITTED SUICIDE

THOMAS CHATTERTON A British poet who poisoned himself on August 24, 1770.

KURT COBAIN The lead singer of the rock group Nirvana, he shot himself on April 8, 1994.

GEORGE EASTMAN American multi-millionaire, founder of Kodak, and philanthropist, who committed suicide on March 14, 1932.

ERNEST HEMINGWAY An American author, he committed suicide (as had his father and brother) with a shotgun on July 2, 1961.

MARILYN MONROE In 1962, the famous American actress was found dead by her housekeeper with a bottle of sleeping pills by her side.

DID YOU KNOW? Many believe that Marilyn Monroe was the victim of murder.

EUPHEMISMS FOR "DEAD"

A euphemism is a polite or pleasant way of saying something rude or unpleasant. Few words have as many euphemisms as "dead" – these are just a few of them:

Answered the final summons • Bit the dust • Breathed one's last Called away • Croaked • Crossed over • Departed • Expired Fallen (used of soldiers) • Gone to meet one's Maker • Gone to the happy hunting ground • Hopped off the twig • Is no more Joined one's ancestors • Kicked the bucket • Laid to rest • Made one's final exit • Passed away • Passed on • Perished • Pushing up the daisies • Six feet under • Turned up one's toes

ASHES TO ASHES: ENDS FOR THE REMAINS OF CELEBRITIES

ALBERT EINSTEIN The German-born mathematician died in Princeton, New Jersey, in 1955. His ashes were scattered in the Delaware River, Trenton, New Jersey.

D. H. LAWRENCE A British author who died in France and was buried there in 1930, but was exhumed and cremated in 1935. His ashes were mixed in concrete to form part of the altar in the memorial chapel at Taos, New Mexico.

VIVIEN LEIGH A British actress, who died in London in 1967. Her ashes were dispersed in the lake at her home.

FAMOUS PEOPLE KILLED IN TRANSPORTATION ACCIDENTS

JOHN JACOB ASTOR III A millionaire and science-fiction author, who went down with the *Titanic* on April 15, 1912.

RUDOLPH DIESEL A German engineer and inventor of the diesel engine, who fell off a steamer in the English Channel on September 29, 1913. His body was found by fishermen who threw it back, after which it was never recovered.

LORD KITCHENER A British soldier famed for his image on the "Your Country Needs You" World War I recruitment posters, who was killed when HMS *Hampshire* struck a mine off Orkney on June 5, 1916.

DENNIS WILSON A singer with the Beach Boys, Wilson drowned while diving to a sunken boat off the California coast on December 28, 1983.

MARC BOLAN The lead singer of the British group T. Rex died when a Mini driven by his American girlfriend, Gloria Jones, crashed into a tree at Barnes Common, London, UK, on September 16, 1977. The tree is now a shrine for T. Rex fans.

ALBERT CAMUS A French Nobel Prize-winning author, who was killed in a car accident, along with his publisher Michel Gallimard, on January 4, 1960.

EDDIE COCHRAN An American rock star, who died following a taxi crash in Wiltshire, UK, on April 17, 1960. The first policeman to arrive on the scene was 16-year-old cadet Dave Dee, who later fronted the group Dave Dee, Dozy, Beaky, Mick & Tich. Cochran's first posthumous single was *Three Steps to Heaven.*

DIANA, PRINCESS OF WALES The British princess died from injuries caused by a car crash in Paris on August 31, 1997.

ISADORA DUNCAN An American dancer, who was strangled on September 14, 1927, when her scarf caught in the wheel of the convertible in which she was a passenger.

GRACE KELLY A former American film actress who became Princess Grace of Monaco, and was killed when her car overturned near Monte Carlo on September 14, 1982.

FAMOUS PEOPLE KILLED BY ANIMALS

KING ALEXANDER OF GREECE Died in 1920 after being bitten by his pet monkey.

ELLEN BRIGHT A British animal entertainer known as the "Lion Queen," was savaged to death by a tiger in 1850.

RUPERT BROOKE An English poet who died in 1915 following a mosquito bite.

EMILY DAVISON An English suffragette who killed herself by running under Amner, a horse owned by the king, during the Derby in 1913.

GENGHIS KHAN A Mongol ruler, who died after falling from his horse in 1227.

WILLIAM III An English king who died in 1701 after a fall when his horse stumbled over a molehill.

ROY KINNEAR A British comedy actor who died in Spain after falling from a horse during the filming of *The Return of the Musketeers* in 1988.

！DID YOU KNOW?
Hannah Beswick of Manchester, UK, was "buried" above ground in a glass coffin. Her corpse was regularly visited from the time of her death in 1758, until 1868.

COUNTRIES WITH MOST CREMATIONS

COUNTRY	% OF DEATHS	CREMATIONS
China	35.20	2,830,000
Japan	98.70	938,777
US	21.31	492,434
UK	71.28	445,934
Germany	37.76	333,373

HEARTS THAT ARE NOT IN THE RIGHT PLACE

ANNE BOLEYN The second queen of Henry VIII was executed at the Tower of London on May 19, 1536. Her heart, secretly buried in a church near Thetford, UK, was found in 1830 and reburied.

LORD BYRON An English poet, who died in Greece on April 19, 1824. His body was buried at Hucknall Torkard, Nottingham, UK, and his heart and brains were placed in a nearby urn.

FRÉDÉRIC CHOPIN A Polish composer who died on October 17, 1849. Before his burial in Paris, his doctor, Jean Cruveilhier, removed his heart and sent it to Poland, where it was buried in the wall of the Church of the Holy Cross, Warsaw.

THOMAS HARDY The ashes of this British writer who died on January 11, 1928, were buried in Westminster Abbey, but there is evidence that his heart, supposedly buried at St. Michael's, Stinsford, UK, was in fact seized and devoured by his sister's cat!

FAMOUS LAST WORDS

JULIUS CAESAR The Roman emperor was assassinated in 44 BC. He is supposed to have said, "Et tu, Brute?" ("You as well, Brutus?"). Brutus was Caesar's friend, who betrayed him by joining the conspirators who stabbed him.

DOUGLAS FAIRBANKS, SR. An American film actor who died in 1939. His last words were "I've never felt better."

VISCOUNT PALMERSTON A British Prime Minister who died in 1865. He said, "Die, my dear doctor? That's the last thing I shall do."

ANNA PAVLOVA A Russian ballerina who died in 1931. Her last words were "Get my swan costume ready."

OSCAR WILDE There are two versions of the Irish author's last words in 1900: "Either these curtains go/that wallpaper goes, or I do," or "I am dying as I have lived – beyond my means."

LAST LISTS

!◯ **DID YOU KNOW?** After 1999, Neptune, not Pluto, will be farthest from Earth, due to a change in orbits.

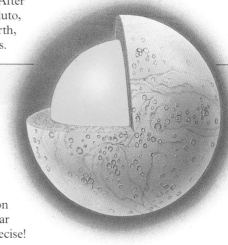

FAMOUS LASTS

CUSTER'S LAST STAND The name given to the final battle fought by American General George Custer against an army of Sioux Indians, at Little Bighorn in the US, on June 25, 1876.

THE LAST JUDGMENT The name given to the prophesied final day, when God judges all Christians.

THE LAST NIGHT OF THE PROMS The final night of a series of classical music concerts held every year in London, UK, and broadcast around the world.

THE LAST OF THE RED-HOT MAMAS The stage nickname of American singer Sophie Tucker (1884–1966), derived from the title of a song she first performed in 1928.

THE LAST SUPPER The final meal eaten by Jesus and his disciples, and the title of Leonardo da Vinci's famous painting of the subject, a mural on the wall of the refectory of Santa Maria delle Grazie, Milan, painted between 1495 and 1498.

THE LAST POST The name of the music traditionally played by buglers at military funerals.

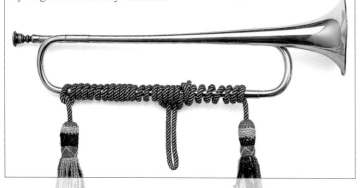

!◯ **DID YOU KNOW?** A bugle is played on the 11th hour of the 11th day of the 11th month to remember the war dead.

LAST BOOKS

CHARLES DICKENS *The Mystery of Edwin Drood* was published in monthly episodes, but Dickens died in 1870, leaving it unfinished.

SHERLOCK HOLMES Sir Arthur Conan Doyle's *The Adventure of Shoscombe Old Place* was published in 1927.

ROALD DAHL *Esio Trot* appeared in 1990, the year Dahl died. *The Minpins* and *The Vicar of Nibbleswick* were both published a year later.

LAST STRUCTURES

LAST OF THE SEVEN WONDERS Built in 280 BC, the 445-ft (136-m) Pharos (lighthouse) of Alexandria, Egypt, was partly demolished by invaders and eventually destroyed by an earthquake.

LONDON BRIDGE Between 1831 and 1832, after 600 years, the old bridge of houses and shops was demolished and the new bridge opened alongside it.

LAST NIGHT OF CRYSTAL PALACE This glass building in London – the world's largest – caught fire in November 1936. The blaze was seen for 50 miles (80 km).

SPACE LASTS

LAST MONTH WITHOUT A FULL MOON This occurred in February 1866. The next will not occur for 2.5 million years – until the year 2,501,991 to be precise!

LAST PLANET TO BE DISCOVERED Pluto was discovered by American amateur astronomer Clyde Tombaugh in 1930. The name Pluto, after the Roman god of the underworld, was suggested by an English schoolgirl, Venetia Burney.

THE FIRST SATELLITE'S LAST DAY The USSR's *Sputnik 1*, the first ever satellite, burned up on its re-entry to Earth on January 4, 1958, three months after its launch on October 4, 1957.

LAST MEN ON THE MOON US *Apollo 17* astronauts Eugene A. Cernan and Harrison H. Schmitt spent three days on the Moon, blasting off on December 14, 1972.

LAST TIME HALLEY'S COMET WAS SEEN Halley's Comet returns to Earth every 76 years. It was last visible to the naked eye in 1986, but was seen by astronomers in Chile as late as 1991. It is scheduled to return in 2061.

THEATER AND FILM LASTS

WILLIAM SHAKESPEARE'S LAST PLAY *The Tempest*, written in 1611, is the last known play by William Shakespeare. The playwright died in 1616, and the play was first published in 1623.

LAST YEAR WHEN ALL FILMS WERE SILENT Films were silent in the early years of the industry, with 1926 being the last year in which films lacked sound. *The Jazz Singer*, starring Al Jolson, which premiered at the Warner Theater in New York on October 6, 1927, was the first full-length feature film containing vocal sound (although it actually contained very little dialogue – its two spoken sequences contain a total of just 354 words). Thereafter, most films had sound.

LAST BLACK-AND-WHITE FILM TO WIN A "BEST PICTURE" OSCAR® *Schindler's List*, directed by Steven Spielberg, contains color, but is predominantly a black-and-white film. Its moving reenactment of ammunition factory director Oscar Schindler's courageous attempt to save Jewish people from Nazi Germany won the 1993 "Best Picture" Oscar®.

MOLIÈRE'S LAST PLAY French actor-playwright Molière (Jean-Baptiste Poquelin) died dramatically on February 17, 1673, after collapsing on stage. He was performing the lead role in *Le Malade Imaginaire* (*The Hypochondriac*).

CRIME LASTS

LAST LIVING WITNESS TO THE ASSASSINATION OF ABRAHAM LINCOLN As a five-year-old boy, Samuel Seymour saw John Wilkes Booth shoot Abraham Lincoln on April 14, 1865. Seymour lived until 1956.

LAST BOW STREET RUNNERS Invented by Henry Fielding in 1750, the Bow Street Runners were London's first police force. In September 1829, they were replaced by the Metropolitan Police.

LAST HANGING IN THE US There were no executions of any kind from 1968 to 1977. In 1972, the Supreme Court declared the death penalty unconstitutional, but changed its mind in 1976. Since 1977, three people have been hanged. Hanging is legal in three states.

LAST DUEL The last to take place in the UK was in 1852, between two Frenchmen, when M. Barthélemey shot M. Cournet in Surrey.

MUSIC LASTS

LAST STRADIVARIUS VIOLIN Antonius Stradivarius (c.1644–1737) is considered the greatest violin-maker of all time. Between 1666 and 1733, when he made his last violin, he is believed to have made more than 1,000 instruments, of which over 700 survive.

BEETHOVEN'S LAST SYMPHONY Ludwig van Beethoven's 9th Symphony was his last before his death in 1827. He promised the London Philharmonic Society that he would write his 10th Symphony for them, but died before he could begin work on it.

LAST BEATLES' CONCERT The Beatles last played in public at Candlestick Park, San Francisco, on August 29, 1966. The only occasion on which the three surviving members have sung together since then was at a memorial service for Paul McCartney's wife Linda in 1998, when they sang *Let It Be*.

SPORTS LASTS

LAST ANCIENT OLYMPIC GAMES The Olympic Games were held at Olympia, on the Greece-Macedonia border, every four years from 776 BC. The 293rd and last was held in AD 392, after which they were banned. The modern Olympics began in 1896.

LAST BARE-KNUCKLE BOXING MATCHES Boxing gloves and strict rules were introduced during the 1870s, but bare-knuckle fighting lingered in the UK until 1885, and in the US until 1889.

LAST OLYMPICS FOR MEN ONLY The 1904 St. Louis Olympics continued the men-only tradition established in 1896, but it was the last such competition: the 1908 Games held in London included women in the tennis events. Thereafter, women competed in more Olympic sports.

VEHICLE LASTS

STAGECOACH After carrying passengers and mail around Britain for two centuries, stagecoaches were gradually replaced by trains during the 19th century. Coaches continued in use in the US until train networks were developed.

HORSE-DRAWN LONDON BUS The last was taken out of service in 1911.

VOYAGE OF THE TITANIC The first and last voyage of the luxury ocean liner *Titanic* ended on April 15, 1912, when it struck an iceberg and sank, killing 1,517 people.

LAST MODEL T FORD After almost 20 years' production, the 15,007,033rd Model T rolled off the US production line on May 26, 1927.

LAST AIRSHIP In 1937, an explosion destroyed the airship *Hindenburg* at Lakehurst, New Jersey, heralding the end of passenger-carrying airships.

ROYAL LASTS

LAST ROMAN EMPEROR Romulus Augustulus was about 14 years old when he was deposed, in AD 476, and the Roman empire split.

LAST AZTEC EMPEROR Montezuma II was deposed by Spanish invaders and killed in June 1520.

LAST KING OF FRANCE Louis Philippe (1773–1850) was ousted in 1848. He escaped to England disguised as "Mr. Smith."

LAST EMPEROR OF CHINA Hsüan T'ung abdicated in 1912. His life is depicted in the film *The Last Emperor*.

LAST TSAR Nicholas II was murdered during the Russian Revolution of 1917.

DID YOU KNOW? The baker of the *Titanic* survived because he had been drinking whiskey and the alcohol in his blood kept him alive in the icy water.

DID YOU KNOW? The *Titanic* was the world's biggest passenger ship.

INDEX

ACKNOWLEDGMENTS

AUTHOR'S THANKS

The author would like to thank the following individuals, organizations, and publications for their help in preparing the lists in this book:

Academy of Motion Picture Arts and Sciences; *Amusement Business*; Amusement & Music Operators Association; *Annual Abstract of Statistics*; Art Sales Index; Caroline Ash; Associated Press; Audit Bureau of Circulations; BMI; *The Bookseller*; BPI; *BP Statistical Review of World Energy*; Richard Braddish; British Broadcasting Corporation; British Library; British Rate & Data; Cameron Mackintosh Ltd; Carbon Dioxide Information Analysis Center; Central Intelligence Agency; Channel Swimming Association; Christian Research Association; Christie's; *Classical Music*; Luke Crampton; Cremation Society; *Crime in the United States; Criminal Statistics England & Wales*; Death Penalty Information Center; Diamond Information Centre; Dr. Stephen Durham; Euromonitor; Federal Bureau of Investigation; Feste Catalogue Index Database/Alan Somerset; *Financial Times*; *Flight International*; Food and Agriculture Organization of the United Nations; *Forbes*; Christopher Forbes; Ford Motor Company Ltd; *Fortune*; Geological Museum, London; Gold Fields Mineral Services Ltd; Russell E. Gough; Higher Education Statistics Agency; Duncan Hislop; Home Office; Indianapolis 500; Institute of Sports Medicine; International Atomic Energy Agency; International Civil Aviation Organization; International Monetary Fund; International Union for the Conservation of Nature; International Union of Geological Sciences Commission on Comparative Planetology; Interpol; Alan Jeffreys; Robert Lamb; Jackie Lane; Library Association; Lloyds Register of Shipping/MIPG/PPMS; Dr. Benjamin Lucas; Meteorological Office; MORI; Ian Morrison; MRIB; NASA; National Basketball Association (NBA); National Football League (NFL); NCAA; Niagara Falls Museum; Nua Ltd; Office of National Statistics; *Oxford English Dictionary*; P&O Cruises; Patent Office; Phobics Society; *Playbill*; Popular Music Database; Professional Golf Association (PGA); Public Library Association; Pullman Power Products Corporation; *Railway Gazette International*; Really Useful Group; Recording Industry Association of America (RIAA); Adrian Room; Royal Aeronautical Society; Royal Opera House; Science Museum, London; *Screen Digest*; Shakespeare Birthplace Trust; Siemens AG; Sotheby's; *Spaceflight*; Sports Council; *Statistical Abstract of the United States*; James Taylor; *Theatre World*; Tidy Britain Group; UNESCO; *Uniform Crime Statistics*; United Nations; Universal Postal Union; US Bureau of the Census; USCOLD; US Department of Justice; US Geological Survey; US Social Security Administration; *Variety*; Tony Waltham; Arthur H. Waltz; World Bank; World Health Organization; World Resources Institute; World Tourism Organization